CISTERCIAN STUDIES SERIES: NUMBER TWO HUNDRED EIGHTY-SEVEN

The Sayings and Stories of the Desert Fathers and Mothers

Volume 1: A–H (Êta)

Translated and Introduced by Tim Vivian

Preface by Kathleen Norris

Foreword by Terrence G. Kardong, OSB†

D0153731

Cistercian Publications
www.cistercianpublications.org

LITURGICAL PRESS
Collegeville, Minnesota
www.litpress.org

5/17/21

A Cistercian Publications title published by Liturgical Press

Cistercian Publications
Editorial Offices
161 Grosvenor Street
Athens, Ohio 45701
www.cistercianpublications.org

1	2	3	4	5	6	7	8	9

Library of Congress Cataloging-in-Publication Data

Names: Vivian, Tim, translator. | Norris, Kathleen, 1947– writer of preface. | Kardong, Terrence, writer of foreword.
Title: The sayings and stories of the Desert Fathers and Mothers / Tim Vivian.
Other titles: Apophthegmata Patrum. English
Description: Collegeville, Minnesota : Cistercian Publications, [2021]– | Series: Cistercian studies series ; number 287, 292 | Includes bibliographical references and index. | Contents: volume 1. A-H (êta) — volume 2. I-Z (zeta) | Summary: "A new translation of the Greek alphabetical Apophthegmata Patrum, The Sayings of the Desert Fathers. Includes expansive notes and glossary texts"— Provided by publisher.
Identifiers: LCCN 2020043299 (print) | LCCN 2020043300 (ebook) | ISBN 9780879071097 (v. 1 ; paperback) | ISBN 9780879072926 (v. 2 ; paperback) | ISBN 9780879075873 (v. 1 ; epub) | ISBN 9780879075873 (v. 1 ; mobi) | ISBN 9780879075873 (v. 1 ; pdf) | ISBN 9780879074920 (v. 2 ; epub) | ISBN 9780879074920 (v. 2 ; mobi) | ISBN 9780879074920 (v. 2 ; pdf)
Subjects: LCSH: Apostolic Fathers. | Christian literature, Early.
Classification: LCC BR60 .A62 2021 (print) | LCC BR60 (ebook) | DDC 271.009/015—dc23
LC record available at https://lccn.loc.gov/2020043299
LC ebook record available at https://lccn.loc.gov/2020043300

To Gregory Boyle, S.J.,
and the Homies and Homegirls
of Homeboy Industries

and to Jim Wallis
and the Sojourners Community

like the ammas and abbas, living the Gospel,

and in Memoriam

Brother Patrick Hart, OCSO
1925–2019

Father Terrence Kardong, OSB
1936–2019

Father John Eudes Bamberger, OCSO
1926–2020

who like the ammas and abbas lived the Gospel

Contents

Monastic community "is also a charism of brotherhood in the wilderness. . . . This closeness is understood as being, at least ideally, a very human and warm relationship, and the charism of the monastic life is, and has been from the beginning, a grace of communion in a shared quest and a participated light. It is then a charism of special love and of mutual aid in the attainment of a difficult end. . . ."

—Thomas Merton, *Contemplation in a World of Action* (1998 edition), p. 18

"The great saints of the monastic tradition, the Desert Fathers [and Mothers] of Egypt . . . read to us now as deeply contemporary. The problems they identify and the disciplines that they suggest are not archeology, not museum pieces, they are directly and profoundly our business."

—Rowan Williams
former Archbishop of Canterbury

"I also came to love the sayings of the desert fathers and mothers, and regretted that I had not found them sooner, for they help me live with myself as I am. I need their stubborn realism, their reassurance that my struggle with bad thoughts does not mean I am a bad person."

—Kathleen Norris, *Acedia*, p. 95.

"Real spirit power isn't something you play with. It's something you get trained in, something you respect, something that can do you damage."

—Grover to Kent Nerburn in Nerburn, *The Girl Who Sang to the Buffalo: A Child, an Elder, and the Light from an Ancient Sky*, p. 240.

Preface

Kathleen Norris

My first encounter with the Desert Fathers and Mothers came about when I purchased Thomas Merton's little paperback *The Wisdom of the Desert*. I found it by happy accident on a less than happy occasion, browsing in a bookstore in St. Paul, Minnesota, on an afternoon when a blizzard was descending on the city. I knew it would be days before I could fly home. I was staying in a big, drafty house with a couple whose marriage was collapsing, and whose young daughter was teething. It promised to be a miserable time for all of us. We managed, but I was glad to go to my room and escape the tension in the household. In those circumstances the desert monastics were the best companions I could have asked for. They lifted my spirits, and took me out of myself and my concerns to an exciting new place that was oddly compelling.

The sayings of these desert Christians were my introduction to the counter-cultural, topsy-turvy world of early monasticism, and I've been an evangelist for this literature ever since. Several years ago I used the desert stories in a course I was teaching at Providence College in Rhode Island. All of my students in the honors program had attended Catholic elementary and high schools, and had read many Christian classics, such as the *Confessions* of Saint Augustine. They were familiar with some of the philosophical and theological concepts of Saint Thomas Aquinas. Not one of them had heard of the Desert Fathers and Mothers, and they were not excited about studying them until they began to read the stories. At our second class a young man exclaimed, "I really love these desert guys!" He explained that he'd always had difficulty with abstract theology but that reading the desert monks he felt as if he was listening to his grandfather. "They do the same thing he does," he said, "giving me advice that might apply in many situations. Like him, they don't tell you what to do; they point you in the right direction and let you find your way."

I'm grateful to Tim Vivian for bringing out a fresh, modern, and accessible translation, but I have to admit that I am an amateur when it comes to this material. I love it, but I have no expertise in Greek, Syriac, or Coptic. I admire Vivian's diligence with the extensive footnotes that I expect will be of use to bona fide scholars of monastic history, but for the most part I have read this book for the stories and ignored the notes. For me it's enough to hear human voices speaking over a distance of some 1,700 years. These are down-to-earth people, our wise, cranky, faith-filled ancestors. Listen to them.

Foreword

Terrence G. Kardong, OSB†

When I ask myself why I find Tim Vivian's translation and commentary on the *Alphabetical Sayings of the Fathers (Apophthegmata)* so satisfying, I have to admit that it is exactly what I would have written. More precisely, it is exactly what I *did* write when I did a commentary on the Rule of Saint Benedict (*Benedict's Rule,* Liturgical Press, 1996). Both of us march through the text and deal with it word by word.

In Tim's case, that means discussing the Greek vocabulary piecemeal. If you are like me, you don't know enough Greek to do this on your own, so here we have an expert to do it for us. This does take an expert, since we are faced with a text that is over a thousand years old, and it is from a spiritual milieu quite different from our own. We need help, and we get it with Tim Vivian's meticulous parsing of the Greek vocabulary.

By this point, some may be muttering that Tim's parsing is a little *too* meticulous for them! Granted, he sometimes seems to err in the direction of repetition and even stressing the obvious. But I think this is the price we pay with this kind of commentary: it is very, very careful. In fact, it is precisely what I need and what I appreciate for *lectio divina.*

By now I suppose I can assume that the reader of this kind of text knows what I am talking about when I use this technical term *lectio divina* from the ancient monastic vocabulary. But in case you need some reminding, *lectio divina* is a special kind of "sacred reading" or "reading from God." I think most of all, you do *not* do this kind of reading rapidly or cursorily. It absolutely does not fit into the category of "speed reading." *Lectio divina* means savoring the text, perhaps something like sipping a fine after-dinner *digestivo* like *Bénédictine.* That is an unpaid political advertisement, but I thought I might slip it in.

Getting back to Tim Vivian's meticulous parsing of the Greek text of the *Alphabetic Sayings,* I find it pretty much ideal for the kind of *lectio* I like to do. He lifts up almost every word for special treatment! We might wonder if every word deserves this kind of scrutiny, but when it comes to *lectio divina,* the answer is YES. We want to take every word seriously because this is a very precious text that has come down to us from the primary origins of monasticism itself in the Egyptian and Palestinian Deserts. We want to know exactly what these people were trying to say.

Of course, it is slow going! And that may not please everybody. Indeed, it may drive some crazy—but that is what *lectio divina* is all about. It has absolutely nothing to do with gobbling the text as we tend to do with so much modern reading. There is no premium here on speed; in fact, that is strictly *verboten!* Slow down! This is not a survey class where the teacher asks us to read a thousand pages of mystical literature *a day!* No, no, we are in no hurry here. Indeed, it is questionable whether anybody can actually absorb this kind of spiritual literature except by going at it word by word.

And if we are willing to trudge along step by step with Tim Vivian as our master, we will find it greatly to our profit. He not only knows his Greek very well (as well as Coptic, and God knows what else!), but he has spent a good deal of time in the Egyptian Desert itself. He has taken student groups to the great monasteries of Scetis (near Alexandria and Cairo) to see for themselves. Granted, the old monks are long gone, but there is a new crop of Coptic monks out there, and they can also teach us a lot.

Just another word about those Coptic monks. Modern scholars like Zachary Smith (*Philosopher-Monks, Episcopal Authority, and the Care of the Self: The* Apophthegmata Patrum *in Fifth-century Palestine* [Brepols, 2018]) think that the occasion of their "publication" in Palestine was probably pressure from the Egyptian bishops. In other words, this literature may well have been produced in a situation of ecclesiastical stress. Sad to say, the Coptic monks, as well as the whole Coptic church, are today again in a situation of religious stress. And so when we read Tim Vivian's exquisite study of their writings, let's keep them in our hearts and our prayers.

Abbreviations

BCE	Before Common Era = BC (Before Christ)
CE	Common Era = AD (Anno Domini, in the year of the Lord)
CF	Cistercian Fathers series. Cistercian Publications.
CS	Cistercian Studies series. Cistercian Publications.
Ger.	German
Gk.	Greek
HB	Hebrew Bible; the Christian Old Testament
KJV	King James Version of the Bible
JSTOR	A digital online library of academic journals, books, and primary sources
Lat.	Latin
LXX	The Septuagint. *Septuaginta*. Ed. Alfred Rahlfs. 2 vols. Stuttgart: Deutsche Bibelstiftung, 1935. <academic-bible.com >.
M. Gk.	Modern Greek
n.	noun
NIV	New International Version of the Bible
NRSV	New Revised Standard Version of the Bible
NT	The New Testament.
PG	Patrologia Graeca. Ed. J.-P. Migne. Turnhout: Brepols, 1857–1866. Patristica.net/graeca/.
PL	Patrologia Latina. Ed. J.-P. Migne. Turnhout: Brepols, 1841–1855. Patristica.net/gape/.
pl.	Plural
sing.	Singular

Sp.   Spanish
vb.   Verb

Journals

ABR   *American Benedictine Review*
BSAC   *Bulletin de la Société d'archéologie copte*
CSQ   *Cistercian Studies Quarterly*
JECS   *Journal of Early Christian Studies*

Dictionaries and Encyclopedias

Anchor   *The Anchor Bible Dictionary.* Ed. David Noel
               Freedman. New York: Doubleday, 1992.
Bauer   Walter Bauer. *A Greek-English Lexicon of the
               New Testament and Other Early Christian Lit-
               erature.* Ed. Frederick William Danker, W. F.
               Arndt, and F. W. Gingrich. 2nd ed. Chicago: Uni-
               versity of Chicago Press, 1979. A 3rd ed. is now
               available.
CE   *The Coptic Encyclopedia.* Ed. Aziz S. Atiya.
               New York: Macmillan, 1991. *The Claremont
               Coptic Encyclopedia.* https://ccdl.claremont.edu
               /digital/collection/cce.
De Vaan   Michiel de Vaan, ed. *Etymological Dictionary of
               Latin and the Other Italic Languages.* Leiden:
               Brill, 2008.
EEC   *Encyclopedia of Early Christianity.* Ed. Everett
               Ferguson. New York and London: Garland, 1990.
Lampe   W. G. H. Lampe. *A Patristic Greek Lexicon.* Ox-
               ford: Clarendon, 1961. Available and download-
               able: archive.org/details/LampePatristicLexicon/
               mode/2up.
Lewis and   *A Latin Dictionary.* Ed. Charlton T. Lewis and
Short   Charles Short. 1879; Oxford: Clarendon, 1975.
               www.perseus.tufts.edu/hopper/text?doc=Perseus
               %3atext%3a1999.04.0059.

Liddell and Scott	Henry George Liddell and Robert Scott, rev. Henry Stuart Jones. *Greek English Lexicon.* Oxford: Clarendon, 1977. www.perseus.tufts .edu/hopper/text?doc=Perseus%3atext %3a1999.04.0057.
Montanari	Franco Montanari, ed. *The Brill Dictionary of Ancient Greek.* English edition eds. Madeleine Goh and Chad Schroeder. Leiden / Boston: Brill, 2015.
OCD	*The Oxford Classical Dictionary.* Ed. N. G. L. Hammond and H. H. Scullard. 2nd ed. Oxford: Clarendon, 1978.
ODCC	*Oxford Dictionary of the Christian Church.* Ed. F. E. Cross and E. A. Livingstone. 2nd ed. Oxford: Oxford University Press, 1988.
ODLA	*Oxford Dictionary of Late Antiquity.* 2 vols. Ed. Oliver Nicholson. 1st ed. Oxford: Oxford University Press, 2018.
OED	*Oxford English Dictionary.* www.oed.com/public /freeoed/loginpage.
Smith, ed.	*The HarperCollins Dictionary of Religion.* Ed. Jonathan Z. Smith. San Francisco: HarperSan-Francisco, 1995.

Editions and Translations

AlphAP	Alphabetical *Apophthegmata Patrum.* Ed. J.-P. Migne. PG 65:75–440. Turnhout: Brepols, 1864. (The translations in this volume are from the PG, with occasional variant PG readings given in the notes.)
AnonAP	Anonymous *Apophthegmata Patrum.* Trans. John Wortley. *The Anonymous Sayings of the Desert Fathers: A Select Edition and Complete English Translation.* Cambridge: Cambridge University Press, 2013.

Antony, Coptic Sayings	*Door of the Wilderness: The Greek, Coptic, and Copto-Arabic Sayings of Antony of Egypt*. Ed. Lisa Agaiby and Tim Vivian. Collegeville, MN: Cistercian Publications, forthcoming.
Antony, Letters	Samuel Rubenson, ed. and trans. *The Letters of St. Antony: Monasticism and the Making of a Saint*. Studies in Antiquity & Christianity. Minneapolis: Fortress Press, 1995.
Arabic Antony, Letters	*Letters of Antony*. Forthcoming in Lisa Agaiby and Tim Vivian. *Door of the Wilderness: The Greek, Coptic, and Copto-Arabic Sayings of Antony of Egypt*. Collegeville, MN: Cistercian Publications.
Guy	*Les Apophtegmes des Pères: Collection Systématique* (=SysAP). Ed. Jean-Claude Guy. 3 vols. SCh 387 (1), 474 (2), 498 (3). Paris: Cerf, 2013.
Historia Lausiaca	Palladius of Aspuna. *The Lausiac History*. Trans. John Wortley. CS 252. Collegeville, MN: Cistercian Publications, 2015.
Hist Mon	*The Lives of the Desert Fathers: The Historia Monachorum in Aegypto*. Trans. Norman Russell. CS 34. Kalamazoo, MI: Cistercian Publications, 1981.
Life of Antony	*Vie d'Antoine*. Ed. G. J. M. Bartelink. SCh 400. Paris: Cerf, 1994. 123–377; *The Life of Antony: The Coptic Life and the Greek Life*. Trans. Tim Vivian and Apostolos N. Athanassakis. CS 202. Kalamazoo, MI: Cistercian Publications, 2003.
Life of John the Little	Maged S. A. Mikhail and Tim Vivian, eds. *The Holy Workshop of Virtue: The Life of John the Little by Zacharias of Sakha*. CS 234. Kalamazoo, MI: Cistercian Publications, 2010.
Life of Syncletica	*The Life and Regimen of The Blessed and Holy Syncletica: Part One, The Translation*. Trans.

	Elizabeth Bryson Bongie. Eugene, OR: Wipf and Stock, 2005; Peregrina Publishing, 2003.
Sbo	*Life of Pachomius.* In *Pachomian Koinonia,* edited by Armand Veilleux. Vol. 1. CS 45. Kalamazoo, MI: Cistercian Publications, 1980.
St Macarius	*St Macarius the Spiritbearer: Coptic Texts Relating to Saint Macarius the Great.* Trans. Tim Vivian. Popular Patristics Series. Crestwood, NY: St Vladimir's, 2004.
SysAP	Systematic *Apophthegmata Patrum.* Ed. Jean-Claude Guy. *Les Apophtegmes des Pères: Collection Systématique.* 3 vols. SCh 387 (1), 474 (2), 498 (3). Paris: Cerf, 2013.

Translator's Reflection

*Engagement with the opaque (even esoteric) biblical text
enables the willing reader to participate in the creation of
a remarkable world of imagination.*[1]

*I rejoice at the hidden wisdom contained in words; this
contradiction helps me break out of the closed circle of my
thoughts.*[2]

I have commented elsewhere that translation is the fine—or not
so fine—art of cutting your losses. Paul Valéry puts it this way:

A work of art is never quite finished because *artists
themselves are never completed,* and the power and agility
that they draw from the work confers them with precisely
the gift of improving it, and so forth. Artists take from it
what they need in order to efface it and remake it—it's in
this way at least that artists must consider things. And they

---

1. Alan Cooper, "Imagining Prophecy," in James L. Kugel, ed., *Poetry and Prophecy: The Beginnings of a Literary Tradition* (Ithaca, NY: Cornell University Press, 1990), 26. I think that what Cooper says applies also to the early monastic sayings and stories in the present volume.

2. Kathleen Norris, *Acedia & Me: A Marriage, Monks, and a Writer's Life* (New York: Riverhead, 2008), 217; see "To Wait and to Hope: At Play with Etymology," 217–22.

arrive at the conclusion that the only satisfying works are those that have taught them something new.[3]

Many years ago, while studying Spanish in grad school, I spent a summer in Guatemala studying and speaking the language. Towards the end of my stay, quite proud of myself, I decided that I was going to read Gabriel García Márquez's *Cien Años de Soledad* (*One Hundred Years of Solitude*). I excitedly "read," oh, four or five pages, and already knew that the novel's syntax and vocabulary, its *acento colombino*, Columbian accent, was way beyond my means.

But what was humbling then has taught me over the years that Valéry has, indirectly, like a set of theses, nailed the potential downside of translation, incompleteness, to a door we're trying to open. Undaunted, though, as we walk through, we can take down the downside—no, not to rip it up, but gently to fold it and keep it in our pocket for reference, perhaps even reverence. Incompleteness and transformation can be identical twins; Norris's (seeming) contradiction is a well-lighted doorway. There *is* an upside, therefore, and I think we should not only nail this upside to every door but also plaster it all over the walls, exterior *and* interior. As Edith Grossman, the eminent translator of García Márquez, so rightly puts it,

> Translation expands our ability to explore through literature
> [and the translations in the present volume *are* literature]

3. "Une œuvre n'est jamais nécessairement finie, car celui qui l'a faite ne s'est jamais accompli, et la puissance et l'agilité qu'il en a tirées, lui confèrent précisément le don de l'améliorer, et ainsi de suite. Il en retire de quoi l'effacer et la refaire—C'est ainsi du moins qu'un artiste libre doit regarder les choses. Et il en vient à tenir pour œuvres satisfaisantes celles seulement qui lui ont appris quelque chose de plus" ("Valéry [Paul] > Les Cahiers," in Régine Detambel, *Conférences, Ateliers, Bibliothérapie*, trans. David Vivian, www.regine-detambel.com/f/index.php?sp=liv&livre_id=1415). Valéry's *mot juste* often appears as W. H. Auden's version, "A poem is never finished; it is only abandoned" (*Collected Poems*, ed. Edward Mendelson, "Author's Forewords" [New York: Vintage, 1976], xxx).

the thoughts and feelings of people from another society or another time. It permits us to savor the transformation of the foreign into the familiar and for a brief time to live outside our own skins, our own preoccupations and misconceptions. It expands and deepens our world, our consciousness, in countless, indescribable ways.[4]

The very word "translation" is a metaphorical gift to English: Latin *trans*, "across," + *latio*, the passive participle of *ferro*, as in "transfer": to set in motion, especially to move onward quickly or rapidly, to bear, carry, lead, conduct.[5] Also, "a handing over." The translator hands a text over, entrusts it, to the reader's keeping. Probably no one's ever thought of rock guitarist Jimi Hendrix as a translator, but Jimi doesn't just redo Bob Dylan's "All Along the Watchtower"; he hands it over to metamorphosis and recreation, giving birth to a whole new song, thus transforming the original into chords and lyrics for a rapidly changing audience.

Transformation. Live outside our own skins—live *into* our own skins. The expanding and deepening of our world, in fact, offers us *worlds*. As Valéry says, "The work is a modification of the author."[6] Not only do the author, and the translator, modify, but the reader also modifies, shapes and reshapes, and, potentially, transforms. As Alan Cooper tells us in the quotation that begins this Reflection, engagement with texts, biblical, literary, monastic, can lead to "the creation of a remarkable world of imagination." What Marvin Meyer says about *The Gospel of Thomas* applies equally to the Bible and to the sayings and stories in this volume: it "is an interactive gospel, and wisdom and knowledge come when readers creatively encounter sayings of Jesus and respond

---

4. Edith Grossman, *Why Translation Matters* (New Haven: Yale University Press, 2010), 14.

5. *A Latin Dictionary*, ed. Charlton T. Lewis and Charles Short (Oxford: Clarendon, 1879, 1975), 737c.

6. Paul Valéry, "L'œuvre est une modification de l'auteur," Detambel, http://www.regine-detambel.com/f/index.php?sp=liv&livre_id=1415.

to the sayings in an insightful manner."[7] Imagination, creativity, response, and insight are, by their very action(s), transformative. Transformation is a major theme, perhaps the overarching theme, in the sayings and stories gathered in the present collection. A number of transformations made the present volume possible; I'll detail them in this Reflection and in the Introduction.

The first one specific to this volume came a while back when I was translating the Coptic sayings of Antony the Great[8] (who, in his Greek guise, appears first in the present volume) and, as the early Christian monastics often put it, an interior voice spoke to me: "These sayings without notes and comments will lose some, sometimes a lot, of their meaning and, thus, their value." Lost in translation. Thus the first impetus for this annotated translation. As I worked on, lived wonderfully with, the texts and their translations, other similar blessings occurred: as I'll discuss below and in the Introduction, while I was working on the translation I was reading Gregory Boyle's *Barking to the Choir*, and that book greatly transformed the Introduction I had planned. (I briefly discuss Boyle's books below and in the Introduction.) Later, while working on the Introduction, I was reading *Acedia* by Kathleen Norris (who had already agreed to write a preface for this book)

7. Marvin Meyer, "The Gospel of Thomas with the Greek Gospel of Thomas," in Marvin Meyer, ed., *The Nag Hammadi Scriptures: The International Edition* (New York: HarperCollins, 2007), 134. He also cites Richard Valantasis's phrase "performative theology"; Valantasis says that "the theology emerges from the readers' and hearers' response to the sayings and their sequence and variety" (Valantasis, *The Gospel of Thomas: New Testament Readings* [Abingdon, UK: Routledge, 1997], 7).

8. My revised Coptic text and translation is "Bohairic Coptic Sayings Attributed to Saint Antony the Great: A New Transcription and First English Translation," *Coptica* 17 (2018 [July 2019]): 55–90; the translations also appear in *More Sayings of the Desert Fathers*, ed. John Wortley (Cambridge: Cambridge University Press, 2019), 118–45. A book dedicated to translations of the Greek, Coptic, and Arabic sayings of Antony is forthcoming: Elizabeth Agaiby and Tim Vivian, *Door of the Wilderness: The Greek, Coptic, and Copto-Arabic Sayings of Antony of Egypt* (Collegeville, MN: Cistercian Publications).

and realized that her book spoke very much to my efforts and to me personally; numerous quotations from and references to her book now occur in this volume. Together, Boyle's and Norris's wisdom and insights confirmed what was already central for me: *these monks still very much speak to us as human beings.*

To better understand, and profit from, the *Apophthegmata Patrum, The Sayings of the Desert Fathers and Mothers*,[9] readers without Greek or Coptic read more satisfactorily when they have a guide, their very own *vade mecum*, a travel guide, if not in person then in book. This travel guide I have done my best to provide here: the notes and comments, the Glossary, the Dramatis Personae, and the Scripture and General Indices provide not just linguistic aid but also historical, biblical, and religious directions, not as mandates but as offerings. At first, readers may well be traversing uncertain terrain, but soon they stop and reflect on what's before them (in this case, texts) and then, with further reflection, what's within. Community is a key part of early monastic spirituality (see III.1 in the Introduction). The texts here can create a community of readers and learners.

As Norris puts it, "languages have a life and wisdom of their own."[10] My intention, then, is to provide help not just with the spoken and written language of these monastics, but to translate, at least partially, imperfectly, the various *languages* they use, that is, the things they take as normal (and abnormal) in the fourth and fifth centuries that are often not the matters of our world. But much more often, I would urge, the normalities and abnormalities that they inhabit, and the ones they confront, are still very much our habitations.

In their Preface and Foreword, Kathleen Norris and Terrence Kardong, respectively, mention the, well, superabundance of notes in this volume. As I've already said and will discuss further in the

9. See the discussion of the *Apophthegmata* in Part II of the Introduction and some of its themes in III–V).

10. Norris, *Acedia*, 2.

Introduction, I believe wholeheartedly that the sayings and stories gathered here still speak to us and can even be transformational. Thus I hope that this volume will reach many kinds of readers: scholars, yes, but, more important, anyone interested in religion, Christianity, early Christianity, early Christian monasticism, monasticism in general, and / or spirituality—in fact, humanity. I believe that the material in this collection can also speak to those who are not Christian, and even to those who don't see themselves as conventionally religious. Perhaps the novelist L. O. Hartley provides the best one-sentence reason for footnotes and comments: "The past is a foreign country; they do things differently there."[11] As a professor, I'm constantly telling my students (probably, to them, *too* constantly), few of whom now regularly attend a place of worship, "With regard to *any* religious text or practice, you don't have to be a 'God-person' to see in the texts you're reading the truths, the values, even the bad truths and values, that make us truly human."

As Terrence Kardong emphasizes in his Foreword, a reader may consult the biblical and linguistic notes as part of *lectio*: slow contemplative reading. English *meditate* doesn't accurately or precisely describe what meditation is for the early monks. For them, it primarily means the quiet, vocal, recitation of Scripture, especially the Psalms, as what we now call a mantra. Scripture's present, and presence, helps the monks attain what they call *hēsychía*, "contemplative quiet," and *anápausis*, "inward stillness," which I discuss in the Introduction (V.4–5).[12]

---

11. L. P. Hartley, *The Go-Between* (Harmondsworth: Penguin, 1953; repr. New York Review Books Classics, 17). In "Sacred Arts: Reading the Great Good Books, from the Torah to the Quran," a review of Robert Alter's new translation of the Hebrew Bible in *The New Yorker* (January 28, 2019), 69–75, Adam Gopnik speaks of "the helpful clarity" of "the greatest feature of Alter's Bible: the commentary, which takes up more than half of nearly every page, seamlessly sliding into the translation proper" ("Sacred Arts," 71). The comments in the present volume are not nearly so voluminous as Alter's, but I hope they're seamless.

12. The translations are my own. For more about the terms, see the Glossary and the General Index, which identify sayings that use these words.

What Kardong emphasizes could well be primary, but another main purpose here is to illustrate how thoroughly biblical these ammas and abbas, mothers and fathers, were—and are.[13] Most translations of early monastic literature footnote only direct quotations from Scripture, but I'm convinced that Scripture, both Testaments, were and are a vital part of the air these monks breathed, the work they did, the ground they sat on, the prayers they made, and the counsel they gave. And now reread the sentence and substitute the present tense for each verb. For every direct quotation from Scripture, there are possibly, probably, ten allusions. Ewa Wipszycka concludes, partly correctly, "If we were to reconstruct [the religious life of the monks] solely on the basis of the sayings, we would conclude that the Bible was of minor importance, since the number of biblical quotations in the sayings is not significant."

"But," Wipszycka immediately adds, "this conclusion would be off the mark, as other sources . . . testify that the Bible was the cornerstone of all religious practices."[14] Scripture was indeed the cornerstone of early Christian practices, but with the Mothers and Fathers of the Desert Wipszycka has restricted herself to quotations, whereas it became clear to me as I translated that the ammas and abbas wove biblical allusions, sometimes consisting of a single word, into the baskets they made (as they prayed while working), the clothes they wore, and the wisdom they offered, and offer still. Close study of their sayings and stories actually tells us that the Bible was central for the ammas and abbas of the desert.[15]

Can we know for certain that these allusions are intentional? No, but that question has two serious problems: (1) In the gospels, thanks to modern scholarship we can sit beside Matthew and Luke

13. See especially Douglas Burton-Christie, *The Word in the Desert: Scripture and the Quest for Holiness in Early Christian Monasticism* (New York: Oxford University Press, 1993).

14. Ewa Wipszycka, *The Second Gift of the Nile: Monks and Monasteries in Late Antique Egypt*, trans. Damian Jasiński, The Journal of Juristic Papyrology Supplements (Warsaw: The University of Warsaw, 2018), 185.

15. For example, see the *Antirrheticus* by Evagrius of Pontus.

especially and watch them shape Jesus (and reshape Mark's Jesus), his acts and words, not into their own image, but into what they thought their respective communities needed. For example, in Matthew's gospel, Jesus says "Blessed are the poor in spirit"; in Luke he says "Blessed are the poor."[16] Depending on how one reads and one's own background and context, that difference of two words can be profound. The gospel writers have given us a simulacrum of Jesus, not Jesus himself. This is true also of the content and language of the sayings gathered in this volume that portray the Desert Fathers and Mothers. (2) Literary critics talk about the "intentional fallacy," pointing to the impossibility of discerning from a text what its author intended. As two scholars long ago pointed out, "The poem is not the critic's own and not the author's (it is detached from the author at birth and goes about the world beyond his power to intend about it or control it)."[17] We can never know, at least fully, the author's intent—she or he doesn't fully know. What we have is the writer's text to make our own.

The more I translated, the more I immersed myself in the texts and their world(s), the more certain I became that primarily through reading / hearing and prayer the early monks steeped themselves in Scripture; it is only natural that its vocabulary, and worldview, became part of who they were, just as the language, and world, of the Hebrew Bible in Greek translation became the referential world

---

16. Matt 5:3 and Luke 6:20, respectively; Burton Mack's translation ("Q: The Lost Sayings Source Burton Mack's translation," www.tonyburke.ca/wp-content/uploads/Burton-Macks-Q-Text.pdf) has Luke as the original: "How fortunate are the poor; they have God's kingdom." The majority understanding now is that Matthew and Luke used a common source, Q, from German *Quelle*, "source," oral or written, and added it to Mark's gospel. Who changed what in the saying here is, at present, unknowable. On Q see John S. Kloppenborg, *Q, the Earliest Gospel: A Introduction to the Original Stories and Sayings of Jesus* (Louisville: Westminster John Knox, 2000), and Kloppenborg, *Excavating Q, The History and Setting of the Sayings Gospel* (Minneapolis: Fortress, 2008).

17. "The Intentional Fallacy," from W. K. Wimsatt, Jr., and Monroe C. Beardsley, *The Verbal Icon: Studies in the Meaning of Poetry* (Lexington, KY: University of Kentucky Press, 1954), faculty.smu.edu/nschwart/seminar/fallacy.htm.

of Paul and the Evangelists, narrators of the Gospel. Some scholars, especially in the early twentieth century, said that the Bible was not important for the monks. But in his translation of the *Conferences* by John Cassian, Boniface Ramsey, O.P, titles his index "Index of Scriptural Citations and Allusions." That "and" is important. I've followed Ramsey's lead with the Scripture Index in this volume. I'm convinced that with annotated references to scriptural quotes and allusions, we understand these monastics much better, and they, in turn, if we're open to it, can help us better understand ourselves.

This sentence points to an equally important purpose of this book, as I suggest above with the use of the present tense: to show the relevance of these monastics and their sayings and stories. In *Tattoos on the Heart: The Power of Boundless Compassion,* and *Barking to the Choir: The Power of Radical Kinship*, Boyle calls the stories he tells "parables."[18] He ministers to current and former gang members; in 1988 he and fellow parishioners founded what became Homeboy Industries.[19] In a Christian context, *parables* walks us right over to Jesus. But Jesus didn't invent the genre; it long preceded him and, as Boyle shows, lives long after him. Boyle's work, like Kent Nerburn's transformational trilogy about his journeys with a Native American elder and his people and geography, like the sayings and stories of the Desert Fathers and Mothers, are fictions in that word's most imaginative, creative, and transforming sense: not something false, but something true, and thus enduring.[20]

---

18. Boyle, *Tattoos on the Heart* (New York: Free Press, 2011), and *Barking to the Choir* (New York: Simon and Schuster, 2017).

19. See homeboyindustries.org.

20. Kent Nerburn, *Neither Wolf Nor Dog: On Forgotten Roads with an Indian Elder* (Novato, CA: New World Library, 1994, 2002), *The Wolf at Twilight: An Indian Elder's Journey through a Land of Ghosts and Shadows* (2009), and *The Girl who Sang to the Buffalo: A Child, an Elder, and the Light from an Ancient Sky* (2013). *Fiction* has a dueling etymology: Latin *fictio* derives from the verb *fingo*, "to touch, handle, stroke," then "form, shape, fashion," with the accessory idea of arranging, adorning," thus "to set to rights, arrange, to adorn, dress, trim." But another accessory meaning is that of untruth, "to alter, change," for the purpose

Fiction is key for me. I spoke earlier in this Reflection of personal transformation that helped lead to the present volume. An anterior transformation, one that I fully realized only when writing this piece, was this: my first three degrees are in English, American Literature, and Comparative Literature (Greek, Latin, Spanish). Thus I bring to the endeavor here a different perspective than would, say, someone trained in history or theology.

Over the past hundred years we've looked at the *Sayings of the Desert Fathers and Mothers* in many different, creative, and helpful ways. But we haven't given one approach much attention—the sayings and stories as literature.[21] This is surprising, given the literary approaches to the New Testament and Hebrew Bible—for example, for the latter, Alter's work on biblical narrative and poetry.[22] Wipszycka summarizes the matter well; she correctly speaks of the sayings as "one specific literary genre," just as the gospels are examples of Late Antique biographies and need, at least in part, to be read as such.[23] She continues, "The compilers of the collection continued to treat their literary material as something malleable: they cut out or added various passages at will, and made changes and corrections whenever the given text seemed to be difficult to understand or simply not to their liking." She

---

of dissembling (Lewis and Short 750c; www-oed-com.falcon.lib.csub.edu/view/Entry/69828?rskey=nDM7rM&result=2&isAdvanced=false#eid4405097).

21. This may be partly because scholars such as C. Wilfred Griggs have not seen the *Apophthegmata* as literature: "of the major sources relating to fourth century monasticism, there are also the non-literary collections of sayings of the desert fathers, or the *Apophthegmata Patrum*" (Griggs, *Early Egyptian Christianity from its Origins to 451 C.E.* (Leiden: Brill, 1990), 149–50.

22. Robert Alter, *The Art of Biblical Narrative*, 2nd ed. (New York: Basic Books, 2011), and *The Art of Biblical Poetry*, rev. ed. (New York: Basic Books, 2011).

23. For an introduction to Late Antique biography, see Ben Witherington III, *Invitation to the New Testament: First Things*, 2nd ed. (Oxford and New York: Oxford University Press, 2017), 58–59. For a full study, see Richard A. Burridge, *What are the Gospels? A Comparison with Graeco-Roman Biography,* rev. ed. (Waco, TX: Baylor University Press, 2018).

adds that the "first heroes of the desert should be regarded as a literary fiction."[24] Wipszycka is correct—though we need to use *fiction* with care and nuance; as many scholars have shown, the *Apophthegmata*, like the gospels, like Paul's letters, are grounded in history and location(s), persons and personalities.[25]

Owen Chadwick calls the *Apophthegmata Patrum* "raw material" that is valuable because it lacks an editor's (or editors') "unifying interest."[26] But (1) a comparison of the sayings in the anonymous *Apophthegmata Patrum* (AnonAP) and the systematic *Apophthegmata Patrum* (SysAP) shows plenty of editorial handiwork.[27] (2) Within the alphabetical *Sayings* it is clear that an editor (or editors) has placed some sayings together, either thematically or linguistically, or both; sometimes a single word connects two sayings. I have noted a number of these occurrences in the notes to the translations. (3) Many of the sayings reflect writerly skill, juxtapositions of words, and places where the vocabulary enhances, sometimes dramatically, the theme(s) of the saying. These, too, I've noted. But let's let a poet have the last word here: Marianne Moore famously said of poetry that we are in the presence of "imaginary gardens with real toads in them."[28]

The monks who handed on the monastic traditions, like Nerburn and Boyle, were not reporters; they were witnesses, recorders, and transmitters, and what they offer is truths (the plural here is important). In Religious Studies we call such truths *myths*,

---

24. Wipszycka, *Second Gift*, 80, 83.

25. For a brief discussion of the historical question, see Zachary B. Smith, "The *Apophthegmata Patrum* in its Historical Context," in *Philosopher-Monks, Episcopal Authority, and the Care of the Self: The* Apophthegmata Patrum *in Fifth-Century Palestine*, Instrumenta Patristica et Mediaevalia 80 (Turnhout: Brepols, 2017), 17–21, chap. 1.3. Smith emphasizes "the compiler" in 5th-century Palestine.

26. Owen Chadwick, *Western Asceticism* (London & Philadelphia: Westminster Press, 1958), 34.

27. See the Bibliography.

28. Moore, "Poetry," poets.org/poem/poetry.

sacred encounters that inform us still.[29] As a saying attributed to a Native American elder has it, "What I'm about to tell you may not have happened, but it's true." Truth is always present tense. As I was working on the third or fourth draft of the translation, I was also reading Boyle's powerful and moving books, mentioned earlier. Now an equally strong voice spoke to me: "Use *Barking to the Choir* and *Tattoos on the Heart* as midrashim on the Desert Mothers and Fathers." In the Introduction I offer a reflection on what that voice asked me to do.

Midrash (plural *midrashim*) is the Hebrew word for "interpretation," "study," "rabbinic Bible interpretation." A midrash can be "the interpretation of a single verse of Scripture" or "a compilation of exegeses of Scripture."[30] Paul offers one (he uses a participle of the verb cognate with *allegory*) on Sarah and Hagar in Galatians 4:21-31. Perhaps the central theme of Boyle's parables is, "How does a person live a Gospel life? How do a people live such a life?" This is the central theme of early monasticism, which the monks often express as "Offer me some counsel. How can I be saved?" They usually don't mean salvation in the sweet hereafter *but in the present*. Homies and homegirls walk into Boyle's office every day and in different words ask that same question. It makes sense, therefore, with this symbiosis between Egyptian desert and urban Los Angeles, to use Boyle's parables to enhance the parables of the monks, and vice versa.

My university studies, as I've said, were first in literature and then in early Christianity. My further graduate studies, to paraphrase Samuel Johnson, tended to focus my mind, in this case on

---

29. "Myth is a much misunderstood and misused word that requires a precise definition"; see "Myth," in Smith, ed., 749. This article for me overemphasizes "supernatural beings," thereby restricting myth. Norris, *Acedia*, 35, offers a pertinent point about myth, especially now: "We have not changed so much that the myth of Narcissus has no relevance today; it is a valid representation of a dangerous aspect of the human personality."

30. See "Midrash" in Smith, ed., 717.

just one or two areas of study, not then connected with literature.[31] When as a Religious Studies professor I began teaching Judaism and the Hebrew Bible, I actually knew little about either. One of my first discoveries, actually a transformational one, was the Talmud: there center stage was a passage of Scripture, and all around it were rabbinic discussions of the text, midrashim—and sometimes the rabbis disagreed![32] I had found a sacred text, and a tradition, where it was not just okay to discuss and differ, it was expected! More important, I found that such discussions, and disagreements, could be transformational, transforming not only the text but also its reader—dare we say making him or her more open-minded. In the Introduction, therefore, I reflect on the sayings of the Desert Fathers and Mothers and with them the thoughts of Greg Boyle as he has lived out his own calling. In this way, adding where apposite insights from Kathleen Norris, I hope to meld the ancient with the modern.

I hope this translation serves these purposes:

1. Language: "Context, context, context." With regard to *any* text, ancient or modern, this is my mantra, both for myself and for my students. When discussing the Bible or early Christian writings (or any writings), with *context* we often think of historical, sociological, religious, and anthropological settings, but we need to add linguistic context too, as any annotated edition of Shakespeare, Chaucer, or Milton shows. As I was translating one day, I remembered how grateful I was in second-year Greek to have a thoroughly annotated edition as I read Plato's *Apology*, his defense of Socrates.

---

31. Johnson: "Depend upon it, sir, when a man knows he is to be hanged in a fortnight, it concentrates his mind wonderfully," from James Boswell, *The Life of Samuel Johnson*, www.gutenberg.org/ebooks/1564.

32. For an example of a page, Google the Vilna Edition of the Babylonian Talmud, Tractate Berachot, fol. 2a.

A significant linguistic example in the New Testament is the Greek word *ánōthen* in John 3:3: "Very truly, I tell you, no one can see the kingdom of God without being born *ánōthen*." The King James Version (KJV) and New International Version (NIV) translate *ánōthen* as "again." The New Revised Standard Version (NRSV) uses "from above."[33] Words indeed matter. How one translates them matters, too. Many words don't translate easily; thus the need for notes and a Glossary.

As someone who grew up in a time when we guys would pool our change for gas, when "groovy" was all the rage, both linguistically and culturally, and as someone who loves Chaucer, Shakespeare, Donne, Herbert, and poetry, I am well aware how language changes and dates. Consider the word *egregious*, with its etymology and shape-shifting character.[34] I've tried with these translations to walk a *via media*, a middle course: I've tried to make the language colloquial, but not too colloquial.[35] I want these monks to sound as though they're speaking, with ease, using contractions. Grossman states the translator's role well:

33. The NIV notes that *ánōthen* also means "from above" and the NRSV notes also "born anew." Walter Bauer places the word with Gal 4:4 as "again, anew" (*A Greek-English Lexicon of the New Testament and Other Early Christian Literature*, ed. Frederick William Danker, et al., 2nd ed. [Chicago: University of Chicago Press, 1979], 92b [4]). To me, the other appearances of the word in John's gospel show that it primarily means "from above," an important theme in John.

34. "Latin *ēgregius*, outstanding, excellent, splendid (also used sarcastically), pre-eminent, illustrious, lit. 'towering above the flock'" (*grex / gregis*). In the mid-16th century *egregious* could mean "distinguished, eminent; great, renowned," "remarkably good; wonderful, extraordinary." But it could also mean "conspicuously bad or wrong; blatant, flagrant"; (later also) "outrageous, offensive," for example, an "egregious foole" [*sic*] (1566). This is the only meaning it has now (www-oed-com.falcon.lib.csub.edu/view/Entry/59939?redirectedFrom=egregio us#eid).

35. Gopnik, "Sacred Arts," paraphrases Alter's belief (in *The Art of Bible Translation*) that biblical translation "should somehow be at once lucid and properly 'estranged,' sounding more like an ancient language" than "like a TV evangelist's homey English" (69–70). In my translations for this volume, I've chosen homey over estranged.

as Ralph Manheim, the great translator from German, so
famously said, translators are like actors who speak the lines
as the author would if the author could speak English. . . .
Whatever else it may be, translation in Manheim's formula-
tion is a kind of interpretive performance, bearing the same
relationship to the original text as the actor's work does to
the script, the performing musician's to the composition.[36]

As I translated I kept asking myself "Would we say it this
way?" Of course that means I'm imposing the way I and we speak,
in the United States, in 2020. But all translation is not only, as is
often noted, interpretation; it is also imposition. But so, too, is
writing. I have, therefore, used contractions, as we do in our con-
versations. Some of the monks—Arsenius, Evagrius, Theodora,
and Theophilus, and others—because of their seeming education
or status (bishop), speak more formally. For biblical quotations,
I have stayed with the more formal translation of the NRSV.

2. Language, Part II: Many of the sayings in Greek, and especially the narratives, have numerous word plays that English cannot adequately capture without notes. I had not before associated
art with the ammas and abbas, but as I translated I discovered that
there is definitely art here. Long gone are the days when scholars
treated these monastics as ignorant, illiterate rubes.[37] I've come
to see that the "rubes," or at least those who told and eventually
wrote down their stories, have become artists, aware of language;
their linguistic gambols reinforce, even undergird, even excavate,
the themes inherent in the stories they're telling.

a. Quotations from and allusions to the Bible: discussed above.

---

36. Grossman, *Why Translation Matters*, 11.

37. Discussing the archeological finds in Egypt, Griggs reports that the papy-
rologist C. H. Roberts "declares that in the first century C.E., writing was pervasive through all levels of society, 'to an extent without parallel in living memory'"
(Griggs, *Early Egyptian Christianity*, 23). See also Griggs, *Early Egyptian Christianity*, 40 n. 65.

b. Extensive glossary: The reader will quickly note that many words have an asterisk after them. These refer to the Glossary, where there is more, often much more, information. The Glossary entries often direct the interested reader, not just scholars, to further primary or secondary sources. The monks, like us if we stop to think about it, have a well-thumbed lexicon of oft-used words, many of which have important meanings that help us better understand their world—words and phrases such as *acedia*, *apatheia*, contemplative quiet, and inward stillness.[38] *Woman* has an asterisk. Why? One wonders. Because some of the (male) monastic views about women are, well, unfortunate, or worse. A little elucidation in the Glossary may help here, and elsewhere.

c. Notes and comments: As is discussed above, many of the notes are biblical references. But notes also direct the reader to other sayings in the volumes, to different textual readings, and to secondary, usually scholarly, works. One could probably comment on each saying, but then the reader would be holding something the size and heft of *The Oxford English Dictionary* (whose hefty volumes some of us have in pre-digital format). Except for one, necessary, long comment, the comments tend to be brief. Here again, a reader can profitably read without either notes or comments, but my hope is that interest or a "Huh?" will ask for further exploration.

Inclusive language: I've done my best to use inclusive language. *Man* appears nowhere in this translation unless the Greek word specifically indicates a male, which, perhaps surprisingly, is rare. (Greek distinguishes between "male" [*anḗr*] and "human / person" [*ánthrōpos*].)[39] With God, pronoun inclusivity is more difficult; usually *he* appears, but I have occasionally substituted *God*.

---

38. See the Glossary and the Introduction for these.

39. I haven't, though, followed the NRSV in making *brothers* "brothers and sisters." The latter wording is anachronistic in an early monastic context where male and female monks rarely interacted.

Greek: The transliterated Greek words in the notes are given in dictionary form; that is, nominative singular masculine for nouns and first person singular present progressive for verbs. Those with Greek will be able to retrofit the transliterations into Greek and use the various dictionaries cited. The sayings in this book often use parataxis: short, simple sentences, with the use of coordinating rather than subordinating constructions (especially *and*). Thus they are much more like Mark's gospel than Paul's letters. This translation will omit many of the instances of *and*, as do modern translations of Mark. I have also often translated *kaí*, "and," as "so," as in "So they went."[40] Some sayings, though, use a more complex syntax and vocabulary, which I've tried to capture.

I'd like to end this Reflection with a story. Many years ago, right after seminary, I had a two-year post-doctoral fellowship at Yale Divinity School. The school was going to pay me to do research and teach only one course on the subject of my research. I thought, "This is pretty cool—being paid to read." There was one problem, though. The post-doc fellows were required to have a subject to work on. And I didn't have one. My first foray proved nugatory when the late Henry Chadwick informed me that one of his doctoral students was already working on it.

Seeking, and not finding, one day early on, to keep up with the Coptic I had learned in grad school, I was reading some Coptic texts, and accidentally, providentially, they were monastic. I had had many years of grad school and seminary and had rarely read an ancient monastic text.[41] Although married, with one child and one in the planning stages, I fell in love. At the same time, with money in my pocket to buy books, I was reading everything I

---

40. Here again I disagree with Alter's approach; Gopnik writes, "This feature [Hebrew parataxis—its rule of connecting phrases with simple 'and's] . . . [is] faithfully reproduced in the King James Version, as it is in Alter's" version ("Sacred Arts," 70).

41. I'm indebted to Prof. Birger Pearson for asking me as a grad student to take his Coptic class at UC Santa Barbara.

could find, pre-Amazon, by Thomas Merton. My parish priest back in grad school had introduced him to me;[42] I was enthralled, and now, after seminary, I had much more free time to read him. I became a very fortunate scholar: I had found a topic, early monasticism, that spoke to me and nourished me well beyond the academic. It turned out that that Coptic text didn't have an English translation; the subsequent—or was it consequent?—translation of it became my first published article.

That was thirty years ago. I'm still journeying with, and within, their communities.

> When I first came out here, I was asleep . . .
> but then I read a few lines from the Desert Fathers and then,
> after that, my whole being was full of serenity and vigilance.
>
> —Thomas Merton[43]

* * *

Acknowledgments

I have many people to thank for helping me with this volume. First, my thanks to the retreat group at St. Andrew's Abbey in Valyermo, California, whose responses to, and questions about, the Desert Mothers and Fathers sowed good seeds on fertile soil: Debby Spaine, Dee Whitley, Mal Schleh, Marilyn Metzgar, and Patricia Puskarich. A big thanks to Kathleen Norris and Terrence Kardong, OSB, for writing, respectively, the Preface and Foreword. Fr. Terrence (1936–2019) died while I was working on this volume. He was my longtime editor at *American Benedictine Review*. He has, as the Lakota Sioux say, traveled on to the Creator. I will always be grateful to him.

---

42. Another thank you: to The Rev. Gary Commins.
43. Thomas Merton, *When the Trees Say Nothing: Writings on Nature*, ed. Kathleen Deignan (Notre Dame, IN: Sorin Books, 2003), 161–62.

Greg Boyle and Kathleen Norris shaped this volume more than they could probably have imagined. Gary Commins, Gwen Hardage-Verger, Rick Kennedy, Maged S. A. Mikhail, and Regina Walton read an almost-final draft of the Introduction. Gary Commins, Gwen Hardage-Verger, and Jack Hernandez read a near-final draft of the Translator's Reflection. The following graciously answered many questions: Lisa Agaiby, Alan Cooper, Sarah Coakley, Gary Commins, Hal Drake, Bob Frakes, Jim Goehring, Vern Hill, Rick Kennedy, Mark Lamas, Andrew Louth, Ruth Meyers, Maged S. A. Mikhail, Andrew Trigg, David Vivian, and Marzena Zawanowska. I wish especially to thank Hany Takla of the St. Shenouda the Archimandrite Coptic Society for generous bibliographical help and Janet Gonzales and the Interlibrary Loan department at CSU Bakersfield for finding the many books and articles I requested.

At Liturgical Press I wish to thank Stephanie Lancour, Colleen Stiller, and Julie Surma for their attention during the publishing process.

Finally, but certainly not least, deep thanks to Marsha Dutton, my wonderful editor at Cistercian Publications, for her initial enthusiasm about this project and then for shepherding a complex manuscript to its home as a book.

Introduction[1]

I. Prologue with Stories

It is impossible to separate the teller from the telling: that whatever I say . . . is a way of saying something about myself.[2]

Given that this present volume contains numerous early monastic stories, I want to begin here with one. Once upon a time I received an invitation to go to Egypt. Since as a scholar I was publishing on the early Christian monks of that country (4th–7th centuries) and had not yet been there, this was, to say the least, an exciting offer.[3] A group was going to the Wadi Natrun*[4] north from Cairo, about halfway between that city and Alexandria, on the Mediterranean, "Scetis"* in the sayings and stories in this volume. The Wadi Natrun today has four active ancient monasteries.[5] This journey was to be a combined archeological-teaching

1. An earlier, considerably briefer, version of this Introduction appeared as "Practices in Transformation: A Reflection on Six Early Monastic Values and Practices in the *Alphabetical Apophthegmata Patrum*, The Sayings of the Desert Fathers and Mothers," CSQ 54, no. 2 (2019): 135–57.

2. David Treuer, *The Heartbeat of Wounded Knee: Native America from 1890 to the Present* (New York: Riverhead Books, 2019), 16.

3. My continuing thanks to Benedicta Ward, SLG, for recommending me.

4. For words with an asterisk, see the Glossary and General Index.

5. For a brief introduction, see "The Monasteries of the Arab Desert and Wadi Natrun," UNESCO, and the website of Saint Macarius monastery (stmacariusmonastery.org/eabout.htm). The Wikipedia article is solid, with links and pictures (en.

1

(ad)venture; I was going to teach the course on early monasticism to students from Evangelical Christian colleges.

We met for the first class in a room spare but replete with beautiful Coptic icons.[6] The texts we were studying was *The Sayings of the Desert Fathers*, the translation of the alphabetical *Apophthegmata Patrum* by Benedicta Ward.[7] I opened the first meeting with a question: "When you hear the word *monk* or *monks,* what first comes to mind?" One young woman responded, "They're agents of Satan." This, I thought, was going to be a tough audience.

As I studied early monasticism more, I came to see that some scholars, to varying degrees, shared that student's reservations, even alarm. The great eighteenth-century historian Edward Gibbon is scurrilous: "the monastic saints, who excite only the contempt and pity of a philosopher," and "The Ascetics [*sic*], who obeyed and abused the rigid precepts of the Gospel, were inspired by the savage enthusiasm which represents man as a criminal, and God as a tyrant."[8] Protestant scholars are conflicted:

- C. Wilfred Griggs is in general positive towards monasticism; he states that monasticism, "adopted as a way of life for

---

wikipedia.org/wiki/Wadi El Natrun).The monastery has a web page. See Tim Vivian, "The Monasteries of the Wadi al-Natrun, Egypt: A Monastic and Personal Journey," in Tim Vivian, *Words to Live By: Journeys in Ancient and Modern Egyptian Monasticism*, CS 207 (Kalamazoo, MI: Cistercian Publications, 2005), 59–108.

6. For "Coptic," see "Copt" and "Coptic Language, Literary," *Coptic Encyclopedia* (CE), 599a–601a and 604a–7a, respectively, though the suggestion in the CE for the "end" of Coptic in the 7th cent. is much too early. Maged S. A. Mikhail via email suggests the 13th cent., "with some exceptional figures and probably villages still around for another century or so. But in the mid-13th c. there is the phenomenon of grammars of the Coptic language, clearly targeting Christians, that use Arabic as the language of reference and instruction."

7. *The Sayings of the Desert Fathers: The Alphabetical Collection*, trans. Benedicta Ward, CS 59 (Kalamazoo, MI: Cistercian Publications, 1975).

8. Edward Gibbon, *The Decline and Fall of the Roman Empire*, vol. II, *The History of the Empire from 395 A.D. to 1185 A.D.* (New York: Modern Library, n.d. [1776–1789]), 363 and 347.

devotional purposes, is a gift of the Egyptian church to the Christian world." But immediately before this, in discussing pre-monastic asceticism, especially with regard to Clement* and Origen,* he calls monasticism "an extreme form of asceticism."[9]

- Kenneth Scott Latourette is first positive: "Monasticism has displayed many variations and has been one of the chief ways in which the vitality of the Christian faith has found expression." But, two sentences later, he declares, "To a certain degree monasticism represented the triumph of ideas which the Catholic Church had denounced as heretical. Into it crept something of the legalism, the belief that salvation can be earned and deserved, which is opposed to grace."[10]

- To his credit, Justo L. González devotes chapter 15 of volume 1 of *The Story of Christianity*, "The Monastic Reaction," to early monasticism, but he places that discussion in "Part II: The Imperial Church" and, as the chapter makes clear, sees monasticism incompletely and too simply as primarily a reaction against the Constantinian Church. He correctly states that "Monasticism was not the invention of an individual," but adds that it was "rather a mass exodus," which is uncertain. But then he calls this "mass exodus" a "contagion," and later says that stylites (pillar saints) used "ostentatious acts."[11]

The above sources, which I read later, helped me understand that student, at least partially, though fortunately Satan does not

---

9. C. Wilfrid Griggs, *Early Egyptian Christianity from its Origins to 451 C.E.* (Leiden: Brill, 1990), 100. Words followed by an asterisk appear in the Glossary.

10. Kenneth Scott Latourette, *A History of Christianity* (New York: Harper & Brothers, 1953), 222.

11. Justo L. González, *The Story of Christianity*, vol. 1, *The Early Church to the Dawn of the Reformation* (San Francisco: HarperSanFrancisco, 1984), 139 and 147.

make an appearance in these scholarly assessments. I don't remember anything else about our first discussion that morning in Egypt, but I clearly remember the decision I made later that day: I decided to abandon traditional classroom pedagogy. Instead, I was going to teach, or try to teach, the students about *lectio, lectio divina*, which the late Terrence Kardong discusses in his Foreword to this volume: attentive silent reading of a text—not so much for information but for transformation. The next day we met in the same room, under the benevolent watch of those sacred icons. We sat on the floor in a circle, with teacher as one of the students (student: Greek *mathētḗs*, "disciple," is cognate with *mathánomai*, "to learn" [English *math*]). Their assignment, and mine, had been to read some of the sayings from Ward's book, so I now asked them to take five to ten minutes, sitting in silence (squirming allowed), to look again at that day's sayings. I asked them to go back to a saying, or even a line or a word, that particularly said something to them—whatever that something was, and then we would share with one another.

It worked. I don't recall any details of the working, but I remember assuredly that it was a great class, that day and thereafter, that we shared with one another, and that, by the end of the course, all of us, even the young woman on the lookout for Satan, had a deeper understanding of the early monastic impulse, its desires and efforts, its hopes and dreams and goals. And, dare one say, its continuing relevance, even necessity? My hope is that you reading this volume will, at least metaphorically, sit within a circle of silence and read both for information and for inspiration, even transformation (see IV.2 below).

As Kathleen Norris writes in her Preface to this volume, she once had the same experience as I, and the same results. When she was teaching an honors course at Providence College, all of her students, unlike mine, "had attended Catholic elementary and high schools, and had read many Christian classics, such as the *Confessions* of St. Augustine. . . . Not one of them had heard of the desert fathers and mothers, and they were not excited about studying them." That is, "until they began to read the stories." Those students intuited something deeply human: "people learn by story," a Native American elder tells Kent Nerburn, "because stories lodge deep in the heart."[12] In talking with Native elders, Nerburn says, apropos of the early Christian monastics, that "what struck me most deeply was the almost sacred value the elders placed on the importance of stories. . . . Stories were not mere entertainment to them, nor were they simple reminiscences; they were the traditional way of handing down the values and the memories of their culture—the way they had been taught by *their* elders—and they approached the task with something close to reverence."[13]

As we've seen, story matters. With regard both to the stories in the gospels and those in the first centuries of Christianity, including early-monastic tellings and tales, scholars once placed too much emphasis on the Ur-text (the oldest, primal text) and *ipsissima verba* (the very words that Jesus or the early monks spoke), and not enough emphasis on *what* the stories are telling (present tense). Scholarship now more humbly acknowledges that we have very little access to Ur-texts or -speech. We have, metaphorically, a Big Bang (the origins of Christianity) and Smaller Bangs (the origins, say, of monasticism). The emphasis shifts, therefore, to what the speakers and writers are saying: What did they want their audiences to hear? What in fact might the audiences have heard?

Jacques van der Vliet has put this very well:

---

12. Kent Nerburn, *The Wolf at Twilight* (Novato, CA: New World Library, 2009), xiv. See the next note.

13. Nerburn, *The Wolf at Twilight*, xii (emphasis his). I've read and taught Nerburn's trilogy—*Neither Wolf Nor Dog, The Wolf at Twilight,* and *The Girl Who Sang to the Buffalo*—many times, and I think that, in deference to his (mostly) non-Native readers, he's being too cautious; in the quotation above, I would change "almost sacred value" to "sacred value," and "with something close to reverence" to "with reverence."

these often colorful stories . . . offer far more and far better than history. . . . storytelling was a common device in late-antique literature in general and in monastic literature in particular. Such stories are not an inferior kind of literature, but an effective means of spiritual communication geared towards communion. . . . they were embedded in the social practices of the communities that selected, acquired, adapted and recited them in order to pass on the shared values of the group. In addition to reproducing these communities, they defined them socially, vis-à-vis other communities, but also teleologically, in a historical perspective, and theologically, in their relation to the supernatural. . . .

Well-told stories allow us to empathize with the heroes of the story and to share a common experience, through an almost physical process designated as "embodiment" in the modern psychology of narrative. Drawing on a repertoire of shared *topoi* and formulas, such stories were a forceful means to forge community. Indeed, as we all know, communities, societies and nations live by stories, and the authors . . . were well aware of this fact, creating their own narrative universe.[14]

Well-told stories. Sacred stories. Religious Studies can help us here: the discipline understands *myth* not as "falsehood," but as story, sacred stories that religious folk pass on because the stories still have meaning. (People and countries also have "secular" myths, which are often sacred to them.)[15] Claudia Rapp, with many others, has made us more aware of the power(s) of story and stories' transformative abilities, "the impact the Holy Scrip-

14. Jacques van der Vliet, "The Apocryphal Mind: Some Reflections on Coptic Literature," presidential address, in *Proceedings of the Eleventh International Congress of Coptic Studies*, ed. Hany N. Takla, et al., Orientalia Lovaniensia Analecta (Leuven: Peeters, forthcoming).

15. See *The HarperCollins Dictionary of Religion*, ed. Jonathan Z. Smith (San Francisco: HarperSanFrancisco, 1995), 749a–51b.

tures could have in bringing about immediate transformation of the reader."[16] Rapp focuses on hagiography/ies, but her insights are appropriate here: we can say that the sayings and stories of the desert fathers and mothers are "little hagiographies," literally "sacred writings," or, more for our purposes here, stories with holy intent, the making of the sacred (or the transforming of the already sacred): "Hagiographical texts play a significant and very particular role in the process that joins the author and his [or her] audience in their participation in the sanctity of the holy man and woman. It is this process which I would like to call 'spiritual communication.'"[17] The spiritual elder, the amma or abba, she observes, is both "beneficiary and proclaimer" of a story, a miracle, a parable, or counsel.

Rapp points to the noun *diḗgēsis* and the much more common verb *diēgéomai*, "to explain, interpret," and / or "to give a detailed account of something in words, tell, relate, describe."[18] For the sayings and stories here, the noun *diḗgēma*, "narrative, account," is apposite.[19] In much of the Septuagint (LXX), the third-century BCE Greek translation of the Hebrew Bible, the verb means "to tell," but, as in Exodus 24:3, it carries deeper import—and impact: *Moses came and told [diēgéomai] the people all the words of the LORD and all the ordinances; and all the people answered with one voice, and said, "All the words that the LORD has spoken we will do."* Perhaps "Moses came and *communicated* to the people"

16. Claudia Rapp, "Storytelling as Spiritual Communication in Early Greek Hagiography: The Use of *Diegesis*," *Journal of Early Christian Studies* 6, no. 3 (1998): 431.

17. Rapp, "Storytelling," 432.

18. Franco Montanari, et al., eds., *Vocabolario della lingua greca* (Turin: Loescher Editore, 2013); English edition: Madeleine Goh and Chad Schroeder, eds., *The Brill Dictionary of Ancient Greek* (Leiden/Boston: Brill, 2015), 527ab; Walter Bauer, *A Greek-English Lexicon of the New Testament and Other Early Christian Literature*, ed. Frederick William Danker, et al., 2nd ed. (Chicago: University of Chicago Press, 1979), 245a. The Greek root gives us *exegesis*.

19. Bauer 245a.

is better. In the New Testament the verb, not surprisingly, occurs almost exclusively in Mark, Luke, and Acts, and almost always in connection with Jesus. In Acts 9:27, Barnabas takes Paul, brings him to the apostles, and describes [*diēgéomai*] for them how on the road to Damascus Paul saw the Lord, who had spoken to him, and how in Damascus Paul *spoke boldly in the name of Jesus*. *Diēgéomai* continues this narratival, relational partnership (as in to relate something in relationship) in the sayings and stories here and 106 times in the systematic *Apophthegmata*.[20]

Appropriately, Latin translates *diēgēsis* as *narratio*, "narrative," "a brief account." "But in the Christian literature of Late Antiquity," *diēgēsis*, Rapp emphasizes, "refers specifically to an anecdote or story that is of edifying character."[21] She cites Palladius's *Lausiac History* and the anonymous *Historia Monachorum*: "Accordingly," the author of the latter says, "since I have derived much benefit from these monks, I have undertaken this work to provide a paradigm and a testimony for the perfect and to edify and benefit those who are only beginners in the ascetic life."[22] The Prologue to the alphabetical *Apophthegmata* (AlphAP) translated in this volume puts it this way: "Most of these who labored, therefore, at different times, have set out in detail [*diēgēma*] both the sayings and accomplishments of the holy elders, in simple and straightforward language, with only this one thing in view—to benefit as many as possible."

Rapp observes that other Classical and Late Antique genres, such as the panegyric, also sought "to edify and benefit," but she

---

20. *Les Apophtegmes des Pères: Collection Systématique*, ed. Jean-Claude Guy, 3 vols., SCh 387 (=1), 474 (=2), 498 (=3) (Paris: Cerf, 2013) [SysAP], 3.301. Citations of sayings in the SysAP using Roman numerals refer to the chapter and saying number (for example, XV.2), while references using Arabic numerals are to the volume and page number(s) (for example, 3.124).

21. Claudia Rapp, "Storytelling," 433.

22. *Historia Monachorum in Aegypto*, trans. Norman Russell, *The Lives of the Desert Fathers: The Historia Monachorum in Aegypto*, CS 34 (Kalamazoo, MI: Cistercian Publications, 1981), Prologue 12 (pp. 50–51). Getting or giving benefit* is key in early monastic practice.

contrasts hagiography and apophthegm; the latter is storytelling, "characterized by two features in particular . . . : its simple and unadorned style and its intrinsic truth-value. The absence of stylistic embellishment enables the audience to focus on the content of the story without the distractions of a lofty style."[23] "What is being communicated," she adds later, "is not simply a story"— and, this is very important—"but a way of life [*politeía*], and it ought to be perpetuated not in words, but in deeds."[24]

Such understandings, ancient and modern, probably to our surprise, connect the early monastics with many modern writers: transformation through story. I don't remember where I first heard or read the term "transformational reading." That is, reading that is not opposite to but includes and transcends informational reading. Because I was fortunate to have a small enrollment in my Native American Religion class the semester I began writing this Introduction, I asked the students to write twice-weekly brief reflections on the reading for each class. We were reading, studying, and discussing the revelatory, insightful, hilarious, moving, and heart-breaking stories about Nerburn, a white author, and his transformational journey with Dan, a Lakota Sioux elder.

This class, like the apophthegmata, illustrated for me Claudia Rapp's insights, what M. M. Bakhtin calls "the dialogic imagination."[25] Four of Bakhtin's statements, I believe, can help us better understand the monastic sayings and stories in this volume:

> Every word is directed toward an answer . . . it provokes
> [that is, calls forth] an *answer*, anticipates it and structures

---

23. Rapp, "Storytelling," 437.

24. Rapp, "Storytelling," 440–41. On *politeía* (from *pólis*, "city"), see "Way of life" in the Glossary.

25. M. M. Bakhtin, *The Dialogic Imagination*, ed. Michael Holmquist, trans. Caryl Emerson and Michael Holmquist (Austin: University of Texas Press, 1981). I wish to thank Stephen Davis for the references to Bakhtin's book in his paper "The Dialogical Function of Shenoute's Monastic Rules: An Archaeology of Practice in the Women's Monastery of Atripe," St. Shenouda the Archimandrite Coptic Society Twentieth Conference, UCLA, July 19–20, 2019.

itself in the answer's direction. . . . [Linguists] have taken into consideration only those aspects of style determined by demands for comprehensibility and clarity—that is, precisely those aspects that are deprived of any internal dialogism, that take the listener for a person who passively understands but not for one who actively answers and reacts. (280, emphasis his)

The more intensive, differentiated and highly developed the social life of a speaking collective, the greater the importance attaching, among other possible subjects of talk, to another's word, another's utterance, since another's word will be the subject of passionate communication, an object of interpretation, discussion, and evaluation, rebuttal, support, further development and so on. (337)

The tendency to assimilate others' discourse takes on an even deeper and more basic significance in an individual's ideological becoming, in the most fundamental sense. Another's discourse performs here no longer as information, directions, rules, models and so forth—but strives rather to determine the very bases of behavior; it performs here as *authoritative discourse*, and an *internally persuasive discourse.* (342, emphases his)

The authoritative word demands that we acknowledge it, that we make it our own; it binds us, quite independent of any power it might have to persuade us internally; we encounter it with its authority already fused to it. (342)

I discovered Bakhtin after that Native American class had ended, but it's clear to me now that those students—and I—were discovering discourse that was both authoritative and internally persuasive. At the beginning of the class one day I looked at each student and praised the group for its brave and insightful reflections on Dan and Nerburn—and themselves: they'd been inspired and given permission by the sacred stories of the Native Americans and the hallowing account of the growing relationship between

Nerburn and Dan to tell their own stories vis-à-vis those in the books. By reflecting and writing, the students were informing themselves of their own journeys and transformations, and sharing them with the class. Their stories are sacred. As one student in that class, a young Latina, wrote about Nerburn, and herself: "It's as if somehow his heart has become his eyes to the world in front of him. I don't see the change only in Nerburn, I see it in myself. Ever since I began the first book, I started to see the world with my heart; it's as if a piece of my heart has become Indian, too."

My hope with this volume is that some of our hearts can become monastic, at least in spirituality. I've read and reread, reflected on, and written about the literature and *politeía* (way of life*) of the early monks over the last thirty years; like that young Latina, I've more and more come to see the ammas* (mothers) and abbas* (fathers) as transformational. Thus, this volume is a result of "contemplative scholarship," scholarship that has sat with others listening to the words in this volume and then reflecting on them within a discipline of silent translation.[26] Without hesitation, even heartily, I can say that they have a great deal to say to us today. Of course, not everything about them is transferable, or even translatable, but if we go beyond the superficial and dive deep, we can see that much of what they lived and tried to live and worked hard at living still speaks to us today—to monastics, yes, but also, potentially, to many, many others.

In *Thomas Merton: The Noonday Demon*, Donald Grayston raises a point apropos here. A reader of the book in manuscript "took issue with the orientation of the book, with what kind of book it was to be. Was it to be a solid piece of scholarship, or, conversely, did it run the risk of being a work of excessive empathy,

26. I owe the phrase "contemplative scholarship" to Edward K. Kaplan, from his essay "Scholarship, Community, and Communion: A Jewish Perspective," in *We Are Already One: Thomas Merton's Message of Hope, Reflections to Honor His Centenary* (1915–2015), ed. Gray Henry and Jonathan Montaldo (Louisville, KY: Fons Vitae, 2014), 52.

a work in which I might be perceived as claiming a closeness with Merton which I don't possess?"[27] The reader's (false) assumption is that "solid scholarship" and empathy are dichotomous, even oppositional. When I read the above, I paused, and then substituted "the desert fathers and mothers" for "Merton," and felt kindred with Grayston. His reader's either / or question assumes that scholarship and empathy can't wed and then bear, nurture, and raise a healthy family. As I hope to show below, scholarship and one's own life and spirituality intertwine.

II. The Sayings of the Desert Fathers and Mothers
(*Apophthegmata Patrum*)

In the desert
dryness promotes the formation
of flower buds. This is not aesthetics,
but survival.[28]

The alphabetical *Apophthegmata Patrum*, the *Sayings of the Desert Fathers [and Mothers]*, is a misnomer—actually, three misnomers: (1) the sayings are not strictly in alphabetical order.[29] Under "A," for example, Antony and Arsenius, probably as the most eminent worthies, are first; strictly alphabetically, a number of their brethren whose names begin with A and who follow them should come before them. The other chapters occasionally have similar ordering. (2) The sayings are not just sayings; they're both sayings and stories. In fact, aren't sayings compressed stories, inviting de-

---

27. Donald Grayston, *Thomas Merton: The Noonday Demon: The Camaldoli Correspondence* (Eugene, OR: Cascade Books, 2015), xvi.

28. Kathleen Norris, "Giveaway," in *Journey: New and Selected Poems 1969–1999* (Pittsburgh: University of Pittsburgh Press, 2001), 91.

29. The chapters follow the Greek alphabet, A through Ω; the present volume includes sayings from A to H (Ēta).

compression? (3) In addition to the fathers (abbas), three desert mothers (ammas) have sayings in the alphabetical collection; one, Theodora, is in volume 2, forthcoming.[30] Hence the subtitle of the present volume is *The Sayings of the Desert Fathers and Mothers.*

The Sayings of the Desert Fathers and Mothers: the key word in this title may be "desert."* Greek *érēmos*, "wilderness" or "desert," is where humans do not normally live and where demons* often do. As Susanna Elm says, "These charismatic *Sayings* were of fundamental importance and are the expression of one of the most vital aspects of desert asceticism."[31] *Asceticism.** A knotty word—and, as with many key monastic words in this Introduction and in the sayings and stories translated here—one on probably few lips and tongues today. The origins of *ascesis* from Greek are athletic: "exercise, practice, training," and by the time of Lucian in the second century CE could mean "mode of life, profession," which fits the way of life* of the ammas and abbas.[32] Inbar Graiver makes a key observation: asceticism is indeed "a practical phenomenon," but, more important, it is "a method for promoting inner transformation" (discussed earlier, and often later; see IV.2,

30. See Laura Swan, *The Forgotten Desert Mothers: Sayings, Lives, and Stories of Early Christian Women* (Mahwah, NJ: Paulist Press, 2001); Susanna Elm, *"Virgins of God": The Making of Asceticism in Late Antiquity,* Oxford Classical Monographs (Oxford: Clarendon, 1996); and Tim Vivian, "Courageous Women: Three Desert Ammas—Theodora, Sarah, and Syncletica," ABR 71, no. 1 (March 2020): 75–107.

31. Elm, *"Virgins of God,"* 255–56.

32. Henry George Liddell and Robert Scott, rev. Henry Stuart Jones, *Greek English Lexicon* (Oxford: Clarendon, 1977), 257b. BCE (Before Common Era) and CE (Common Era) are more inclusive replacements for BC and AD. Since my intention with this Introduction is to focus on monastic spirituality, I will not discuss here *ascesis* and the origins of monasticism; for the former see Susan Ashbrook Harvey, "Asceticism," *Late Antiquity* (1999): 317a–18a, and for the latter, Tim Vivian, "The Origins of Monasticism," in *T&T Clark Handbook to the Early Church*, ed. Piotr Ashwin-Siejkowski, Ilaria L. E. Ramelli, and John Anthony McGuckin (New York: T&T Clark / Bloomsbury, forthcoming 2021).

"Paths to Transformation"). Geoffrey Galt Harpham calls this "the ascetic imperative": "the broadest description of the project of asceticism is that it recognizes and manages drive or impulse, commonly called desire [for the early monks the "passions"*], by harnessing and directing resistance."[33]

Two modern writers make important observations about the desert. As Gail Fitzpatrick says, "It is the very nature of the desert to introduce the monk to its element of the wild. Those who seek its peace find instead a raw encounter with all that is untamed and unregenerate *in their hearts*."[34] In conversation with her, I would suggest that "those who seek *only* its peace," in other words, spiritual short-time visitors, will be very disappointed. She is absolutely right about what's "untamed" in our hearts, but the monks in this volume would not say that some things in their hearts are "unregenerate." As we'll see, regeneration and transformation are key to early Christian monasticism. Teresa M. Shaw summarizes the matter very well:

> Although modern studies of early Christian asceticism have tended to emphasize self-denial of bodily pleasures and the battle between flesh and spirit, it should become clear that such a view does not do justice to the complex meaning of such terms as *askesis* and *enkrateia*.[35] Rather, ancient in-

33. Geoffrey Galt Harpham, *The Ascetic Imperative in Culture and Criticism* (Chicago and London: University of Chicago Press, 1987), 61; see xiii for "the ascetic imperative." For a discussion of "resistance / repression," see Inbar Graiver, *Asceticism of the Mind: Forms of Attention and Self-Transformation in Late Antique Monasticism*, Pontifical Institute of Mediaeval Studies, Studies and Texts 213 (Toronto: Pontifical Institute of Mediaeval Studies, 2018), 96–128, esp. 114–19.

34. Cited in Norris, *Acedia*, 137; full source not given. My emphasis. For a compelling interreligious reflection on wilderness, see Steven Charleston, a retired bishop of Alaska in the Episcopal Church and a Native American, *The Four Vision Quests of Jesus* (New York: Morehouse Publishing, 2015), esp. chap. 3, "The Voice," 42–59, and chap. 6, "The Wilderness," 92–112. Although he doesn't address the matter directly, his work makes a compelling case to relabel Matt 4:1-11 // Luke 4:1-13, "The Temptation of Jesus" (NRSV), to "The First Vision Quest of Jesus."

35. See "Ascetic practice" and "Control / Get control of," respectively, in the Glossary.

sights concerning the control of desires that lead to pleasure (and pain) and concerning the careful management and training of the body with the soul . . . give much of the shape and contours to early Christian understandings of the body, creation, and, indeed, salvation.[36]

Within a comparative religion context, one can think of these ammas and abbas, as Shaw shows, going on a vision quest, as some Native Americans do as the passageway from childhood to maturity.[37] For the early monastics, the quest is lifelong.

As with so much of the vocabulary of the Egyptian and Palestinian monks of the fourth and fifth centuries, terms such as *áskēsis* and *enkráteia, érēmos*, "wilderness, desert," are biblical: this is where John the Baptist emerges from, *the voice of one crying out in the wilderness [érēmos]* (Matt 3:3; Isa 40:3).[38] Matthew Kelty expresses well the monastic understanding of John and desert: "John the Baptist has always been a favorite of those in monastic life. His feast comes at the time when the sun first begins its journey down [June 24]. We know this dying will lead to eventual life, and the monks see in the plunge into night their own way into the darkness of God. The inward journey has all the dressings of death, a decrease, which like death hides the truth of growth in life. John was prelude to Jesus also in this: there is no greater road."[39]

---

36. Teresa M. Shaw, *The Burden of the Flesh: Fasting and Sexuality in Early Christianity* (Minneapolis, MN: Fortress Press, 1998), 7.

37. The article in *The HarperCollins Dictionary of Religion*, ed. Jonathan Z. Smith, defines vision quest as an "institutionalized activity characteristic of but not limited to the Plains tribes, by which a special relationship with transcendent powers is sought" (Smith, ed., 1124b–25a). See Steven Charleston, *The Four Vision Quests*, esp. chap. 1, "The Quest: the Meaning of Spiritual Quest." The four quests are based on Matt 4:1-11; 17:1-8; 26:36-46; and 27:32-55.

38. See *áskēsis* ("Ascetic practice"), *enkráteia* ("Self-control"), and *érēmos* ("Desert") in the Glossary.

39. Matthew Kelty, *My Song is of Mercy: Writings of Matthew Kelty, Monk of Gethsemani*, ed. Michael Downey (New York and Oxford: Rowman and Littlefield, 1995), 25.

The literal and spiritual wilderness is where Jesus goes out to *a deserted place* (*érēmos*) to pray (Matt 14:13, 15). In the late-nineteenth century, indefatigable scholars published the monumental series The Nicene and Post-Nicene Fathers, Series 1 and 2, in twenty-eight volumes.[40] The desert fathers and mothers have no place in them, not even the *Life of Antony*, well-known among post-Nicene Christians. In 1960 Thomas Merton was prophetic, at least in English, when he published *The Wisdom of the Desert*. There are now in English hundreds of articles and dozens of books on early Christian monasticism, with as many more in French and German, both scholarly and for a wider audience outside the academy.

Apophthegmata is the plural of Greek *apóphthegma*, "maxim, saying" and, in the Septuagint (LXX), can mean "oracle, prophecy" (Ezek 13:19). It comes into English as "apophthegm" (also spelled "apotegm"); this noun is cognate with the verb *apophthéngomai*, "to declare one's own opinion," "to express a maxim."[41] *Apóphthegma* dates back to Xenophon (428/7–354 BCE) and Aristophanes (ca. 457 / 445–ca. 385 BCE). The verb occurs in the New Testament only in Acts 2:14 and 26:25.[42] I will not discuss here the very complicated, polylingual transmission of the texts of these alphabetical sayings,[43] translated here

---

40. Repr. Grand Rapids, MI: Eerdmans, 1979.

41. Montanari 279c for both n. and vb.

42. Bauer 125a. Translated in the NRSV as, respectively, *say* and *said*.

43. See Graham Gould, *The Desert Fathers on Monastic Community*, Oxford Early Christian Studies (Oxford: Clarendon, 1993), 17–25; and, for recent discussions, Ewa Wipszycka, *The Second Gift of the Nile: Monks and Monasteries in Late Antique Egypt*, trans. Damian Jasiński, The Journal of Juristic Papyrology Supplements (Warsaw: The University of Warsaw, 2018), 179–89, and Zachary Smith, chap. 1, "The Text and Production of the *Apophthegmata Patrum*," in Zachary Smith, *Philosopher-Monks, Episcopal Authority, and the Care of the Self: The* Apophthegmata Patrum *in Fifth-Century Palestine*, Instrumenta Patristica et Mediaevalia 80 (Turnhout: Brepols, 2017), 24–64.

from the text of J.-P. Migne.[44] The textual transmission of the *Apophthegmata*, or *Sayings*, is still very uncertain; on advice of scholars in the field, and lacking a definitive text, I've chosen to use Migne, with the use of variant readings in that text and comparisons with parallels in the *Systematic Apophthegmata* (SysAP).[45] As Elm, quoting a great scholar of the *Sayings*, Jean-Claude Guy, succinctly points out, "Exactly when the written tradition began is not certain, but a rudimentary corpus existed before 399."[46]

What became written, as with the gospels, began as oral. Opening lines such as the following are common: "Abba Poemen used to say that Abba John the Little," "They also used to say," and "Abba Poemen, speaking about Abba Isidore." In Islam's Hadith, sayings of and stories about Muhammad and the first Believers or Muslims, the *isnad* or chain of narrators is very important; with regard to the *Sayings*, Derwas Chitty speaks of a saying's "pedigree." Quoting Guy, Elm adds, "Naturally, this oral, then written, corpus became enlarged and altered in the process of accumulation, presenting the scholar with 'the philological problem,' . . . one of the most complex that the publication of patristic texts poses."[47]

Other translations of the alphabetical collection in English are, as noted earlier, Ward's *The Sayings of the Desert Fathers*, and John Wortley's *Give Me a Word*.[48] Wortley has also done good translations of the two other major collections, the anonymous *Apophthegmata Patrum* (AnonAP) and the systematic *Apophthegmata Patrum*

44. Alphabetical *Apophthegmata Patrum*, ed. J.-P. Migne, PG 65:75–440 (play .google.com/store/books/details?id=-ieFkWHbhgIC&rdid=book--ieFkWHbhg IC&rdot=1).

45. SysAP. With Antony's sayings I also refer to some Coptic readings. For ongoing work on the Apophthegmata, see *Monastica*, a dynamic library and research tool, Centre for Theology and Religious Studies, Lund University, monastica.ht.lu.se/.

46. See Evagrius, *Praktikos* 91–100 (pp. 339–42).

47. Elm, *"Virgins of God,"* 256. I've translated the quotation from Guy's French.

48. John Wortley, *Give Me a Word: The Alphabetical Sayings of the Desert Fathers*, Popular Patristics Series (Yonkers, NY: St Vladimir's, 2014).

(SysAP), the former with the Greek texts and English translation on facing pages.[49]

In addition to what Rowan Williams and Kathleen Norris say at the front of this volume about the vitality and importance of the *Sayings* for today, let me adduce two scholars on the importance of the *Apophthegmata*:

> Peter Brown, the great scholar of Late Antiquity, reminds us of the importance, then and now, of monastic spirituality: he speaks of "a further, and more radical ramification of the Christian response to the breakdown of the old solidarities"; the ammas and abbas "came to analyze the tensions among their fellow [human beings] with anxious attention. They spoke about these with an authority and an insight that make *The Sayings of the Desert Fathers* the last and one of the greatest products of the Wisdom Literature of the ancient Near East."[50]

> Graham Gould: "there can be no doubt . . . that the most important single source for the knowledge of monasticism of fourth- and fifth-century Lower Egypt is the *Apophthegmata Patrum*."[51]

In this Introduction I emphasize the spiritual aspect of the sayings and stories (III–V).[52] Three sensitive readers and explorers of early monastic spirituality give a good start.

---

49. John Wortley, trans., *The Anonymous Sayings of the Desert Fathers: A Select Edition and Complete English Translation* (Cambridge: Cambridge University Press, 2013); John Wortley, trans., *The Book of the Elders: Sayings of the Desert Fathers: The Systematic Collection*, CS 240 (Collegeville, MN: Cistercian Publications, 2012). For the Greek texts, see AnonAP, SysAP, and Wortley in the Bibliography.

50. Peter Brown, *The Making of Late Antiquity* (Cambridge, MA: Harvard University Press, 1978), 82.

51. Gould, *The Desert Fathers on Monastic Community,* Oxford Early Christian Studies (Oxford: Clarendon, 1993), 4.

52. For good briefer introductions, see Ward, *Sayings*, xvii–xxvii, and Wortley, *Give Me*, 13–22. In English, the most wide-ranging discussion of background

Douglas Burton-Christie: "The desert fathers and mothers of fourth-century Egypt created a spirituality of remarkable depth and enduring power from their reading of Scripture."[53]

Graham Gould speaks of "the pattern of personal relationships" and of "orally transmitted recollections of answers which different spiritual fathers or abbas [and mothers or ammas] gave to the questions which they were asked by their disciples."[54] In other words, communal spiritual direction.[55]

As Gould further states, the texts "see obedience and self-disclosure as heroic activities directed to the end of personal development in the virtues of the monastic life, not as something supine, passive, or signifying immaturity or lack of individuality."[56]

Kathleen Norris speaks of the relevance of the *Apophthegmata* and their application to her life: "I continue to be inspired by the ways in which the ancient monastic story intersects with and informs my own, orienting me and directing me in ways I could not have anticipated."[57]

III. An Introduction to Some Early Monastic Themes in the *Apophthegmata Patrum*

1. Community

Thomas Merton famously wrote,

---

with texts is Harmless, *Desert Christians*, 167–273.

53. Burton-Christie, *Word*, vii. His book is seminal for studying the relationship between the ammas and abbas and the Bible.

54. Gould, *The Desert Fathers*, 17.

55. I give a brief introduction about this in the Translator's Reflection.

56. Gould, *The Desert Fathers,* 57.

57. Norris, *Acedia*, 275.

In Louisville, at the corner of Fourth and Walnut, in the center of the shopping district, I was suddenly overwhelmed with the realization that I loved all these people, that they were mine and I theirs, that we could not be alien to one another even though we were total strangers. . . . There is no way of telling people that they are all walking around shining like the sun. It was like waking from a dream of separateness, of spurious self-isolation in a special world, the world of renunciation and supposed holiness. The whole illusion of a separate holy existence is a dream.[58]

The themes in the monastic sayings and stories, the themes discussed here, are not neatly numbered and segregated as a linear introduction necessarily makes them; they're much more like marrow and bone, bone and sinew, sinew and muscle, muscle and movement. Here I will make connections where I can. With a different metaphor, the themes are like a quilt on a bed, seen whole from a distance; *and* they're the threads and cross threads one studies and appreciates when looking at the quilt close up.[59]

The sayings and stories in this volume come mostly from anchorites* and semi-anchorites,* those who lived alone (anchorites) or mostly alone (semi-anchorites), rather than those who lived in a cenobium,* a community much like most monasteries today.[60] Cenobia, however, do figure in the alphabetical *Sayings* gathered in this volume. Pachomius* (292–346) founded the Koinonia, "Community," a collection of affiliated monasteries.[61] Most of the

58. Thomas Merton, *Conjectures of a Guilty Bystander* (New York: Doubleday / Image, 1968), 153–54.

59. For a powerful spiritual reflection by a monk on weaving, which is "especially suited to a life of prayer," see Kelty, *My Song*, 18.

60. The pl. of *cenobium* is *cenobia*. In the texts in this volume it's not clear what kind of community the term is defining. For a presentation of a modern semi-anchorite in Egypt, see Vivian, *Words to Live By*, 75–85.

61. See CE 1859a–64b.

sayings and stories here originated in Scetis,* Kellia,* and Nitria* in the fourth–fifth centuries, with additions and editing, most probably in Palestine, in the fifth–sixth centuries.[62]

While at the Wadi Natrun / Scetis during the archaeological-teaching sojourn that I related earlier, I was standing one day atop a sand-commandeered wall of the long-abandoned Monastery of John the Little. As I looked out over the desert, I could see dozens of circular areas where the sand was darker. These, someone told me, were *manshubia*, Arabic for the Coptic *manshōpe*, "place of being / living." Only one had been excavated.[63] The monks of John's monastery lived in these simple manshubia of two to three rooms outside the monastery walls and came to the monastery for work,* occasional meals, and the synaxis.* What's important in that vista (beside the sadness that comes when one realizes that only one manshubia had been excavated) is both the panorama and the intimacy: even the anchorites and semi-anchorites we encounter in these pages are an integral part of community, *koinonia*; these monks could well have used the phrase "the communion of saints."[64] Thus in this Introduction I look first at

62. Two good, but now aging, volumes on Scetis are Derwas Chitty, *The Desert a City* (Crestwood, NY: St Vladimir's, 1966); and Hugh G. Evelyn-White, *The Monasteries of the Wâdi 'N Natrun*, vol. II, *The History of the Monasteries of Nitria and Scetis*, ed. Walter Hauser, The Metropolitan Museum of Art Egyptian Exhibition (New York: Metropolitan Museum, 1932; repr. Arno Press, 1973); online: alinsuciu.com/2011/09/24/nitria-and-scetis-h-g-evelyn-whitethe-monasteries-of-the-wadi-n-natrun/. On the Palestinian editing, see most recently Smith, *Philosopher-Monks*, 31–35, chap. 1.2.

63. See G. Pyke and D. Brooks Hedstrom, "The Afterlife of Sherds: Architectural Re-use Strategies at the Monastery of John the Little, Wadi Natrun," in *Functional Aspects of Egyptian Ceramics in their Archaeological Context: Proceedings of a Conference Held at the McDonald Institute for Archaeological Research, Cambridge, July 24th–July 25th, 2009*, ed. B. Bader and M. F. Ownby, Orientalia Lovaniensia Analecta 217 (Leuven: Peeters, 2013), 307–25; and Yale Monastic Archaeology Project, Yale Monastic Archaeology Project North (Wadi al-Natrun), www.yale.edu/egyptology/ae_al-natrun.htm.

64. The phrase apparently dates to the 4th–5th cents.

community, then the self—the opposite of the current American template. The two, of course, don't live in splendid isolation—even the anchorites in these sayings wouldn't be here today unless another monk had recorded his or her words for use within community.

In *Contemplation in a World of Action,* Merton, joining desert with community, puts it eloquently. He says that monastic community "is also a charism of brotherhood in the wilderness," and continues, "This closeness is understood as being, at least ideally, a very human and warm relationship, and the charism of the monastic life is, and has been from the beginning, a grace of *communion* in a shared quest and a participated light. It is then a charism of special love and of mutual aid in the attainment of a difficult end."[65] A participated light: a beautiful phrase illuminating a deep truth, one that's not solely monastic. We can apply Merton's words to any intentional community and communion. Worthwhile ends are, in my experience, often difficult. Self not *in se ipso* but in community. Community not *in se* but in selves; not *in se* alone but also *in aliis*, in others.

One such early monastic community was the Monastery of Apa Jeremias at Saqqara, just south of modern Cairo. Wall paintings there depict, perhaps, Ama Sibylla; more certainty comes at the monastery at Bawit, where two rooms (apparently) contained paintings of Ama Sibylla with the Virtues: Chapelle III and VI with ten and twelve Virtues, respectively, surrounding Ama Sibylla.[66] Sibylla is a somewhat mysterious figure, but it's clear that the Virtues at Bawit were important presences to the monks and represented an important spiritual concept: they tried to cultivate the virtues in themselves and in others. We could say that the virtues were the loyalties that the monks lived individually and in community. These Virtues, portrayed, were sometimes grouped together, with some

65. Thomas Merton, *Contemplation in a World of Action* (New York: Doubleday, 1965, 1973), 18 (emphasis his).

66. See Tim Vivian, "Ama Sibylla of Saqqara: Prioress or Prophet? Monastic, or Mythological Being?" in Vivian, *Words to Live By,* 377–93.

names in Greek and some in Coptic: *Pistis* (Faith), *Elpis* (Hope), *Agapē* (Love), *Parthenia* (Virginity), *Thbbio* (Humility), *Tbbo* (Chastity), *Mntrmrash* (Gentleness), *Gratia* (Grace), *Hypomonē* (Patience / Patient Endurance), and *Sophia* (Wisdom).[67]

"Virtue," with its rare utterance these days, and the lack of discussion around it, seems like an antique word or, worse, a long-forgotten relic left behind in the shuttered Museum of Superannuated Language. Yet forms of the word occur well over one hundred times in Shakespeare's writings. The following couplet is apropos to the monastic sayings in this volume: "O infinite virtue, com'st thou smiling from / The world's great snare uncaught?"[68] From the world's great snare uncaught. It's a chilling question, itself worthy of *lectio* and discussion. As Antony cries out, "I saw all the snares of the Enemy stretched out like a net over the earth" (7). Shakespeare and Antony ask, What in the world (so to speak) seizes and captures virtue, hogties and muzzles her? But Shakespeare suggests, and the early monks show, that virtue can escape captivity, and "come smiling." Again, a question: "By what agency?" Well, with inherent and gifted grace, ours.

In Antony 7, Antony calls "the snares" those set by "the Enemy," that is, Satan, so he cries out "Who, then, can escape them?!" The one-word answer he gets is "Humility."* The use of "humility" is probably as rare as "virtue" in the United States these days! "Humility" (discussed below) is one of the Virtues / virtues at ancient Bawit, and the virtues that the early monastics taught in community can act as signposts that say to stop, look, listen, *pay attention*! *Attendite et videte!* Pay attention and look![69] Breathe, reflect, act, and *enact*. For the purposes of this volume, these signposts serve as guide to what the ammas and abbas are saying, and enacting, major themes in the *Apophthegmata*.

---

67. Latin *gratia*, "Grace," instead of Greek *cháris*, or its Coptic equivalent, *hmot*, puzzles me.

68. Shakespeare, *Antony and Cleopatra* IV.8.

69. From "O vos omnes," sung during Holy Week; numerous versions are on YouTube.

2. Exquisite Mutuality

The Jesuit Gregory Boyle ministers to, lives with, weeps with, and loves young men and women, mostly Latinos and Latinas, in Los Angeles; they are, or were, members of gangs, the homies and homegirls whose stories Boyle relates (*diēgéomai*; see above, p. 8) in *Tattoos on the Heart* and *Barking to the Choir*. In *Barking to the Choir*, Boyle speaks of "exquisite mutuality": "Truth be told, we are all in need of healing; we are all a cry for help."[70] One cries for help to another person, and / or to God, as we saw Antony do earlier; one seeks healing, a major theme in the *Sayings*, *from another person*, a doctor, a priest or pastor, a counselor or therapist, a loved one, a friend, an amma, an abba. Mutuality. I grew up on Air Force bases in the '50s and '60s during the years of "Mutually Assured Destruction" (MAD), hiding under my desk with other students during air raid drills at school.[71] In contrast, Boyle and the ammas and abbas offer us "mutually assured construction."[72] "Assured," given us humans, is undoubtedly optimistic, but the monks' entire enterprise is optimistic. It's worth noting that *optimism* comes from Latin *optimus*, the superlative form of *bonus*, *good*; thus optimism is thinking things for the best, and *towards* the best. Both are prophets of, and pilgrims to, hope (see V.6), hope not solipsistic but communal, where *all* are community.

As Rowan Williams points out, citing Paul Evdokimov,

> the Fathers of the Desert have paved the way for [not flight and abandonment, but rather] *a return to history, to the city, to society*; once the reality of the desert has been seen, in

70. Greg Boyle, *Barking to the Choir: The Power of Radical Kinship* (New York: Free Press, 2017), 172. See also Greg Boyle, *Tattoos on the Heart: The Power of Boundless Compassion* (New York: Free Press, 2011).

71. See Tim Vivian, "The Bomb(s) This Time: A Meditation on Thomas Merton's *The Cold War Letters*," CSQ 55, no. 1 (2020): 19–54.

72. Boyle, *Tattoos*, 178. Since Boyle (b. 1954) is like me a child of the Cold War and MAD, I'm sure his phrase is an echo, and reversal, of Mutually Assured Destruction.

the city and in the wilderness, the resultant deep transformation of the human consciousness becomes, to a greater or
lesser degree, independent of external circumstances.
Human consciousness was different before the ascesis of
the desert from what it was after.[73]

Evdokimov undoubtedly overreaches, but we can connect him with
the ammas and abbas in their quest for transformation in both desert
and city. The monastics in this volume live on the edge, geographi-
cally, socially, and spiritually. They are often attentive to the poor
and outcast but, at least as the sayings and stories here portray them
(and, we need to remember, all presentations are partial), their daily,
hourly, focus is to excavate the rubble within, not to throw it away
but to build a habitude, a simple one, a *manshubia*, a good foundation for the soul from which to work for self and others.[74]

Community, and its discontents—and salvation. In Achilla 1,
three monks come to see the abba. One of them, like one of
Boyle's homies, has "a bad reputation." "Bad" here, *kakós*, can
mean "evil": the monk has an evil reputation—which means that
other monks believe he's bad or evil, therefore an outcast. But, as
the celebrity culture so dominant and domineering now attests,
reputation is often not reality. The two complaining monks ask
Achilla for something he's made, at least one like a spiritual tourist
looking for a sacred souvenir. He tells them no. When the third
monk, bad or evil, asks, Achilla quickly says "I *will* make *you*
one." We can virtually hear the agitating and vexing of the pots
boiling over inside the other monks: bewilderment, possibly anger,
self-righteousness, judgmentalism. We have met them, and they
are ours. They can even *be* us.

These other two, stunned, ask what's going on. Achilla, probably
quietly and gently, explains that if he doesn't give the other monk

---

73. Rowan Williams, *A Silent Action: Engagements with Thomas Merton*
(Louisville, KY: Fons Vitae, 2011), 29.

74. In monastic terms, then, a habitation can also be a habitude, "habitual
disposition or mode of behavior or procedure" (Webster's).

something, the monk will say "It's because of my sin; the elder's heard about it, so he refused to make me a net." Achilla then adds, "If we do this, we're quickly cutting the rope. So I raised up his soul so someone like this wouldn't be swallowed by sorrow." Swallowed by sorrow, in the maw of Jonah's whale. Achilla is metaphorically speaking about cutting the rope that connects the sinful monk with the three of them, that is, with the community. I once asked a wise old Episcopal priest if, in some forty years of ministry, he'd ever excluded anyone from Communion. His simple reply: "No." *Rope* in this story translates *schoiníon*, a rope used in sailing, one that holds a ship in place. Thus we can see it here as a lifeline: if the monks cut it, they'll set the sinful monk adrift, isolated from community, perhaps to drown (the metaphor of drowning occurs twice below in other sayings).

Ammonas 10, with a bit of comedy, *la comédie humaine*, concerns another sinful brother. The elder Ammonas goes to a monastic community where "one person . . . had a bad [or: evil] reputation." It so happens, the story tells us, that a woman* enters the cell of this disreputable fellow. When the monk's brethren find out, instead of having one of them quietly and responsibly go see the brother about it, they tell Ammonas, apparently thinking that he'll act as judge and jury, and perhaps executioner: he'll excoriate the monk, and drive his woman away. When the monk finds out that Ammonas and the monks are on to him and are coming after him (we can imagine the torchlit villagers in *Frankenstein*), he hides the woman "in a very large jar"! Ammonas, "for God's sake," says nothing (now cue the laugh track)—and goes and sits on top of the jar. The monks, undoubtedly let down now that they're not going to see harsh punishment meted out, look all over for the woman, but find nothing.

Ammonas now, surely to their amazement, tells them "God will forgive you." They—and we—now exclaim "Forgive *us*?! For *what*?!" After the brothers leave, Ammonas now tells the monk only "Watch out for yourself, brother." Keeping watch* is a key monastic practice, but it's almost always to watch, guard, protect* *oneself* (*phylássō* means all three), often from the Devil and, as here, often from oneself. *Phylássō doesn't* mean to watch, spy on, others in community. Logs and specks.[75] We'll see later that judging not others but rather oneself is an important part of living in community. The monks in the story above show that, as Boyle says, "It's sometimes plain hard to locate the will to be in kinship even though at the same time it's our deepest longing."

We'll look later (III.3–4) at tales of community and kinship, and community and kinship's concomitant need for forgiveness. Perhaps these monastic sayings and stories are remarkable precisely because they're *not* about miracles and because they *are*. They show that an ever-present danger within community is being judgmental, putting gates outside *and within*. We often look for spectacular miracles, theophanic Fourth of July fireworks shows. Let's call the wonders here "quotidian miracles," a mother breast-feeding, a father carrying his beloved on his shoulders. Conception and giving birth and spiritual parenting are vital, life-giving, to the desert monks' communities. But what will they and we conceive and give birth to?

3. Helping Others: Neighbor and Stranger

Love depersonalizes when it treats the neighbor as significant primarily in relation to myself; it is rightly directed toward the unique reality of the person when it sees the other in relation to God—as, in the proper sense, symbolic, a living sign of the creator, irreducible either to generalities or to the other's significance and usefulness for me.[76]

75. See Matt 7:5.

76. Rowan Williams, "The Theological World of the *Philokalia*," in *The* Philokalia: *A Classic Text of Orthodox Spirituality*, edited by Brock Bingaman and Bradley Nassif (Oxford: Oxford University Press, 2012), 104. I wish to thank Sarah Coakley for referring me to Williams's piece.

Community means neighbor,* and neighbors. For Jesus, "Love your neighbor" is not secondary to loving God; it's concomitant.[77] I live in a middleclass suburb in California where most neighbors rarely see one another. As someone who grew up with great rock 'n' roll in the '60s, I also lived during the Vietnam War, the Cold War, riots, assassinations, and segregation, and now witness our recrudescent and recidivist racism, so I'm usually not a nostalgist. But I often wonder what the garage-door opener and disappearance of the front porch has done in many of our communities, to many of us. An attentive reader doesn't read Marilynne Robinson's *Gilead* series for the nostalgia (the characters there are too much us for that) but for the joy of reading about, experiencing, community, both its travails and its achievements, and receiving the learning, informational and transformational, that comes with it.[78] I've begun Part III with community, built on the good foundation of what Boyle terms mutuality and kinship. If monastic, and homeboy, community is the home, then neighbors are those without and within.

As Boyle notes, "As misshapen as we feel ourselves to be, attention from another reminds us of our true shape in God."[79] As he emphasizes above, we'll see later that attention to another also shapes us. A key monastic virtue for monks in Late Antiquity, as for the folks in the Bible much earlier, is hospitality. One welcomes* and receives* a stranger* as one receives the sacraments. Abraham welcomed strangers; as Hebrews says about that welcoming, "Do not be forgetful to entertain strangers: for thereby some have entertained angels unawares."[80] As Abba Apollo says,

---

77. See Mark 12:29-31 // Matt 22:36-40.

78. Marilynne Robinson, *Gilead* (New York: Farrar, Straus and Giroux, 2004); *Home* (New York: Farrar, Straus and Giroux, 2008); and *Lila* (New York: Farrar, Straus and Giroux, 2014). Her most recent addition to this series is *Jack* (Toronto: McClelland & Stewart / Penguin Random House, 2020).

79. Boyle, *Tattoos*, 55.

80. Gen 18:1-19; Heb 13:2 (KJV).

"We must respectfully welcome brothers who come to visit us because we're not welcoming them but rather God" (3).[81]

Antony both puts this succinctly and moves deeper: "We have life and death through our neighbor. If we gain* our brother, we gain God, but if we cause our brother to sin, we sin against Christ." This saying, Antony 9, is the only saying attributed to him where the word *Christ* appears. Maybe this fact should grab our attention. At first this unique instance puzzled me. Why not more? Yet Christ's only explicit appearance in Antony's 39 sayings in this volume strongly puts the focus on and reinforces Jesus' redefinitions of Torah in Matthew's gospel: *You have heard that it was said, "You shall love your neighbor and hate your enemy." But I say to you, love your enemies and pray for those who persecute you, so that you may be children of your Father in heaven. . . . and "You shall love the Lord your God with all your heart, and with all your soul, and with all your mind." This is the greatest and first commandment. And a second is like it: "You shall love your neighbor as yourself." On these two commandments depend all the law and the prophets.*[82] This is the monastic commandment: Love your neighbor. It's a matter of life and death. And, as we'll see, monastic neighbors include even, perhaps especially, outcasts and lepers (for Jesus' "the least of these," see Matt 25:40).

Neighbor and self. Self and neighbor. Theodore of Pherme 11 exegetes an inherent monastic and human problem—a problem that in our culture may now be a pathogen. A brother asks Theodore what "the work* of the soul" is. "Work," *érgon*, and its cognates are key to early monasticism for many reasons, but perhaps the most important is that work, especially in one's cell, is the venue for prayer. One of work's siblings, *ergasía*, means "action,

81. See further discussion of this saying below.

82. Matt 5:43-45a; 22:37-40. Beginning with his birth narrative, Matthew presents Jesus as the new Moses, who metaphorically inscribes with his finger on new tablets. "Love your neighbor" is from Lev 19:18. "Hate your enemy" does not occur in the Hebrew Bible.

activity," and the insistence of Theodore here is activity and action *for our neighbor*. This action, he insists, is the work of the soul— not the work of the hands (as important as that is), working for oneself. It may be hard for us to hear the seismic rumbles of culture shock here. Working with one's hands for the monks was vital and necessary, both physically and spiritually. But *no* work or activity, even praying, Theodore is saying, matters more than helping a neighbor. Praxis as prayer.

But Theodore goes further, much further, and what he narrates in Saying 18 was assuredly countercultural then, and is preposterously so now. Theodore tells a brother about Abba Theonas, who "wants always to be predisposed to God." But what does such predisposition mean? This: Theonas goes off to the bakery to bake bread, a quotidian activity (it isn't overreach to hear "staff of life" throughout this enacted parable). After he's done and is heading home, "some poor people" ask him for bread—and he gives them *everything* he's baked. We may condescendingly smile at this— Oh, isn't that sweet—but the story has barely begun. The saying is terse, but clearly Theonas is now heading home, with his empty baskets, perhaps feeling hungry. Now some others, seeing the bread baskets, also ask him for bread; having none, "he gave them his little baskets and the cloak he was wearing." If the clash of cultures was gently ringing before, it now clangs and reverberates: once he's back in his cell, Theonas finds fault *with himself* and says "I haven't fulfilled God's commandment."

What commandment?! "Thou shalt go hungry"? Theonas's behavior certainly seems extreme. But after we wince at Theonas's thinking, we're faced with a difficult truth—or truths: Why are *we* so greedy? And Why *are* we so greedy? And Why are we *so* greedy?[83] Why do so many of us in our culture do obeisance to the concomitant commandments of consumerism: "You are what

83. See Cassian, *Institutes* 7, in *John Cassian: The Conferences*, trans. Boniface Ramsey, ACW 57 (New York: Paulist Press, 1997), 167–89.

you consume. You are the money you make. On these two depend all our profits and economic growth".[84] Theodore's enacted parable confirms what Antony says earlier about neighbor and life and death. After saying the Trisagion ("Holy, Holy, Holy"), the monk should immediately add "Neighbor, Neighbor, Neighbor." As should we.

In John the Little 39, John puts into saying form what we've seen in Theodore's parable: John, channeling Jesus, says, "It isn't possible to build a house from the top to the bottom but only from the foundation up."[85] When the brothers, like Jesus' disciples, ask John what he means, he simply, and profoundly, says, "The foundation is your neighbor; you lay it in order to gain your neighbor. He ought to come first. All the commandments of Christ depend on him." Not "depend on *it*," but "depend on *him*." Since the monks ask so often about salvation, we should pause to see that there's nothing here about future and heavenly salvation, gaudy thrones being prepared at Jesus' right and left hand:[86] salvation is here and now, incarnated in our brother and sister, a realized eschatology, a realized soteriology.[87] When a lawyer asks Jesus, *What must I do to inherit eternal life?* Jesus tells him to love God and his neighbor: *do this, and you will live.* Norris adds, "For the early Christian abbas and ammas, both heaven and hell were to be found in present reality" (*Acedia*, 111). One should not take my statement and Norris's to mean that the fathers and mothers weren't concerned with heavenly salvation. They were, but their emphasis is on being saved here and now. If we're attentive, they can help us redefine ourselves, here and now.

---

84. A sarcastic inversion of Matt 22:37-40.

85. See Luke 6:46-47.

86. See Luke 9:46-48.

87. See Luke 10:25-28. "Realized eschatology" was popularized by a number of scholars in the 20th century to emphasize the "presentness" in the kingdom that Jesus preached and enacted; see Donald K. McKim, *Westminster Dictionary of Theological Terms*, 2nd ed. (Louisville, KY: Presbyterian Publishing, 2014), 106.

4. Judging, and on to Discernment and Compassion[88]

Now there are varieties of gifts, but the same Spirit. . . .
To each is given the manifestation of the Spirit for the
common good. To one is given through the Spirit the utter-
ance of wisdom . . . to another the discernment [diákri-
sis] *of spirits.*[89]

Always watch first, with a still heart and mind; then you will
learn. When you have watched enough, then you can act.[90]

We saw earlier that at the Monastery of Apa Jeremias at Bawit
a wall painting depicts Ama Sybilla with the Virtues, such as Faith,
Hope, Love, Humility, and Patience / Patient Endurance. Discernment, perhaps surprisingly, is not in their company. But, as we'll
see, discernment is central to early monastic spirituality and community. Perhaps, again surprisingly, the most extended saying by
Abba Antony on discernment occurs not in the Greek or Coptic
sayings but rather the Arabic (unattested elsewhere).[91] Some brothers "were with Abba Antony, and they were discussing which
virtues are best for protecting the monk from falling into the traps
of the Devil." The brothers list fasting, keeping vigils, humility,
asceticism, and mercy, "the most honorable."

From a dramatic viewpoint, the monks are all sitting; what
they're discussing is a Prologue that allows Antony now to stand

---

88. See these terms in the Glossary and General Index. For a lengthy teaching
on discernment in the Arabic tradition of Antony's sayings, see Arabic Antony,
Letters 62 in Elizabeth Agaiby and Tim Vivian, *Door of the Wilderness: The
Greek, Coptic, and Copto-Arabic Sayings of Antony of Egypt* (forthcoming from
Collegeville, MN: Cistercian Publications).

89. 1 Cor 12:4-10; see 1 John 4:1: *Beloved, do not believe every spirit, but test
the spirits to see whether they are from God.*

90. Dan to Kent Nerburn in Nerburn, *Neither Wolf Nor Dog*, 65.

91. Arabic Antony, Letters 61; a translation will be available in the forthcoming book by Agaiby and Vivian; see n. 88. The translation here is Agaiby's. See
also Antony, *Letters* 3.5 (p. 206).

and face them: "Indeed, all the virtues you mention are beneficial for those seeking God and wanting to draw near to him." But then he enunciates the excesses such virtues may have; they can wreak such havoc that all the monks' "virtues were lost and even rejected." Why? Because, Antony continues, these monks "lacked discernment. Discernment is what teaches a person how to walk on the royal path[92] and avoid the wrong way." It's a good metaphor: discernment as a roadmap, or a GPS app, or, better, Discernment, the name of an experienced guide who walks beside a person. Before Antony explains to the monastics "how King Saul lacked discernment,"[93] he looks from face to face and offers this soliloquy: "Discernment is what teaches a person not to be deceived by the right hand of virtue,[94] or turn aside to the vices on the left hand.[95] Discernment is the eye and lamp of the soul, in the same way that the eye is the lamp of the body,[96] and so the Lord warns us to take care that the light within is not darkness.[97] Discernment makes a person examine his will, his language, and his deeds, and separate good from bad."

Antony doesn't explicitly say that discernment is a virtue, but it's clear that he believes that a monk must practice discernment in order to practice the virtues. In III.3 we saw compassion at work in hospitality and helping others. But the monks, like Antony above, are very aware of toxicity (we've seen it in action), both in community and in each person (on the latter see III.5 below). To deny this would be like someone standing on the beach in New

92. See Num 20:17; 21:22; Matt 11:30. Compare AlphAP Benjamin 5 (below) / SysAP VII.5 (Wortley, *Book,* 99); AlphAP Poemen 31 (Wortley, *Give Me*, 233) / SysAP X.61 (Wortley, *Book,* 157–58).

93. See 1 Sam 15.

94. Right hand of virtue: literally "right attack." In monastic literature this refers to deeds such as fasting, vigils, asceticism, etc.

95. Left hand: literally "left attack." In monastic literature this refers to vices such as gluttony, lust, laziness, etc.

96. Matt 6:22; Luke 11:34.

97. Matt 6:23; Luke 11:35.

Jersey just as Hurricane Sandy hits, obliviously painting a halcyon, imaginary, sunrise.

Probably the greatest toxicity that the monks diagnose is judging, being judgmental, whose noxious effects we've already seen. As Anna Freud says, "Sometimes we become all too sure of ourselves, all too willing to denounce others, renounce what they said—a measure of our passion to control things and, I regret to say, hear only the echoes of our own voices!"[98] But in the language the early monastics speak, lexical, spiritual, and practice-able, connected with judgment is *discernment*, judgment recollected in tranquility and prayer and, thus, sanctified, judgment sacramentally transformed. In Greek, *to judge** is *krínō,* and *judgment* is the cognate *krísis* (which can also mean, we should note, "charge, accusation," "trial," and "condemnation").[99] But in one of language's pregnant elucidations, "to discern" is *diakrínō,* and "discernment," a central practice, is *diákrisis*, both "to judge *through* (*diá*)," to judge through what's instant and importunate, with immediate gratification, and to move on towards a deeper, fully realized, judging. Discernment requires both duration of time and endurance.[100] Buddhism teaches that one faced with assault (of any kind) should, most importantly, practice patience.

Etymologically and realistically, practically (that is, praxis, *practice*), one must judge to discern, one must make judgments. But they must be *discerning* judgments, not our common (usual?) ones rising out of ignorance, fear, arrogance, and anger. One of the most

98. Freud to Robert Coles in conversation, cited by Coles in his Foreword to *Thomas Merton, Contemplation in a World of Action*, ix (see n. 65).

99. Montanari 1178b. That *krísis*, "judgment," comes into English as *crisis* offers fair warning.

100. The preposition *diá* with the accusative case can show extent of time, "during," as in *dià núkta*, "through the night," thus emphasizing the time needed for discernment. In Latin, "endurance," *indurare*, "to harden, make lasting," and "duration," *durare*, "to last," are related (www-oed-com.falcon.lib.csbu.edu/view/Entry/62033?redirectedFrom=endurance#eid and www-oed-com.falcon.lib.csub.edu/view/Entry/58626?redirectedFrom=duration#eid).

stunning instances of tough discernment in this volume is when a monk comes to Theodore of Pherme, "asking to hear some counsel"* (4). Abba Theodore, however, doesn't respond, so the brother leaves, saddened. In the monastic world, such a lack of response should tip us off, as the monastic disciples often do, that something's not right: Theodore's disciple, surprised, and standing in for us, now asks him, "Abba, why didn't you offer him counsel? He went away saddened." The elder says to him, "It's true that I wouldn't respond to him—he in fact traffics in what elders say and wants to be acclaimed for others' words of counsel." What Theodore says here strongly suggests that in his world there's nothing worse than a spiritual forger, a trafficker in easy grace, a charlatan miming the community's hard-won wisdom, monastic mummery.

The ammas and abbas in the present volume prize discernment, even tough discernment like Theodore's. But let's be honest, as with us it's where-there's-smoke-there's-fire discernment. We all know in our selves, in our communities, how toxic judgmentalism is. And in our nation: many people with no, or fake, evidence, have preemptively judged brown-skinned refugees to be criminals, rapists, and terrorists; such judgment, stooped over, carries with it on its back a trunk filled with venomous snakes, its lid wide open. Toxicity and sin. Toxicity *as* sin. We know what happened when the Germans, and much of Europe, dehumanized Jews. We know what happened when white Americans dehumanized Africans and Native Americans in this country. We see what happens now when whites dehumanize Blacks, Latinos, and Muslims; we see it too when Buddhists do the same with the Rohingya and the Chinese with the Uighurs. The early monastics gathered here don't speak, at least directly, of original sin,[101] so perhaps we should

---

101. Rom 5:12 is the usual first source: *Therefore, just as sin came into the world through one person, and death came through sin, and so death spread to all because all have sinned.* (NRSV, revised), though I think what Paul says is ambiguous ("*so . . . because*"). I haven't seen any allusions to Rom 5:12 in the sayings in this volume and Guy, SysAP 3.232, cites only one reference in the more voluminous SysAP, a saying not in the AlphAP (XI.51 [2.164–65]; Wortley, *Book*, 199).

say that judgmentalism is a *besetting* sin, concerns about which occupy many sayings.

The irony, and truth, here is acute. The monks have withdrawn* from "the world"* to live holy lives. The young monks in the sayings usually don't realize, but the elders do, that sins of anger, violence, hatred, and self-righteous judging, and judging's off-spring, condemnation, have come right along with them into the desert. Philoxonos, the sixth-century Syrian ascetic, says that the monk follows Christ into the desert "to fight the power of error." Then he adds, "And where is the power of error? We find it was after all not in the city, but in *ourselves*."[102] Kathleen Norris's statement is salutary, both for the monks and for us: "I regard sin as a viable concept, one that helps explain the mess we've made of our battered, embattled world, and the shambles we make of so many personal relationships."[103] As they sit in their spare cells and live in community, the monks, though far from the world, nevertheless dwell amidst mess and shambles; they *do* see that toxicity can grow, even in the aridity of Egypt, like poisonous mushrooms in damp, fertile soil.

Perhaps the greatest desert toxicity is judging others, judgmentalism (see III.5). Jesus speaks forcefully about judging: *Do not judge [krínō], so that you may not be judged. For with the judgment [kríma] you make you will be judged, and the measure you give will be the measure you get. Why do you see the speck in your neighbor's eye, but do not notice the log in your own eye?*[104] Judging, we can say, comes with monastic—that is, human—territory. Perhaps the major theme of this Introduction is to show that this monastic land-scape, depressions and flat spaces, deserts and waterways—and

102. Philoxonos, cited by Thomas Merton, *Raids on the Unspeakable* (New York: New Directions, 1966), 19; cited by Williams, *A Silent Action*, 29. There are spiritual semantics in what Philoxonos says: monks flee "the world,"* the city (*pólis*), only to find error in themselves, in their new way of life* (*politeía*).

103. Norris, *Acedia*, 34; see 33–39.

104. Matt 7:1-3; see Luke 6:37.

attainable mountains—is ours. They, like us, are its pilgrims. Antony 21 has what may be the best metaphor in the sayings gathered here for the consequences, and costs, of judging others: a brother "one time" succumbs to a deliciously non-specified "temptation," so his fellow monks (all sinless, presumably) drive him out of the monastery. This brother goes to stay with Antony awhile (we don't know what transpires there), and then Antony sends him back. But now, apparently without any restorative encounter, the monks give him the boot once again.

So, yet again, Antony sends him back; a motif in many sayings is that it often takes more than one try to get matters, especially spiritual matters, right.[105] We can picture this brother metaphorically carrying this message, Gospel and gospel, in his hands, as Jesus often holds the gospels in icons. "A ship shipwrecked at sea," Antony informs the judgmental monks, "and lost its cargo; after great hardship, it came safely to shore. You monks, however, want to throw into the sea to drown what has been safely brought to shore."[106] In Greek, "safely," *esṓthē*, is literally "was saved," from *sṓzō*, "to save," and cognate with *sōtēría*, "salvation," and *sōtḗr*, "savior / Savior." Now we know we're walking through the vast and imaginative landscape of monastic parable. As Alan Cooper says of biblical texts, quoted at the beginning of the Translator's Reflection earlier, "Engagement" with such texts "enables the

---

105. A good friend of mine signs off his emails with "O God of second chances, here I am again."

106. In ancient Mesopotamian-Semitic religions, water often stands for chaos. In Gen 1:2 when God begins to create, "darkness was over the surface of the deep." "Deep" in Hebrew is *tᵉhom*, cognate with Tiamat, the monster in the Babylonian epic *Enuma Elish*. See John J. Collins, *A Short Introduction to the Hebrew Bible*, 2nd ed. (Minneapolis: Fortress Press, 2014), 46. In discussing the Hebrews' crossing of the Red / Reed Sea in Exod 15 and the drowning of Pharaoh and his army, Collins observes, 70, "The imagery of sinking in water is used elsewhere in Hebrew poetry as a metaphor for distress (e.g. Psalm 69). . . . In these cases, sinking in the depths is not a description of physical condition, but simply a metaphor for distress."

willing reader to participate in the creation of a remarkable world of imagination." This world, realized (at least briefly) in what Antony says above, is salvific.

The judgmental monks, of course, when they hear this vivid metaphor from the great Antony himself (but did they hear the lexical admonishment?), "accepted [the brother] back—immediately." Perhaps *too* immediately. Perhaps the ending is a little too pat, especially for us moderns; we're not quite happy with a Fortinbras coming in at the end of *Hamlet*, bucket and mop in his hand, cleaning up the bloody mess. But let's imaginatively look a little closer at the closing scene here. The picture is one of all the monks, perhaps, standing outside the monastery doors as if to welcome Antony himself. Imagine them in their freshly washed clothes, waving palm fronds (as the ancients did, and not just for Jesus), the head of the monastery ready to receive the eminent Antony.[107] When they open the doors to let the transgressive monk back in, *and* hear Antony's words, they, symbolically, welcome *themselves* back home, presumably penitently, back from the alienation that they've made with their very own hands, back from the lack of salvation that condemnation brings with it. Now, and only now, can the monastic vision of work,* and prayer,* peace,* patient endurance,* contemplative quiet,* and inward stillness* truly dwell (see V.1–5).

There are many more stories like this, a fact that tells us that if we're firewatchers, we'd better sound the alarm, because in parable, and absolutely certainly in fact, there's a lot of billowing smoke from the monasteries in these sayings and stories. Concurrently, these stories not only tell but show us that each of us often has smoke roiling around within, often pouring forth. A similar story in Antony 29 about judging presents another wonderful metaphor, a garment both clean and dirty that we can take off the rack at the monastery and, like them, humbly wear. In this saying, a brother

107. Jesus: Matt 21:8 // Mark 11:8 // John 12:13. See 1 Macc 13:51.

is "falsely accused of sexual sin."* He denies it and hightails it off to see Abba Antony. Unlike the monk in the previous story, this monk has self-excluded himself from community.

At Antony's, it's not the wise and discerning Antony who commands the monastic stage but Paphnutius Kephalas,* "who happened to be there." So Paphnutius, instead of giving a lecture on judging, tells this parable: "I saw on the riverbank a person who had been thrown down into the mud up to his knees, and some people came to give him a hand—and they shoved him further down into the mud, up to his neck!" I wish the story ended here, to let the monks and us meditate on it a bit. But the saying provides a punch line: "So Abba Antony said this to them about Abba Paphnutius [Coptic: *papnoute*, the one of God, *noute*]: '*Here* is a real human being, someone who *can* heal and save souls.'" Despite my wish for a conclusion with more dramatic punch, Antony's final words "save souls" do nicely connect us with "safely," that is, healing and, thus, saving, salvation.

Paphnutius, like Antony, has shown discernment, thinking things through. The K-12 for discernment is learning honesty and self-honesty, the former like arithmetic, the latter like advanced algebra; college is learning calculus, humility.[108] We see this in bright illumination in John the Little 8, where John is valedictorian: one time an elder, with jealousy waging war against him, turns to Abba John as the latter is counseling the brothers and says, "Your jug, John, is filled with poison." John doesn't react angrily at this, indignantly jumping up and grabbing the guy by his monastic lapel; he does what is normally counterintuitive and countercultural: "So it is, abba, and you've said this while seeing only the outside. If you saw the inside, what would you say?" Can *any* honest person not say this? Can any honest person *not* say this? As a friend of mine recently said, "I don't

---

108. With a very different, and vivid, metaphor, a friend said recently that humility is the manure that we spread around our spiritual plantings.

do Facebook; I have a hard enough time keeping track of myself."
The questions above contain multitudes. Perhaps each of us
should wear John's response as tefillin and also place it as a
mezuzah not just on the front door of our homes but at every
doorway, which is, in monastic terms, the door of heart and mind,
soul and spirit. Judging—compassion is a coin. It seems that
judging all too often faces up. But its flipside is empathy and
compassion. We carry both sides on each coin we carry in our
quotidian, spiritual, pockets. We're like a Roman coin: on one
side is an admiring self-portrait, on the other *LIBERTAS*. We can
pull a coin out and, as opposed to a regular coin toss, decide
which side to place face up.

I want to close this section with one of the most memorable
sayings-stories of the early monks on judging and not-judging.
Context is important: in Moses 3, which is contemporarily ours,
monks belittle Moses because he's Ethiopian ("Moses the Black"),
that is, *the other*, of a darker skin than they, from across the south-
ern border.[109] But in Moses 2, he plays a venerable participant at
a council: a "severe assembly" as Thomas Merton might call it,
is taking place at Scetis about a brother who has transgressed in
some way, and the monks invite the estimable abba to come and
take part, that is, give his imprimatur and nihil obstat to their
condemnation of the monk.[110] He declines. So the priest (presumably, it's important to note, a spiritual leader in the community) pulls rank and sends for him. Thus asked, commanded,

---

109. See Bauer 626b. As early as the *Epistle of Barnabas* 4.9 (ca. 120–130) in
Christian literature, "the Black One" (*ho mélas*) indicates the Devil. Black can be
an "apocalyptic color" (Rev 6:5 with a "black horse"). Black "as the color of evil,
forming a contrast to the world of light (evil, malignant in the moral realm)," occurs in Classical Greek (Solon, Pindar). As early as *Iliad* 2.834 death itself is black,
pain can be black (4.117), and *Iliad* 1.103 describes ominous and threatening anger
as black. I wish to thank Apostolos Athanassakis for the references to the *Iliad*.

110. Thomas Merton, *The Wisdom of the Desert: Sayings from the Desert
Fathers of the Fourth Century* (New York: New Directions, 1960), 19.

Moses comes—but he comes counterculturally. He puts sand in a basket with a lot of holes in it and carries it with him, probably on his back (as a cross?). When the monks come out to greet him, they ask what's going on with the basket. Moses says: "My sins are running out like sand through the holes in the basket, and I don't see them, but you've asked *me* to come judge someone else?" (Or: "My sins are running out like sand through the holes in the basket, and I don't see them, but you've asked me to come judge *someone else?*") Shamed, they don't say a word of judgment to the brother and forgive him. Moses has just healed one deleterious habit of the heart.

5. Habits of the Heart

God asks for the heart, but the heart is oppressed with uncertainty in its own twilight.[111]

It is in the depths of the heart that we discover not only our own humanity, but all human nature and humankind.[112]

"Heart," in fact, may be the key that unlocks all kinds of gates. *Heart* is a much more flexible and deeper word in Coptic than it is in Greek or English. A story about Antony in the Coptic Sayings shows this. Coptic *hēt* (pronounced "heat"), "heart," is not only the last word in the story, it's part of other words: "mercy," "consideration" (the virgin acknowledges that God has "taken into consideration [-*hēt*] all our sins"), "merciful," and "repentance" (literally "the eating of the heart"). In fact, there could well be a play on words at the beginning of the story: Antony "sets out" for the monastery; in Coptic, "sets out" is *–er hēts*, "to begin," from

111. Abraham Joshua Heschel, *God in Search of Man* (New York: Farrar, Straus and Giroux, 1976), 296–97.
112. Kelty, *My Song*, 40.

hē, "forepart, beginning," no linguistic relation to *hēt*, "heart, mind." But in Coptic the close homophone *er nhēt*, with *hēt*, "heart," at its center, means "reflect on, criticize, repent, regret," all of which are apropos to this story.[113] "Setting out" thus foreshadows future events in the story: Antony (whether he knows it or not, more likely the latter) is on his way to reflecting on his judgmentalism, then criticizing it (even if we don't see the self-criticism), then regretting and repenting.

For "compassion," Coptic doesn't use *hēt*, but it does use the Greek loanword *splánchnon* / pl. *splánchna*, "guts," as in the verb *splanchnízomai*, "to have compassion." We should follow the Greek and say that "to have compassion" first requires the guts to do so.[114] *Splanchnízomai* returns us to Jesus: when Jesus sees a crowd, he has *compassion for them* because they're *harassed and helpless* (Matt 14:14); moved with compassion *for two blind men*, Jesus touches their eyes, and they immediately gain their sight (Matt 20:34); having compassion for a widow, he raises her dead son (Luke 7:13). Boyle reminds us that dropping "the enormous inner burden of judgment," as Antony does, "allows us to make of ourselves what God wants the world to ultimately be: people who," like Antony again, "stand in awe. Judgment, after all, takes up the room you need for loving."[115] To take Boyle's metaphor a bit further (metaphors like to travel), things would be much clearer if each of us wore a reversible sign: one side says NO VACANCY; the other, within a heart, VACANCY.

The iterations of "compassion" in Antony, Coptic Saying 36 make me want to move right away from the fog of judging to sun-illuminated compassion. Antony kills something when—even *if* the revelation is from God—he sets out to "severely rebuke and

113. Walter Ewing Crum, ed., *A Coptic Dictionary* (Oxford: Oxford University Press, 1962); repr. (Eugene, OR: Wipf & Stock, 2005), 714a–17b.

114. In Hebrew, *compassion* is cognate with *womb*.

115. Boyle, *Barking*, 57.

condemn" a female monastic. A sorrowful, difficult thing it is to realize and admit that we humans all too easily turn the territory we inhabit—geographical, moral, and spiritual—into killing fields. Anger bedevils the ammas and abbas as much as it does us. They intuitively sense, or come to know, Rowan Williams's insight: "The essential point is simply that anger used against any other person is unnatural—not least because it implies that the source of our problems or failures is in someone else's acts and dispositions."[116] When I first read that sentence, I was startled. Unnatural? Seems *all too natural* to me. But then I saw the wisdom in Williams' statement: "anger used against any other person" is key. *Against* someone else. As I reflected further, what hit me was *used.* We use a tool; so we can use anger, like a club, a bat, a knife, even a gun, both metaphorically and, unfortunately, not. And, in doing so, we use it against ourselves.

The ammas and abbas see anger in several ways: when Antony elsewhere defines "humility" too simply, perhaps simplistically, another monk says that "humility neither gets angry nor provokes someone to anger."[117] Abba Agathon even warns, "If someone prone to anger were to raise the dead, even this would not be acceptable in God's sight."[118] Ammonas is realistic: "I spent fourteen years in Scetis asking God night and day to give me the grace* to defeat anger."[119] When asked what anger is, Abba Isaiah simply, yet deeply, replies, "Strife, lying, and ignorance."[120] (We should reflect on those unexpected instances of *lying* and *ignorance.*) And Abba Isidore wisely counsels: "I went to the marketplace one time to sell a few things, and when I saw anger getting near me, I dropped what I had and fled."[121] The ammas and abbas offer

116. Williams, "Theological World," 109.
117. SysAP Prologue 5 (line 94); Wortley, *Book*, 4.
118. Agathon 19.
119. Ammonas 3.
120. Isaiah 11.
121. Isidore 7.

lived-out midrashim on Matt 5:21-26: here Jesus teaches, force-fully, that anger is as bad as murder; more important than making an offering at the altar is reconciliation. And reconciling is an act of compassion towards another—and oneself. There *is* healing: compassion is both poultice and antibiotic.

6. The Wallpaper of the Soul: Compassion*

Worship without compassion is worse than self-deception;
it is an abomination.[122]

Antony, as we saw, a canonized saint in Orthodox, Anglican, and Roman Catholic Churches, learns compassion the hard way. That makes me wonder if that's *always* the way. Many of the monks in this volume do likewise. Apparently for us humans judging is easy, compassion far more difficult. Judging is turning an immediate and glaring spotlight on an offense (or presumed offense); compassion is taking the time and holding a flickering candle to find the light that was there before the darkness over-came it.[123] Antony, in what is a monastic set-piece (though no less valuable for that), has an awe-filled experience that allows him to learn or, more likely, relearn, compassion. Antony's flickering candle can, with faith and hard work (*ascesis*, "training"), become a sanctuary lamp behind the altar table always kept lit, a sign of both Real Presence and hope. This means there is always the presence and possibility of a consequent Eucharist of gracious fragility and grace-filled compassion.

As Boyle says, "When we share . . . shards of excavation with each other, we move into the intimacy of mutual healing."[124] Bread and wine transfigured from shards of excavation. Bread and wine transfigured *into* shards of excavation. Aren't we all spiritual and

---

122. Abraham Joshua Heschel, *The Insecurity of Freedom: Essays on Human Experience* (New York: Farrar, Straus & Giroux, 1966), 87.

123. See John 1:5.

124. Boyle, *Barking*, 56.

moral excavators, gathering our shards together to make not fragments shored against our ruins, nor a perfect whole—that's extremely rare in archeology—but to build enough of a semblance of wholeness to call it a guide towards our true selves?[125] As we'll see in IV.3 with the "true" and "false" selves, healing within is also mutual, the former self healing the latter (the former self-healing the latter). What Boyle says elsewhere applies both outwardly and inwardly: "Compassion is always, at its most authentic, about a shift from the cramped world of self-preoccupation into a more expansive place of fellowship, or true kinship," and "Compassion is not a relationship between the healer and the wounded. It's a covenant between equals."[126]

Much of Buddhism stresses *anatta* (*anatman*), "no self," "not-self," and disavows the Western construct of self (see below at IV.1).[127] But much of Buddhism also emphasizes what the Vietnamese Zen Buddhist Thich Nhat Hanh calls "engaged Buddhism," taking compassion, a deep emphasis of both the Buddha and Jesus, out into the world, to others.[128] Thus individual *and* community. An emphasis on community responds to the radical individualism in America that's long been part of our DNA, now a dominant and domineering gene, with manifest, and manifestly dangerous, results. As we turn in Part IV to the self, we should always keep community and kinship in mind, self *and* community.

125. Fragments shored against our ruins: see T. S. Eliot, *The Wasteland*, Part V, "What the Thunder Said," near the very end (The Poetry Foundation, www. poetryfoundation.org/poems/47311/the-waste-land).

126. Boyle, *Tattoos*, 77.

127. See James A. Wiseman, "Thomas Merton and Theravada Buddhism," in *Merton and Buddhism: Wisdom, Emptiness, & Everyday Mind*, ed. Bonnie Bowman Thurston (Louisville, KY: Fons Vitae, 2007), 35.

128. See Wiseman's discussion of Walpola Rahula (1907–1997) vis-à-vis Thomas Merton in the essay above, 41–49; Thich Nhat Hanh, *Living Buddha, Living Christ*, Twentieth Anniversary Edition (New York: Riverhead Books, 2007); and Robert H. King, *Thomas Merton and Thich Nhat Hanh: Engaged Spirituality in an Age of Globalism* (New York: Continuum, 2003).

IV. Ego & Self: The Awe-filled Rowing towards the True Self[129]

Mystics ask God to remind them they are nothing. This is irritating to the ego's need for self-satisfaction.[130]

1. Ego & Humility

To transcend one's own self-centeredness is not a virtue [but] a saving "necessity."[131]

An elder was asked "What is humility?" He replied, "If your brother sins against you and you forgive him before he asks forgiveness from you."[132]

The monks in this volume, like Buddhists with "no-self,"[133] talk about the nothingness of the self, the "Nothing that is not there and the nothing that is," as the poet Wallace Stevens puts it.[134]

---

129. Borrowed from the poet Anne Sexton: "The Awful Rowing Toward God." Graiver, *Asceticism,* 70, notes that "Whereas a soul-body dualism has proven too simple a model by which to understand early monastic notions of selfhood, a distinction between ideal or normative selfhood and the actual constitution of embodied selves allows us to reconstruct a more complex and dynamic picture of monastic notions of selfhood and the ways in which they were formed and employed." See her next paragraph for a good discussion. See "Demons and the Human Mind: Two Phenomenologies of Mental Life," in *Asceticism,* 65–71.

130. Boyle, *Barking,* 94.

131. William James, quoted by Norris, *Acedia,* 23; source not given.

132. AnonAP 304 (SysAP 15.78); Wortley, *Anonymous Sayings,* 202–3, my translation.

133. No-self: Sanskrit *anatman,* "Buddhist doctrine positing the lack of an indwelling individual essence. . . . the basic idea is simple: what appears as a unitary agent and subject of experience is in fact a collocation of psychophysical events, and the goal of meditation is to 'realize' the truth of selflessness, both to understand it and make it real" (Smith, ed., 803a).

134. Stevens, "The Snow Man," The Poetry Foundation, www.poetryfoundation.org/poems/45235/the-snow-man-56d224a6d4e90. The poem ends, "The

However alien and mysterious the teaching of the no-self is for most Westerners, it can be tonic for our ego-plagued culture, as we watch one "poor player" after another "that struts and frets his hour upon the stage."[135] The monks' "nothing," like the Buddhist "no-self," seems to focus on humility. As Boyle reminds us, "Humility returns the center of gravity to the center. It addresses the ego clinging, which supplies oxygen to our sufferings."[136] Humility. Many of us have had preachers (guilty as charged) inform us that "humility" comes from Latin *humus*, "earth, ground, soil."[137] Ashes to ashes and dust to dust. But what if we see ashes, the ashes of the ego, not as death and detritus, but as purifying agents, available with and without cost every day? Norris makes a very important point for us in an age and culture that often equates humility with groveling, hair shirts, and metal-tipped flagellants; she points out that the early monks "were suggesting that people become not doormats wallowing in self-abnegation, but individuals with a realistic perception of their place in the world." A *realistic* perception. As Norris and Boyle point out, we should, all the time, be asking ourselves if T. S. Eliot was right when he said "Humankind cannot bear very much reality."[138] The early monastics are nothing if not realistic. Our problem, it seems, is that all too often we can't stand too much reality.

Norris speaks here of our "cracks and fissures" as not just indicating our misery but also "as places where the light of promise shines through."[139] As Leonard Cohen memorably expresses it,

---

listener, who listens in the snow, / And, nothing himself, beholds / Nothing that is not there and the nothing that is."

135. Shakespeare, *Macbeth* V.5.2381–82.

136. Boyle, *Barking*, 102. Chap. 5, "Sell Your Cleverness," 91–105, is on humility.

137. Lewis and Short 870c. For *humilitas*, "lowness, meanness, insignificance," "meanness, baseness, abjectness," the dictionary does not give a positive sense until ecclesiastical Latin: Sulpicius Severus in the 4th–5th cents. (870bc).

138. Eliot, "Burnt Norton," *The Four Quartets* (1936).

139. Norris, *Acedia*, 139.

"Ring the bells that still can ring / Forget your perfect offering / There is a crack in everything / That's how the light gets in."[140] Realism allows us to take that humus and become spiritual gardeners: "We want to prepare a good soil in which grace can grow."[141] The "nothingness" that humility offers can be restorative. But, used wrongly, it can maim, even destroy. Translators can get transfixed by words. I was stunned, then moved, even shaken, one day by one word in a text I was translating: *exouthenéō* (= *exouthenízō*) is a later variant of Classical Greek *exoudenízō*, "to value not at all, to hold of no account at all, scorn." "Not" and "no" in those definitions capture it well: *outhén/oudén* in Greek means "nothing."[142] So we can also add "denigrate," "put down," as definitions. To denigrate a person, therefore, to have contempt or scorn for that person, is to consider her as nothing, to *make* her nothing. What else does the racism of so many do today? I have an African-American friend who not long ago told me, "You're the first white person I've ever trusted." He's 82. In Saying 13 Theodore of Pherme says it very well: "There is no other virtue than not being disdainful [*exouthenéō*]."

But another Greek word can help us here. In the Greek texts translated in this volume, one of my favorite words lexically is *katanússomai*. Its basic meaning is "to sting." But it also means, as we say, "stung to the heart." An older word for this in English (maybe we should dust it off) is *compunction*, partly from Latin *pungo / punctum*, as in *puncture*. Another word not readily available to us now is *contrition*; as Psalm 51:17 says, "The sacrifice acceptable to God is a broken spirit; / a broken and contrite heart,

140. Cohen, "Anthem," music and lyrics online. For an appreciation of Cohen pertinent to the discussion here, see Donald Grayston, "Thomas Merton and Leonard Cohen: Soul-Brothers and Spiritual Guides" (www.leonardcohenfiles .com/grayston.pdf).

141. Norris, *Acedia*, 169.

142. Bauer 729a. Related words supply resonance: *oxoudénēma*, "object of scorn"; *exoudenismós*, "disparagement"; *exoudénōma*, "contempt."

O God, you will not despise."[143] Rowan Williams, vis-à-vis the *Philokalia*, puts it well: "the dual habits of contrition and gratitude keep before us the nature we had almost lost and preserve us from defeat by the passion* of lust and anger which—to use an awkward but helpful phrasing—de-realize other things and persons, making them either objects for possession and manipulation or objects of hatred and fear."[144] Contrition *and* gratitude. Williams' insight captures well the spirituality of the monastics gathered in this volume.

Similarly, as we saw above, Boyle says, "You learn with the years to abide in the sting." Now he continues, "then move quickly away to the equanimity of humility." A good, if etymologically redundant, phrase here is "equanimity of spirit."[145] But how does one get from A (the sting) to B (equanimity of spirit)? I will discuss this in V.4–5. A good start, says Boyle, an experienced spiritual director (and who goes to one), is to ask ourselves, "What is my 'core wound?' "[146] The ammas and abbas ask this same question, though more indirectly; it's part of their common question "How can I be saved?" The scriptural *locus biblicus* for the monks' question is Acts 16:31: a jailer asks Paul and Silas, "Sirs, what must I do to be saved?" They answer, "Believe in the Lord Jesus, and you will be saved, you and your household." John Wortley emphasizes: "*not once*" is Paul and Silas's "answer cited (or even obliquely referred to)" by the monks. "Scriptural quotations abound in the Fathers' responses, but this is never one of them."

---

143. *Contrite* comes from Lat. *contritus < contero*, "to grind down." *Contritio*, "a grinding," "contrition, grief," equals Gk. *thlípsis*, "grief" (Lewis and Short 459).

144. Williams, "Theological World," 106. The *Philokalia* "is a collection of ascetic and mystical writings dating from the 4th to the 15th centuries, dealing in general terms with the teaching of Hesychasm and more particularly with the Jesus Prayer," ODCC 1084b.

145. "Equanimity": Lat. *aequanimitās,* equivalent to *aequ(us)*, "even, plain, equal," + *anim(us)*, "mind, spirit, feelings," + *-itās*, "-ity."

146. See Boyle, *Tattoos*, 81–82.

Apparently all of the time, therefore, we can translate the monks' question as "How can I be saved *from my wound(s)*, most of them self-inflicted? How can I be *healed*?"[147]

Amma Theodora posts a seemingly daunting job description for such spiritual directors:

> stranger to the love of power, alien to vanity and self-delusion, far from haughtiness and pride; the person who teaches should not seek out flattery, be blinded by gifts, conquered by the belly, or be ruled by anger. Instead, the person who teaches should be patient and even-tempered, courteous and forbearing and, as far as possible, completely humble. The one who teaches should be approved for the position, accommodating, prudent, and a lover of souls. (Theodora 5)

The pedagogical virtues that Theodora enumerates are virtues that the monks seek to live out, as can we. In the gospel of Luke, shortly after calling the first disciples (5:1-11), Jesus cleanses a leper (5:12-16): *one day*, but narratively next, while Jesus is teaching, some men lower a paralytic with his bed through the tiles of the roof into the middle of the crowd in front of Jesus (5:17-26). By positioning the two scenes back-to-back, Luke immediately connects call and ministry with compassion and healing. According to Luke, when the first disciples don their apostolic clothing, it symbolizes not power and authority but humility and service to others.

Theodora 6 summarizes the importance of such humility in a few sentences: echoing the prophets and Jesus about true sacrifice, internals rather than externals, Amma Theodora says to her fellow (female) monastics that neither "ascetic practice nor keeping vigils nor all kinds of toil and suffering will save us without genuine

---

147. The quotations are from a draft of an article that the late John Wortley sent me (emphases his). I had already come to the same conclusion about the meaning of "being saved" in the *Apophthegmata*; I'm grateful to have his corroboration. See also Wortley, "What the Desert Fathers meant by 'being saved,'" *Zeitschrift für Antikes Christentum* 12 (2008): 322–43.

humility." As I've emphasized, monastic thinking is often countercultural; it was then, and is now. Here Theodora is countercul-
turaling the counterculture; her counsel* with warning echoes the
prophets' and Jesus' concerns and admonitions about the primacy
of morality and ethics over outward observance. Her audience,
like theirs, must be shaking their heads in disbelief: "What?! But
that's what we do! Ascetic practices, vigils, toil, and suffering."[148]
So, like a good teacher, she tells them a story: "A certain anchorite
. . . used to drive away demons."* She's got 'em hooked now.
Oh boy, demons! But this is not a fairly typical good guys vs. bad
guys shoot 'em up. As this monk drives away demons, apparently
out of curiosity he pauses in his expulsions and questions them:
"Why do you come out here?" He then suggests, fasting? *No, we
demons don't eat.* To keep vigils? *Nope, we don't sleep.* To withdraw* from the world?* *Nah, we already live in the desert.**

   "Why then," our monk asks, perhaps in exasperation, "do you
come out here?"[149] They respond, "Nothing defeats us except
humility. Do you see that humility means victory over the demons?" For the early monks, demons assault them in myriad ways;
if humility defeats such miscreants and malefactors, we today
might call it a "wonder drug." But wonder drugs are manufactured;
the monks know that defeating demons is internal struggle. It
requires transformation. Antony often takes a physical beating
from demons in the *Life of Antony*; but before we roll our eyes at
monastic demonology, we should remember that we say, "I'm
really beaten up *inside*." Antony's bruises and lacerations symbolically, that is, spiritually, are our own.

---

148. The monks' response reminds me of Israel's, and our, usual reply to the
prophets chastising them for what we now call social injustice: *But we observe
the Sabbath, we sacrifice, we tithe*, ad nauseum. See Matt 23:23, where Jesus
says to those opposing him, *you tithe mint, dill, and cumin, and have neglected
the weightier matters of the law: justice and mercy and faith. It is these you ought
to have practiced without neglecting the others.*

149. One could read this sentence three ways, depending on whether one
emphasizes "do," "you," or "here."

We also know, though, that interior beatings can, if not attended to and healed, beat up our bodies, "psychosomatic" in the original sense: soul-body. Healing is, in fact, transformation. Before we go on to the latter, we should look briefly at the multivalent nuances of Greek *sṓzō*, whose translation only as *save* is anemic. The verb can also mean "save / free from disease," as in the disease(s) of the soul. But the verb's other meanings are important: "to preserve or rescue from natural dangers and afflictions, save, keep from harm, preserve, rescue"; "bring out safely"; "keep, preserve in good condition"; "thrive, prosper, get on well"; and "save or preserve from transcendent danger or destruction, save / preserve from eternal death."[150] As we can see from *sṓzō*, transformation is eschatological, both now and in the future.

2. Paths to Transformation

Weaknesses make us strong, because they make us stand up to ourselves.[151]

The early desert monastics knew, and emphasized, that transformation was hard work. It's striking that, in an utterly different context, the philosopher of religion William James understands this reality. The monks' word for such "hard work" is *áskēsis*, "ascetic practice," discussed earlier. James uses "strenuous": the "strenuous mood" or "strenuous life." Todd Lekan summarizes for James what any amma or abba would agree with:

> For James, it is not enough to reflectively endorse, with passion, an ideal. One must put the ideal into practice with vigor. James' main point is that people living significant lives are *serious* about their ideals, and are willing to make sacrifices

---

150. Bauer 982ab. Latin *salus*, related to Greek *hólos*, "whole, entire," is instructive: "being safe and sound, a sound or whole condition, health, welfare, prosperity, preservation, safety, deliverance" (Lewis and Short 1621c).

151. Dan to Nerburn in Nerburn, *Neither Wolf Nor Dog*, 178.

for them, braving dangers on their behalf. Such risk-taking is part of what makes devotion to ideals meaningful enough to give significance to lives.[152]

Using modern psychological vocabulary to discuss "virtues," Lekan sounds very monastic:

> I propose thinking of "strenuousness" as a concept that encompasses a variety of what might be called "executive virtues"—integrity, devotion, discipline, patience, bravery and so forth. Such virtues are second-order dispositions that take other first-order value commitments to ideals as their objects. . . . A person leads a strenuous life when he or she pursues ideals with an energetic devotion made possible by the possession of such executive virtues.[153]

The takeaway here, and for the whole Introduction, is that early Christian monasticism, in essence, is not at all antique and superannuated, as we see even more fully in Inbar Graiver's recent work.

Graiver helpfully uses psychology to better understand the monastic imperative. She has pointed out that "Many religious practices are aimed at transformation of the self and often operate to support these transformations. Comparative studies in the history of religion suggest that the need for such a change is a universal theme at the heart of all the major religious cultures." She distinguishes between "passive" transformation and "gradual transformation based upon an active effort over years of intentional and systematic practice. Asceticism belongs to this gradual

---

152. Todd Lekan, "The Marriage of Ideals and Strenuous Actions: Exploring William James' Account of Significant Life," *Transactions of the Charles S. Peirce Society: A Quarterly Journal in American Philosophy* 52, no. 4 (Winter 2016): 583 (emphasis his). On "mood," Lekan notes, "Even though James tends to use the phrase *strenuous mood*, it is clear that he means to apply the notion to *lives* and not simply feelings" (583, emphasis his).

153. Lekan, "Marriage," 583.

mode of self-transformation."[154] Transformation is a, if not *the*, key theme in the works of Gregory Boyle, Kathleen Norris, Kent Nerburn, Thomas Merton, Matthew Kelty, and Steven Charleston (discussed below). It is also, and importantly, biblical. Graiver cites Romans 12:2: *Do not be conformed to this world* [aíōn, or "age"], *but be transformed* [metamorphóō] *by the renewing of your minds, so that you may discern what the will of God is—what is good and acceptable and perfect.*[155] She says that in "Paul's epistles and in the Deutero-Pauline letters,[156] we find for the first time in the early church the development of a language of self-transformation, which had a profound influence on the subsequent development of the Christian ascetic tradition."[157]

154. Graiver, *Asceticism*, 18–19; see 18–21, "Asceticism and Self-Transformation."

155. With "conformed" (*schēmatízō*), an early monk might have heard 1 Pet 1:14: *Like obedient children, do not be conformed to the desires that you formerly had in ignorance.* Desires, *epithymíai*, at least inordinate desires, are what monastics need to get under control.

156. "Deutero-Pauline" is a term many New Testament scholars use for the pseudonymous Pastoral Epistles: 1 and 2 Timothy and Titus; some scholars also add Colossians and Ephesians as works not by Paul but his followers. See Marcus J. Borg and John Dominic Crossan, *The First Paul: Reclaiming the Radical Visionary behind the Church's Conservative Icon* (New York: HarperCollins, 2009), esp. 45–48. Pseudonymous works were common in Antiquity and Late Antiquity. See also the work of Richard A. Horsley (*Jesus and Empire, Jesus and the Powers, In the Shadow of Empire*, and *Paul and Empire*); and Walter Wink (*Naming the Powers: The Language of Power in the New Testament, Unmasking the Powers*, and *Engaging the Powers: Discernment and Resistance in a World of Domination.*

157. Graiver, *Asceticism*, 30; she points specifically to Paul's "formula demanding renewal of the 'old man.'" "Man" here and elsewhere is *ánthrōpos*, "person, human being," not "male." For Rom 6:6, Eph 4:2, and Col 3:9 the NRSV uses "old self," which is preferable but, as Graiver points out, "The category of 'self,' however, is the product of historical development, and neither classical Greek nor Latin had a word denoting 'self' in the sense in which the term has come to be used in the modern era" (30). See 30, n. 2 for references. Perhaps "our old person" is the best we can do, that is, who we were.

In ancient and modern monastic thought, transformation occurs in dialogue with, and argument against, the world.* We can all too easily misunderstand the biblical and early monastic understanding of "the world" (Gal 4:3: *while we were minors, we were enslaved to the elemental spirits of the world**), projecting upon it a dualism that self-insulates, and even exculpates, us from seeing the necessity of living "life in the spirit" in the world (see Gal 5:25), and from seeing also the detriments of what happens when we don't, a blindness that can lead to lives of detritus. What Aldous Huxley acutely and presciently observed seventy-five years ago is even more true today:

> it is upon fashions, cars, and gadgets, upon news and the advertising for which news exists, that our present industrial and economic system depends for its proper functioning. For . . . this system cannot work unless the demand for non-necessaries is not merely kept up, but continually expanded; and of course it cannot be kept up and expanded except by incessant appeals to greed, competitiveness, and love of aimless distractions, which are the original sin of the mind; but never before today has an attempt been made to organize and exploit distractions, to make of them, because of their economic importance, the core and vital center of human life.[158]

If we construe broadly what Matthew Kelty says about "noise," we can see that he summarizes what Huxley says in one memorable sentence: "I suspect seriously that the single most effective weapon of Satan in our times is noise."[159] And yet—both the early monastics and modern psychology show us the tools we have in order to move from "noise" into spiritual depth, literal and

---

158. Aldous Huxley, "Distractions—I," in *Vedanta for the Western World*, ed. Christopher Isherwood (Hollywood: Vedanta Press, 1946), 129. One assumes that Huxley appreciated the irony that such words were published in Hollywood.

159. Kelty, *My Song*, 22.

figurative silence. As Graiver has shown in *Asceticism of the Mind*, modern psychological terms often coincide with early monastic, biblical, understandings: "(mental) training" (*áskēsis*), "self-formation," "paying attention to oneself"* (*prosochḗ*), "knowledge"* (*gnōsis*), and, finally and repeatedly, "transformation" (*metamorphóō*). As she concludes, "in an early Christian context the inner self and its relation to God were . . . more important . . . than the material world and more practical to control. Monastic asceticism is a direct result of that choice."[160] The monastics' choice is, importantly, also ours. Steven Charleston shares a very important insight about transformation:

> transformation is not necessarily about transcendence. In fact, it can be just the opposite. Transformation can mean a grounding into reality, a deepening into the finite. Transformation is a process forming a human life from the substance of that life itself. Seen in this context, the quest is not an escape from reality, but a passage into an even deeper reality. . . . The quest is an invitation to go deeper.[161]

Transformation can lead to what Thomas Merton calls "final integration." As Donald Grayston says of Merton's article "Final Integration: Toward a 'Monastic Therapy,' " "he was pointing toward what he thought should be the result of the vow of *conversatio morum* (literally, 'conversion of morals or mores,' that is, of ongoing transformation) . . . : the journey to the true self, liberation, transformation, rebirth."[162] Given the discussion earlier

---

160. Graiver, *Asceticism*, 188.

161. Charleston, *The Four Vision Quests*, 17.

162. Donald Grayston, *Thomas Merton: The Noonday Demon*, 51. *The Rule of Benedict* 58.17-18 defines *conversatio* thus: *conversatione morum suorum et oboedientia, coram Deo et sanctis eius* ("a person seeking the monastic life promises ongoing transformation and obedience before God and his saints" [my translation]. As Georg Holzherr comments, "It includes a renunciation of the former worldly way of life and the assent to Christ." See Holzherr, *The Rule of Benedict: An Invitation to the Christian Life*, trans. Mark Thamert, CS 256

about present salvation, I suggest that as we read the ammas and abbas in this volume we often translate "being saved" as "being transformed," and "salvation" as "transformation." As Greg Boyle says, "Scripture reminds us, constantly, . . . not to wait for salvation but to watch for it today."[163] And, I think he would with the early monastics add to *watch: and work.* Yes, the monks *do* speak, often, of future salvation, but they also, as we've seen, often speak of and act out a realized soteriology, salvation, transformation here and now. In communion with Buddhist teaching, Boyle says that "[t]his present is eternal and the only eternity that counts is now." "The time for any of us to be returned to ourselves is now."[164]

The alphabetical *Sayings* actually open with this theme of present salvation-as-transformation: "When Saint Abba Antony was dwelling in the desert one time, he became dispirited, and his thoughts were extremely dark and gloomy. He was saying to God, 'Lord, I want to be saved, and my thoughts won't leave me alone! Afflicted like this, what will I do? How will I be saved?'" (Antony 1). It's a dark opening. Antony's *cri de coeur* is very often our own.[165] A little later, going outside, Antony sees someone like him: he's sitting and working; then he stands up from his work and prays. Then he sits down and plaits rope; then once again he stands to pray. We discover that he's an angel of the Lord, sent to set Antony right and strengthen him. Antony hears the angel saying, "Do what I am doing, and you will be saved."

(Collegeville, MN: Cistercian Publications, 2016), 437 and 452, respectively. See the General Index, 584, under "*conversatio.*" I wish to thank Marsha Dutton for this reference. For a recent thoughtful reflection on the *Rule*, see Terrence Kardong, *Benedict Backwards: Reading the Rule in the Twenty-First Century* (Collegeville, MN: Liturgical Press, 2017).

163. Boyle, *Barking*, 82.

164. Boyle, *Barking*, 88 and 90.

165. A very powerful and moving expression of "dark and gloomy" in song is Lindsey Buckingham's "I'm so Afraid," lyrics online and video at "Fleetwood Mac—I'm So Afraid—The Dance—1997." For a good personal, spiritual reflection, see Norris, *Acedia.*

Work* and prayer,* work *with* prayer, may not sound all that dramatic to us—but how often do we do it? The basic monastic *modus vivendi* was, and is, a life of work and prayer, prayer and work. But we can sum up the parable above with what Paul says: *Pray without ceasing* (1 Thess 5:17). Three words (two in Greek). Praying without ceasing may seem impossible, but Paul Philibert offers another way of seeing it: "we don't always have to *say* a prayer, we can *live out* a prayer"; this is how ceaseless prayer "comes to be achieved in [one's] life."[166] As Boyle says, as "homies embark on the journey to turn their lives around [a better translation of *metanoia*, usually translated "repentance"] . . . they become accustomed to speaking of paths."[167] Greek *hodós* means both "path" and "way," as in John 14:6 where Jesus says "I am the way, and the truth, and the life." As John 1:23 shows, where John the Baptist is quoting the prophet Isaiah (40:3), "I am the voice of one crying out in the wilderness, 'Make straight the way of the Lord,' " *way* in the Hebrew Bible and New Testament can be metaphorical. Commenting on the early-Christian use of "the way," Boyle speaks of the way as "not necessarily a secret formula, but a path of trans-formation," and says that this effort, deepening transformation, is "a commitment to abide fully in our complete humanity."[168]

3. The True Self and its Practices[169]

The awakening is
to transformation,
word after word.[170]

---

166. Quoted by Norris, *Acedia*, 263 (emphases Philibert's); source not given.

167. Boyle, *Barking*, 112.

168. Boyle, *Barking*, 113.

169. See further Williams, *A Silent Action*, chap. 2, " 'Bread in the Wilderness': The Monastic Ideal in Thomas Merton and Paul Evdokimov," 23–39.

170. Denise Levertov, "The Unknown," from *The Sorrow Dance*, in Denise Levertov, *Collected Poems*, ed. Paul A. Lacey and Anne Dewey (New York: New Directions, 2013), 244.

Boyle's "complete humanity" is undoubtedly related to Thomas Merton's "true self." But what is *incomplete* humanity? Possibly Merton's "false self." Kathleen Norris uses "superficial me" when she reflects on her incomplete, false, self: it "may show a confident face to the world but inwardly is plagued by fears and compulsions, and remains blind to its true condition."[171] Thomas Merton indelibly and, like a desert father or mother, confrontationally, states, "Every one of us is shadowed by an illusory person: a false self." Merton's foot is already on the gas pedal here, but he presses down further as he immediately continues with an even tougher statement: "This is the man that I want myself to be but cannot exist, because God does not know anything about him. And to be unknown of God is altogether too much privacy." With this second sentence, Merton surprises us with humor. But he's very serious: now he goes pedal to the metal: "All sin starts from the assumption that my false self, the self that exists only in my own egocentric desires, is the fundamental reality of life to which everything else in the universe is ordered."[172]

I very often tell my students (way too often for them) not to use the passive voice ("Mistakes were made"). Why? Because a statement in the passive voice omits the actor or actors—and, as we see with "mistakes were made," often hides, thereby exculpating, both them and their malfeasances ("the exculpatory passive," as I call it). What Merton, contextually, is saying is that *he* is ordering "everything else in the universe," in his own image—which means, not God's.[173] But . . . as Merton implies here, there

---

171. Norris, *Acedia*, 139.

172. All three references are to Merton, *New Seeds of Contemplation* (New York: New Directions, 1961), 34–35; for a nice appreciation, see Ilia Delio, "Discovering the True Self in God with Merton's Guidance," *National Catholic Reporter* (www.ncronline.org/blogs/ncr-today/discovering-true-self-god-mertons-guidance). For a full treatment, see James Finley, *Merton's Palace of Nowhere: A Search for God through Awareness of the True Self* (Notre Dame, IN: Ave Maria Press, 1978; repr. 2003).

173. Writing on Merton is voluminous; on the topic here, a good, brief, accessible essay is David Odorisio, "Rediscovering the True Self through the Life and Writings of Thomas Merton" (merton.org/ITMS/Seasonal/28/28-2Odorisio.pdf).

is a true self, a God-given self that knows nothing of false fronts, aggrandizements, and admiring mirrors. Our true self is like a snake, but we're shedding our multitude of false skins *continually*. As Robert Barron says of Merton: "Merton felt in his bones that his own life constituted a battleground between conflicting interests, warring tendencies, mutually exclusive 'selves.' For him, the spiritual life could be defined as the awakening to the true 'I,' the Christ living in me, and the dying to the vaporous and destructive ego created by fear."[174] Merton heard the early monastic demons jabbering, squawking, and dancing outside and within each person (see Michelangelo's *Temptation of St. Antony*). The ammas and abbas lived long before the psychological "discovery" of the self and its companions, but we can say, without anachronism, that their journey is one, often painfully slow, from the false self to the true self. As they and Merton show, it's ours, too.

Thomas Merton calls this "final integration."[175] But, as we know all too painfully from history, segregation precedes integration—often, as history teaches, for a very long time. We earlier saw the story of Antony, the judgmental monks, and the cast-out brother whom Antony sends back. In Antony, Coptic Saying 36 a judgmental Antony himself returns home, both literally and figuratively, a journey that began with his false self and ended with the return of his true self, his integral self.[176] Often our true self is adjunct or appendage, even vestigial, to our ego and false self. Thus we can read these parables as our own. When the true self

---

174. Robert Barron, *And Now I See: A Theology of Transformation* (New York: Crossroad, 1998), cited by Matt Emerson, "Merton and the 'True Self'" (www.americamagazine.org/faith/2013/11/22/merton-and-true-self).

175. Merton, "Final Integration: Toward a 'Monastic Therapy,'" in Merton, *Contemplation in a World of Action*, 200–215.

176. Integral: OED Online, "Of or pertaining to a whole. Said of a part or parts: Belonging to or making up an integral whole; constituent, component; *specially* necessary to the completeness or integrity of the whole; forming an intrinsic portion or element, as distinguished from an adjunct or appendage" (emphasis mine) (www.oed.com.falcon.lib.csub.edu/view/Entry/97344?redirectedFrom=integral#eid).

returns, it now finds on the open and unguarded monastery gate, RETURNEES TO THEIR TRUE SELVES—WELCOME! But our self-serving bastions are legion, perhaps innumerable: monastery, church, religion, "race" (a false construct), class, gender, country, politics (often false, and falsifying constructs). Where, then, do we go? As Williams has said, the journey becomes "the refusal of falsehood and the search for identity-in-God."[177]

The rest of this Introduction offers paths, the monks' transformative ways. Their ways can indeed be ours.

V. Practices in Transformation

Rowan Williams has written two helpful comments: "For the authors of the *Philokalia*, revelation was essentially the gift of a wisdom that opened up fresh possibilities for human action—or, more accurately, that restored possibilities lost by human sin and ignorance."[178]

"The repeated practice of various strategies of attention management eventually enabled ascetic practitioners to transform their entire mental disposition and cultivate new psychological capacities. This optimistic vision of human potential is supported by current research on brain neuroplasticity."[179]

1. Love* (*agape*)[180]

Thomas Merton "learned that the deepest meaning of solitude was love.[181]

If love is the answer, community is the context that others can follow, and tenderness the methodology.[182]

177. Williams, *A Silent Action*, 38.
178. Williams, "Theological World," 102. On the *Philokalia*, see n. 144.
179. Graiver, *Asceticism,* 177.
180. *Agápē*.
181. Grayston, *Thomas Merton*, 3.
182. Boyle, *Barking*, 85.

First, the bad news. Greg Boyle offers this insight: "gangs are bastions of conditional love—one false move, and you find yourself outside."[183] I'm pretty sure that most of us, you reading this, and I, have never thought of ourselves as gang members. But, spiritually, we often are: like them, we are good at pushing away people, and our true self, thus making love conditional. Boyle's "one false move" is chilling. But it should prompt each of us to ask, "How many of *my* loves are conditional?" I'll discuss below four other key early monastic virtues and practices: peace, patient endurance, contemplative quiet, and inward stillness (V.2–5). But as Paul says of the virtues, the greatest is love (*agape*) (1 Cor 13:13), so we'll begin with love. In the '60s, Thomas Merton told social justice activists—whom he in general supported—that they had better be grounded spiritually, firmly planted in their, God's, true self, before they told and showed others how to do what's just and right. Otherwise, they'd be taking their own inner demons, false selves of self-righteousness, anger, and violence, along with them, and using them as placards and signs to beat "the enemy" over the head.[184]

Here again, the oft-supposed dichotomy between prayer and action breaks down. As the monks in this volume show, those who desire a life of prayer, quiet, and stillness *must act*.[185] The monastic cell is the redoubt of an early monk, where he or she worked, prayed—and confronted demons. As Abba Moses instructs, "Go, stay in your cell; your cell will teach you everything."[186] But, as

183. Boyle, *Tattoos*, 94.

184. Norris, *Acedia*, 116–17, agrees: "Anger over injustice may inflame us, but that's a double-edged sword. If our indignation feels too good, it will attach to our arrogance and pride and leave us ranting in a void." In the New Testament and in the sayings in this volume, Gk. *dikaiosúnē* can mean "justice" and / or "righteousness."

185. See Merton's seminal *Contemplation in a World of Action*.

186. AlphAP Moses 6.

the ammas and abbas show (not tell) us, we need both love of the (true) self *and* the love of others, and we must have love for *the other*, who, really, is not other, but a mirror image of our true self, a mirror that, in fact, we can walk through.

Ancient Israel did a very good job of welcoming the stranger, the other, but its welcome mat spread only so far: one of the Jubilee requirements was the manumission of slaves—but only Israelite slaves, not foreign ones.[187] So, too, with early Christians: Paul declares, *There is no longer Jew or Greek, there is no longer slave or free* (Gal 3:28; see 1 Cor 12:13), and in Philemon he sends the slave Onesimus back to his master, whom he urges to free his property. But by the time of the later, pseudonymous epistles 1 Timothy (6:1) and Titus (2:9), in capitulation to conformity and the ways of empire, modern capitulations still, Christians have long forgotten, or now ignore, Paul's words.[188] What happened among the first followers of Jesus tells us to ask ourselves, "Where are my boundaries? Who's out of bounds? The refugees, the homeless, the poor, the prisoners, the transgender . . . ? Who are the victims of *my* fear?" And for Christians: "Why do I ignore what Jesus and Paul say?"

Agápē, love, is absolutely central to early Christian monasticism; it, and its cognate verb, *agapáō*, occur over 160 times in the

---

187. Lev 25:39-46.

188. See also Col 3:22-41. 1 Tim 6:1: *Let all who are under the yoke of slavery regard their masters as worthy of all honor, so that the name of God and the teaching may not be blasphemed*; Titus 2:9: *Tell slaves to be submissive to their masters and to give satisfaction in every respect; they are not to talk back, not to pilfer, but to show complete and perfect fidelity, so that in everything they may be an ornament to the doctrine of God our Savior.* My assessment is based on Borg and Crossan, *The First Paul*. See n. 155; see also the work of Richard A. Horsley (*Jesus and Empire, Jesus and the Powers, In the Shadow of Empire*, and *Paul and Empire*); and Walter Wink (*Naming the Powers: The Language of Power in the New Testament; Unmasking the Powers*; and *Engaging the Powers: Discernment and Resistance in a World of Domination*).

sister systematic *Apophthegmata*.[189] Love isn't all you need, but it most certainly comes first. We're often so besotted, understandably, with the wedding march of 1 Corinthians 13 that we forget that in 1 Corinthians 11:17-22 Paul harshly berates the Christians in Corinth for abuses at the Lord's Supper; *only then* does he teach them about the institution and practices of that Supper (23-36).[190] Love, then, as we know if we reflect on it, has both background and foreground; in each of us, it has history. And not just one-and-done history. From my work translating this volume, I see the ammas and abbas using *love* three main ways (there may well be more):

- As Paul does in 1 Corinthians 13 when he adumbrates all the things that love is, the monks see the iterations of love in Paul's list as virtues and practices.

- In the *agape* feast, where all the monks gather to celebrate love in community with worship and a eucharistic meal. See Arsenius 39 and John the Little 9.

- In what the monks call the "act of love" (*agape*). It's the last that I'll focus on here.[191]

Whoever edited Agathon 25–30 in the present collection was a genius, theologically, pastorally, and mimetically. Of all the sayings and stories in this volume, I find these the most remarkable and memorable—and challenging, even confrontational. They take the *lectio* that Terrence Kardong speaks of in his Foreword to this volume and do open-heart surgery on the heart, mind, soul, and spirit. *Lectio* here has become workshop, retreat, daily prayer, a lifelong companion who tells the reader or listener both the bad

---

189. Guy, *Les Apophtegmes des Pères*, 3.253.

190. We often also forget (or ignore) that in 1 Cor 13:1-3 Paul says what love *isn't*.

191. For all three, see the Glossary and General Index.

news and the very good news. Agathon 25 opens with the brothers "talking about love." Talking. What we do so well. Then submit a report about our findings that will sit unread in a bottom drawer or digital file. But an Abba Joseph quickly translates talk into action. Numerous monks in the sayings and stories in this volume give love without measure. As Saint Francis de Sales says, "The measure of love is to love without measure."[192] In Agathon 25, Joseph speaks of Agathon's having a knife: "A brother came to see him, and praised the knife, and Abba Agathon wouldn't let him leave unless he took the knife with him." Unstated, enacted, giving and self-giving love.[193]

With one sentence, Agathon 26 then both intensifies 25 and provides a foretaste of Sayings 27–29a and 30. The abba, astounding us, says "If it were possible for me to find a leper, give him my body, and take his, I would gladly do so: this is real [or: perfect] love."[194] I believe him. To see Agathon's statement as hyperbole is to be in denial. *Love* as a word doesn't make an appearance in Saying 27, but it doesn't need to: Agathon *enacts* love, which is far more important: the saying essentially midrashes *Seek, and you will find* (Matt 7:7 // Luke 11:9) to "Seek to do good, and you will." One day Agathon is headed to the city to sell his wares, a common monastic practice. On the way he finds "a person, someone he doesn't know"—the very definition of a stranger, "the other," whom the Bible repeatedly says, even commands, to welcome.[195] "Stranger" in this story equals "leper," as we'll see below.

---

192. fatherkevinestabrook.blogspot.com/2013/01/homily-january-24-st-francis-de-sales.html.

193. One could ask whether the brother should even admire and want the knife that much. Agathon could well see the monk's desire as inordinate (that is, a passion*), but he chooses not to judge that desire. Whatever the case, his action demonstrates voluntary poverty.

194. Being astounded and amazed* is a common occurrence in the sayings and stories.

195. See Deut 10:18-19; Rom 12:13; Heb 13:12.

This stranger has been "cast out into the street, sick and weak," and, the story continues, no one's paying attention to him. Much like the homeless in our cities. Agathon stops and stays with him, and then finds a place for the stranger and outcast to stay. Significantly, the author calls the place a monastic "cell." Agathon pays for this now-monastic space with part of the money he earns. All the rest of the money he spends "for the care of the sick man." And, as if we weren't already amazed, he stays with him four months. But now comes the most significant line: "And this way the elder went back home to his cell in peace." "Peace," "contemplative quiet,"* and "inward stillness"* are central to monastic spirituality (see V.2, 4–5). Agathon now, like Theonas earlier, comes home with his pockets empty but his heart full.

Agathon 28 and 29 are not a loud intermission before Saying 30 but a quiet pause for the spiritual dramatics of the latter. In Agathon 28, the elder loves (*agapáō*) Abba Alexander because— and this is important—he's "gentle and forbearing," important monastic virtues (see "humility" in IV.1). Alexander is washing his rushes in the river for basketweaving. A bucolic scene, but cue the ominous music: now the villains enter—and they're fellow monastics. For some reason we're not privy to (probably jealousy because Agathon loves Alexander, and not, they think, them), they trashtalk Abba Alexander: "Brother Alexander isn't doing anything." Now, again a surprise. Agathon gently corrects not the brothers but *Alexander*, in order to "benefit"* the others: "Brother Alexander, wash them carefully, because they're flax."

When Alexander hears this, he becomes sad. Agathon now "comforts" Alexander: "Don't you think I knew that you were doing your washing carefully? I said that to you for the benefit* of the others in order to correct what they were thinking* concerning your obedience,* brother." I'm not quite sure what's happened here, but it looks like, because he loves him, Argathon has, briefly, used Alexander to teach the backbiters a lesson. Apparently, the lesson matters more to the elder than Alexander's brief hurt feelings. This is, in more ways than one, tough love. What we have here, perhaps a bit obscurely for us who don't have the monastic context, is pastoral care acting out of love. But, as we've seen, there is a price; perhaps we have here a very small example of the cost of discipleship.

With Agathon 29a, while we're pondering the previous enacted saying, for Act II the theater's property crew has changed the scenery: the elder shows love by boarding a boat and being "the first one to grab an oar." Later, when brothers come to visit Agathon, after prayer "he himself," showing humble hospitality, sets the table. It appears in the *Apophthegmata* that normally an elder asks a disciple to do this. These are small things, but small things eventually change mountains. The story concludes, "He did these things because he was filled with the love of God." And Agathon's cup thus runs over with love and care *for others*.[196] As Kathleen Norris says, caring is "an assertion that no matter how strained and messy our relationships can be," and I would add our relationship(s) with our own selves, "it is worth something to be present, with others, doing our small part."[197]

In Saying 30 Agathon is again headed to the city to sell some wares. This time he finds "a leper by the side of the road," the outcast now as leper. As with the earlier fellow, he brings the afflicted man with him into town, perhaps even carrying him. The monks who first heard and read this story knew exactly what *leper* meant: unclean, outcast, ostracized. But they also knew that Jesus healed lepers. Isn't this story, then, a parable about what the Christian life should be? Although I might use a stronger word than *jostled* here, Gregory Boyle gets purity codes right, because he connects what Jesus is doing with the kingdom of God: "Jesus jostled the purity codes of the shot callers of His day. He recognized that it was precisely this code that kept folks from kinship." "Maybe success," he continues (and, I would suggest, other causes almost *ad infinitum*), "has become the new purity code. And Jesus

196. See Ps 23:5.
197. Norris, *Acedia*, 3–4.

shows us that the desire for purity (nine times out of ten) is, in fact, the enemy of the gospel."[198] This story reminds me of another boundary-breaker, Saint Francis of Assisi, who is very much like Abba Arsenius: "Then the holy lover of complete humility went to the lepers and lived with them, serving them diligently for God's sake."[199] Abba Serapion, seeing a pauper on the streets of Alexandria, puts it bluntly: "How can I, who am supposed to be an ascetic* and one who works,* be wearing a coat while this pauper—or, rather, Christ himself—is dying of cold?"[200]

The impure leper in the mini-drama of Agathon 30 becomes an antagonist of sorts and creates dramatic tension. He is, given his situation, a bit importunate. No, he's downright pushy. Extremely pushy. As such, he's pushing not only Agathon's limits *but our own.* But the abba never acts as though he's being shoved. Twice after Agathon sells something, the leper demands that the monk buy him something. And Agathon does so, without comment or complaint. After the second time, we're mumbling to ourselves, "Why, you. . . . How dare you . . . ?" But after Agathon sells everything and is leaving, the leper asks / tells him, "Do another act of love [*agape*] and take me where you found me." Agathon, without demur, does so, and the leper declares, "Agathon, you have been blessed by the Lord in heaven and on earth." Now, with a nice dramatic flourish in the drama, we find that when Agathon leaves he raises his eyes, and no one's there: "it was an angel of the Lord who had come to test* him."[201]

When I first read this story, I could've done without another *deus ex machina monastica*; I wanted the story to end with, "Abba

198. Boyle, *Tattoos*, 179.

199. Thomas of Celano, *The First Life of St. Francis* 17, Vatican documents, www.vatican.va/spirit/documents/spirit_20001103_tom-da-celano_en.html. I wonder if Francis knew the *Sayings.*

200. SysAP 15.117 (= AnonAP 566), Wortley, *Book*, 276, altered.

201. In one version of the story about Francis and the lepers, it's less clear that it is an angel who visits him.

Agathon carried him and brought him back to where he'd been before." In some of the stories in this collection it looks as though someone, either the original author or a later editor, has tacked on a conclusion or moral to make the point obvious, as some of Jesus' parables in the gospels receive Cliff Notes explanations from the Evangelists. But testing, and being tested, are very important to the monastic ethos (see the Glossary and General Index). The key here, though, is "act of love," an *agape*. Love in action.

John the Persian 2 provides an apt conclusion to the sayings above about Agathon. John has "borrowed a gold coin from a brother and bought some linen in order to make something." Then he freely gives away to other brothers all the items he's made. The monk who loaned the money asks John for it back, several times. John doesn't have it, but he finds a gold coin on the road. Instead of using that to repay the loan, he gives it to an elder, Abba James, and asks him to find the owner. When Abba James can't find him, John asks the elder to give the coin to his creditor. The story concludes: Abba James

> was amazed that Abba John, since he was in debt, didn't immediately return [the gold coin] once he had found it. And this is what's so amazing—if someone came to borrow something from him, no matter what, he himself wouldn't hand it to him but would say to the brother, "Go and help yourself to whatever you need." And if the brother returned it Abba John would say to him, "Put it back where you found it."

The (perhaps) idealization of Acts 4:32 finds incarnation among the first monastics: *All the believers were one in heart and mind. No one claimed that any of their possessions was their own, but they shared everything they had.*

Now the story moves from gentle counsel about freely giving to quiet, and thunderous, exhortation: "But if someone who had borrowed something didn't return it, he wouldn't say a word." At first, the story about John may not seem to connect with those about Agathon, as for Theonas earlier, but I've adduced this story because it shows absolute, and ready, giving; for Agathon and John such giving is routine, the quotidian imbued with grace, and love. And *this* astounds us. The assumption behind this story is implicit in the tales of Agathon: although the stories don't make the following explicit, seeing Christ or God's image in another human being, especially in the hurting and outcast, is to incarnate God's love. But I don't want to end with the impression that the sayings are all about love in action. That theme is hugely important but, as we saw earlier, Merton advised the social-justice activists in the '60s that love-in-action must be grounded in a deep spirituality. For the early monks, the next four topics show essential components of that grounding.

2. Peace* (*eirḗnē*)²⁰²

In Agathon 21 a brother asks Abba Agathon about sexual sin,* and the elder says to him, "Go, throw your weakness before God, and you'll be at peace." Agathon's reply probably echoes Psalm 54:23: *cast your care upon the Lord, and he will support you.* "Casting" and "throwing" here are actions: in other words, don't sit on your butt feeling sorry for yourself. Do something! For yourself. What is so often striking about the ammas and abbas is that when they're doing something for or counseling others they almost never say, "The Bible—or God, or Christ—is telling me (or you) to do this." They act because of their *immersion* in God, Christ, and the Bible, and how they live out this trinity in community; there's no need to turn an interior (im)pulse into a parade with confetti and marching bands. Earlier we saw Abba Agathon care for "someone he didn't know, cast out into the street, sick and weak," without anyone to care for him. He does so *for four months*, and then goes "back home to his cell in peace." Perhaps this is the peace that passeth all understanding.²⁰³

---

202. *Eirḗnē.* It, like *agápē*, is a feminine noun in Greek; peace, with the other feminine nouns—love (V.1), patient endurance (V.3), contemplative quiet (V.4), and inward stillness (V.5)—combine into a sacred monastic feminine.

203. See Phil 4:7 (KJV).

As we just saw, peace don't come easy, whether through exterior or interior action. In a dramatic story in Achilla 4, a certain elder visits Abba Achilla and observes him spitting blood from his mouth, so he asks him, "What's going on, father?" The elder says to him, "It's what a brother is saying;* it's saddened me." Not wanting to confront the other monk, Achilla says, "I struggled not to report this to him. I begged God to take this away from me, and what the brother had said became like blood in my mouth, so I spat it out, and I found myself at peace, and I forgot about my sorrow." What are we to make of this? My first thought was, "Well, if you tell him, you can work things out." Because of my own tendencies, and as a veteran of parish ministry, I want to yell, "Watch out for passive-aggressiveness!" But Achilla evinces no such behavior.

I think there's something deeper here: "what a brother is saying" is very vague. But in Greek a listener or reader might hear a lot more going on. "Saying" and "had said" in Greek use *lógos*. A junior monk would often ask an elder, literally, "Give me a word" (*lógos*), that is, "tell me something spiritually profitable, offer instruction, wise counsel." So the mouthy brother here is offering an "anti-word," and it has saddened Achilla; this brother is not only hurting Abba Achilla; he's clawing at the very fabric of early monastic spirituality, spiritual direction, and community. "Saddened," *lupéō*, can also mean "injured," "angered." No wonder that what the monk said has become blood in Achilla's mouth; the abba is symbolically hemorrhaging. But once he spits out the clot obstructing his peace, he finds peace.

Ah, but our monks are ever on the alert: laurels, and their accoutrements and accountants, an Olympics medal stand and thousands of cheering fans, are banned here. Abba Bessarion warns, "When you find yourself at peace and not at war,* that's especially the time to be humble"* (Bessarion 9). Really? Yes. Bessarion is fully aware that something can quickly "come along with it so that we brag about it and get handed over to warfare." He concludes optimistically, however: "Oftentimes, on account of our weaknesses, God won't allow us to be handed over to warfare;

otherwise, we'd be lost." Oftentimes. Bessarion and the desert fathers and mothers know that peace, however hard-earned, is temporary, fragile, and frangible. Each of us in our life knows this, but we may not be as aware as the ammas and abbas that that something that's a-comin', like the Devil, is a powerful train—powered by our egos, ever arriving, ever at the station blowing its horn, biding its time (Luke 4:13).

In the monastic worldview, peace *can* bear out Isaiah's promise (11:6):

> The wolf shall dwell with the lamb,
>   and the leopard shall lie down with the young goat,
> and the calf and the lion and the fattened calf together;
>   and a little child shall lead them.

As if fulfilling Isaiah's vision, James S1 offers this remarkable, and moving, story. An elder says,

> When I was in the desert, living there, I had a neighbor, a boy, dedicating himself to living alone. Making a visit to see how he was doing, I saw him praying and asking God to live in peace with the wild animals. When he finished praying, a hyena came close; she was suckling her young. The boy got under her and began suckling with them.

Perhaps Paradise *can* be regained.

3. Patient Endurance* (*hypomonḗ*)

We can't get love, peace, and transformation from a spiritual fast-food drive-through; the ammas and abbas tell us that we need patient endurance.* In John the Little 11, the monks "used to say about him that one time he plaited cord for two large baskets and stitched it together into a cord for a single basket without noticing it until it reached the wall. This was because his thoughts were so intent on spiritual contemplation" (*hēsychía*; see V.4).[204] In the 1960s Merton, again prophetic, began to bring people of faith from Eastern and Western religions together in conversation, especially mystics and monastics, to share the practices and goals they had in common.[205] What John is doing in his cell has affinities with *samadhi*, "concentration," "absorption." The term contains multitudes: one aspect is a "meditative concentration . . . gradually calming the mental whirlwind." In Buddhism, *samadhi* is "a state of consciousness leading to higher forms of meditation (*dhyana*) that finally result in non-dualistic consciousness." (Smith, ed., 955b). One teacher of *samadhi*, metaphorically sitting in a circle with ammas and abbas, lists "five great obstacles to *samadhi*": "laziness; forgetfulness; mental wandering and depression [aka *acedia**]; failure to correct any of the above problems when they arise; and applying meditative opponents to problems that are not there, that is, they are purely imaginary."[206] The reader will find each of these, and practices for resolving them, in the *Sayings of the Desert Fathers and Mothers*.

Abandon the ego, all ye who enter here.[207] In the saying above, John is so absorbed in contemplative quiet* (another way I've

---

204. Spiritual contemplation: or contemplative quiet.* See John the Little 1 for a memorable story about patient endurance; the fact that this is the first of John's forty sayings speaks of the importance that *hypomonḗ* has for the monks.

205. See Thomas Merton, *The Asian Journal* (New York: New Directions, 1975); Thomas Merton, *Zen and the Birds of Appetite* (New York: New Directions, 2010 [repr.]); Thomas Merton, *The Way of Chuang Tzu*, 2nd ed. (New York: New Directions, 2010); and Thomas Merton and Thich Nhat Hanh, *Contemplative Prayer* (New York: Image Classics; Penguin/Random House, 1971 [repr.]). Merton's essay "Nhat Hanh is My Brother" (*Collected Essays*) is online (www.buddhistdoor.net/features/nhat-hanh-is-my-brother). For good reflections on Merton and Buddhism, see Thurston, ed., *Merton and Buddhism,* nn. 127–28..

206. Lama Yeshe Wisdom Archive, "Teachings," "Developing Single-pointed Concentration," online.

207. This is a play on "Abandon all hope, ye who enter here," Dante, *Inferno*, Canto III.

translated *hēsychía* in this volume) that he's not thinking about what he'll do later that afternoon or about the nasty thing so-and-so said about him. In SysAP VII.14 (p. 117 below), Abba Macarius the Great visits Abba Antony where he's living. When Macarius knocks on the door, Abba Antony, with dramatic nonchalance for the monastic rubric commanding hospitality, comes out and says, "Who are *you*?" Macarius replies, "I'm Macarius." (Pause. We need to note here that Macarius is "Macarius *the Great*.") Abba Antony goes inside, closes the door, and leaves him standing there. But when he sees Abba Macarius's patient endurance, he opens the door so Macarius can come inside, graciously welcomes him, and says, "For a long time now I've very much wanted to see you; I've heard about the things you're doing."

As so often, Antony here is countercultural and, we can add, counter-expectational: if we were inside the cell rather than Antony, we would probably throw the door wide open, rejoice, and embrace the great elder. So, what's the point of this little enacted parable? I think it's that Antony offers *hypomonḗ*, and Macarius accepts it. Greatness does not put one above the need for patient endurance. But early monastics make it very clear that patient endurance isn't a form of abject resignation or torture; it's something very positive. In Theodora 1 the amma asks Pope* Theophilus what the Apostle means when he says "making the most of the opportune time* [*kairós*]" (Col 4:5). With an ingenious, imaginative, exegesis, Theophilus replies:

> The phrase means "making a profit." For example: when the time [*kairós*] comes that someone insults you, with humility and patient endurance purchase that time of insult and make a profit for yourself. Has there been a time when you have felt humiliated? With forbearance purchase the opportunity, and make a profit. If we wish, we can profit from every adversity.

A holy profit-making.

In addition to *hypomonḗ*, a key word here is *kairós*, yet another biblical-monastic term: "a period characterized by some aspect of special crisis" (see "Opportune time" in the Glossary). In Romans 3:26 Paul says that *at the present time* [kairós] God has shown through Christ that *he himself is righteous [and just] and that he justifies the one who has faith in Jesus.* That "special crisis" can also be eschatological, one "of the chief terms relating to the endtime."[208] Jesus warns a crowd, "Beware that you are not led astray; for many will come in my name and say, 'I am he!' and, 'The time [*kairós*] is near!' Do not follow after them" (Luke 21:8, modified). Paul seconds Jesus: "Therefore do not pronounce judgment before the time [*kairós*], before the Lord comes, who will bring to light the things now hidden in darkness and will disclose the purposes of the heart" (1 Cor 4:5). What is so striking among the monks is that, as the sayings above show, as with salvation and being saved (see III.4), they make *kairós* present, here and now, in the hurly-burly day-to-day, a realized chronology: dealing with ego and profiting from adversity. And a—perhaps the—key way to do this is through contemplative quiet.

4. Contemplative Quiet* (*hēsychía*)

[Hēsychía] has little to do with the absence of conflict or pain. It is a rest in God in the midst of a very intense daily struggle.[209]

As with much monastic practice and teaching, the ammas and abbas talk about contemplative quiet both negatively and positively. By these adverbs I mean that the early monastics, as with the Buddhist counsel earlier about meditation, warn about what can distract us, what pulls us away from practicing quiet contemplation, even

208. Bauer 498ab.
209. Henri Nouwen, quoted in Norris, *Acedia*, 6; source not given.

from our true selves (see IV.3).[210] As Norris cautions, "But when distraction becomes the norm, we are in danger of becoming immunized from feeling itself."[211] Aldous Huxley was prescient (see p. 55 above); a superabundance of things in our lives now, including our cellphones, should carry a Surgeon General's warning: "Repeated distractions are dangerous for your mental and spiritual health." In Antony 10 the abba warns his monastic brothers (with something of a mixed metaphor) that "fish die if they stay too long on dry land," and it's the same with monks: "if they stay outside their cells too long . . . they unstring the bow of contemplative quiet and thus lose its tautness. So, then, just as fish need to hurry back to the sea, in the same way we too need to hurry back to our cells so we don't stay too long outside and forget all about our interior watchfulness."

Abba Doulas generalizes what Antony says and makes the strung bow of contemplative quiet part of the fight against the Devil: "If the Enemy* [that is, Satan] is committing violence against us, preventing us from practicing contemplative quiet, let's just not listen to him. There's nothing like contemplative quiet. And fasting—when the two join forces, they fight as allies against him and provide us with keen interior vision" (Doulas 1). In Theodora 3, where *contemplative quiet* occurs four times, the amma backs up what Doulas says, "know this for a fact: if someone sets out to practice contemplative quiet, the Evil One* quickly comes and weighs down that person's soul: with acedia,* with discouragement, with thoughts."* Is this Luke's warning to Jesus, and us, that even after Jesus defeats the Enemy's temptations, the latter departs "from him until an opportune time"?[212]

---

210. The metaphor of a tractor is fitting for "distraction": Latin *dis-* ("away") + *tractum*, the passive participle of *traho*, "to draw, drag, pull." Thus, etymologically and spiritually, distractions are what pull one away from God.

211. Norris, *Acedia*, 46.

212. Luke 4:13; Matthew's parallel lacks this, concluding, "Then the devil left him, and suddenly angels came and waited on him" (4:11).

Thus the need for patient endurance.* In early monastic literature, demons* often incite distraction and discouragement. We often are too concerned with whether the Devil, the demons' Boss, is "real," that is, whether Satan is an external "person," but to paraphrase Pogo, with regard to anger, self-righteousness, and judgmentalism, the enemy we meet is all too often ourselves. Kathleen Norris wisely asks, "Why, if we have effectively banished the word *demon*, we are still so demon-haunted."[213] I deeply appreciate the monks' *realism* about the spiritual life.[214] First Peter 5:8, some 250 years before the desert fathers and mothers, warns, *Like a roaring lion, your adversary the Devil prowls around, looking for someone to devour.* Second Timothy 4:17, however, declares, *But the Lord stood by me and gave me strength. . . . So I was rescued from the lion's mouth.* And the author of Hebrews says that faith shuts *the mouths of lions* (11:33). This demonic bestiary lives not in some external and infernal landscape, but within the heart, soul, mind, and spirit of each human being.

The lion's mouth is now shut. But . . . what *is* contemplative quiet?* In what could be maddening for a modern reader, the ammas and abbas are not prescriptive; they don't sell, or even give away free, self-help manuals on the practice.[215] Although "Contemplative Quiet" is not in one of the medallions of the Virtues we saw earlier at Bawit and Saqqara, John the Little, seeming to emulate one of the Apostle Paul's lists, places contemplative quiet as one of many, many virtues: "with fasting, with repentance and weeping, fighting as in war, with discernment,* with purity of soul, engaging in goodness, keeping contemplative quiet as you work with your hands,[216] keeping vigil at night . . ." (34). The saying

---

213. Norris, *Acedia*, 131 (emphasis hers).

214. See Graiver, *Asceticism*, 90–105, "The Realism of the Desert."

215. For help with practicing contemplative quiet, see Thomas Keating's teaching on centering prayer, for example, *Intimacy with God: An Introduction to Centering Prayer*, 3rd ed. (New York: Crossroad, 2009).

216. 2 Thess 3:12.

to follow both shows the monastic union of contemplative quiet with action (helping self and others) and wisely comments on, and corrects, our binary, dichotomous, often all-or-nothing zero-sum minds. An unidentified abba learns about the seemingly disparate practices of two great elders, Arsenius and Moses: "Lord, show me what this means: one [Arsenius] flees from people for your name's sake, while the other one [Moses] welcomes people with open arms for your name's sake." Suddenly he's "shown two great ships on the Nile": he sees "Abba Arsenius and the Spirit of God sailing together in contemplative quiet." He also sees "Abba Moses and the angels of God sailing together, and they were feeding him honeycombs" (Arsenius 38). Contradictory as it may seem, Arsenius and Moses together are a model for the spiritual life.

5. Inward Stillness* (*anápausis*)²¹⁷

Wrong solitude vinegars the soul,
*right solitude oils it.*²¹⁸

I mentioned at the beginning that one concern about an inevitably linear presentation of some aspects of early monastic spirituality is that it can seem to set up a separation between, say, contemplative quiet* and action, a dichotomy that usually isn't in the sayings and stories. Kathleen Norris reminds us of the mystics of the quotidian, those who "search for God in a life filled with noise, the demands of other people, and duties that can submerge the self."²¹⁹ The ammas and abbas in this volume are both mystics of the quotidian and mystics of contemplative quiet and inward stillness, each potentially daily, even hourly. Another, equally important, problem is that a linear presentation can be a hot iron that

217. *Anápausis*. I wish to thank Gould, *The Desert Fathers*, 131, for the phrase *inward stillness* (not referring explicitly to *anápausis*).

218. Jane Hirshfield, "Vinegar and Oil," *Come Thief* (New York: Knopf, 2011), 6, and at poets.org/poem/vinegar-and-oil.

219. Norris, *Acedia*, 188.

the presenter is using to smooth out the wrinkles of differences, even conflicts, in the monastic clothing. Sometimes more than wrinkles: tears, rips, even gashes. In Alonius 1 the Abba says unilaterally and categorically, "If a person doesn't say in his heart 'I alone and God are in the world,' he won't have inward stillness."

Abba Apollo, however, reinforcing Scripture, tells his fellow brothers, "We must respectfully welcome brothers who come to visit us, because we're not welcoming them but rather God. If you've seen your brother," he says, "you've seen the Lord your God."[220] "And this," he adds, "we've received from Abraham, and when you welcome brothers, you're sustaining them with inward stillness.[221] This we've learned from Lot, who prevailed on the angels to enter his home."[222] In addition to "inward stillness," the key word here is *welcome*. *Proskuneō* means more than just "welcome":[223] "to express in attitude or gesture one's complete dependence on or submission to a high authority figure, (fall down and) worship, do obeisance to, prostrate oneself before, do reverence to, welcome respectfully."[224] The wise men "pay homage" (*proskunéō*) to newborn Jesus (Matt 2:2); a person "worships" (*proskunéō*) God (John 4:21-22). Alonius and Apollo here show us both dimensions of inward stillness.

In Arsenius 6, from his own wellspring of inward stillness, the abba is able to give it *to others*: "a certain monk" is "stealing the elders' things." So Abba Arsenius takes "the thief into his cell, wanting to win him over[225] and get the elders some inward stillness."

---

220. See 1 John 4:20-21.

221. The story of Abraham welcoming the three visitors (Gen 18:1-8) is the archetype of monastic hospitality.

222. See Gen 19:3.

223. *Déchomai* is the usual word for "welcome."

224. Bauer 882b–83a.

225. Win him over, *kerdaínō*: or "gain." In the NT the verb can mean gain someone for the kingdom of God (Matt 18:15; 1 Cor 9:19-22); a person can also "gain Christ" (Phil 3:8). The word undoubtedly had this biblical resonance for many monastics.

He tells the monk, "If you want something, I'll get it for you—only, don't steal." So he gives him "money, both gold and bronze, and clothing, and everything he needed." But—and here's our reality check: the thieving brother starts stealing again, so the other monks drive him out. Here's another, perhaps even tougher, reality check: a brother tells Theodore of Pherme that he finds inward stillness neither alone nor with people.[226] So Abba Theodore asks, "How many years have you worn the monastic habit?" The brother replies, "Eight." Theodore now brings out the metaphorical bucket of cold water, pours it over the brother, and tells him, "The fact is I've worn the habit for seventy years, and I haven't found one day of inward stillness. And *you* want to have inward stillness in *eight*?" The saying tacks on a heart-warming conclusion, but I think it's a later, jejune, addition.[227] And, as we know, most moral and spiritual learning is not immediate; like good, strong coffee, it requires slow brewing, with the ever-present possibility, even danger, that we, or someone else, will unplug the pot mid-percolation. The bracing statement that Theodore concludes with reflects a common monastic awareness: the spiritual life ain't easy—and you'll be working at it till the day you die.[228]

Difficulty, however, does not mean impossibility. Abba Poemen says, "If you want to find inward stillness* wherever you are, in every situation say 'I, who am I?' and do not judge* anyone."[229] When a brother asks Abba Joseph of Panephysis about whether he

226. Theodore of Pherme 2.

227. "When he heard this, the brother left, firmly established in the monastic life." The saying's parallel, SysAP VII.9, lacks the sentence, which makes it doubly suspect to me.

228. Antony says that a person should expect temptation until his or her last breath (4); in Agathon 9, Antony tells the brothers: "Every ascetic activity that a person pursues and perseveres in brings peace and tranquility, but prayer requires struggle until the very last breath." See also John the Little 13. In *My Song is of Mercy* Matthew Kelty is very clear about this.

229. On judging and discernment, see III.4; discernment (*diákrisis*) is patient, reflective judgment (*krísis*). Sometimes the commandment against judging can

should leave the cenobium and go live by himself, Joseph offers some wise counsel: "If you find inward stillness in the cenobium and in living by yourself, weigh the two as though they were in a balance. Live where you see that one is better than the other and where your thoughts lead you" (2). Once again, as with contemplative quiet, the ammas and abbas aren't prescriptive. To be honest, when I began writing on the terms in Part V, I thought the monks would be definitive, or at least *a little more defining* than what I've found. One thing I've learned, though, is that early monastic spirituality is much more an open hand than a closed fist, gently opening doors rather than pounding on them. Thomas Merton, to our benefit, ceaselessly inquired about and sought inward stillness; his use of Latin *quies* sounds very much like what the early monastics strive for: "I have an immense need for that silence, for that *quies* in which the soul rests, unmoving, in the obscurity of an immense and simple activity which is God himself."[230]

6. Hope and Joy

We must accept finite disappointment, but never lose infinite hope.[231]

The fruit of the Spirit is love, joy, peace, patience, kindness, generosity, faithfulness, gentleness, and self-control.[232]

I hope that with an open hand, or two, I've extended an invitation to explore a world that may at first seem daunting and formidable,

---

be scandalous, especially for us, who are so much more aware of, say, child abuse, much of it, sorrowfully, unreported; see John the Persian 1.

230. Grayston, *Thomas Merton and the Noonday Demon*, 70. Grayston glosses *quies*, 70 n. 4, as "A prayerful and nonverbal resting in God."

231. Martin Luther King, Jr. (www.guideposts.org/inspiration/inspiring-stories/stories-of-hope/martin-luther-king-jr-on-infinite-hope).

232. Gal 5:22-23.

even, possibly, prohibitive. When we first enter the world of the desert fathers and mothers we imagine a pretty austere landscape and monastic way of life.* And we're right to do so. Very few of us could—and perhaps even should—live the life they did. But my hope is that as readers hike their way through these stories, past brambles and even sidetracks, pausing for quiet, reflection, challenges, and even beauty, in these stories and sayings they will see also the hope and the joy. I want to conclude with these partly because the monks are very often joyful and are almost always hopeful.

Hope and *to hope* occur only a couple of times in the sayings and stories in this volume, but, to echo Paul, hope abides with faith and love.[233] Norris has a good insight here: "How far we have come since Søren Kierkegaard spoke confidently of despair as evidence of our 'superiority over the animal.' We seem to have lost a sense of the reverse, that it could be hope rather than despair that sets us apart."[234] At first, Bessarion 12 doesn't seem like a good place to look for a monastic read on hope, but upon reflection I think it's exactly that: a folk tale as parable on hope; it's also a biblical palimpsest. Instead of the Wandering Jew we have the Wandering Monk; Diogenes' lantern here has faith as the wick and hope as the fire.

Elm's comment on *xeniteía*, "solitude,"* gives us a good start: the idea that "the one who wants to imitate Christ has to be a stranger* [the root meaning of *xénos*] on this earth found its expression in Egypt not only in an exodus into the alien world of the desert, but also in its more literal sense: asceticism as a continuous exile, a perpetual pilgrimage, a life of wandering."[235] In Bessarion 12, the abba symbolically externalizes spiritual wandering, becoming "a wandering Aramean," going "down into Egypt," and living "there as an alien."[236] With echoes from Scripture, Bessarion's life

233. 1 Cor 13:13.
234. Norris, *Acedia*, 271.
235. Elm, *"Virgins of God,"* 276.
236. Deut 26:5. The LXX uses *Syrian* instead of *Aramean*, and doesn't use *xeniteía*.

is an unending journey; perhaps it's a tale told to reinforce what the monks have shown earlier in this Introduction: the spiritual life ain't no picnic, and it's not take-out; it's a life where nourishment comes primarily, even overwhelmingly, not from without but from within. And it requires *áskēsis*, ascetic training.

All this is prologue to Abba Bessarion. The story, a biblical recollection, says that Bessarion seems to be

> completely free of all the bodily passions,* nourished by the hope of things to come,[237] safe inside the stronghold of faith;[238] he would remain as steadfast as a prisoner here or there,[239] enduring cold and nakedness, being roasted by the scorching flame of the sun,[240] always in the open air. Pushing himself into the crags of the desert like a person who's lost, he took great delight in having himself carried along through uninhabited sandy expanses, like a person being tossed about in the sea.

The closing metaphor, a mixed one, seems odd: being tossed about in the ocean brings fear and panic, not hope. But perhaps the author of this saying is imagining someone on a boat throwing out a tethered lifesaver. Or even Jesus in that same boat commanding the waters to still.[241] I won't turn Bessarion's story into an allegory, but it does, very imaginatively, limn, and then deeply color, the challenging contours and landscapes of early Christian monasticism, its realities—and its hope(s).

"Joy," by comparison with the explicit occurrences of *hope*, is a luxuriant, yet implicit, perennial blooming within both desert heat and cold. The ammas and abbas hear what Hugh Feiss warns,

237. See Heb 11:1.

238. Stronghold: see Prov 10:29; 2 Cor 10:4.

239. It looks as though the author is comparing Bessarion to Moses in Heb 11:23-28, with some of the same language; see also Paul as a prisoner (Acts 23:18; Eph 3:1; Phil 1:1, 9).

240. See 2 Cor 11:27; Heb 11:38.

241. Matt 8:28-29 // Mark 4:35-41 // Luke 8:22-25.

heed his warning, and live "contrary" lives of real joy: "the confused heart, having lost joy with itself, seeks . . . consolation . . . outside itself. The more it seeks exterior goods, the more it lacks interior joy to which it can return."[242] Abraham Heschel puts it this way: "joy is not self-centered like pleasure."[243] It's worth noting here that judgmentalism is pleasurable. The monks in this volume live, and die, with very few of what we call *pleasures*— and yet, with so very much, which, as we've seen, they willingly share with others, and with us.[244]

When Abba Agathon is dying, the brothers gather around his bed, seeking wisdom. But when they try to ask him yet another question, he says to them, "Keep doing acts of love [*agápē*], but don't discuss them with me anymore; I'm occupied." And he dies "with joy." The brothers now see "him set off the way someone says goodbye to friends and loved ones" (Agathon 29b). The monks remind us that joy can have a simplicity—not a naïveté but a simple sincerity—about it: "There was a certain elder at Kellia by the name of Apollo, and if someone even began to ask him to do some kind of work or another, he would go off joyfully, saying, 'Today I have Christ working with me on behalf of my soul! He is the soul's reward'" (Apollo 1). I want to repeat: *If someone even began to ask him.* As T. S. Eliot says, "In my beginning is my end."[245]

Hope and joy, as we know, are often scarce. So to conclude, and yet to open doors rather than close them, let's turn to a poet who gives us numerous images that can help us both to imagine hope and keep her close by our side:

> "Hope" is the thing with feathers –
> That perches in the soul –

---

242. Quoted by Norris, *Acedia*, 124; source not given.
243. Heschel, *God in Search of Man*, 385–86.
244. See "Possess / Possessions" in the Glossary and General Index.
245. The line opens the second section of *The Four Quartets*, "East Corker" (www.davidgorman.com/4quartets/2-coker.htm).

And sings the tune without the words –
And never stops – at all –

And sweetest – in the Gale is heard –
And sore must be the storm –
That could abash the little Bird
That kept so many warm –

I've heard it in the chiliest land –
And on the strangest Sea –
Yet – never – in Extremity,
It asked a crumb – of me.[246]

---

246. Emily Dickinson, Poem 254, in *The Complete Poems of Emily Dickinson*, ed. Thomas H. Johnson (Boston: Little, Brown, 1960), 116; Poetryfoundation .org/poems/42889/hope-is-the-thing-with-feathers-314. "Hope," *elpís*, is a feminine noun in Greek.

The Sayings of
the Desert Fathers
and Mothers

Prologue for the Book

About the Ascetic Practices of the Blessed Fathers[1]

[72] [SysAP Prologue][2] In this book are inscribed the virtuous ascetic practice,* the awe-inspiring* way of life, and the sayings*

1. This Prologue, vis-à-vis the sayings that follow, is like the "Dedication to Theophilus" in Luke 1:1-4 vis-à-vis the gospel of Mark; the former uses a long periodic sentence (four verses: one sentence grammatically), with the main clause or predicate at the end, while the latter employs a paratactic style, that is, short, simple *sentences*, with the use of coordinating ("and") rather than subordinating conjunctions. I have tried to convey the style of the Prologue in English here. The Prologue employs numerous doublets (repetition of a word or of a close cousin), and even one triplet; the effect of some of these in Greek is lost in translation. I have paragraphed in accordance with the paragraphing in the SysAP version (*Les Apophtegmes des Pères: Collection Systématique*, ed. Jean-Claude Guy, 3 vols., SCh 387, 474, 498 [Paris: Cerf, 2013], 1.92–94); the SysAP Prologue continues to p. 100.

2. Bracketed Arabic numerals before the sayings indicate the alphabetical *Apophthegmata Patrum* (AlphAP) in Migne's edition (PG 65:75–440). Bracketed Roman numerals followed by Arabic numerals (e.g., XII.3) identify the chapter and saying number in the systematic *Apophthegmata Patrum* (SysAP) (Jean-Claude Guy, ed., *Les Apophtegmes des Pères: Collection Systématique* [Paris: Cerf, 2013]). Other references in the work to Guy's edition (for example, Guy 3.219) give the volume and page number of the citation. AnonAP references come from the anonymous *Apophthegmata Patrum*, from John Wortley, trans., *The Anonymous Sayings of the Desert Fathers: A Select Edition and Complete English*

89

of the holy and blessed fathers, for the ardor and instruction and emulation of those who wish to attain the heavenly way of life* and who wish to follow the way that leads to the kingdom of heaven.[3]

It is necessary, therefore, to understand that the holy fathers, those who became zealous adherents and teachers of the blessed life of the monks, once they had become enflamed with godly and heavenly desire,[4] who considered as nothing all those things that people call good and worthy of honor, who made it their practice, above everything else, to do nothing for the sake of being ostentatious, also hiding most of their achievements, through extraordinary humility* concealed their achievements, thereby completing the path that is in accordance with God.

Because of such practice, no one has been able to write down in full the virtuous life of these elders,[5] but those who have labored mightily with regard to these matters[6] have handed down a few of the words* and deeds*[7] that these elders accomplished, not so they could please them but so they could afterwards rouse those who are zealously making every effort.[8] Most of these who labored, therefore, at different times, have set out in detail both

---

Translation (Cambridge: Cambridge University Press, 2013). For a complete list of abbreviated entries, see Abbreviations (pp. xix–xxiii).

3. way, *hodós*: see John 14:6; *path* at the end of the second paragraph.

4. desire: *érōs* (English *eros*) occurs only once in the SysAP, in the Prologue, as here. But see Tim Vivian, "A Spirituality of Desire: A Meditation on the *Life of Pshoi* vis-à-vis *The New Asceticism* by Sarah Coakley," CSQ 53, no. 1 (2018): 9–31.

5. the virtuous life of these elders: I have followed the suggestion in PG 65:73 n. 2, confirmed by the Prologue in the SysAP (Guy, *Les Apophtegmes des Pères*, 1.92). But I have added *elders*; the masculine genitive pl. pronoun assumes a noun. The text reads "this virtuous life." The difference between the texts is one letter: *toútōn* vs. *toúton*, omega vs. omicron.

6. I have supplied *matters*; one could substitute *elders*. See the previous note.

7. *Words* and *deeds* are singular in SysAP Prologue.

8. That is, making every effort to zealously live the monastic life.

the sayings* and the accomplishments of the holy elders,[9] in simple and straightforward language, with only this one thing in view—to benefit* as many as possible.

But since the details that many have set out are confused and disorderly, they present a certain difficulty to the reader's ability to understand; as a result, the mind and its memory cannot sufficiently grasp the variegated bits and pieces scattered about in the book. Because of this circumstance, we have been moved to present the exposition in an alphabetical arrangement[10] that, because of its orderliness and comprehension,[11] will be able to provide both the clearest and the most accessible format to those who wish to benefit* from it. [12]A saying brought forward by many virtuous* individuals provides no small inducement for virtue.*[13] Thus, beginning with the letter A is material concerning Abba Antony, Arsenius, and Agathon. Following alphabetically comes B, with material about Basil, Bessarion, and Benjamin, and so matters proceed until Ω.[14] But since there are also other sayings* and practices of the holy elders where the names of those who spoke or

---

9. Most of these who labored, therefore, at different times, have set out in detail both the sayings* and the accomplishments of the holy elders: SysAP Prologue, These who labored, therefore, at different times, have set out in detail most of the sayings and accomplishments of the holy elders.

10. alphabetical arrangement: SysAP Prologue, arrangement by chapters. The change in wording shows the different approach of the SysAP, which an editor has arranged by topics ("headings").

11. orderliness and comprehension: SysAP Prologue, orderliness and comprehension in equal measure.

12. SysAP Prologue continues with this sentence.

13. Beginning with this sentence, the SysAP Prologue is very different, so I have not included variations from it in this translation; nor have I translated its considerably longer prologue. For it, see Guy 1.94–100; John Wortley, trans., *The Book of the Elders: Sayings of the Desert Fathers: The Systematic Collection*, CS 240 (Collegeville, MN: Cistercian Publications, 2012), 4–6.

14. Ōméga, the last letter of the Greek alphabet.

accomplished them are omitted, we have arranged them under headings after the completion of those arranged alphabetically.[15]

After seeking out and tracking down numerous books, whatever we could find we placed at the end of the material with headings so that, gathering them together for the soul's benefit,* and taking pleasure in the sayings* of the fathers, which are sweeter than honey and the honeycomb,[16] having lived a way of life* worthy of the call to which the Lord has called us, we might gain* God's kingdom. Amen.

15. This must be referring to the Systematic Collection; see Guy, SysAP, and Wortley, *Book*.
16. Ps 19:11 (LXX 18:11).

Chapter 1

A / Álpha / A[1]

Concerning Abba Antony[2]

1. [76] [VII.7][3] When Saint Abba Antony was dwelling* in the desert* one time, he became dispirited,* and his thoughts* were extremely dark and gloomy.[4] He was saying to God, "Lord, I want to be saved,* and my thoughts* won't leave me alone! Afflicted* like this, what will I do? How will I be saved?"*

---

1. Each chapter is labeled with three characters: the first is English, the second is the Greek name of the letter, and the third gives the letter in Greek.

2. Gk. *Antōnios*. See Antony in Dramatis Personae (pp. 319–22).

3. Bracketed Arabic numerals before the sayings indicate the page numbers in the alphabetical *Apophthegmata Patrum* (AlphAP) in Migne's edition (PG 65:75–440). Bracketed Roman numerals followed by Arabic numerals (e.g., XII.3) identify the chapter and saying number in the systematic *Apophthegmata Patrum* (SysAP) (Jean-Claude Guy, ed., *Les Apophtegmes des Pères: Collection Systématique* [Paris: Cerf, 2013]). Other references in the work to Guy's edition (for example, Guy 3.219) give the volume and page number of the citation. AnonAP references come from the anonymous *Apophthegmata Patrum* (John Wortley, trans., *The Anonymous Sayings of the Desert Fathers: A Select Edition and Complete English Translation* [Cambridge: Cambridge University Press, 2013]). For a complete list of abbreviated entries, see Abbreviations (pp. xix–xxii). All the sayings regarding Antony except Antony 5, 25, 26, 28–31, and 34 are in the SysAP.

4. Words followed by an asterisk are discussed in the Glossary (pp. 261–322).

A little later, going outside, Antony saw[5] someone like him: he was sitting and working;* then he would stand up from his work* and pray.*[6] Then he would sit down and plait rope;[7] then once again he would stand to pray.* It was an angel of the Lord, sent* to set Antony right and strengthen him.[8] Antony heard the angel saying, "Do what I am doing, and you will be saved."*

Hearing this,[9] he was filled with joy and courage. So, doing what the angel had said, he was saved.*[10]

2. [XV.1] The same Abba Antony, intently studying the depths of God's judgments,* wanted an answer, so he said, "Lord, why do certain people live short lives and die while others live to be really old? And why are some poor* and in need while others get rich? And why do those who are neither righteous nor just* get rich while the righteous and just* are in need?"

A voice came to him,[11] saying, "Antony, pay attention* to yourself; to be sure, these are God's judgments,* and it will not do you any good[12] to inquire about these matters."

---

5. saw: literally "sees." Greek often uses the historical present in narrative where English requires the past. The historical present occurs often in the sayings.

6. pray: this shows that the monks prayed standing up, the *orans* position.

7. plait rope: SysAP VII.1, work (with) the rope; perhaps an insignificant difference, but with "work" instead of "plait," SysAP further reinforces the theme of "work."*

8. strengthen him, *diorthóō* (*orthós*: "straight, right," as in English *orthodoxy*): correct, set right, amend, "of moral and spiritual amendment" (Lampe 373b). See n. 300.

9. Hearing: *akoúō* can also mean "hear and understand," "receive instruction, be taught," "be a disciple," and "give heed to, hear inwardly" (Lampe 64a), all apposite here.

10. he was filled with joy and courage. So, doing what the angel had said, he was saved: Antony, Coptic Saying 32, he thoroughly rejoiced. He received the strength to continue and would do what he saw the man doing all the days of his life.

11. A voice [*phōnḗ*] came to him: this is a common topos in the AlphAP; see Antony 7 and 26.

12. it will not do you any good: and / or "it is not your place," reminiscent of God's response to Job in Job 38:4-7.

3. [I.1] Someone asked Abba Antony, "What sort of practices*
do I need to maintain* in order to please God?"[13]

In reply the elder said, "Practice* what I'm prescribing* for
you: Wherever you go,[14] keep God right before your eyes—always. Whatever you're doing, hold on to[15] the testimony of the
holy Scriptures.*[16] Wherever you're living,* don't be in a hurry
to move on. Keep these practices* and you'll be saved."*

4. [77] [XV.2] Abba Antony said to Abba Poemen:[17] "This is
the greatest work*[18] a person can do when he trips up: own his
error[19] in God's presence,[20] and expect temptation* until his last
breath."

13. The need for a spiritual guide, as in Sufism and Buddhism, is key for the
early monks; the classic work for early Christianity is Irénée Hausherr, *Spiritual
Direction in the Early Christian East*, CS 116 (Kalamazoo, MI: Cistercian Publications, 1990); see p. 418 for Antony's appearances in the book. See also Graham Gould, *The Desert Fathers on Monastic Community*, Oxford Early Christian
Studies (Oxford: Clarendon, 1993), esp. chap. 2, "The Abba and His Disciple."

14. go: *apérchomai* means "depart, leave" (*apó*: away from), so the sense is:
wherever you go when you leave your cell / the monastery.

15. Both "keep" and "hold on to" translate the imperative of *échō*, "to have."

16. Whatever you're doing, hold on to the testimony of the holy Scriptures:
Antony, Coptic Saying 44 differs, may the holy Scriptures bear witness in everything you do.

17. Antony, Coptic Saying 25 does not have Antony speaking to Poemen, but
SysAP XV.2 does.

18. See Antony 1. This is the greatest work: Antony, Coptic Saying 25, Courage consists entirely of this.

19. error: *sphálma* can mean "sin," but is a "misstep, mistake, error, fault"
(Lampe 1353a); "lose one's footing, slip, stumble, fall" (Bauer 979b). The cognate
verb *sphállō* means "to make to fall, throw down; to trip up (as in wrestling)," in
the passive voice, "err, go wrong, be mistaken" (Liddell and Scott 1739a). The
usual word for "sin" is *hamartía*.

20. to own his error in God's presence: the phrase is a bit elliptical; I have taken
my cue from the Latin: *ut culpam suam super se ponat coram Deo* ("put on his
guilt before God"). Wortley, *Give Me*, 32, is good: "to take responsibility for his
own shortcoming."

5. He said, "No one will be able to enter the kingdom of heaven without facing temptation.*[21] Remove temptations,"* he said, "and no one will be saved."*

6. [I.2][22] Abba Pambo asked Abba Antony, "What should I do?"

The elder said to him, "Don't be won over[23] by your own righteousness,* and don't feel bad about something you did in the past,[24] and get control* of both your tongue and your belly."[25]

7. [XV.3] Abba Antony said, "I saw all the snares[26] of the Enemy* stretched out like a net over the earth, and I cried out and said, 'Who, then, can escape them?!'[27] And I heard a voice saying to me: 'Humility.' "*[28]

21. without facing temptation: *apeírastos*; the word combines *peirasmós*, "temptation," with a prefixed alpha-negative (negation).

22. Antony, Coptic Saying 3, has one sentence: Abba Antony said to Abba Pambo, "Don't insist on your own righteousness."

23. won over: or "persuaded."

24. something you did in the past: the Greek is less explicit, literally "a deed that's gone by," so "don't feel bad about something that happened in the past" is also possible. Wortley, *Give Me*, 32: "have no regrets about a past action."

25. tongue: Jas 3:1-12; belly: Matt 12:40; 15:17.

26. snares: or "traps," *pagís*; see Luke 21:34-35; Rom 11:9 (Ps 35:8; 69:22-23).

27. stretched out like a net: *haplóō*, "stretch out," can be used of nets (Lampe 187b.2.5), so I have chosen to use the metaphor. Who, then, can escape: this is reminiscent of Jesus' discourse on wealth (rich folk and the eye of the needle) in Luke 18:18-27: those who hear what Jesus has said exclaim, *Then who can be saved?* Jesus replies, *What is impossible for mortals is possible for God.*

28. The end of the saying is very different in Antony, Coptic Saying 43: A voice came to me, saying, "By being humble and sticking with God, a person will overcome all these snares. They will not be able to prevail over the person who possesses humility and perseverance, nor will they be able to inflict any kind of violence on such a person." Humility, *tapeinophrosúnē*: that is, one can escape the Devil's snares by practicing humility. See Antony 15, 17, 19, and 27. Voice: see Antony 2 and 26.

8. [X.1] Again he said: "There are some who've worn out their bodies doing ascetic* practices,[29] and, because of this, they've lost the power of discernment* and have become far from God."

[30]9. [XVII.2] He also said: "We have life and death through our neighbor.* If we gain* our brother, we gain God, but if we cause* our brother to sin we sin against Christ."[31]

[32]10. [II.1] Again he said, "Just as fish die if they stay too long on dry land, so too with monks: if they stay outside their cells too

29. worn themselves out: with regard to property, *katatríbō* means "squander," a meaning apposite here.

30. Antony 9 is similar to a passage in Antony, Letters 6.53. Samuel Rubenson, *The Letters of St. Antony: Monasticism and the Making of a Saint*, Studies in Antiquity & Christianity (Minneapolis: Fortress Press, 1995), 219, suggests that vis-à-vis Letter 6, the Syriac version of the saying is more original: "our destruction is of our neighbor, and also our life is of our neighbor." In 219 n. 11 he states that the "meaning of the verse is obscure at several points." See his discussion.

31. Antony, Coptic Saying 4 is considerably different: If [a person] does what is evil for the other, he'll give birth to death. But if he's done what is good for the other, he'll give birth to life. Antony 9 is the only time in Antony's sayings that "Christ" appears. "Jesus" occurs not at all, though in twenty footnotes I have shown allusions to him; "Lord" almost always refers to God, only once to Jesus. John Wortley informs me that in the entire AlphAP, the name "Jesus" appears only 11 times, and 25 in the AnonAP; "Christ" occurs 15 and 56 times, respectively. In the SysAP "Jesus" occurs 18 times (SysAP III.42) and "Christ" 75 times (Guy 3.250). Perhaps the speakers / writers knew that their audience would hear the allusions, and so they did not need to use the proper names.

32. This saying is strikingly similar to an analogy Antony offers in Life of Antony 85 (pp. 239 and 241) to a "military commander" or "Duke." What is most striking is that, although the passage in the Life is almost word for word with Antony 10, it lacks four key words: *kellíon*, "cells"; *kosmikós*, "those living in the world";* *hēsychía*, "contemplative quiet";* and *phylakḗ*, "watchfulness."* Rubenson, *Letters of St. Antony*, 161–62, argues for the priority of the version in the Life: "A decisive argument for the priority of the text of the Vita is that the word *óros* for a monastic site is attested in the early fourth-century documents, while *kellion* with this meaning is first attested in texts from the late fourth century." I am not so sure, for two reasons: (1) as far as early sources, what we do not know is vaster, perhaps far vaster, than what we know. (2) *Cell* occurs six

long, or spend too much time[33] with those living in the world,*
they unstring the bow of contemplative quiet* and thus the bow
loses its tautness.[34] So, then, just as fish need to hurry back to the
sea, in the same way we too need to hurry back to our cells so
we don't stay too long outside and forget all about our interior
watchfulness."*[35]

11. [II.2] Again he said, "The person who dwells in the desert*
and practices contemplative quiet* frees himself from three wars:
hearsay and gossip, chatter, and keeping an eye out for visitors.[36]
But really he wages only one war: against sexual sin."*[37]

---

times in Antony's sayings (10 [2x], 34 [3x], and 38), *óros* ("mountain" / "monastic
settlement") twice (21 and 34). Rubenson, *Letters of St. Antony,* 153 n. 1, divides
the Sayings of Antony into those that "should be considered genuine," the "probably genuine," and those that "should be considered in all probability spurious."
Of the sayings with *cell* he places Saying 10 in the "genuine" category, and
Sayings 34 and 38 in the "probably genuine" category; of the sayings with "mountain / monastic community," he sees Saying 21 as "genuine" and Saying 34 as
"probably genuine" (193–94). It is very difficult to "define" authenticity in the
sayings.

33. spend too much time: *diatríbō* more neutrally means "spend time," but can
also mean "waste time," the implication here.

34. they unstring the bow of contemplative quiet and thus the bow loses its
tautness: the metaphor of the bow is not explicit in Greek but could certainly be
implied: *eklúō* can mean to loosen or even unstring a bow, and *tónos* can mean
"tightness" or "tension," as in the tension or tautness of a bow. See Saying 13.

35. And forget all about our interior watchfulness: Antony, Coptic Saying 12,
and forget about the interior life, that is, persevering in a life with God.

36. hearsay and gossip, chatter, and keeping an eye out for visitors: I have taken
considerable—but, I think, justifiable—license here. The text literally says "listening, speaking, and looking," but these seem quaint (and very imprecise) as
preludes to sexual sin. Hearsay and gossip, idle chatter, and keeping an eye out
(for visitors) are vices that the elders often warn against..

37. sexual sin: Rubenson points out, *Letters of St. Antony,* 155, that "only the
Greek text [here] gives 'fornication' as the remaining temptation for the monk,
whereas" four other traditions "give the temptations 'of the heart.'" SysAP II.2
also has "of the heart." Rubenson suggests that the original reading was "the
genitals."

12. [X.2] Some brothers approached[38] Abba Antony to let him know about visions* they'd been seeing and to learn from him whether these visions* were true, or came from demons.*[39] They had had an ass, and it had died on the way. Antony had anticipated their arrival, and when they came to visit the elder he said to them, "How did the little ass die on the way?"

They said to him, "How do you know this, abba? Where'd you get your information?"

He said to them, "The demons* pointed it out to me."[40]

They said to him, "Because of what you're saying,[41] we've come to ask you about what happened, because we saw[42] visions,* and often they turn out to be true, but we want to know if we've been deceived somehow."

The elder [Antony] demonstrated for them from the example of the ass that such visions come from demons.*[43]

38. approached: there may be a play on words here: "approached" is *parébalon*, from *parabállō*, and later "anticipated" is *prólabōn*, from *prolambánō*. The similarity in sound may be emphasizing that while the brothers were approaching, Antony had foreseen them.

39. In Life of Antony 11.2 (pp. 85 and 87), "the Enemy . . . cast onto the road the illusory shape of a large silver dish"; in 12.1 (87) Antony sees "real gold, not another illusion," but the text then wonders "whether it was the Enemy who showed it to him," or a divine "mighty power."

40. to me: or "for me," if one takes the dative as dative of advantage.

41. Because of what you're saying: literally "Because of this," that is, because of what Antony said about the demons, or they knew already about his gift of foreknowledge—or both.

42. saw: literally "see," so this may be the historical present for the past, or they may be saying that they are still seeing visions.

43. The Coptic is quite different. The monks say: "For our part, we came to ask you about this because we saw something unreal, and it's so happened that they've [the demons] told the truth any number of times. We don't want to be led astray." Then Antony "agreed that what they had seen came from demons. They left him, giving glory to God."

13. [X.3] There was a certain man, a hunter,[44] who hunted wild animals throughout the wilderness region,[45] and he saw Abba Antony laughing and joking [80] with the brothers and was scandalized.*[46]

The elder [Antony], wanting to assure him, because he needed to accommodate himself[47] from time to time to the level of the brothers,[48] said to him, "Put an arrow in your bow and stretch the bow tight," and this he did.

Antony said to him, "Stretch it tight some more," and he stretched it some more.

Again he said, "Stretch it."

The hunter said to him, "If I stretch it too tight, the bow will break."

The elder said to him, "it's the same with doing God's work:* with regard to the brothers, if we stretch them too tight, they'll

---

44. Antony, Coptic Saying 7 makes the hunter an elder (an experienced abba), which is not likely, and its beginning differs considerably: An elder asked Abba Antony, "Is it OK to meet with the brothers?" and the elder [Antony] wanted to assure him, saying, "It's OK occasionally to meet with the brothers." While he regarded the hunter of wild animals, Antony said to him, "Put an arrow in your bow . . . ."

45. wilderness region: I have chosen to translate *érēmos* here as *wilderness* rather than the usual "desert."* *Wilderness* is where humans do not normally live and is where John the Baptist emerges from: "The voice of one crying out in the wilderness [*érēmos*]" (Matt 3:3; Isa 40:3).

46. Because of the context, I have followed a variant reading, PG 65:79–80 n. 3 and SysAP X.3, which continue with "and he was scandalized."

47. he needed to accommodate himself: *sunkatabaínō*. Lampe notes, 1267b, that the verb can refer to teachers and pupils or, significantly, "God's dealings with" humankind. In Acts 25:5 it means "come with," "accompany," which gives a nice pastoral gloss to what is happening here.

48. he needed to accommodate himself from time to time to the level of the brothers: Wortley, *Give Me,* 33, "The elder wanted to convince the hunter that he had to come down to the level of the brothers from time to time." Wortley has taken *chrē̌,* "needed to," "had to" with "the hunter" (he has supplied these words).

quickly break into pieces.[49] It's necessary, then, to come down to the brothers' level from time to time."[50]

When the hunter heard what Antony was saying, he was deeply moved* and, having benefited* greatly from the elder, departed. The brothers, strengthened and feeling supported,[51] withdrew* to their monastic settlement.*

14. [VIII.1] Abba Antony heard about a certain young monk who had performed a miracle[52] while on the road: when the young monk saw some elders who were traveling and were wearied by their journey, he ordered wild asses to come and carry the elders until they reached Antony. So the elders informed Abba Antony about what had happened.

He said to them, "It seems to me that this monk is a ship filled with goods;[53] I don't know whether he's going to make it to shore."

After a while Abba Antony suddenly began to weep[54] and pull out his hair and mourn. His disciples said to him, "Why are you weeping, abba?"

The elder said, "A great pillar of the church has just now fallen!" (He was talking about the young monk.) "But go," he said, "until you reach him and see what's happened."

49. break: *prosréssō* (= *prosrégnumi*). The verb means "dash or beat against," as a river dashing against a house, or bursting a vein or sinew (Liddell and Scott 1525a). The image of an athlete rupturing an Achilles tendon is analogous for us.

50. Antony, Coptic Saying 7 picks up the theme of meeting with the brothers: "It's the same, then, with doing God's work: if someone goes too far, in such a way that he strains the abilities of the brothers, they will soon break—it's OK to meet with them occasionally." Then it concludes, "Through the analogy of the bow, what Antony had said greatly edified the elder, and so he left."

51. strengthened and feeling supported, *stērízō*: "to fix firmly in place, set up, establish, support," "to cause to be inwardly firm or committed, confirm, establish, strengthen" (Bauer 945a). The verb occurs often in the New Testament.

52. miracle, *sēmeíon*. John's gospel calls the miracles or wonders that Jesus does *sēmeía*, "signs"; see John 2:11, 18, 23; 20:30.

53. a ship filled with goods: SysAP VIII.1, a ship filled with all kinds of goods.

54. weep: *klaíō* also means "wail, lament," and below.

So the disciples left and found the monk sitting on a mat, weeping[55] over the sin he had committed.[56] When he heard the elder's disciples, he said, "Tell the elder to implore* God to grant me just ten days and I hope* to make amends."[57]

And within five days, he died.[58]

15. [VIII.2] The brothers praised a certain monk to Abba Antony. Abba Antony questioned the monk, testing* him to see if he could stand being criticized.[59] Finding that the monk could not take it, he said to him, "You're like a village out in the country: on the outside it looks all nice and pretty while inside it's being plundered by bandits."*[60]

16. [X.4] A brother said to Abba Antony, "Pray* for me."

The elder said to him, "Neither I nor God will have mercy* on you if you yourself don't make the effort and ask God."[61]

55. weeping, *klaíō*: see the previous note; thus the monk is, unknowingly, emulating Antony.

56. committed: *ergázomai* is cognate with *érgon* and *ergasía* (see Antony 1 and Work in the Glossary), a greatly valued monastic virtue. Thus, ironically, the young man has "worked a sin," which really makes his action anti-érgon. See nn. 178, 204, 292, 304, 579.

57. to make amends: *apologéomai* (English "apology"). SysAP VIII.1 to make amends and repent. Antony, Coptic Saying 15 agrees with AlphAP Antony 14.

58. It is a common monastic topos for a person to die shortly after repenting, but the monk's death here after five days (thus *not* making amends in ten?) seems cruel.

59. "Praised" and "testing" are much closer in sound in Greek than in English: "praised" is *epēnéthē* and "tested" is *epeírasen*. In Greek at this time the first two syllables of the words were pronounced the same.

60. There is an echo here of the epithet "whitewashed tombs" that Jesus hurls at the Pharisees in Matt 23:27-28.

61. if you yourself don't make the effort and ask God: SysAP X.4 is significantly different, if you yourself don't have mercy and please God. In Gen 5:22 LXX, Enoch pleases God.

17. [XV.4] Elders visited Abba Antony one time, and Abba Joseph[62] was with them. The elder,[63] wanting to put them to the test,* put forward[64] a passage[65] from Scripture* and, beginning with the least advanced, asked them what the passage meant.

Each would speak to the best of his ability.* The elder would say to each one, "You haven't found the answer yet." After speaking with all of them, he said to Abba Joseph, "And you—what do you think[66] this passage[67] from Scripture* means?"

He answered, "I don't know."

So Abba Antony said, "Clearly Abba Joseph has found the way ahead because he said 'I don't know.' "

18. [81] [IV.1] Brothers from Scetis* were going to visit Abba Antony, and, boarding a boat to go see him, they found an elder who also wanted to go there. (The brothers didn't know him.) Sitting in the boat, they were talking about the sayings* of the fathers and passages from Scripture,* and afterwards they were doing their handiwork. The elder remained silent.[68] After they had entered the harbor, they discovered that the elder had gone off to see Abba Antony.

---

62. Perhaps Joseph of Panephysis, who has eleven sayings in the AlphAP (he is the only Joseph therein); Joseph figures prominently in Cassian, *Conferences* XVI and XVII.

63. elder: that is, Abba Antony.

64. put forward, *probállō*: "visited" translates *parabállō*. A visit naturally includes a passage or passages of Scripture.

65. passage: *rhēma*, which has a wide variety of meanings in the New Testament: "word, saying, expression, or statement of any kind," or "an event that can be spoken about, object, matter, event" (Bauer 905a). If we take it more broadly, a translation could be, "What do you think is going on here?" Wortley, *Give Me*, 34, "verse." *Rhēma*, then, can mean here a verse, a saying, a passage, a parable, or a story.

66. what do you think: literally "how do you say."*

67. passage: the text has switched from *rhēma* to *lógos*; see Counsel in the Glossary.

68. The elder remained silent: SysAP IV.1: The elder remained completely silent.

When the brothers reached Abba Antony's, he said to them, "You found a good companion to voyage with in this elder." He also said to the elder, "You found good brothers to travel with you, abba."

The elder said, "They're good companions, but their courtyard doesn't have a gate, and anyone who wants to can enter the stable and set the ass loose." He was saying this because the brothers would talk about whatever came into their heads.[69]

19. [XVI.1] Brothers came to visit Abba Antony and said to him, "Offer us some counsel:* How can we be saved?"*

The elder said to them, "Have you listened to[70] the Scripture?*[71] You'll be fine."

But they said, "We also want to hear from you, father."

The elder said to them, "The Gospel says, *If someone strikes you on the right cheek, offer the other cheek also.*"[72]

They said to him, "We can't do this."

The elder said to them, "If you can't offer the other cheek, at least patiently endure it when the one is being struck."

They said to him, "We can't do this, either."

The elder said, "If you can't do even this, at least don't hit back."

They said, "We can't do this, either."[73]

The elder said to his disciple, "Make them some hot cereal; they're weak."[74]

"If you can't do this, and refuse to[75] do that, what will I be able to do for you? It's prayers* that you need."

---

69. This last sentence could be an editorial gloss.

70. Listened, *akoúō*: or "heard," or "obeyed."

71. Antony's question could also be a statement.

72. Matt 5:39.

73. We can't do this, either: or perhaps "We can't do even this."

74. weak: *asthenéō* can mean "be sick, weak." The noun *asthénia* (English *neurasthenia*), "weakness," can also indicate "frailty of the flesh, not necessarily denoting sin" (Lampe 243a).

75. refuse to, *thélō*: or "don't want to," but *thélō* with a negative can mean "refuse."

20. [VI.1] A brother renounced* the world* and distributed his possessions* to the poor,* but kept a little for his own needs,[76] and went to visit Abba Antony. When the elder learned about this, he said to him,[77] "If you want to become[78] a monk, leave, and go to this certain village. Buy some meat, and cover your naked body with it. Once you've done this, come back here."

When the brother did what Antony had told him, the dogs and the birds tore his body to pieces. When he returned to meet with the elder, Abba Antony inquired of the brother whether he had done what he had advised.[79] When that brother showed[80] Abba Antony his lacerated body, Saint Antony[81] said, "This is the way that demons* wage war* against those who renounce* the world* yet want to keep some money:[82] they shred them to pieces."

21. [IX.1] A brother one time succumbed to temptation*[83] in the cenobium* of Abba Ēlít.[84] Driven out[85] of the monastery, he left for the monastic community* of Abba Antony.

---

76. See Acts 5:1-11, where Anianas and Sapphira do this, with bad consequences.

77. A brother renounced the world. . . . When the elder learned about this, he said to him: the beginning of Antony, Coptic Saying 23 is considerably different, A brother paid a visit to Abba Antony and said to him, "Teach me to be a monk." The elder said to him . . . .

78. become: *gí(g)nomai* can mean both "be" and "become"; given the situation here, "become" has more punch.

79. whether . . . advised: literally "whether what he had advised had come into being," with "come into being / become" translating *gí(g)nomai*, as above.

80. showed: or "displayed."

81. Saint Antony: SysAP VI.1, Abba Antony.

82. money, *chrḗmata*: *chrḗma* can also indicate "goods" or "property."

83. succumbed to temptation, *peirasmós*: literally "temptation happened to a brother."

84. Ēlít: a variant reading, PG 65:81–82 n. 10: Ēlíou; that is, Elijah, which is the Septuagint's rendering (3 Kgs = 1 Kgs 17:1). Neither name occurs in the SysAP (Guy 3.241).

85. Driven out: *diṓko* has a wide range of additional meanings: "chase away, banish," "pursue, chase," as in war, and, as a legal term, "prosecute, bring an action against" (Liddell and Scott 440b).

After the brother had stayed there a while with him, Abba Antony sent him back* to the cenobium* that he'd come from. When the monks there saw him, once again they drove him away. He returned to Abba Antony, saying, "They refused to welcome* me back, father."

The elder then sent* him back,[86] saying, "A ship shipwrecked at sea and lost its cargo; after great hardship,[87] [84] it came safely [88] to shore. You monks, however, want[89] to throw into the sea to drown what has been safely brought to shore."[90]

When they heard that it was Abba Antony who had sent* the brother back, they accepted him—immediately.

22. [V.1][91] Abba Antony said, "After reflection,*[92] I've concluded that the body has a natural movement kneaded in with

86. Aptly, and ironically, the once-excommunicated brother, now "sent out" (*apostéllō*) by Abba Antony, is his apostle (the cognate noun *apóstolos*) to the judgmental monks. SysAP IX.1: sent him back to them.

87. hardship: in monastic Greek, *kámatos*, "labor," can indicate the labor of spiritual discipline (Lampe 699b), apposite here.

88. safely, *esóthē*: literally, "was saved," from *sōzō*, "to save,"* and below. The aorist passive participle "saved," *esóthē*, has the root *–sōt*, cognate with *sótēr*, "savior," English *soteriology*, and *sōtēría*, "salvation."

89. want, *thélō*: earlier, "refused" translates *thélō* with a negative. The monks earlier refused to welcome the brother; now they, Antony accuses, want to throw him into the sea to drown. In other words, the sinful monk has been saved, but the monks are too hard-hearted to see it.

90. In ancient Mesopotamian-Semitic religions, water often stands for chaos. In Gen 1:2 when God begins to create, "darkness was over the surface of the deep." *Deep* in Hebrew is *tᵉhom*, cognate with *Tiamat*, the monster in the Babylonian epic *Enuma Elish*. See John J. Collins, *A Short Introduction to the Hebrew Bible*, 2nd ed. (Minneapolis: Fortress Press, 2014), 46. In discussing the Hebrews' crossing of the Red / Reed Sea in Exod 15 and the drowning of Pharaoh and his army, Collins observes, 70, "The imagery of sinking in water is used elsewhere in Hebrew poetry as a metaphor for distress (e.g. Psalm 69). . . . In these cases, sinking in the depths is not a description of physical condition, but simply a metaphor for distress."

91. See Antony, Letter 1.27–41 (Rubenson, *Letters of St. Antony*, 199), for a very similar version of this saying.

92. After reflection: SysAP V.1, After reflection; Antony, Coptic Saying 22 lacks these words.

it,[93] but it isn't active* unless the soul wishes it;[94] it signals in the body only a movement free from sinful passions.*

"But there is also another movement that nourishes the body and with food and drink causes it to flourish. From these the blood's heat[95] stimulates the body so it can function.[96] Therefore the Apostle used to say, 'Do not get drunk on wine;* this leads to debauchery.'[97] Additionally, in the Gospel the Lord commands* the disciples, saying, 'Be careful. Don't let your hearts get weighed down with dissipation[98] and drunkenness.'[99]

"There is a certain movement for those who spiritually contend;* this movement comes upon them because of the plotting and ill-will of the demons.*[100] So then, we need to recognize that

93. natural movement, *physikós*: or "innate," "essential" movement (Lampe 1494a–95a).

94. unless the soul wishes it: possibly "if the soul refuses it." *Thélō* with a negative can mean "refuse." But the next sentence suggests that a person would not refuse this movement.

95. Andrew B. Lumb notes that "Galen's writings strengthened the analogy between the heart and a flame, and several pages of *On the Use of Breathing* are concerned with the similarities between the two" ("The History of Respiratory Physiology," in *Nunn's Applied Respiratory Physiology,* 8th ed. (Amsterdam: Elsevier Publishing, 2017) (booktree.mg/nunns-applied-respiratory-physiology-pdf).

96. function, *enérgeia,* and "active" earlier render the verb *energéō.* See "Work" in the Glossary.

97. Eph 5:18. Debauchery: *asōtía,* the word that the author of Ephesians uses; Bauer 148a: "wild living." Lampe 255b offers "profligacy" and "concupiscence." The NRSV translates *asōtía* as "debauchery." Ephesians continues, importantly, *but be filled with the Spirit,* which a biblically aware person might hear here. The verb *asōténomai* means, "To lead a profligate, wasteful life"; the adjective *ásōstos* means "having no sobriety, abandoned," "having no hope of safety, in desperate" straits, "past recovery." All are cognate with *sōtēría,* "salvation,"* and *sṓzō,* "to save,"* preserve." See Liddell and Scott 267b; Bauer 148a; Lampe 255b.

98. dissipation: *kraípalē* can mean a "drunken bout" or even a "hangover." Latin *crapula* came into English as *crapulous, crapulent,* excessive drinking or eating.

99. Luke 21:34. Don't let your hearts get weighed down: SysAP V.1, Don't let your hearts ever get weighed down. The Greek NT has the same reading.

100. Evagrius, *Chapters on Prayer* 12 (p. 57) speaks of the "disordered movement" of anger* and retaliation and how to heal it with prayer and mindfulness of judgment.

the body has three movements: one is natural, one comes about from foods neither good nor bad, but[101] the third comes from the demons."*

23. [X.5] He also said, "God doesn't allow wars*[102] against this generation as he did against those who went before; no doubt he knows that those of this generation are frail[103] and can't bear* them."[104]

24. [XVIII.1] To Abba Antony it was revealed in the desert:* In the city there is a certain person like you, a doctor by profession, who gives his excess income to those in need, and every day he sings the Trisagion[105] with the angels.[106]

25. Abba Antony said, "A time* is coming when people will go insane, and when they see someone who's not insane they'll rise up against that person, saying, 'You're insane, you! You're not like us!' "

26. Brothers visited Abba Antony, and they cited him a verse* from Leviticus. Because of this, the elder[107] went out into the desert;* Abba Ammonas secretly followed* him, knowing his practice.[108] When the elder was quite a distance away,[109] standing

---

101. but, *dé*: or "and."

102. wars: SysAP X.5, the wars of the Enemy, that is, Satan (see Antony 7), so a good translation could be, "God doesn't allow the Enemy to wage war."

103. frail: *asthenḗs*; the word leads off the clause and is thus in Greek emphatic. See Antony 19, where the translation is *weak*.

104. frail and can't bear them: or "weak and can't endure them," or other combinations. There may be echoes here of Luke 7:31; 11:19; Acts 2:40; and / or Phil 2:15. On the "nostalgia" of this saying, and others, see John Wortley, "Nostalgia and the Desert Fathers," CSQ 58, no. 3 (2018): 267–78.

105. On the Trisagion, see Andrew Louth, "Trishagion" [*sic*], in *Theologische Realenzyklopädie*, ed. Gerhard Müller, Bd. 32 (Berlin-New York: Walter de Gruyter, 2002), 121–24. See Isa 6:3; Rev 4:8. Louth and Lampe 1409a cite Proclus of Constantinople (d. 446) as the earliest instance; Proclus introduced it into the liturgy in 438.

106. the angels: SysAP XVIII.1, the angels of God.

107. elder: that is, Antony.

108. practice: or "habits."

109. quite a distance away: either in the distance or far away from the monastery.

in prayer,* he cried out[110] in a loud voice,[111] "My God, send*
Moses,[112] and he will teach me what this verse* means!"

And a voice came to him[113] and was speaking with him. Abba
Ammonas said,[114] "I heard the voice that was speaking with him,
but I couldn't understand the meaning of the words."*[115]

27. [XVII.5] Three of the fathers had the custom to go see the
blessed Antony each year. Two of them would ask him about their
thoughts* and the salvation* of their souls,[116] but the one always
remained silent and wouldn't ask anything.

Quite a while later, Abba Antony said to him, "Look, you've
been coming here all this time, and you never ask me anything."

He responded, saying to him, "It's enough for me just to see
you, father."

28. They used to say that a certain one of the elders asked God
to see the fathers. When he saw them, [85] Abba Antony was not
among them, so he said to God, who was showing them to him,
"Where is Abba Antony?"

---

110. When the elder was very far away, standing in prayer, he cried out: or one
could punctuate as, "When the elder was very far away, standing in prayer he
cried out."

111. he cried out in a loud voice: the Greek is essentially the same (two variants
of the same verb) in John 11:43 when Jesus cries out to Lazarus. In Mark 15:34,
when Jesus cries out in a loud voice, the Greek has the same adjective and noun
but a different verb.

112. In Lev 1:1, *The Lord summoned Moses and spoke to him from the tent of
meeting, saying*, and then for most of the book the Lord instructs Moses what to
tell the people.

113. And a voice came to him: see Antony 2 and 7.

114. Abba Ammonas said: this is elliptical; it probably means, "When Abba
Ammonas returned [to the monastery], he said."

115. I couldn't understand the meaning of the words: literally "I didn't learn
the power* of the word* / speech" (*lógos*).

116. the salvation of their souls: literally "the salvation of soul." I have supplied
"their," but the monks may more generally be asking about the salvation of souls
or, possibly, the salvation of the soul. Monks often ask, "How can I be saved?"

God said to him, "Wherever God is, Abba Antony is there."

29. A brother in the cenobium* was falsely accused of sexual sin,* so he got up and went to see Abba Antony. The brothers from the cenobium* came too in order to heal[117] him and seize[118] him. They began to berate him, "You committed sexual sin!"*

He defended himself: "I did no such thing!"

Abba Paphnutius* Kephalas happened to be there, and he told this parable: "I saw on the riverbank a person who had been thrown into the mud up to his knees and some people came to give him a hand—and they shoved him further down into the mud,[119] up to his neck!"

So Abba Antony said this to them about Abba Paphnutius:* "Here is a real[120] human being, someone who can heal and save* souls."

Stung,* therefore, by what the elders had said,* the brothers from the cenobium* prostrated* themselves before the brother.

Comforted* by the fathers, they took the brother back to the cenobium.*

---

117. heal: *therapeúō*, "heal, cure," given the context, seems odd here: the brothers berate the "sinner" and have come to seize him. Lampe says the verb can be used "of reconciliation," "of treating gently, consoling," and "care for, look after" (all 645a), but these do not fit, either. Antony, Coptic Saying 10 is clearer: "The brothers left their monastery to seize him; they cast aspersions on him and beat him." Given the (ironic, sarcastic) reoccurrence of "heal" below, "heal" here suggests "ostensibly in order to heal him."

118. seize: *lambánō* can mean "to seize violently"; it can also mean "catch," or it can simply mean here "take (back)," but Greek has a word for this: *apolambánō*.

119. shoved him further down: *katapontízō* means "engulf, swallow up, overwhelm"; the noun *katapontismós* means "drowning" (Lampe 715a). So there is a suggestion that the person could drown in the mire.

120. real (or: true): *alēthinós*, cognate with *alḗtheia*, "truth." John 8:32 is apposite here: Jesus says, "Then you will know the truth, and the truth will set you free."

30. Some people[121] were talking about Abba Antony: "He has become a Spiritbearer,[122] but he's refused to speak about people."[123] It's a fact: he would reveal[124] what was happening in the world* and what was going to happen.[125]

31. One time Abba Antony received a letter from Emperor Constantine*[126] to come to Constantinople.*[127] He was considering what to do, so he said to his disciple Abba Paul,[128] "Am I obligated to leave here?"

Abba Paul said to him, "If you go away, you'll be called 'Antony,' but if you don't go away, 'Abba Antony.' "

121. Some people: Antony, Coptic Saying 1, The elders.

122. Spiritbearer: *pneumatophóros* became an appellation of Macarius the Great (Macarius of Scetis); see Tim Vivian, *St Macarius the Spiritbearer: Coptic Texts Relating to Saint Macarius the Great*, Popular Patristics Series (Crestwood, NY: St. Vladimir's, 2004). The only occurrence in the SysAP is in III.19 (AlphAP Macarius 38), where a skull says to Macarius, "You are Macarius the Spiritbearer." Historia Lausiaca 11.5 (p. 26) describes Evagrius as "discerning" (*diakritikós*) (see Discernment in the Glossary) and a "Spiritbearer" (*pneumatophóros*). Lampe 1106a also translates the word "inspired"; in Patristic Greek it was used of biblical prophets, John the Baptist, monks, scriptural writers, and doctors of the church. Prophet here, as now, seems to indicate foresight rather than the social critique given by the biblical prophets.

123. to speak about people: or "on account of people" or "for the sake of people."

124. reveal, *mēnúō*: or "disclose." Justin,* *Apology* 59.1 says that "through Moses . . . the prophetic spirit . . . revealed how God created" (Lampe 868a).

125. he would reveal what was happening in the world and what was going to happen: Antony, Coptic Saying 1, He knew [people] from a distance and knew what they represented.

126. Constantine the Great, d. 337, became emperor in 306. Antony died in 356, so it is certainly possible that the emperor sent him a letter asking him to visit—and, if he did, it is even more likely that Antony did not go.

127. The infinitive in Greek and in English leaves it open whether Constantine is asking or commanding Antony to come.

128. This is Paul the Sincere (or: Simple), who has one saying in the AlphAP. He was a disciple of Antony; see Historia Lausiaca 22 (pp. 58–62) and Hist Mon 24 (pp. 114–15).

32. Abba Antony said, "I[129] no longer fear* God. No, I love* God, because *Love* casts out fear.*"[130]

33. [III.1][131] He said, "Keep right in front of you[132] at all times the fear* of God.[133] Keep in mind the one who causes death and gives life.[134] Hate the world* and everything in it.[135] Hate every kind of worldly* leisure.[136] Renounce* this life in order to live for God.[137] Remember* what you vowed[138] to God:[139] God will ask you [pl.][140] about it on the Day of Judgment.* Hunger, thirst, be

129. I: in Greek the pronoun "I," *egṓ*, unlike in English, is not necessary, so it may be emphatic here, something like "as for me, I."

130. 1 John 4:18: "There is no fear in love. But perfect love casts out fear."

131. There are 19 verbs in this saying directed to "you." The first two are singular, and all the rest are plural. SysAP III.1 is significantly different: all the verbs are first-person plural subjunctive / cohortative: "let us keep in mind," etc.

132. Keep right in front of you: literally "before your eyes." The command is "you" singular; SysAP has the plural.

133. With the theme of fear, an editor undoubtedly put Saying 33 with Saying 32, or vice versa, but this sentence is jarring after Saying 32. This saying emphasizes ascetic requirements.

134. causes death and gives life: this may be a compression of Deut 30:15: "See! I have set before you today life and prosperity, and death and adversity." "Causes death" and "gives life" have more resonance together in Greek: *thanatoûntos* and *zōonoûntos* (English *thanatology* and *zoology*). SysAP III.1 is considerably different: Keep in mind / be mindful of death.

135. "Hate," *misḗsate* is a strong word, but see Luke 14:26, where Jesus uses the same verb in the singular.

136. This is a compressed and multivalent command. "Worldly," *sarkikós* here rather than *kosmikós* (see World in the Glossary), is literally "fleshly," "of the flesh."* "Leisure," *anápausis*, is actually a condition or state much desired by the monks (see Inward stillness in the Glossary), but here, combined with "worldly," it is not.

137. for: or "with, in." The dative case can mean any of them.

138. vowed: *epangéllō* can mean to make monastic profession; its primary meaning is "announce, proclaim."

139. Remember what you vowed to God: SysAP II.1 lacks.

140. you [pl.]: SysAP III.1, us.

naked,[141] keep vigil,* mourn, weep and wail,[142] sigh deeply within yourselves.[143] Scrutinize whether you're worthy of God.[144] Despise[145] the flesh* in order to save your souls."

34.[146] Abba Antony one time paid a visit to Abba Amoun at the monastic settlement* of Nitria.* At the end of their conversation,[147] Abba Amoun said to him, "Since, because of your prayers,* the brothers have increased in number and some of them want to build cells far away in order to practice contemplative quiet,*

141. be naked, *gymnēteúō*: Lampe does not include this verb, suggesting that it does not have special patristic meaning. See 1 Cor 4:11: *To the present hour we are hungry and thirsty, we are poorly clothed* [gymniteúō] *and beaten and homeless.* Bauer 208a agrees with the NRSV and notes, 208b, that it can mean "inadequately clothed, poorly dressed," or "lightly clad, without an outer garment." With "naked," I am following 2 Cor 11:7, where Paul recites his hardships: *in toil and hardship, through many a sleepless night, hungry and thirsty, often without food, cold and naked.* I believe that this passage had particular resonance with the monks. The root *gymnós* (originally "naked"; [male athletes competed naked]) nourishes a tree of many branches: *gymnasía,* "exercise, training"; *gymnásion,* "exercise, training, discipline" or "spiritual training and discipline"; *gymnastikós,* what is suitable for spiritual training; *gymnḗteusis,* "nakedness, poverty" (Lampe 324b).

142. weep and wail: SysAP III.1 lacks.

143. sigh deeply within yourselves: literally "sigh in your heart."

144. worthy of God. Despise . . . : SysAP III.1, worthy of God. Let us love affliction* so we can find God. Despise. . . .

145. Despise, *kataphronéo*: or, more neutrally, "disregard, pay no attention to" (Lampe 726a).

146. This saying tells the story of the founding of Kellia* (Cells). See Derwas Chitty, *The Desert a City* (Crestwood, NY: St Vladimir's, 1966), 29–30; Hugh G. Evelyn-White, ed., Walter Hauser, *The Monasteries of the Wâdi 'N Natrun,* vol. II, *The History of the Monasteries of Nitria and Scetis,* The Metropolitan Museum of Art Egyptian Exhibition (New York: Metropolitan Museum, 1932; repr. Arno Press, 1973), 50.

147. At the end of their conversation: literally, "After they (had) met with one another," but Amoun then speaks, so it is not really "after."

what are your orders? How far from here do you want these cells constructed?

He said, "Let's eat at the ninth hour;[148] then let's leave and walk out into the desert* and take a look at the place."

[88] They walked out into the desert* until the sun was setting, at which time Abba Antony said to Abba Amoun, "Let's pray* and set up a cross[149] here so that those who want to build cells here can do so, and so when those back at the monastery want to visit the ones here, the monks from the monastery can eat a little bread* at the ninth hour and so visit, and when those here leave to visit the monks at the monastery they can do the same. That way they'll remain undistracted[150] when they visit one another."

The distance was twelve miles.[151]

35. [XI.3] Abba Antony said, "The person hammering a piece of iron first considers[152] what he's going to make: scythe, sword, axe. It's the same with us, too: we need to consider[153] which of the virtues*[154] we're seeking so we don't labor in vain.[155]

---

148. ninth hour: about 3 p.m., calculated from the time of sunrise; the time varied throughout the year.

149. set up a cross: Lampe 1254ab does not explicitly cite "setting up" a cross, but the uses of the cross he cites are instructive: "veneration of the Cross," "sign of the cross" on the body, and "as standing for mortification."

150. undistracted: *anerispástos* can also mean "unwavering, continuous," as of prayer (Lampe 184a).

151. Unless this saying is hagiographical, which seems unlikely to me, it shows, as Gould notes, 13, the "interdependence of some of the founders of monasticism."

152. considers: in Patristic Greek *skopéō* can mean "contemplate spiritually" (Lampe 1241), which is more than suggested here because the metaphorical craftsman is literally "contemplating his thought"* (*logismós*).

153. consider, *logízomai* (verb): "considers" earlier translates *skopéō tòn logismón* (noun); see Thoughts in the Glossary.

154. which of the virtues: literally "what sort of virtue."

155. so we don't labor [*kopiáō*] in vain [*kenós*]: See Phil 2:16: "It is by your holding fast to the word of life that I can boast on the day of Christ that I did not run in vain [*kenós*] or labor [*kopiáō*] in vain [*kenós*]." See nn. 158, 168.

36. [XIV.1] He also said: "Obedience* with self-control* subdues[156] the wild beasts."[157]

37. [XI.1] He also said, "I know monks who, after great
exertions,[158] fell and lost their minds*[159] because they put their
trust* in their own work* and didn't consider[160] the commandment* that says 'Ask your father,*[161] and he will inform you.' "[162]

38. [XI.2] Again he said: "However many steps[163] the monk
takes, or however many drops of water he drinks in his cell, he
ought, if at all possible,[164] to confide these things to his elders to
see if he's doing wrong[165] by doing them."

156. subdues: *hypotássō*; its cognate noun *hypotagḗ* is earlier in the sentence
translated *obedience*. SysAP XIV.1, with *hypakoḗ* (also "obedience") instead of
hypotagḗ, loses the wordplay.

157. wild beasts, *thēríon*: in the letter to Titus 1:12, the author, quoting Epi-
menides, *De Oraculis*, proclaims "Cretans are always liars, vicious brutes
[*thēríon*], lazy gluttons." See Bauer 455b–56a.

158. exertions, *kópos*: its verb, *kopiáō* is translated as "labor" in Antony 35.
See nn. 155, 168.

159. lost their minds: literally "came to separation [*ékstasis*] of mind." Lampe
438b notes that *ékstasis* can mean both "separation, alienation of mind," and,
mystically, "ecstasy,"* literally "standing out of / away (from)."

160. didn't consider: or "reckon with." *Paralogízomai* can mean "leave out of
reckoning" and even "condemn," and its cognate noun *paralogismós*, can mean
"craftiness" (Lampe 1021b). On *logismós* and *logízomai*, see n. 153 and Thoughts
in the Glossary. They've put their trust in their own work and didn't consider:
SysAP XI.1, they've put their trust in their own work, thinking that it was pleasing to God, and didn't consider.

161. ask your father: that is, your spiritual father, *ábba*; see Antony 38.

162. Deut 32:7 LXX.

163. steps, *bḗmata*: *bḗma* (the singular) can mean "way of life" (Lampe 295b–
96a).

164. if at all possible: *dynatós*, "if possible," is cognate with *dýnamis*, "power."*
The phrase "if possible" emphatically begins the sentence in Greek, so I have
tried to make it more emphatic.

165. doing wrong: *ptaíō* can also mean "sin, lapse" and, with the genitive, "fall
away from." The basic meaning of the verb is "stumble, trip, fall" (Bauer 894b);
its cognate noun is *paráptōma*, of offenses against humans (Matt 6:14) or God

[XI.2][166] Again he said, However many steps the monk takes, or however many drops of water he drinks in his cell, he ought, if at all possible, to confide these things to his elders to see if he's doing wrong by doing them. This is because a brother found a place* in the desert* appropriate for withdrawal* from the world* and for the practice of contemplative quiet,*[167] and he entreated* his father, saying, "Let me live there: I have hope that through God and through your prayers I'll work[168] extremely hard."

The abba did not allow him to go, saying, "I know that you will, in fact, work very hard, but because you won't have an elder you'll put your confidence in your work, thinking that it pleases God; because of this, you'll be confident[169] that what you're doing is really and truly monastic, and you'll destroy[170] the work* you've done and defeat your purpose."[171]

(Rom 5:15) (Bauer 770b). Since the standard verb for "to sin" is *hamartánō* (see Antony 9), I have chosen not to use *sins* here.

166. After Antony 38 concludes, SysAP XI.2 continues at length, so I have added it as a complete saying here. Either someone truncated Antony 38 or combined two sayings with "this is because" to make SysAP XI.2.

167. appropriate . . . contemplative quiet: thirteen words here translate three Greek words: withdrawn (*anachōréō*), and (*kaí*), quiet (*hēsychía*). I have made the expansion in English in order to capture the monastic sense of *anachōréō* and *hēsychía*.

168. work, *kopiáō*: see nn. 155, 158.

169. *Confident* and *confidence* here translate the same verb, *tharréō* (*tharséō*), as does *confide* in the first sentence. *Confide* will not work for the two later uses of the Greek verb, but the cognate words *I hope* capture the sense of the Greek. The etymology of all three English words, Latin *confidere*, "put your trust in" (*fides*: "trust, faith in"), captures the sense. See n. 215.

170. destroy, *apóllumi*: or "ruin."

171. purpose: *phrḗn* can be a difficult word to translate (English *diaphragm* and *frenetic*), "the parts about the heart," then "heart, mind" (Liddell and Scott 1954b). I have used it the way Liddell and Scott cites Sophocles' use, though the playwright is much earlier. Lampe does not cite the word. A possible translation is "lose your mind." In the plural, the word occurs twice in 1 Cor 14:20; both the NRSV and NIV translate it as "thinking."

Appendix

Significant Sayings Concerning Abba Antony in the Systematic *Apophthegmata Patrum*[172]

1. [Prol. 5] When Abba Antony says that humility* allows a person to elude all the snares of the Devil,[173] and someone else adds that humility* is a tree of life[174] rising up high into the sky, and another that humility* neither gets angry* nor provokes someone to anger,* while another adds that if someone with humility* says to someone else "Forgive me," it burns up the demons*— from all of these the mind* of the reader receives assurance and confidence as he zealously pursues humility*. . . .

2. [VII.14] Abba Macarius the Great visited Abba Antony where he was living.[175] When Abba Macarius knocked on the door, Abba Antony came out and said, "Who are *you?*"

Abba Macarius said, "I'm Macarius."

Abba Antony went inside, closed the door, and left him standing there.

When he saw Abba Macarius's patient endurance,* he opened the door so Abba Macarius could come inside, graciously welcomed* him, and was saying, "For a long time now I've very much wanted to see you; I've heard about the things you're doing." . . .

3. [VII.41] A brother asked an elder, "What can I do, father? I'm not doing[176] anything befitting a monk; instead, I'm indifferent

---

172. These are sayings where Antony appears, independent of those in AlphAP Antony. In some of the sayings below, I have included only the portions that deal with Antony.

173. This is a summary of Antony 7.

174. tree of life: see Prov 3:18; 11:30; 13:12; 15:4; Rev 2:7; 22:2, 14, 19.

175. where he was living: literally "at / on the mountain" (*óros*), translated earlier as "monastic community,"* but it is not clear here that Antony is at a monastic settlement. In Saying 4 below, *óros* clearly means a monastic community.

176. doing, *ergázomai*: an important monastic term, translated as "thing" later and, further on, as a plural, "works";* thus the repetition of the terms in Greek reinforces what the elder is saying to the brother.

and neglectful[177]—I eat and drink and sleep; I'm prone to shameful thoughts,* and I'm very upset, very unsettled, moving from one thing[178] to another and from one thought* to the next."

The elder said, "Sit in your cell, and whatever you're able to do, do, without getting upset about it. Here's what I think: the little bit that you do now is like the great works* that Abba Antony used to do in the desert,* and it's my belief that the person who sits in his own cell for the sake of the name of God[179] and keeps watch over[180] his conscience—that person, too, will be found where Abba Antony is."

4. [XV.62] A certain brother paid a visit to Abba Sisoës at the monastic community* of Abba Antony, and while they were having a conversation he said to Abba Sisoës, "Haven't you now reached the stature of Abba Antony?"

The elder said, "In what way could I reach the stature of the saint? If I had one thought* that Abba Antony had, I would become all fire.[181] But I do know a person who, with great effort, can carry[182] his thought.*

5. [XVII.3] Abba Amoun of Nitria* visited Abba Antony and said to him, "I see that I work* harder than you do.[183] So why is your name held in greater esteem than mine?"

---

177. indifferent and neglectful: *ameleía* means both; using the cognate verb, *ameléō*, Heb 2:3 and 1 Tim 4:14 offer biblical resonance: the brother is indifferent about and neglectful of what God gives.

178. thing, *érgon*: usually a monastic work;* in other words, the brother lacks monastic stability. See nn. 56, 204, 292, 304, 579.

179. for the sake of the name of God: Matt 18:4-5 may be apposite here: Jesus says, "Whoever becomes humble* [*tapeinóō*] like this child is the greatest in the kingdom of heaven. Whoever welcomes one such child in my name welcomes me." God's name is very important in the HB; the Psalms* often speak of God's name.

180. keeps watch over: *tēréō* can specifically mean "keep unharmed or undisturbed" (Bauer 1002a), apropos here; see John 14:21. See nn. 243, 246.

181. I would become all fire: see Arsenius 27 and Joseph of Panephysis 7.

182. carry, *bastázō*: the verb used for Jesus' carrying the cross (Luke 14:27).

183. work: it may mean here "work harder at being a monk."

Abba Antony said to him, "Because I also love* God more than you."[184]

6. [XVII.4][185] Abba Hilarion from Palestine*[186] visited Abba Antony where he was living, and Abba Antony said to him, "I'm glad you've come, morning star that rises at dawn."

In reply Abba Hilarion said to him, "Peace be with you, pillar of light that supports* the whole world."[187]

7. [XX.7] They used to say about Abba Sisoës that when he was about to die, while the fathers were sitting around him his face lit up like the sun, and he said to them, "Look! Abba Antony has come!" A little later, he again spoke to them, "Look! The choir of prophets has come!" Once again, remarkably, his face lit up even more and he said, "Look! The choir of the apostles has come!"

Concerning Abba Arsenius[188]

1. [88] [II.3] Abba Arsenius, when he was still at the palace, prayed* to God, saying, "Lord, guide me: How can I be saved?"*

A voice came to him,[189] saying, "Arsenius, flee* people, and you will be saved."*

2. [II.4] The same Arsenius, after he had withdrawn* from the world* to live as a solitary, prayed* once again, asking the same question, and he heard a voice saying to him, "Arsenius, flee,*

---

184. See Amoun 1.

185. This saying occurs in fragmentary form as Antony, Coptic Saying 5 and also as AlphAP Hilarion.

186. Antony, Coptic Saying 5 says he is from Syria.

187. morning star that rises at dawn: in Isa 14:12 the prophet speaks of down-fallen Babylon: "O Day Star, son of Dawn! / How you are fallen from heaven." On the pillar of fire: see Exod 13:17, 21, 22.

188. Gk. *Arsénios*. See Arsenius in Dramatis Personae.

189. A voice came to him: see also Antony 2 and 7 and Arsenius 2 and 33. This is a common topos.

maintain silence, live a life of contemplative quiet.* These are the roots of being without sin."

3. [XV.5] The demons* appeared one time to Abba Arsenius in his cell and were afflicting* him. Those who ministered to him came to visit him; standing outside the cell, they heard him crying out to God and saying, "Do not forsake me![190] I have not done one thing in your sight that is good! But treat me in accordance with your goodness and kindness so I can at least begin!"[191]

4. [XV.6] They used to say about him that just as no one in the palace wore finer raiment than he did,[192] so too in the church no one had lived more simply and frugally.[193]

5. [X.7] Someone said to blessed Arsenius,[194] "Why is it that we, highly educated and learned in wisdom, have nothing, while these [88] rude peasants, these Egyptians,[195] have come to possess* so many excellent virtues?"*

Abba Arsenius said to him, "We have kept nothing from our worldly education, while these peasants, these Egyptians, because of their own toil, have come to possess the virtues."*

6. [90] [XV.7] When Abba Arsenius one time was asking a certain Egyptian elder about his thoughts,* another person, seeing this,

190. forsake, *enkataleípō*: the same verb that Jesus uses on the cross in Mark 15:34 // Matt 27:46 (Ps 22:1; LXX 21:2); thus Arsenius's cry has deep resonance.

191. Beginning anew, even each day, even to one's dying breath, is an important monastic theme.

192. wore finer raiment than he did: SysAP XV.6 continues, when he was in the palace. For a vivid description of Arsenius's palatial life, see Arsenius 33.

193. "Wore" and "lived": each translates *phérō*, so a first translation is "no one bore finer raiment" and "no one bore (himself) more simply and frugally." Simply and frugally: I have used both words to translate *entelés*, which carries both material and ascetic tones: "thrifty, frugal, simple," and "insignificant, slight, unimportant" (Lampe 577b).

194. Someone said: SysAP X.7, An elder said.

195. these rude peasants, these Egyptians: literally "these rude peasants and Egyptians." On the distinction between (Coptic) Egyptians and, it appears, Greeks, see also Arsenius 6.

said, "Abba Arsenius, why are you, so highly educated in Roman and Greek learning, asking this peasant about his thoughts?"*

Arsenius said to him, "I am highly educated in Roman and Greek learning, but I have not yet learned the alphabet of this peasant."

7. [II.6] One time blessed Archbishop Theophilus* visited Abba Arsenius, along with a certain official.[196] He[197] asked the elder to hear something edifying* from him.

The elder stayed silent for a while; then he answered him:[198] "And if I say something to you, will you follow[199] what I say?"

They promised to do so.

Then the elder said to them, "Wherever you hear Arsenius is, do not go near there."[200]

8. [II.7] Another time, the archbishop wanted to visit him again, so first he sent someone to find out whether the elder was opening his door. The elder made it clear to him, saying, "If you come, I am going to open the door to you. And if I open the door to you, I am going to open it to everyone. And then I will not live here anymore."

196. a certain official: it is possible that Greek *tis*, "someone, a certain person," can mean here "along with some official or other," a snide remark.

197. He: the Greek is also ambiguous; SysAP II.6, the archbishop. The story soon switches to "they."

198. him: SysAP II.6, them.

199. follow, *phylássō*: see Protect in the Glossary.

200. At first glance, Arsenius's final words seem to say "Leave me alone" to my life of contemplative quiet. But since humility* is a cardinal monastic virtue, and if we read the story at a symbolic / spiritual level, as Origen* would have us do, a translation of the last sentence could be "If you think Arsenius is a paragon, thus paradigm, of virtue, think again." Smith, *Philosopher-Monks*, 243 n. 171, emphasizes the countercultural aspect of asceticism: "visitors expect monks to behave in certain ways, and the monks problematize these assumptions by acting as they see fit." See Theodore of Pherme 28.

When the archbishop heard these words, he said, "If my going is going to drive him away,[201] I am not going to see him anymore."[202]

9. [XI.4] A brother asked Abba Arsenius to hear something beneficial* from him. The elder said to him, "With every ounce of strength you have, fight,*[203] in order that your interior* way of life[204] will be in accordance with God. Then you will defeat the exterior passions."*

10. [XI.5] Again he said, "If we seek out God, he will make himself known to us, and if we hold tight to him, he will remain by our side."

11. [VII.34; AnonAP 195] Someone said to Abba Arsenius,[205] "My thoughts* oppress* me, saying,[206] 'You don't have the fortitude[207] either to fast* or to do your work.* At least go visit[208] the sick—this, at least, is an act of love!' "*

The elder, knowing the intentions of the demons,* said to him, "Go. Eat, drink, sleep—and do not work.*[209] Only, do not leave your cell."

---

201. drive him away: *diōkō* can also mean "expel," even "persecute" (Lampe 376b).

202. him: SysAP II.7, the saint.

203. See Arsenius 15.

204. Way of life, *ergasía* here instead of the usual *politeía* (see Way of Life in the Glossary), generally means "work, action" (*érgon*), especially working to keep and fulfill the commandments; see Work in the Glossary. See Lampe 545b and Arsenius 33.

205. Someone said to Abba Arsenius: SysAP VII.34, A brother said to a certain elder, "What should I do . . . ?"

206. My thoughts oppress me, saying: AnonAP 195, What can I do? My thoughts oppress me, saying.

207. You don't have the fortitude, *ou dýnamai*: literally "you cannot" or "you're not able." *Dýnamai* is cognate with *dýnamis*, "power,* strength."

208. go visit, *episképtomai*: or "take care of."

209. Go. Eat, drink, sleep—and do not work: SysAP VII.34 and AnonAP 195, Eat, drink, sleep.

He said this because he knew that the patient endurance* of the cell brings the monk to where he can keep his monastic rule.[210] When the monk had done this for three days, he lost patience and grew discouraged,[211] so, finding a few palm fronds, he split them and again the next day began plaiting them.[212] When he got hungry, he said, "Look, there are a few more fronds here; I'll plait them, and then I'll eat." When he was working with the fronds, he said again, "I'll read a little, and then eat." When he was done reading he said, "I'm going to say a few psalms,* and then I'll eat, free from anxiety."

And so, little by little,[213] he made progress, with God working* right alongside him,[214] until he returned to the monastic rule and so, gaining confidence[215] against his thoughts,* he defeated them.

12. [X.8] Abba Arsenius used to say,[216] "A foreign monk in a country not his own must not interfere[217] in matters; if he refrains from doing so, he will find inward stillness."*

13. [92] [II.5; XVII.6 (Lat.)] Abba Mark said to Abba Arsenius, "Why do you stay* away from us?"

---

210. Arsenius 11 ends here; I have supplied the rest of the saying from SysAP VII.34 and AnonAP 195.

211. he lost patience and grew discouraged: *akēdiáō < akēdía*; see Acedia in the Glossary.

212. the next day he began plaiting them: SysAP VII.34, Next day because he had soaked the fronds in water overnight, he began plaiting them.

213. little by little: *katà mikrón*. The Greek text linguistically emphasizes the theme of patience with the repetition of *mikrós*: "a few [*mikrá*] palm fronds," "a few more [*mikrá*] fronds," "I'll read awhile [*mikrón*]," "a few [*mikroús*] psalms," and "little by little [*katà mikrón*]."

214. with God working right alongside him: literally "God working with him," so one could translate "because God was working with him."

215. "gaining confidence," *thársos* occurs only once in the NT (Acts 28:15), but its cognate verb *tharséō* occurs five times in the gospels: "take heart" (NIV: "take courage"); see Matt 9:2, 22; 14:27; Mark 10:49; John 16:33 (Bauer 444a). See n. 169.

216. Abba Arsenius: SysAP X.8, The blessed Abba Arsenius.

217. interfere, *mesázō*: or "act as a middleman."

The elder said to him, "God knows that I love all of you. But I cannot be with God and with people. The spiritual realities,[218] numbering in the thousands and tens of thousands, have one intention, but people have a multitude of intentions.[219] I cannot leave God and come be with people."

14. [IV.2] Abba Daniel used to say about Abba Arsenius that he would keep vigil* all night, and, around dawn, out of necessity[220] he wanted to lie down.[221] He would say to sleep, "Go away, wicked servant!"[222] Sitting, he would grab a little sleep and then immediately set about doing his work.

15. [IV.3] Abba Arsenius would say that one hour of sleep is plenty for the monk, if he wants to be a fighter.*[223]

16. [XV.8] The elders used to say that one time a few dried figs were given to the monks in Scetis,* and because the figs didn't amount to much the elders didn't send* any to Abba Arsenius so he wouldn't feel insulted.[224]

---

218. spiritual realities, *hai ánō*: "the things above," thus "heavenly things" and "spiritual things." "From above," *ánōthen*, is a key word in John's gospel; see John 3:7, 31; 8:23; Jas 1:17; 3:15.

219. intention / intentions, *thélēma*: "will," "that which is willed" or "object of an act of willing" (Lampe 620b–21b).

220. out of necessity, *kata phýsin*: according to nature.

221. wanted, *thélō*. I have used the variant reading of PG 65:91–92 n. 24 and SysAP IV.2 of *éthele* instead of the text's similar-sounding *élthe*, "came," "when it was [came] around dawn," because the infinitive "to lie down" requires a previous modal verb. The variant reading *éthele* < *thélō* also connects with the previous *thélēma*, "will"; see n. 219.

222. wicked servant: or "slave," *doúlos*. The phrase "wicked servant / slave": Matt 18:32; 24:48; 25:26; Luke 19:22.

223. See Arsenius 9.

224. he wouldn't feel insulted, *húbrin páthē(i)*: literally "so he wouldn't suffer hubris." "Suffer" is cognate with *páthos*, pl. *páthei*, "suffering, passion," pl. "the passions."* *Húbris* has a wide range of meanings, but its verb, *hubrízō*, is more apposite here: "insult, outrage" (Lampe 1422a).

When the elder heard about this, he didn't go[225] to the synaxis,*
saying, "You have excluded me by not giving me the gift* that
God sent to the brothers—which, apparently, I was not worthy to
receive."[226]

They all heard this and benefited* from the elder's humility.*[227]
So the priest left and took him the dried figs and brought him back
to the synaxis* with joy.

17. [IV.4] Abba Daniel used to say,[228] "He [Arsenius] lived with
us all those years, and we would prepare for him only one basket*
of bread* per year.[229] When we visited him we would eat some of
this bread."*

18. [IV.5] He also used to say about this same Abba Arsenius[230]
that except for once a year he would not change the water that he
soaked palm branches in; he would only add to it. He would plait
rope and twine branches together until noon.[231]

The elders summoned him, saying, "Why don't you change the
water for the palm branches? It stinks."

He said to them, "In return for the fragrances and aromatics that
I enjoyed in the world,* I now need to receive in return this stink."

19. [IV.6] Again he said that when he used to hear that the
harvest season for all of the different fruits was drawing to a close,

225. he didn't go (*érchomai*): a variant reading, PG 65:91–92 n. 25 and SysAP
XV.8, he didn't leave his cell to go; literally "he didn't go out," *exérchomai*.

226. which, apparently, I was not worthy to receive: I have added "apparently";
context suggests that it is appropriate here.

227. SysAP XV.8 lacks *all*.

228. used to say: SysAP IV.4, used to say about him.

229. basket of bread, *thallís* (Bauer 923a): *sítos* can mean "grain, wheat" or
"bread." Wortley, *Give Me*, 43, translates *sítos* as *grain*, but since the verb is "we
would *prepare* (or 'make')," I have chosen to render it as *bread*.

230. He also used to say about this same Abba Arsenius: SysAP IV.5, He also
said.

231. The alternation, and simultaneity, of work and prayer is extremely important. Regnault's comment is apropos here (*Day-to-Day Life*, 99): "It seems
that basketry was taken up very early by the monks as the ideal solitary work in
their cells." See especially Antony 1.

he would say for his part, "Bring them to me." Each year he would taste only a little bit of each kind of fruit, giving thanks to God.

20. [VI.3] One time Abba Arsenius was ill in Scetis,* and he didn't have anything, not even a single bedsheet.[232] Since he didn't have the means to buy one, he accepted one as an act of love* from someone and said, [93] "Thank you, Lord. You considered me worthy to receive this act of love* for the sake of your name."[233]

21. [II.9] They used to say about him that his cell was thirty-two miles distant.[234] He didn't readily leave it because others ministered to his needs. When Scetis* was laid waste,[235] he left weeping and would say, "The world has lost Rome and the monks Scetis.*"[236]

22. [X.9] Abba Mark asked Abba Arsenius a question, "Is it good for someone not to have comfort and consolation* in his cell? I ask this because I saw a certain brother who had a few vegetables planted, and he was pulling them up by the roots."

Abba Arsenius said, "It *is* good, but only according to the person's ability:[237] if he does not have the strength for such a serious practice,[238] he will plant them again."

---

232. bedsheet, *línos*: SysAP VI.3, loaf of bread, *silígnion*, "bread made from fine wheaten flour" (Lat. *siligo*) (Lampe 1233b); see Historia Lausiaca 13.2 (p. 28) where such bread is one of the things "sick people need."

233. your name: see Matt 7:22; 18:20; John 15:16; Rom 10:13, among many. See Arsenius 38.

234. thirty-two miles: SysAP II.9, two. The Roman mile was 4,850 feet; thus 32 Roman miles equals 27.56 miles / 44 kilometers, and 2 Roman miles equals 1.8 mile / 3.2 km.

235. laid waste, *erēmóō*, "to turn into a desert or wasteland." The sad irony here is that *erēmóō* is cognate with *érēmos*, "wilderness, desert,"* the habitat of John the Baptist (Matt 3:1), the *desert* of the monks of Egypt. On the despoliation(s) of Scetis, see "Barbarians" in the Glossary.

236. In Greek "has lost" begins the sentence and is thus emphatic. Rome fell in 410. On Scetis, see note 146.

237. ability: *héxis* can also mean "an acquired habit, strength" (Lampe 497a).

238. such a serious practice, *toioúto(i) trópō(i)*: this is a pregnant phrase. *Trópōs* can mean "way of life, habit, custom" (Liddell and Scott 1827a) and "method,

23. Abba Daniel, the disciple of Arsenius, told this story: "One time I found myself standing near Abba Alexander when pain gripped him and laid him out. Because of the pain, he was looking heavenward.[239]

"It just so happened that blessed Arsenius came to speak with him and saw him laid out on his back. When he spoke, therefore, Abba Arsenius said to him, 'And who was the person from the world* whom I saw here?'

"Abba Alexander said, 'Where did you see him?'

"Abba Arsenius said, 'When I was coming down from my monastic settlement and getting close to your cave here, I saw someone laid out on the ground, looking up to heaven.'

"Abba Alexander got up and prostrated himself* before Abba Arsenius, saying, 'Forgive me, it was me. Pain had gotten me in its grip.'

"The elder said to Abba Alexander, 'So it *was* you? Very well, then. As far as I could tell, I thought it was someone from the world.* So I asked.'"

24. [XIV.2] Another time Abba Arsenius said to Abba Alexander,[240] "When[241] you've separated your palm branches,[242] come eat with me, but if strangers* come, eat with them."

So Abba Alexander set about working,* deliberately and patiently. When the time came to eat, he still had palm branches to

---

form of faith or piety" (Lampe 1414b–15b). *Toioútos* here has an intensive sense: "so great, so noble" (Liddell and Scott 1802a). Therefore I have used *serious*, because it can suggest both "a grand practice or way of life" and a "serious, even a huge, undertaking."

239. heavenward, *ánō*: See Arsenius 13 and n. 218 on "spiritual realities."

240. Abba Arsenius: SysAP XIV.2, blessed Arsenius.

241. Using SysAP XIV 2 *hótan* instead of the text's *hóti án*.

242. palm branches: *thállos* indicates a young shoot, a young branch, but it also seems to indicate a basket or bag made from palm branches, as in Arsenius 17. Later in the text a variant reading (PG 65:93 n. 28) is *báïs*, "palm branch." See Arsenius 19.

finish but, wanting to fulfill*[243] what the elder had told* him, he stayed to finish his work.*

Abba Arsenius, therefore, when he saw that Abba Alexander was delayed, went ahead and ate, thinking* that perhaps Abba Alexander had strangers* to accommodate. When Abba Alexander finished quite a while later, he left. When he reached Abba Arsenius's cell,[244] the elder said to him, "Did you have visitors?"[245]

He said, "No."

Abba Arsenius said to him, "Why, then, did you not come earlier?"

[96] He said, "Because you told me to come when I finished dividing the palm branches and, doing what you had told me to do,[246] I didn't come because I hadn't yet finished my work."*

The elder marveled at his conscientiousness and said to him, "Break your fast* earlier so you can keep your synaxis,* and drink some water. If you do not, you will quickly get sick."[247]

25. [II.8] Abba Arsenius one time went to visit the monastic settlement.* There were reeds there, and they were being moved by the wind. The elder said to the brothers, "What is this commotion?"[248]

They said, "They're reeds."

So the elder said to them, "Of course. If someone is sitting in contemplative quiet* and hears the chirping of a sparrow, his heart

---

243. wanting to fulfill: literally "keeping the word" (*tēréō* + *lógos*); instead of this, SysAP XIV.2 uses *plēróō*, with the same meaning except that it loses the biblical resonance of Matt 19:17, where Jesus says, "If you want to enter life, keep [*tēréō*] the commandments." *Finish* soon after translates *plēróō*. See Arsenius 7 and nn. 180, 246.

244. When he reached Abba Arsenius's cell: I have added this phrase as a segue.

245. visitors, *xénos*: or "strangers,"* as above. See nn. 325 and 527.

246. doing what you had told me to do, *tēréō* + *lógos*: see nn. 180, 243.

247. you will quickly get sick: literally "your body will quickly get sick [or: weak]; *asthenéō*."

248. commotion: *seismós*, as with English *seismic*, can also indicate an earthquake.

no longer rests in contemplative quiet.* How much more is that true of you, who have the commotion of these reeds?"[249]

26. Abba Daniel used to tell about some brothers who wanted to go to the Thebaid* to get some linen.* They said, "Let's take this opportunity to see Abba Arsenius,[250] too."

After they had arrived,[251] Abba Alexander entered Abba Arsenius's cell and said to the elder, "Brothers have come from Alexandria who want to see you."

The elder said, "Find out from them the reason for their visit." When he found out that they had come to the Thebaid* to buy linen, he told the elder.

Abba Arsenius said, "They are certainly not going to see the face of Arsenius: they have not come on account of me but on account of their work.* Let them rest, and send them off in peace,* saying to them, 'The elder is unable to meet with you.'"

27. [XVIII.2] A certain brother left his monastery to go see Abba Arsenius in his cell in Scetis.* He was looking through a small window and saw the elder completely like fire.[252] (The brother was worthy to see this.)

When he knocked, the elder came out, saw that the brother was standing there utterly astonished,*[253] and said to him, "Have you been knocking a long time? You did not see anything here, did you?"

He said, "No."

So, after talking with him, the elder sent him off.

---

249. How much more . . . : the sentence could also be an exclamation.

250. The sayings do not say or suggest that Arsenius was in the Thebaid, but Arsenius 32 says that the elder went to the southern Sinai. Perhaps these brothers were coming from the north and stopped to see Arsenius in Scetis.*

251. After they had arrived: I have added this phrase for continuity.

252. See Joseph of Panephysis 7.

253. utterly astonished, *ekthambéomai*, like *thaumázō*, "be amazed,* marvel." See Mark 9:15, when a crowd sees Jesus, "they were immediately overcome with awe." In Acts 3:1-11, when a crowd sees Peter heal a lame man who then jumps up and walks, they are "utterly astonished [*ékthambos*]" (see Bauer 303a).

28. [II.10] One time when Abba Arsenius was living in Canopus,* a very wealthy woman,* one who was a virgin and of senatorial rank and who feared* God, came from Rome to see him.[254] Archbishop Theophilus* received her. She implored* him to persuade the elder to receive her.

The archbishop went to him and implored* him to receive her, saying, "A certain woman,* of senatorial rank, has come from Rome and wants to see you."

But the elder did not receive her or meet with her. When the archbishop conveyed to her the elder's response, she ordered the horses and pack animals to be readied, saying, "I have faith* in God that I will see him. To be sure, I have not come to see just anyone;[255] we have numbers of people in our city. No, I have come to see a prophet."[256]

When she drew near the elder's cell, by the governing grace of God[257] the elder happened to be outside. When she saw him, she threw herself at his feet. He raised her up to her feet—angry. Regarding her, he said, "If you want to see[258] my face, [97] look: here it is."

---

254. The stories of high-ranking women like Melania the Elder and Melania the Younger give credence to this story; see ODLA 2:1000 for entries on both.

255. I have not come to see just anyone: literally "I have not come to see a person" (*ánthrōpos*). "People" then translates the plural. SysAP II.10 lacks this sentence.

256. Thus, the import of her words could be, I have not come to see a *human being*; I have come to see something more than a mere human being: a *prophet*. See Matt 11:9.

257. by the governing grace of God: or "in accordance with God's plan." Governing grace / plan: *oikonomía* (English *economy*), cognate with *oíkos*, "house," primarily means "management, governance, supervision." An *oikónomos* is a "steward, manager." *Oikonomía* can also mean "dispensation, ordering" and "divine grace or operation in the sacraments" (Lampe 940b–43a). Bauer 697b, citing Eph 3:9, suggests "state of being arranged, order, plan" and "of God's unique plan . . . plan of salvation, i.e. arrangements for redemption of humans."

258. see, *horáō*: there is a play on words here. Twice earlier, the verb *see* has the idea, as in English, of "meet with." Here it is literal: Arsenius is allowing the

She, out of modesty,[259] would not look into his face.[260]

The elder said to her, "Have you not heard about the work* I do? Look to that, then. How did you have the courage[261] to make such a long voyage? Don't you know you're a woman?* Don't you know you should never go *anywhere*? Or did you come so that when you go back to Rome you can say to the other women,* 'I have seen Arsenius!' so that they[262] as a result will turn the sea into a roadway filled with women coming to see me?"

She said, "If the Lord wills it,[263] I will not allow anyone to come here. But, please, pray* for me, and remember me always."[264]

He responded by saying to her, "I pray* to God that memory of you be eradicated from my heart!"

After hearing this, she left, shaken.*

When she returned to the city, in her distress and grief she became feverish, and blessed Archbishop Theophilus*[265] was informed that she was ill. Coming to visit her, he urged her to tell him what had happened.

She said to him, "I wish I had not gone to visit him in Egypt! When I said to the elder 'Remember me,' he said to me 'I pray*

---

woman to see his face, but the reader does not yet know whether he will allow her *to meet* with him. On Arsenius's modesty, see Arsenius 26 and 42.

259. modesty: *aischúnē*, "modesty, reverence to someone," just as appropriately means "shame"* or, not likely here, even "disgrace" (Bauer 29b–30a).

260. would not look into his face: or "meet eyes with him." *Katanoéō* seems unusual here: "to contemplate" and its noun, *katanóēsis*, "intellectual comprehension," "contemplation" of God or divine truth (Lampe 713a; Bauer 522b), but Bauer 1067b has "Look at, observe."

261. have the courage, *tolmáō*: or "dare."

262. they: SysAP II.10, you (sing.)

263. Lord: SysAP II.10, God.

264. On the implied efficacy of the holy person's presence, thoughts, and prayers, see Peter Brown, *The Cult of the Saints: Its Rise and Function in Latin Christianity* (Chicago: University of Chicago Press, 2014). But see also Life of Antony 90 (p. 249).

265. blessed Archbishop Theophilus: SysAP 28, the archbishop.

to God that memory of you be eradicated from my heart!' And now, look! I am dying of grief."

The archbishop said to her, "Do you not know that you are a woman?* And that because of women* the Enemy* wages war* against the saints?[266] This was why the elder said that. He is praying* for your soul all the time."[267]

On account of this, therefore, her attitude[268] was healed, and she returned to her home and family with joy.

29. [VI.2] Abba Daniel told this story about Abba Arsenius: One time an official on the staff of the *magister officiorum** brought the will of a certain high official,[269] a relative of Arsenius. The official had left Arsenius an exceedingly large inheritance.

Taking the will, Arsenius was about to tear it in two. The official fell at Arsenius's feet, saying, "I beg you, do not tear it apart![270] If you do, they will behead me!"

Abba Arsenius said to him, "I died before he did; he died just now."[271] He didn't accept the will, and handed it back.

30. [XII.1] Again they used to say about him[272] that late in the day on Saturday, when Sunday's dawn was approaching,[273] he would put the sun at his back, facing east, and stretch out his hands

---

266. See Elaine Pagels, *Adam, Eve, and the Serpent* (New York: Vintage, 1989).

267. all the time (*diapántos*): she had earlier asked him to pray for her always (*diapántos*), so the archbishop's word picks up her earlier request—but not for the reason she probably intended.

268. attitude, *logismós*: see Arsenius 6.

269. high official: *synklētikós* indicates a senator in Rome or Constantinople or a high official elsewhere. In Arsenius 28, the wife of a Roman senator (*synklētikḗ*) visits Arsenius. Amma Syncletica (*synklētikḗ*), who has 28 sayings, may have been from a noble family.

270. I beg you: SysAP VI.2 lacks.

271. he died just now: SysAP VI.2 lacks.

272. him: SysAP XII.1, Abba Arsenius.

273. Saturday and Sunday: in Patristic and Modern Greek, Saturday and Sunday, as well as Friday, retain biblical resonances. Saturday and Sunday are *Sábbaton* and *Kyriakḗ* (the Lord's Day), respectively; Friday is *Paraskeuḗ* (preparation; the day before the Sabbath).

to heaven as he prayed,* until the sun once more shone on his face, and then he would sit down.[274]

31. [VIII.3] They used to say about Abba Arsenius and Abba Theodore of Pherme* that more than anything else, they hated it when people praised them. Abba Arsenius, for his part, would not readily go to meet someone, while Abba Theodore would meet with people—but he was like a sword, long and broad.

32. [XV.10] One time when Abba Arsenius was living lower down in Egypt[275] and was being mobbed by people there, it seemed to him [100] that he ought to leave[276] his cell. Taking nothing from there with him, he went to his Pharanite* disciples Alexander and Zoïlos.[277] When there, he said to Alexander, "Get up, sail north." And he did so. To Zoïlos he said, "Come with me to the Nile[278] and find me a boat sailing downstream for Alexandria.*[279] This way you will sail to find your brother."

Zoïlos, upset at what Arsenius had said, kept silent. And so he and Arsenius went their separate ways. Arsenius went downstream to the region of Alexandria*[280] and became sick and very weak. The attendants* there said to one another, "Maybe one of us saddened the elder and that's why he separated himself from us," but

274. and then he would sit down: since *kathézomai* can also mean "dwell, live," the sentence has also the sense of "and this is the way he lived."

275. lower down in Egypt: because the Nile flows south to north, *lower* indicates northern in Egypt. Technically, Abba Arsenius would be between the Wadi Natrun* and Alexandria,* but it is vague here, "once upon a place," as it were. In Arsenius 34 he is in "Petra of Troë."

276. leave: *kataleípō* in addition to meaning "relinquish, leave behind," can also mean "abandon, forsake" and "give up, renounce" (Lampe 710b). Bauer 520b–21a does not suggest that it has the stronger meanings in the NT: "leave behind."

277. he went to his Pharanite disciples: the text is incomplete, so I have followed the variant reading, PG 65:99–100 n. 34 and SysAP XV.10.

278. Nile: monastic literature designates the Nile "the River."

279. find me: SysAP XV.10, let's find.

280. the region of Alexandria: Arsenius 42 says that he spent "three years in Canopus* of Alexandria."

between them they couldn't figure out the reason—nor did they ever find out the reason, even by chance.

When he got well, the elder said, "It is time for me to go see my fathers." So he left; sailing upstream, he went to Petras* where those who tended to him were. Since he was near the Nile, a certain young Ethiopian* girl[281] came and touched his sheepskin coat.*[282]

The elder rebuked her, so the young girl said to him, "If you're a monk, go to the monastery."

The elder, stung* to the heart at what she had said, was thinking to himself, "Arsenius, if you *are* a monk, go to the monastery!"

And there Alexander and Zoïlos met him, and fell at his feet. The elder, too, then threw himself to the ground, and all of them were weeping. The elder said,[283] "Did you not hear that I was sick?"

They said to him, "Yes."

The elder said, "So why did you not come see me?"

Abba Alexander said, "The reason for your leaving us wasn't plausible,[284] and a lot of people got nothing edifying from it and were saying, 'If they hadn't disobeyed the elder, he wouldn't have separated from them.' "

He said to them,[285] "So, people are going to say once again that the dove has not found a resting place for her feet and has returned[286] to Noah in the ark."[287]

---

281. young girl: *paidiskḗ*, from *país*, "child," can also mean "young slave" or even "courtesan" (Liddell and Scott 1287b).

282. sheepskin coat, *mēlōtḗ*: in Life of Antony 92.1 (p. 255), before his death Antony leaves his sheepskin coat and worn-out cloak to his disciples, "who keep them and treat them as great valuables." See Arsenius 42. In the gospels, a woman touches Jesus' cloak, seeking healing (Mark 5:25-34 // Matt 9:20-22 // Luke 8:43-48).

283. The elder said: SysAP XV.10, The elder said to them.

284. The reason for your leaving us wasn't plausible (*pithanós*): SysAP XV.10, we weren't happy (*harmódios*) with the reason you gave for leaving us.

285. SysAP XV.10 continues, "In fact, I knew that."

286. has not found . . . and has returned, or "did not find . . . and returned."

287. Gen 8:9. The Greek is a direct quotation from the LXX.

And so they were reconciled,[288] and he remained with them until his death.[289]

33. [XVIII.3] Abba Daniel[290] said, "Abba Arsenius told us a story as though he were talking about someone else, although he may have been talking about himself: A certain elder was sitting in his cell when a voice came to him,[291] saying, 'Come on, I'll show you what human beings do.'[292]

"So he got up and left. The voice brought him away to such and such a place and showed him an Ethiopian* chopping wood; he was stacking so much wood in a carrier that it was almost too heavy to bear.[293] In fact, he was trying to carry it, but he couldn't. But instead of removing some wood from the load, he set about once again cutting wood—and adding it to the load. And he went on doing this for a long time.

288. they were reconciled, *therapeúō*: the usual meaning is "heal" (thus English *therapy*); thus "they were healed." The verb can also mean "reconcile, make restitution, smooth something out" (Lampe 645a). SysAP XV.10 differs: they were convinced [*plērophoréō*]. See Rom 4:21.

289. In SysAP XV.10, the text parallel with Arsenius 40 continues, "When he [Arsenius] was about to die." Either an editor of the AlphAP broke up SysAP XV.10 into disparate sayings, or an editor of SysAP gathered separate AlphAP sayings into XV.10.

290. Abba Daniel: SysAP XVIII.3, The disciple of Abba Arsenius.

291. when a voice came to him: see Arsenius 1, 2, and 33.

292. what human beings do: literally "the works [*tà érga*] that human beings do." The singular, *tò érgon*, means "work,"* a work that someone does, as in Jas 2:14-26. It is an important monastic term. So here, the monks already do good and salubrious work(s). The works that humans do here, although (as we will find out), are anti-works. See nn. 56, 178, 204, 304, 579.

293. too heavy to bear: the key word in this sentence is *phortíon*, from *phérō*, "to carry, bear," which I have translated *carrier* here. *Phortíon* evolved into "*hard* to carry, bear." The adjective *phortikós* means "burdensome, hard to bear" (Lampe 488b). In the NT *phortíon* neutrally means "load" (Acts 27:10) and also "burden" (Matt 23:4; Luke 11:46ab; Gal 6:5).

"Going on a little further,[294] the voice showed him another person,[295] this one standing beside a lake; he was pulling buckets of water from the lake and pouring the water into a large jar full of holes—and the water poured out, back into the lake.

"The voice said to him again, 'Come on, I'll show you something else.' And the elder found himself looking at a temple and two men seated on horses, and they were carrying a crossbeam between them. They wanted to go in through the doorway but couldn't because the wood, carried like that, wouldn't go through the door.[296] But neither one would lower himself[297] and ride behind [101] the other in order to carry the wood together to the side—so there they remained, outside the door.

" 'These are those who,' the voice said,[298] 'bear* things as if they were carrying the yoke[299] of righteousness—but they do so with arrogance: they have not humbled* themselves and put themselves right[300] and traveled Christ's path of humility.* They, therefore, remain outside the kingdom of God. The person cutting wood has a multitude of sins and, instead of repenting, he piles on top of his sins[301] transgression* after transgression.* The person drawing water is doing good works, but, since he is compounded with

294. Going on a little further: the Greek is clear that it is the voice "going on."

295. person, *ánthrōpos*: the singular of *ánthrōpoi*, translated as "human beings" above.

296. between them. . . . through the door: SysAP XVIII.3 lacks, but the sentence is needed for the story.

297. lower himself, *tapeinóō*: a monastic listener would immediately get the point. The noun, *tapeinós*, means "humility, modesty" (Lampe 1373b), a key monastic virtue. See Humility in the Glossary. Being humble, therefore, is to emulate Christ; Christ's "path of humility" occurs a bit further.

298. said: without a noun or pronoun, the verb is ambiguous: it could refer to the voice or Arsenius, or even Daniel.

299. yoke, *xúlon*: "wood" above. In the NT it can mean "cross" (see, for example, Acts 5:30; 10:39; Gal 3:13).

300. put themselves right, *diorthóō*: see n. 8.

301. sins: SysAP XVIII.3, transgressions.

evil,[302] he has lost his good works.* So, then, every person needs to be sober-minded, keeping control[303] of himself in everything he does[304] so he doesn't labor in vain.' "[305]

34. Abba Daniel told the story that one time some of the fathers came from Alexandria* to see Abba Arsenius, and one of them was the uncle of Timothy,* former archbishop of Alexandria, who had been called "the poor."*[306] He had one of his nephews with him.

The elder at that time was sick and didn't want[307] to meet them, fearing* that others would come and cause him a great deal of trouble.[308] (At that time he was in Petra of Troë.) So they returned, disappointed.

There occurred an invasion of barbarians,* so he left[309] and stayed in Lower Egypt. The people heard about this and once again came to see him. With joy he welcomed them, and the brother who was with them said, "Don't you know, father, that we came to see you in Troë and you didn't greet us?"

302. since he is compounded with evil: this is a difficult phrase. It might suggest the possibility that one can be free of evil, or that all humans are evil (at least in part), or that the person is doing evil deeds. See the next sentence.

303. sober-minded, keeping control, *néphō*: I have used both phrases to capture the sense. The verb means "not drinking wine," therefore "sober." For the use in the NT, Bauer 672b offers "be well-balanced, self-controlled." In the NT it occurs only in 1 Thess (3:3, 8); 1 Pet (1:13; 5:8), and 2 Tim 4:5.

304. in everything he does: in all his works,* *érgon*. See Arsenius 9. See nn. 56, 178, 204, 292, 579.

305. labor in vain, *kenòn kopiázō*: Phil 2:16; 1 Thess 3:5.

306. "the poor," *aktḗmenos*: literally "without possessions." The usual word for "poor" in the NT and monastic literature is *ptōchos*. *Aktḗmenos* here points to a person of high estate who gives up everything (see Matt 19:21).

307. didn't want, *ouk ethélō*: or "refused."

308. trouble, *parenochlês*: the root of the verb is *óchlos*, "crowd, mob." See "mobbed" in Arsenius 32. In the NT, at the Council of Jerusalem (Acts 15), James says to the assembly that the Jewish followers of Jesus "should not trouble those Gentiles who are turning to God."

309. left: using the variant reading *elthṓn* instead of the text's metathesis, *thélōn* ("wanted / wanting to").

The elder said to them, "All of you ate[310] bread* and drank water. I, on the other hand, my child, as is my nature, tasted neither bread* nor water; nor did I sit down with you to eat,[311] punishing myself until I was sure that you had reached your destination. I did this because it was on account of me that you had gone to all that trouble. But now, please forgive me, brothers."

Comforted,* they returned home.

35. [XI.6] Abba Daniel used to say, "Abba Arsenius summoned me one day and said to me, 'Help your father be at peace* so that when he leaves to be with the Lord he will appeal*[312] to the Lord on your behalf, and things will go well with you.' "

36. They used to say about Abba Arsenius that he was sick one time in Scetis.* The priest came, got him, took him back to the monastery,[313] and brought him inside the church; he placed him on a mat and put a small pillow under his head. And here is what happened: one of the elders came to look in on him. When he saw Abba Arsenius lying on the mat, with a pillow under his head, he was scandalized* and said, "This is Abba Arsenius?![314] And he's lying here on a mat with a pillow!"

Taking the elder aside, the priest said to him, "What work* did you do in your village?"

The elder said, "I was a shepherd."[315]

---

310. ate: "tasted"; see immediately below for *tasted*, which is the more cutting word in Arsenius's reply.

311. sit down with you to eat: I have supplied *to eat*. The phrase can also mean "sit (to meet) with you."

312. appeal, *parakaleō*: SysAP XI.6 *dysōpéō*, with essentially the same meaning, "importune, win over," but without the biblical resonance of *parakaléō*. See Appeal in the Glossary.

313. got him, took him back to the monastery: I have added these words for continuity; presumably, Arsenius was in his cell 32 miles away.

314. "This is Abba Arsenius!": or "Is *this* Abba Arsenius?!"

315. shepherd, *poimēn*: the tale could intend a huge irony here. The word for "shepherd" here is the same as the gospel of John uses in the parable of the sheepfold and the good shepherd (John 10:1–21). Jesus, then, is the good shepherd,

"So, what was your life like?" the priest asked.

"It was a really hard life."

The priest said to him, "So, what's your life like now in your cell?"

He said, "I have a much more peaceful* life now."

The priest said to him, "Do you see Abba Arsenius here? [104] He was the tutor[316] of emperors[317] when he lived in the world,* and thousands of slaves with gold waistbands, all wearing golden armlets and silken clothing, waited on him. Extremely valuable carpets lay beneath his feet. But you, as a shepherd, while living in the world,* didn't have the inward stillness*[318] you now have. Arsenius here had luxuries in the world; he doesn't have them here. Look: you're at peace.* And Arsenius over there's in distress."*

When the elder heard what the priest was saying, he was conscience-stricken;* he repented and begged for forgiveness,[319] saying, "Forgive me, father, I've sinned.[320] You're right: this is the

---

as opposed to this judgmental elder who is, metaphorically, a bad shepherd. A monastic audience might hear an additional irony: Poimén (Poemen) was one of the greatest abbas of early monasticism; he has 186 sayings in the AlphAP.

316. tutor: *patḗr* is "father." I have not found "tutor" as a meaning for *patḗr*; I am following Evelyn-White, *Monasteries*, 123, 162.

317. emperors: Arcadius and Honorius.*

318. See Arsenius 18 for Arsenius's asceticism vis-à-vis his former, luxurious, life.

319. he repented and begged for forgiveness: *metánoia* means both "repentance" and "forgiveness," so I have used both words here. See Arsenius 23.

320. I've sinned: Greek can distinguish between a simple past action (aorist past), "I sinned," and, as here, a past action with ongoing consequences (present perfect): the present perfect here says "I have sinned (and I stand before you a sinner)." In Greek, "he is dead" is "he has died (and remains dead)," present perfect. When the monks refer to "what is written," they use either *tò gegramménon* or *gégraptai*, the perfect passive participle and present perfect, respectively, of *gráphō*, "to write." Thus, "what is written" is, as it were, still writing itself (on the human heart). In John 19:30 Jesus on the cross utters "It is finished" (*tetélestai*

true path.[321] This man came from riches to lowliness and humility*
while I came from hardship to comfort and rest."

Benefiting* from this, the elder departed.

37. One of the fathers came to see Abba Arsenius, and, when
he knocked on the door, the elder opened it, thinking that it was
one of the monks who ministered to him. When Abba Arsenius
saw that it was someone else, he fell on his face.

The father said to him, "Stand up, abba, so I can greet you."

Abba Arsenius said to him, "I am not getting up unless you
leave."

Although the father at length urged him to get up, Abba Arsenius wouldn't until the father had left.

38. They used to say about a certain brother that he would come
to Scetis* to see Abba Arsenius and, going into the church, would
urge the clergy to take him to meet with the elder.

So they would say to him, "Rest a little, brother, and eat
something,[322] and you'll see him."

But he said, "I won't eat anything unless I first meet with him."

So they sent a brother [105] to go with him because Abba
Arsenius's cell was far away.[323] After they'd arrived, they knocked
on the door and went in; after greeting[324] the elder, they sat down
and remained silent. The brother from the church said, "I'm leaving. Pray* for me."

< *teléō*). It can mean "it is finished," but a better rendering is "it is consummated
/ completed": my work is brought to completion (and its effect will continue).

321. true path, *alēthinè hodós*: in John 14:6 Jesus says, "I am the way [*hodós*],
the truth [*alḗtheia*], and the life [*zōḗ*]." At the beginning of the sentence I have
translated *alēthṓs*, "truly," as "You're right."

322. Rest a little, brother, and eat something: I have added "and eat something"
because the monastic practice was first to feed a visitor, and because of the visitor's response coming up.

323. Arsenius 21 says that his cell "was 32 miles distant."

324. greeting, *aspázomai*: or "embracing, hugging."

When the brother, the foreigner,* discovered that he didn't have the confidence* or courage to approach the elder, he said to the brother, "I'm going with you!" So they left together.

Now the foreigner* fervently said to the brother, "Take me also to see Abba Moses, who used to run with bandits."*

So they went to see Abba Moses. He welcomed them with joy and, receiving them with kindness,[325] sent them on their way.

The brother who had brought the visitor to see Abba Moses said to the guest, "You see? I took you to the foreigner* and to the Egyptian.[326] Which of them pleased you more?"

He responded by saying, "So far I've gotten more out of seeing the Egyptian."

When one of the fathers heard about these matters, he prayed* to God, saying, "Lord, show me what this means: one flees* from people for your name's sake, while the other one welcomes* people with open arms for your name's sake."[327]

And suddenly he was shown two great ships on the Nile: he saw Abba Arsenius and the Spirit of God* sailing together[328] in contemplative quiet.* He also saw Abba Moses and the angels of God sailing together, and they were feeding him honeycombs.

39. Abba Daniel used to say that when Abba Arsenius was going to die soon he gave us an order, saying, "Do not worry about

---

325. kindness: *philophonéō* can also mean "receive with honor" (Lampe 1484b–85a). A variant reading, PG 65:105 n. 33, has *philoxenízō*, "welcome as a stranger* [*xénos*]"; see nn. 245, 527. This verb does not occur in the NT, but its cognate nouns do, meaning "hospitality,"* "hospitable" (Bauer 1058b).

326. the foreigner and to the Egyptian: that is, Arsenius and Moses, respectively. It is interesting that the monk refers to Moses, an Ethiopian, as an Egyptian, but perhaps the contrast is between one person, Arsenius, who speaks Greek, and another person, Moses, who speaks Coptic.

327. for your name's sake: the phrase is used of God often in the HB, especially in the Psalms* and the prophets; in Matt 19:29 Jesus uses it of himself.

328. sailing together: the idea of sailing "as one" is also present, and later.

holding an *agápē** on my behalf: if I have done an *agápē*,* an act of compassionate charity that also benefited me,* I will be able to find it there."[329]

[330]40a. [XV.10, Guy 2.290][331] When Abba Arsenius was going to die soon, his disciples were upset.* He said to them, "My hour has not yet come;[332] when the hour does come, I will let you know. I will be judged,* along with you, at the fearful Judgment* seat[333] if you give my remains to anyone."[334]

They said, "What should we do, then? We don't know how to do a burial."[335]

The elder said to them, "Do you not know how to throw a rope around my foot and drag me to the monastery?*"[336]

---

329. The Greek of Arsenius's response is elliptical and not perfectly clear to me. My translation is more of a paraphrase that I hope has captured the sense. I have added "there," presumably meaning heaven, as does Wortley, *Give Me*, 51.

330. I believe Arsenius 40 has three distinct sayings that have coalesced, so I have used 40b and 40c for the latter two.

331. On 2.290 of the SysAP, the text continues from the end of AlphAP Arsenius 32.

332. My hour has not yet come: see John 2:4.

333. fearful judgment seat: a variant reading, PG 65:105–6 n. 43 and SysAP XV.10, have "the judgment seat of Christ," which Wortley, *Give Me,* 51, adopts. See Rom 14:10 and 2 Cor 5:10; the HB refers to the "mercy seat" (Exod 25:17; 40:20), as does Heb 9:5.

334. It is possible that Arsenius is fending off having his remains become relics. As Brown notes, *Cult*, 1, "The cult of the saints, as it emerged in late antiquity, became part and parcel of the succeeding millennium of Christian history." See *Life of Antony* 92.2 (p. 255), where two monks bury Antony, and "To this day no one knows where [his body] is buried except those two alone."

335. This seems odd; perhaps it is a stage prop to further the narrative.

336. Since Arsenius lived 32 miles away from the community (see Arsenius 21), I am taking his last wishes to mean he wants to be taken to the monastery (*óros*) for burial. But it could also mean away from the monastery, to a (distant) mountain* (*óros*; though, in Egypt, not a "mountain" as we commonly understand the word).

[337]40b. [XV.10, Guy 2.292] This was what Arsenius said:* "Arsenius, why did you leave the world?"[338]

He replied, "I have often regretted[339] having spoken—having kept silence, never."

40c. [XV.10, Guy 2.290] When he was about to die,[340] the brothers saw him weeping, so they said to him, "Are you really afraid* too,[341] father?"

He said to them, "Yes I am."[342] The fear* that is with me now in this hour has been with me[343] since I became a monk."

So this way he went to his rest.[344]

[345]41a. [III.3] They used to say that as he[346] sat doing his work* his whole life, he had a rag in his lap because of the tears that would fall from his eyes.

41b. [XV.10, Guy 2.292] When Abba Poemen heard that Abba Arsenius had gone to his rest, he wept and said, "Blessed are you,

337. It is not clear here who the speaker/s is / are. AlphAP 40b and SysAP XV.10 are identical. By adding "He replied," I have translated it as Arsenius speaking to himself and replying; an alternative translation could have an unidentified elder saying, "Arsenius, why did you leave the world?" and Arsenius replies. Another possibility is that they are two separate sayings, with 40b being a rhetorical question from Arsenius to himself, that is, "Why did you leave the world, Arsenius? You are no different now than you were then."

338. leave: since *exérchomai* can mean to leave secular life (Lampe 495b), and since this is a major theme in early monasticism, I have added *the world.**

339. regretted, *metamél(e)ō*: the cognate noun *metaméleia* means "repentance, penitence" (Lampe 853b).

340. When he was about to die: An alternative reading, PG 65:105–6 n. 44 and SysAP XV.10, give up the spirit; which Wortley, *Give Me*, 51, adopts.

341. too: "too" translates *kaí*, which can also mean "even," thus giving us "Are even you afraid?" Both meanings are highly likely here.

342. Yes I am: *en alḗtheia(i)*: "truly," which I have earlier translated as *really.*

343. this hour has been with me: perhaps an allusion to Mark 14:35.

344. went to his rest, *koimáomai*, "to fall asleep," a euphemism.

345. We have two separate sayings here, too (Guy, SysAP 3.219, concurs), joined together by the theme of weeping.

346. he: SysAP III.3, Abba Arsenius.

Abba Arsenius: you wept and wailed for yourself in this world*
here. The person who doesn't weep and wail for himself here will
do so there, eternally.[347] So whether someone weeps and wails
here, willingly, or there, because of torments,[348] it's impossible
not to mourn and lament."[349]

42. [XV.11] Abba Daniel used to relate these details[350] about
Abba Arsenius: He never wanted to speak about any problem of
interpretation[351] concerning Scripture,* although he could have
spoken if he'd wanted to. Nor would he readily write a letter.
When he'd come to church from time to time, he'd sit behind a
pillar so [108] no one would see his face; nor would he look at
anyone else's face. This was his practice, angelic, like Jacob's.[352]
His hair completely gray, he was noble in his bearing, austere[353]
in appearance. He had a long beard reaching almost to his belly.
He had lost his eyelashes because of his weeping.[354] He was tall
but stooped over from age. He died at the age of ninety-five.[355]
He'd spent forty years in the palace of Theodosius the Great* of

347. eternally: see Matt 18:8; 25:41, 46.

348. torments: *básanos* can also mean "torture" and the act of torture used to
question a prisoner (Liddell and Scott 309a; "inquiry by torture").

349. mourn and lament: once again "weep and wail."

350. used to relate these details, *diēgéomai*, translated earlier as "to tell a story,"
but this saying is more description than story.

351. problem of interpretation: *zétēma*, like *zétēsis*, can more neutrally mean
"question, inquiry," especially about Scripture (from *zētéō*, "seek, inquire"), but
often it more particularly means "exegetical problems" (Lampe 591b).

352. Possibly an allusion to Gen 32:29, where Jacob, after wrestling the man,
declares, "I have seen God face to face" (that is, he has seen God's face). Or,
more remotely, Jacob's dream at Bethel, Gen 18:10-22.

353. austere: *xērós* has a wide variety of meanings. Its basic meaning is "dry,"
then "dried out" as in "withered, lean, haggard," and "fasting, austere" (Liddell
and Scott 1190b). With regard to ascetic practices, it is the adjective in "dry bread,"
a monastic staple.

354. See Arsenius 41.

355. He died at the age of ninety-five: accepting the variant reading of PG
65:108 n. 46 and SysAP XV.11, instead of "he was 95." Ninety-five could be

godly memory,[356] and he became tutor[357] to the most godly Arcadius and Honorius.*

He spent forty years in Scetis* and ten in Troë* of Upper Babylon*[358] opposite Memphis,* and three years in Canopus* of Alexandria;* then for the other two years he returned to Troë, and there he went to his rest. He completed his course in peace* and in the fear* of God because he was a good man, one filled with the Holy Spirit and faith.*[359] He left me his coat* made of skins,[360] shirt of white wool, and sandals of palm-fiber. Although I'm unworthy, I've worn them in order to be blessed.[361]

43. [XV.11] Abba Daniel also used to tell this story about Abba Arsenius: One time he summoned my fathers, Abba Alexander and Abba Zoïlos.[362] Humbling* himself, he said to them, "Since the demons* wage war* against me and I do not know whether they are stealing me[363] in my sleep, tonight do your best to toil beside me and keep watch* with me to see whether I doze off during the night vigil."* So they sat with him, one at his right and one at his left, keeping silent late into the night.

My fathers told me this: "We fell asleep, and, when we woke up, we couldn't tell whether he had dozed off. Early in the morning (God knows if he did this on his own so we'd think he had

---

hagiographical, but very long monastic lives were not uncommon; for example, Antony (250–ca. 356) and Shenoute (ca. 348–ca. 466).

356. godly, *theíos*: SysAP XV.11, sainted, *hósios*.

357. See n. 317.

358. Troë of Upper Babylon: on Troë see Arsenius 34.

359. filled with the Holy Spirit and faith: see Acts 11:24.

360. See Life of Antony 92.3 (p. 255) and Arsenius 32.

361. He left me his coat . . . that I might be blessed: SysAP XV.11 lacks. Influenced by the Life of Antony, an editor might have added these last two sentences; see the previous n.

362. Abba Alexander and Abba Zoïlos: see Arsenius 32.

363. stealing, *kléptō* (English *kleptomaniac*, *kleptocracy*): the translation here is literal. Perhaps "stealing my soul" or "stealing from me." Or, perhaps, the demons are snatching him away physically as well as spiritually.

nodded off or if sleep really had overcome him), he exhaled three deep breaths and immediately stood up, saying, 'I must have taken a nap.' We responded, saying, 'We don't know.' "

44. [II.11] Some elders came one time to see Abba Arsenius and urged him over and over to let them meet with him. He opened the door for them, and they urged him to tell them something beneficial* about those living the contemplative life* who meet with no one.[364]

The elder said to them, "When the virgin is in her father's house, many men come, wanting to woo her. But when she takes a husband,[365] it does not please[366] all the others. Some despise her, while others applaud her. Because of this, she does not have the honor she had formerly when she was sequestered. So, too, with matters pertaining to the soul: once she[367] makes herself public,[368] she will never make everybody happy."

45.* [XV.9] [AnonAP 15][369] They used to say about Abba Arsenius that no one could grasp[370] his monastic way of life.

364. urged him over and over to let them meet with him. He opened the door for them, and they urged him to tell them something beneficial about those living the contemplative life who meet with no one: SysAP II.11, urged him to tell them something beneficial about those living the contemplative life who meet with no one.

365. when she takes a husband: SysAP II.11, if she proceeds to do so.

366. it does not please: since Greek verbs do not require nouns or pronouns, the verb here could mean "she does not please."

367. she: again Greek does not have a pronoun here; I have used *she* because it nicely indicates the young woman or the soul (feminine in Greek).

368. Once she makes herself public: SysAP II.11, if she proceeds to expand her territory.

369. These last two Sayings attributed to Arsenius are not present in Guy's edition of the SysAP, but he includes them in his earlier collection of Greek Apophthegmata, *Recherches sur la tradition grecque des Apophthegmata Patrum* (Brussels: Bollandistes, 1962), 119. Although he numbers them simply S 1 and S 2, for ease of reference I number them to follow 43, so 44* and 45*.

370. grasp: one of the primary meanings of *katalambánō* is "seize, catch, grasp," so also "understand, comprehend." The use in John 1:5 is different: "The

46.* [SysAP X.6] [AnonAP 568] A brother asked Abba Arsenius, "Why are there some good people who, when they're dying, suffer terrible affliction,* their bodies stricken?"

The elder replied, "So that even as they are salted here,[371] they will go there purified.

Concerning Abba Agathon[372]

1. [108] [X.11] Abba Peter, the disciple of Abba Lot, said, I was in Abba Agathon's cell once, and [109] a brother came to see him and said, "I want to live with the brothers. Tell me, what do I need to do in order to live with them?"

The elder said, "Just as you were a stranger* the first day you joined them, see that you remain* a stranger*[373] all the days of your life so you don't go around talking with everyone."*[374]

Abba Macarius said to Abba Agathon, "Why? What will talking freely with everyone do?"

The elder said to him, "It seems to me that talking freely like this is like a roaring fire: when the fire flares up, everyone runs away from its scorching heat[375] as it consumes the trees and their fruit."[376]

---

light shines in the darkness, and the darkness did not overcome it." But perhaps the darkness cannot grasp (understand) the light.

371. See Mark 9:49-50.

372. Gk. *Agáthōnos*. See Agathon in Dramatis Personae.

373. remain a stranger: literally "guard your foreignness / stranger-ness."

374. go around talking with everyone, *parrēsiázomai* (vb), cognate with *parrēsía* (n): see Confidence in the Glossary. It is striking that such a valued monastic word is negative here, in the very first saying for Agathon. The verb occurs five times in this saying; I have used three different translations: "go around talking with everyone," "talking freely with everyone," and "talk his head off."

375. heat: literally *face*. The verb cognate with "fire" can mean "scorch, burn up."

376. trees and fruit: see Agathon 8.

Abba Macarius said to him, "So, talking freely to everyone is harmful, even evil?"

Abba Agathon said, "There isn't a single other passion* more destructive[377] than going around talking* to everyone; in fact, this gives birth to all of the passions.* The monk who is working* at being a monk[378] is not to talk his head off, even if he's alone in his cell.[379] I know for a fact that one brother spent all his time living in his cell. His cell had a small side bedroom. He said, 'I could have moved around in my cell and not known about this small bedroom, if someone else hadn't told me about it.'

"Such a person is both a monk who works at being a monk and a warrior."[380]

2. [XI.8] Abba Agathon said: "The monk must not allow his conscience to accuse him about any matter whatsoever."

3. He also said: "Without keeping*[381] the holy commandments,* a person doesn't make progress, not even in a single virtue."*

4.[382] [XVII.8] Again he said, "I never went to bed holding anything against anyone, nor, to the best of my ability, did I allow someone to go to bed holding anything against me."

---

377. destructive, *chalepós*: earlier translated as "harmful, even evil." *Chalepós* means both "harmful" and "evil," so I have used both words.

378. working at being a monk: literally "the worker."

379. SysAP X.11 (Guy 2.20) ends here. It is possible that an editor has appended another saying here.

380. Early monastic cells often had two rooms: a small bedroom and a larger room for prayer and visitors. So this monk, by ignoring the other room and living in the "prayer room," spatially lived a life of prayer, praying without ceasing (1 Thess 5:17).

381. keeping, *phylakē*: in Agathon 1 "see that" translates the cognate verb *phylássō*. See Protect / Protection in the Glossary.

382. SysAP XVII.8 also gives this saying to Agathon; Epiphanius 4 attributes it to Bishop Epiphanius of Salamis in Cyprus. See Cassian, *Conferences* 4, for the same idea. See Eph 4:26. In Syncletica 13, before quoting part of Eph 4:26

5. [X.12] They used to say this about Abba Agathon: some people, having heard about his great abilities of discernment,* came to see him. Wanting to test* him to see whether he would get angry,* they said to him, "Are you Agathon? We hear that you sin sexually* and are arrogant."

He said, "Yes, there you have it."

Then they said, "Are you the Agathon who gossips and tells tales about people?"³⁸³

He said, "That's me."

Yet again they said, "Are you Agathon the heretic?"

He responded, "I am not a heretic!"

So they pleaded* with him, "Tell us why, when we said such terrible things about you, you just accepted them, but you wouldn't stand for it when we asked whether you're a heretic."

He said to them, "With regard to the first charges, I file charges against myself: it's good for my soul. But as for being a heretic— that separates³⁸⁴ a person from God, and I don't want to be separated from God."

When they heard what he had said, they marveled at his power of discernment* and so left, edified.³⁸⁵

---

the amma puts the matter bluntly: "It is good not to get angry, but, if you do, Paul has not allowed you to hold on to this passion* for even twenty-four hours."

383. tells tales about people: Lampe's translation of *katálos* is nice, "scandal-monger" (710a). See Agathon 1.

384. separates: *chōrismós* can also mean "divorce" and even "excommunication" (Lampe 1539ab). In Rom 8:35, 39, Paul uses the cognate verb *chōrízō* to affirm that nothing can separate the faithful from the love of God. Here, apparently, heresy can.

385. edified: see the next note. Antony D. Rich, *Discernment in the Desert Fathers: Διάκρισις in the Life and Thought of Early Egyptian Monasticism*, Studies in Christian Theology and Thought (Waynesboro, GA: Paternoster, 2007), 136–37, has a good discussion of this saying, observing that Agathon denies being a heretic because of "his commitment to his ultimate goal of union with God," while he accepts the other charges "without demur" because he "was committed to his proximate goal," *apatheia*,* being free from sinful emotions.

6. [VI.4] They told this story about Abba Agathon: he spent a considerable amount of time building a cell with his disciples.[386] After they finished their cell they later came to live there, but he saw something the very first week that was of no benefit* to him.[387] He said to his disciples, "Get up. We're leaving this place."[388]

The two were very upset* and said, "If your intention* all along was to move away, why'd we have to endure*[389] such hard work building the cell? People are going [112] to be scandalized* by us and say, yet again,[390] 'Look! The vagabonds[391] are moving— again!' "

386. An editor probably put Saying 6 after 5 (they are in separate chapters in the SysAP) because of the theme of discernment in both (in 6 Agathon discerns that something is "of no benefit to him") and linked them with each other, either intentionally or unintentionally, with a word play: in 5, the people go away edified, *oikodomēthéntes*, and in 6 Agathon and his disciples are building, *oikodoméō*. For the cognate noun *oikodomḗ*, see 2 Cor 10:8; 13:10; Eph 4:12, 16. AnneMarie Luijendijk notes that the word may be catechetical in 4th-cent. Egypt; see *Greetings in the Lord: Early Christians and the Oxyrhynchus Papyri*, Harvard Theological Studies (Cambridge: Harvard University Press, 2008), 121–23. As with English *edifice* and *edify* (from Lat. *aedis*, "dwelling" + *facere*, "make"), the two Greek words are cognate, "to build up" in English. The NT has both meanings (Bauer 696ab). At the end of 6, Agathon's disciples too are edified, though the word used previously does not occur.

387. no benefit to him: perhaps a circumlocution for something that harmed him in some way.

388. See John 14:31.

389. endure, *hypoménō*. Bauer 1039ab suggests that the verb as a possible variant reading at Rom 8:24 means "put up with," which fits here.

390. The early monastic ideal was to stay put; sayings disapprove of monks gallivanting about or changing locations. Neither the Latin nor Wortley, *Give Me*, 55, translates *pálin* as "again, once more." Since *pálin* occurs again in what the people say, it could be an accidental redundancy. Or it could be that people were bothered, even offended (*skandalízō*), the first time, when Agathon built a new habitation, and, now, when Agathon is moving—*again*.

391. vagabonds: there is a significant play on words in the Greek. "To live" at the beginning of the saying translates *kathízomai*, "to sit, dwell, live"; "vaga-

When Abba Agathon saw that they were disheartened,[392] he said to them, "If some[393] are indeed scandalized,* nevertheless, others will, once again, be edified, and they'll say, 'Blessed are people like these: they've moved on account of God, and haven't paid any attention at all to what people say.'[394] But . . . if you want to come, come; I'm leaving in a bit."

So they threw themselves to the ground, asking him to take them with him, until Abba Agathon gave them permission to travel with him.[395]

7. [VI.5] Again, they said about him that oftentimes he moved from one place to another having only his knife[396] in his basket.

8. [X.13] Abba Agathon was asked: "Which is better, manual labor[397] or safeguarding* the interior* spiritual life?"

The elder said, "A human being is like a tree: as such, manual labor is the leaves, while the interior* spiritual life, that which keeps watch,* is the fruit. Since according to what is written, 'Every tree that doesn't produce good fruit gets cut down and thrown into the fire,'[398] it's clear that all of our diligence and zeal is for the fruit, that is, safeguarding* the mind.* But we also need

---

bonds" renders *akáthistoi* (literally "not-sitting / dwelling"), alpha-privative (negation) + *káthistoi*, cognate with *kathízomai*.

392. disheartened, *oligopsychéō*: *óligo*, "small," + *psychḗ*, "soul, spirit," so also "downhearted," "discouraged"; 1 Thess 5:14: "fainthearted" (NRSV). Colloquially: down in the dumps.

393. some, *tines* < *tis*: "someone," or, edgier, "certain people."

394. to what people say: I have added this phrase.

395. Douglas Burton-Christie, *The Word in the Desert: Scripture and the Quest for Holiness in Early Christian Monasticism* (New York: Oxford University Press, 1993), 225, observes, "This story, with its echoes of biblical language, conveys well the importance of being willing to leave everything for the sake of the Gospel and how this was related to freedom from care."

396. knife: SysAP VI.5 has *mēlōtḗ*, "sheepskin," "sheepskin cloak" (Lampe 868a). In Life of Antony 91.8–9 (p. 253), Antony, dying, gives his two sheepskin cloaks to Bishop Athanasius and Bishop Serapion.

397. manual labor, *kópos*: or "bodily suffering."

398. Matt 3:10.

the protective shade and beauty[399] of the leaves, that is, manual labor."[400]

9. [XII.2] Once again the brothers asked him, "What virtue* is it, father, among the things we do in our way of life* that requires the most effort?"

He said to them, "If you'll allow me, I think nothing requires more effort than praying* to God.[401] It never fails: when a person wants to pray,* the enemies*[402] want to cut him off at the knees. They know that nothing else gets in their way except praying* to God. Every ascetic activity[403] that a person pursues[404] and perseveres in brings inward stillness,* but prayer* requires struggle* until the very last breath."

10. [X.14] Abba Agathon was wise in his understanding of things, unflagging in his bodily efforts, and moderate and content[405] in everything, in both the work* he did with his hands and with regard to food and clothing.[406]

---

399. beauty: *eukosmía* can also mean the "good order" and "harmony" (*eu-*, "good," + *kósmos*, "order") of the universe (Lampe 566a). For the Greeks, what is in good order (*tò kósmon*) is beautiful.

400. On this unity, see Agathon 10.

401. praying to God: SysAP XII.2, praying to God without distraction.

402. enemies, *echthroí*: SysAP XII.2, the Enemy.* That is, Satan (Lampe 589a); see Luke 10:19. In Arsenius 28 the Devil is "the Enemy."

403. ascetic activity, *politeía*: I have translated *politeía* a bit earlier as "the things we do in our way of life." See Way of life in the Glossary.

404. pursues, *metérchomai*: or "practices," an understanding seconded by the variant reading *meletáō* (PG 65:112–13 n. 31), "practice, train oneself in" (Lampe 840b). English "pursue a vocation," a calling.

405. moderate and content: *autárkēs* suggests "self-sufficiency, frugality," "moderation, contentment, satisfaction with little" (Lampe 266a); see Agathon 7. *Autarky* has come into English: "self-sufficiency."

406. Rich, *Discernment*, 147, comments on Agathon's holistic spirituality: "his own life was an example of an inner and outer life unified and supporting the development of each other." On this theme, see Agathon 8.

11. The same elder was out walking with his disciples, and one of them found a small green pea plant in the road. He said to the elder, "Father, do you want me to take it?"

The elder looked at him, astonished,* and said, "Did you put it there?"

The brother said, "No."

So the elder said, "Why, then, do you want to take something that you didn't put there?"

12. A brother came to see Abba Agathon and said, "Let me live with you."

When he was walking on the road, he found a small amount of natron[407] and brought it with him. The elder said, "Where did you find the natron?"

The brother said, "I found it on the road, while I was walking, and brought [113] it with me."

The elder said to him, "If you've come to live with me, why didn't you leave there what you had found?"

And he sent him to take it back where he had found it.[408]

13. [VII.2] A brother asked[409] the elder, "I've just received an order* to go somewhere, but there's fighting[410] going on where

---

407. natron: *nítron* means both niter (potassium nitrate, or saltpeter) and natron (sodium carbonate decahydrate, or soda ash). Natron contains sodium bicarbonate, baking soda. The ancient Egyptians mined natron in the Wadi Natrun* (hence its name).

408. Chitty, *Desert,* 42 and 18 n. 66 reports that a version of the story "in the Syriac collection (clearly translated from the Greek)" says that the monk has to walk back twelve miles. He states that "Agathon 12 is a shortened variant of the story."

409. Despite "asked," there is no question, so I have supplied it later in brackets.

410. fighting: *polemós* also means "war."* SysAP VII.2 (Guy 1.336) has a significant difference: "there's fighting going on *with me*," thus, spiritual warfare. I take the dative *moi* here as a dative of disadvantage, meaning it is not in the monk's interest to go. The story supplies no specifics.

the command* came from. So, I want to go,[411] because of the order, but I'm afraid of the fighting. [What should I do?]"

The elder said to him, "If it were me, I'd do what I was ordered,* and put an end to the fighting."

14. [X.15] When a council took place at Scetis* about some matter and it had come to a decision, the same Abba Agathon appeared afterwards and said to the abbas, "The decision you reached concerning this matter isn't a good one."

They said to him, "Who are you to talk this way at all?"

He said, "I'm a simple human being; it's written, 'If you truly speak justly, mortals,[412] you will judge* correctly."[413]

15. [IV.7] They used to say about Abba Agathon that for three years he kept a stone in his mouth until he learned[414] to keep silent.[415]

411. I want to go, or "I'm willing [*thélō*] to go." "I'm willing" works better with the text in SysAP VII.2 (see the previous note).

412. mortals: it and "simple human being" translate "son of man / humanity," *huiòs anthrṓpou*. Bauer says that the "plural form appears frequently in the LXX to render 'mortals,' " as I have translated the plural in the last sentence (Bauer 1026a). Jesus applies the singular phrase to himself many times (no one ever addresses him as such). For "simple human being" (or "mere mortal"), I have followed James L. Kugel, *How to Read the Bible: A Guide to Scripture, Then and Now* (Boston: Free Press, 2008).

413. Ps 57:2 LXX. Rich, *Discernment*, 210, makes a good observation about this saying: Agathon "regarded sound judgement, and therefore *diákrisis* [*discernment**], as an expression of righteousness. *Diákrisis* could thus be used assertively to uphold the truth."

414. learned, *katorthóō*: as the root—*órthos*, "straight, right"—shows, the verb has a number of apposite nuances here that are difficult to convey in English: "set right, establish," "perform, carry out precepts," "attain to, live a good life" (Lampe 735b). The verb does not occur in the NT but occurs about 25 times in the LXX.

415. In "The Life of Demosthenes" 11.1 in *The Parallel Lives*, Plutarch reports that the "indistinctness and lisping in [Demosthenes'] speech he used to correct and drive away by taking pebbles in his mouth and then reciting the speeches" —the opposite of Agathon! (Loeb Classical Library: Penelope.uchicago.edu).

16. They also used to say about him and Abba Amoun that when they were selling an item they would state the price once, taking whatever was given to them, with silence and equanimity.*

And again, any time they wanted to buy something, they in silence paid whatever price was stated to them and took the item, without saying a word.

17. [AnonAP 353] The same Abba Agathon said, "I've never done an act of love.* No, giving and receiving was itself for me an act of love.* As I see it, whatever benefits⁴¹⁶ my brother is a work* that bears fruit."⁴¹⁷

18. When the same Agathon saw something and wanted to rush to judgment,*⁴¹⁸ he said to himself, "Agathon, don't you do it!" Calming himself this way, he found peace and quiet.*⁴¹⁹

19. [X.16] The same person said, "If someone prone to anger* were to raise the dead, even this would not be acceptable in God's sight."⁴²⁰

20. One time Abba Agathon had two disciples who had withdrawn* from the world,⁴²¹ each living by himself. One day, then, Abba Agathon asked one of them, "What sort of life do you live in your cell?"

---

416. whatever benefits: *kérdos* especially indicates a moral or spiritual benefit (Lampe 748a); see Phil 1:21 and 3:7 (NRSV: "gain").

417. bears fruit: *karpophoría*. AnonAP 353, which may be parallel with Agathon 17, "bears fruit for me." See Rom 7:4 and especially Matt 13:23 (*karpophoréō*, the cognate verb).

418. wanted to rush to judgment: literally "his thought* wanted to judge."

419. he found peace and quiet: literally "his thought* found peace and quiet" [*hēsychía*]." English: "his mind was put at rest."

420. See 1 Cor 13:1-3. Rich, *Discernment*, 157, observes that "anger is not regarded as justified if it arises from the arrogance or violence of a *confrère*, but appropriate 'if he separates you from God'" (AlphAP Poemen 117). On this separation, see Agathon 5.

421. withdrawn from the world: I have added "from the world"* to "withdraw," but one could also translate "withdrawn from the monastery."

He said, "I fast* until evening and then I eat two small loaves of dried bread."*

Abba Agathon said to him, "That's a good way to live, not overdoing it by working too hard."

He said to the other one, "And you, how about you?"

The disciple said, "I fast* every other day; then I eat two small loaves of dried bread."*

[116] The elder said to him, "That's hard work, fighting a battle on two fronts,[422] because if someone eats every day but doesn't eat his fill, he's working hard. But another person wants to fast* every other day, and then eat his fill. But you fast* every other day and don't eat your fill."

21. A brother asked Abba Agathon about sexual sin,* and the elder said to him, "Go, throw your weakness before God,[423] and you'll be at peace."*

22. Abba Agathon was sick one time, along with a certain other elder. While they were lying down in the cell, the brother was reading Genesis aloud and came to the passage where Jacob says, "Joseph is no more, Simeon is no more, and you [pl.] will take Benjamin away . . . and you will take my gray hairs down to Hades in grief."[424]

In response, the other elder said, "The other ten aren't enough for you, Abba Jacob?"[425]

Abba Agathon said, "Elder, stop. If God says it's right, who's to judge?"*

---

422. fighting a battle on two fronts: I wish to thank John Wortley, *Give Me*, 57, for this image; literally "bearing up under two wars* / battles."

423. throw your weakness before God: Ps 54:23 has "cast your care upon the Lord, and he will support you."

424. Gen 42:36, 38.

425. Jacob (Israel) has 12 sons (the twelve tribes of Israel); in Gen 49 he blesses them.

23. Abba Agathon said, "If my feelings for someone whom I love very much[426] become excessive and I realize that they're becoming a problem,[427] I cut the person out of my life."

24. He also said, "A person needs always to keep in mind God's judgment."*[428]

25. [XVII.7] When the brothers were talking about love,* Abba Joseph would say, "Do we know what love* is?" And he told them about Abba Agathon, that he had a knife: "A brother came to see him and praised the knife, and Abba Agathon wouldn't let him leave unless he took the knife with him."

26. Abba Agathon used to say, "If it were possible for me to find a leper,[429] give him my body, and take his, I would gladly do so: this is real[430] love."*

---

426. love very much, *agapētós*: "beloved"; see Matt 3:17, where God says it of Jesus (NRSV: *with whom I am well pleased*). See Love in the Glossary. *Agapētós* is the first word in this sentence, and thus emphatic. In Agathon 28 he "loved Abba Alexander because he was an ascetic and was gentle and forbearing."

427. problem, *eláttōma*: Lampe uses *defect* and notes that the word can indicate a moral defect, one corrected at baptism (445b). The noun does not occur in the NT, but the verb *elattóō* does: "make lower, inferior," "be worse off, be in need," "diminish, become less" (Bauer 313b–14a).

428. judgment, *kritḗrion*: as English *criterion* shows, *kritḗrion* differs from its cognate *krísis*, "judgment," in that the former has the meaning of "criterion, standard, means for judging," even "test." So a good translation could be "A person needs always to keep in mind what God wants." *Kritḗrion* can also mean "a court of judgment, tribunal" (Liddell and Scott 997a). In Patristic Greek it can mean God's judgment seat, and can refer to an ecclesiastical court. See nn. 440 and 442.

429. leper, *kelephós*; Agathon 30 uses a different word.

430. real, *téleios*: the usual translation is "perfect," and it can mean that, but, as Bauer demonstrates, the word has a wide range of nuances applicable both in the NT and here: "meeting the highest standard," "full-grown, mature, adult," "being fully developed in a moral sense, perfect" (995b–96a).

27. They also used to say about him that going one time to sell his wares in the city, he found a person,[431] someone he didn't know, cast out into the street, sick and weak, and no one was paying any attention to him.[432] So the elder stayed with him, rented a place for a cell, and paid for it with the money he made from selling his handiwork. All the rest he spent for the care of the sick man. He stayed there four months, until the sick man got well. And this way the elder went back home to his cell in peace.*

28. Abba Daniel used to say: Before Abba Arsenius came to stay with my fathers, they were staying with Abba Agathon. Abba Agathon loved Abba Alexander[433] because he was an ascetic* and [117] was gentle and forbearing. It happened that all of his disciples were washing rushes in the river. Abba Alexander was also conscientiously washing his rushes, but the other brothers said to the elder, "Brother Alexander isn't doing anything."

Wanting to care for them,[434] he said to him, "Brother Alexander, wash them carefully; they're flax."

When Abba Alexander heard this, it saddened him.

Afterwards the elder comforted* him, saying, "Don't you think I knew that you were doing your washing carefully? I said that to you for the benefit* of the others in order to correct[435] what they were thinking* concerning your obedience,* brother."

---

431. An editor has connected this saying with Agathon 26 both thematically and lexically: in both, Agathon "finds," essentially redefining "Seek, and you will find" (Matt 7:7 // Luke 11:9) to "Seek to do good, and you will find."

432. and no one paid any attention to him: *epimeléomai* here can also mean "with no one to care for him."

433. See Agathon 23.

434. care for: *therapeúō* usually means "heal" (English *therapy, therapeutic*) and can also suggest "heal spiritually," for purposes of reconciliation, and "care for, look after" (Lampe 645a).

435. correct: *therapeúō* again; see the previous note.

29a. [XI.9–10][436] The abbas[437] used to recount that Abba Agathon made every effort to keep all the commandments:* if he boarded a boat, he was the first one to grab an oar, and when brothers visited him, immediately after prayer* he himself set the table. He did these things because he was filled with the love* of God.

29b. When he was about to die, he remained in bed for three days without moving, with his eyes open. The brothers nudged him, saying, "Abba Agathon, where are you?"

He said to them, "I'm standing before the Judgment* seat[438] of God."

They said to him, "And are you afraid,* father?"

He said to them, "All this time I've done everything in my power* to keep* God's commandments.* But I'm a human being. How do I know if my work* has been pleasing[439] to God?

The brothers said to him, "Aren't you confident* about your work?* Don't you think it's what God wants?"

The elder said, "Unless I meet God, I'm not sure. God's standards[440] are one thing, people's another."

When they wanted to ask him another question, he said to them, "Keep doing acts of love,* but don't discuss them with me anymore; I'm occupied."

And he died with joy.

They saw him set off the way someone says goodbye to friends and loved ones.[441] He kept careful watch* about everything and

---

436. Agathon 29 consists of two sayings that an editor has joined. SysAP XI.9–10 (Guy 2.140) confirms this observation because Agathon 29a is not there.

437. The abbas: literally "they."

438. Judgment seat, *kritḗrion*; see nn. 440, 449.

439. pleasing, *euarestéō*: see Heb 11:5-6.

440. standards: *kritḗrion* again, or "judgments." See nn. 438 and 449.

441. loved ones, *agapētós*: see Love in the Glossary. Set off: *anágō* can mean "launch a ship into water" or "set off on a boat" so, whether intended here or not, there is the nice image of a person on a boat waving goodbye to friends and fam-

used to say, "Without keeping a careful watch,* a person does not make progress, even in a single virtue."*[442]

[443]30. One time Abba Agathon went to the city to sell some small wares, and he found[444] a leper[445] by the side of the road. The leper said to him, "Where are you going?"

Abba Agathon said to him, "Into the city to sell some wares."

The leper said to him, "Do an act of love* and take me there."

So Abba Agathon carried* him and brought him into the city. The leper said to him, "Take me where you sell your wares," and this he did. Whenever Abba Agathon sold something, the leper said, "How much did you sell it for?" and Abba Agathon told him the amount. So the leper would say, "Buy me some flatbread," and Abba Agathon bought it. Then he sold another item, and the leper said, "How much did you get this time?" and Abba Agathon would tell him the amount. So the leper said to him, "Buy me such and such," and he'd buy it.

So after Abba Agathon had sold all his wares and wanted to leave, the leper said to him, "You're going?"

He said to him, "Yes."

"Do another act of love* and take me back where you found me."

---

ily on shore. It could possibly be echoing the Greek myth of Charon, who ferries the souls of the dead across the rivers Styx and Acheron.

442. keep a careful watch *phylakḗ*: see Protect in the Glossary. At the beginning of the saying, Abba Agathon "made every effort to keep [*phylássō*, cognate with *phylakḗ*] all the commandments."

443. For a longer story about Abba Eulogius helping "a cripple," see Historia Lausiaca 21 (Wortley, *Lausiac History*, 52–58).

444. found, *heurískō*: thus continuing the theme of finding and doing good; see Agathon 26 and 27.

445. leper, *lelōbaménos* < *lōbáō*: literally "one maimed / mutilated"; Lampe notes that it was used particularly of lepers. *Lṓbē* equals *lépra*, "leper" (818a).

So Abba Agathon carried* him and brought him back to where he'd been before. The leper said to him, "Agathon, you have been blessed by the Lord in heaven and on earth."[446]

When Agathon raised his eyes, he didn't see anyone—it was an angel of the Lord who had come to test* him.

Concerning Abba Ammonas[447]

1. [120] [III.4] A brother asked [*sic*] Abba Ammonas, "Give me some guidance."*

The elder said, "Go, and think* the way evil-doers do—you know, those who are in prison: those who are always asking people 'Where's the governor?'* and 'When's he coming?' And as they wait for the governor,* they weep. In the same way, the monk always needs to be concerned* about himself and accuse and discipline himself,[448] saying, 'How will I ever stand before the Judgment seat of Christ?[449] How will I defend myself before him?' If you reflect* on these things all the time, you can be saved."*

446. See Ps 115:15: "May you be blessed by the Lord, who made heaven and earth."

447. Ammonas, Gk. *Ammōná*: the text has *Ammona*, but SysAP has *Ammonas*, which is the common spelling in the literature. See Ammonas in Dramatis Personae.

448. accuse and discipline, *elénchō*: I have used two words to try to capture the sense. The verb and its cognate noun *élenchos* occur often in the NT but only a few times in the gospels; see Luke 3:19: "rebuke" (NRSV). The words have numerous meanings and ascetic implications of self-examination and correction: "charging with wrongdoing, accusation," "reproof, censure, correction," "expose, set forth," "convict, convince of wrongdoing," "reprove, correct," "punish, discipline" (Bauer 315ab).

449. the judgment seat of Christ, *bēma* here: *kritērion* earlier; see nn. 438, 440. In Rom 14:10 Paul speaks of the Judgment seat of God; a variant reading there has "the Judgment seat of Christ." In 2 Cor 5:10 Paul uses "the Judgment seat of Christ."

2. They used to say about Abba Ammonas that he had killed a basilisk.[450] Here's what happened: he'd gone into the desert to draw water from a body of water. When he saw the basilisk, he threw himself on his face and said, "Lord, am I going to die, or this basilisk?" Immediately, through the power* of Christ,[451] the basilisk burst into pieces.

3. [VII.3] Abba Ammonas said, "I spent fourteen years in Scetis* asking God night and day to give me the grace* to defeat anger."*

4. [X.20] One of the fathers told this story: There was a certain hard-working monk living in Kellia,* and he would wear a little mat.[452] He went to pay a visit to Abba Ammonas. When the elder saw him wearing the mat, he said to him, "This won't be of any benefit* to you."

In reply the elder asked Abba Ammonas, "Three things crowd my thoughts:* should I wander the desert,*[453] or go away to a foreign country where no one knows me, or shut myself up in a cell where I'll meet no one and eat every other day."

Abba Ammonas said to him, "None[454] of the three will do you any good if you do them. Instead, sit in your cell, eat a little every day, and keep in your heart at all times what the tax collector said,*[455] and you can be saved."

450. basilisk: according to Pliny the Elder, *Natural History* 8:33 (upenn, The Online Books Page), the basilisk ("little emperor") is a serpent native to Cyrene; it is a fantastic creature that destroys shrubs, burns up grass, and breaks stones, "so tremendous is its noxious influence."

451. The phrase "the power of Christ" does not occur in the NT; in 1 Cor 1:14 Paul calls Christ "the power of God."

452. wear a little mat: SysAP X.20, only a little mat.

453. wander, *plázōmai*: a variant reading, PG 65:119–20 n. 24 and SysAP X.20.5, *pelázōmai*, "approach, draw near," which must be a spelling mistake.

454. None: SysAP X.20, not one; not a single one.

455. what the tax collector said: literally "the word* [*lógos*] of the tax collector." In Luke 18:13 the tax collector beats his breast and says, "God, have mercy on me, a sinner."

5. It happened that some brothers were suffering affliction* where they were living and wanted to abandon the place.* They left to go see Abba Ammonas. By chance, the elder was sailing downstream, and when he saw them walking on the river bank he said to the boatmen, "Put me ashore." He called to the brothers and said to them, "It's me, Ammonas, the one you want to see." After comforting and strengthening* their hearts, he sent the brothers back where they had come from. He did this because what was damaging them was not a matter of the soul; rather, the affliction* was caused by people.

6. One time Abba Ammonas came to the Nile in order to cross it; he found a ferry ready to go and sat down beside it. Now another boat came and docked and boarded the people who were there. They said to him, "Come on, abba, you too. Cross the river with us."

He said, "Unless it's a public ferry, I won't take it."

He had a bunch of palm fronds, so he sat down and plaited rope [121] and then loosened it, until the ferry sailed across. [He did this until a public ferry came,] and that was how he crossed the river.

When the brothers heard about this,[456] they prostrated* themselves and said, "Why did you do that?"

The elder said to them, "So I don't always go around with my thoughts* hurrying me along as I walk."[457]

This, too, offers us an example of how we should take our time walking,[458] walking God's path in a settled, orderly, fashion.[459]

---

456. When the brothers heard about this: I have added this phrase as a segue.

457. hurrying me along: *spoudázō* means "to be busy, eager, zealous; hurry, hasten" (Lampe 1250b); one could be tempted to translate the phrase, anachronistically, as "with his thoughts in high gear."

458. take our time walking: *badízō* means "walk, march," but it also means "walk slowly," connected with *bádēn*, which can mean "step by step, gradually" (Liddell and Scott 300b).

459. It is possible that Ammonas, rather than the narrator, is speaking this final sentence. Or it could be a moral that an editor has tacked on.

7. One time Abba Ammonas went to see Abba Antony, and he lost his way. He sat down and slept a little. Rising from sleep, he prayed* to God, "I'm begging you, Lord my God, do not let what you have formed[460] perish."

There appeared to him something like a human hand extending from heaven,[461] showing him the way[462] until he came and stood before Abba Antony's cave.[463]

8. Abba Antony prophesied[464] to this same Abba Ammonas, "You have the ability to make progress in the fear* of God," and he led him out of the cell and showed[465] him a rock and said to him, "Insult this rock and hit it."

He did so and Abba Antony said to him, "Did the rock say anything?"[466]

---

460. what you have formed, *tò plásma*: see Ps 102:14 LXX and Isa 29:16 LXX.

461. It's common in the HB for suppliants to hold out their hands to heaven; with his plea, Ammonas is figuratively holding out his hands to God, and God's hand responds.

462. When Ammonas loses his way (*hodós*, the same word as in John 14:6, where Jesus says he is the way), the verb is *planáō*, "to wander" (English *planet*); in the NT (Bauer 821b–22a) and in Patristic Greek the word can have a moral sense, "lead astray," "deceive" (Lampe 1088b–89a). See also Ps 119:176 LXX 118:176. The text does not say that Ammonas has gone astray, but we could easily read it as a parable: God's guiding hand points the way for those who have gone astray. "Rising from sleep" lends credence to this suggestion: the participle for "rising" is *anastás* (English *stand*, Lat. *stare*, Ger. *standen*) < *anístēmi*; *anastás*, "risen," gives *anástasis*, "resurrection."

463. On Antony's cave, see Tim Vivian, "St. Antony and the Monastery of St. Antony at the Red Sea, ca. 350–ca. 1322 / 1323," in *Monastic Visions: The Wall Paintings at the Monastery of St. Antony at the Red Sea,* edited by Elizabeth S. Bolman (New Haven, CT: Yale University Press, 2002), 3–20.

464. prophesied: in the NT *prophētúō* has the two basic senses it has in English: (1) "to proclaim an inspired revelation, prophesy" (Matt 7:22), and (2) "to foretell something" (Matt 15:7) (Bauer 890a).

465. *Showed* here and *showing* at the end of Ammonas 7 are forms of the same verb in Greek, linking the two sayings.

466. The negative *mḗ* at the beginning of the sentence expects a negative answer.

He said, "No."

So Abba Antony said to him, "You too will attain this ability," and that's what happened.

Abba Ammonas made such progress with regard to what Antony had said that because of his great goodness,[467] he no longer knew evil. So after he had become a bishop,* a young woman who was pregnant was brought to him, and the people said to him, "Look what so-and-so did! Punish her!"

But he made the sign of the cross* on her belly and ordered six fine linen sheets[468] be given to her and said, "Do this in case the birth goes awry and she or the baby dies and there's nothing to do the burial in."

Those there who were against her said to him, "Why'd you do that?! Punish her!"

He said to them, "Look, brothers: she's near death. What else can I do?" And he released her. The elder did not presume[469] to judge* her.

9. They used to say about him that some people came to be judged* by him, but the elder acted[470] as though he didn't understand what was going on. Just then one of the women stood near him and was saying,[471] "This elder's an imbecile."

467. goodness: *agathótēs* (< *agathós*, "good") does not occur in the NT, but the LXX often uses it of God.

468. fine linen: *sindónion* (*sindōn* in the gospels; Matt 27:59 // Mark 15:46 // Luke 23:53) indicates the linen cloth used to wrap Jesus' body after the crucifixion.

469. presume, *tolmáō*: in the NT the verb more often means "dare, have the courage, be brave enough," but often also means "presume." *Dare* could work here if the sense is "he did not dare to judge her out of fear of the Lord."

470. but the elder acted: SysAP X.20, but when he heard [what they wanted] he acted.

471. Just then one of the women stood near him and was saying: a variant reading, PG 65:121 n. 67 and SysAP X.20, Just then a woman was saying to her neighbor.

The elder heard her and called out to her, "All those years I worked so hard in desert* places to acquire this imbecility—and because of you I'm going to lose it today!"[472]

10. One time Abba Ammonas went to a monastic settlement* to share a meal, and there was one person there who had a bad reputation.[473] It so happened that a woman* came and went inside the cell of the brother with the bad reputation. When therefore those living in that settlement learned about this, they were upset and disturbed,* so they gathered together to drive the brother out of his cell. Knowing that Bishop Ammonas was there in the community, they went and appealed* to him to come and support them.

When the brother found out, he took the woman* and hid her in a very large jar. When the crowd arrived with[474] Abba Ammonas, the bishop* saw [124] what was going on and for God's sake covered the matter up. Going inside, he sat on top of the jar and ordered the cell to be searched. So they searched around[475] and, when they didn't find the woman,* Abba Ammonas said, "What's the problem?[476] God will forgive you."[477]

472. lose: a chief meaning of *apóllumi* is "to ruin, destroy" (Lampe 200b). In the NT the word has this meaning, as well as "lose out on, lose," "perish, be ruined" (Bauer 115b–16a).

473. bad reputation: *kakós*, "bad," also means "evil," its primary meaning. The Devil is "the evil one" (Matt 5:37; 6:13); see Mark 7:21; Luke 6:45. See n. 485.

474. arrived with: *paragínomai* means "to be(come) beside" (*pará*); it can also mean "stand beside, support," as translated two sentences earlier.

475. searched around, *psēlapháō*: there may be an intended or unintended irony here. The verb can also mean "grope." In Acts 17:27 Paul says that God has made it so that the nations "would search for God and perhaps grope for him." These monks, then, are—linguistically and spiritually—searching in all the wrong places.

476. Literally, "What is this?"

477. God will forgive you: instead of the future tense, a variant reading, PG 65:123–24 n. 70, has an infinitive that, if not a typo, must be acting as an imperative: "God forgive you," "May God forgive you." See F. Blass and A. Debrunner, rev. Robert W. Funk, *A Greek Grammar of the New Testament and Other*

After praying,* he made everyone leave.[478] Taking the brother's
hand, he said to him, "Watch out* for yourself, brother."
Having said this, he withdrew.*[479]

11. [X.116] Abba Ammonas was asked, "What is the way that's
narrow and difficult?"[480]

He answered, "The 'way that's narrow and difficult' is this:
forcefully to constrain your[481] thoughts* and for God's sake cut
off your own will.[482] This explains the saying 'Look! We've left
everything and followed you.' "[483]

Early Christian Literature (Chicago: University of Chicago Press, 1961), ‡‡389,
"The imperatival infinitive," 196–97.

478. leave: there is another irony here. *Anachōréō* is a key monastic term:
"withdraw* (from the world to be with God)." Here the monks are leaving with
their tails between their legs. After completing his pastoral care, Ammonas himself withdraws.

479. We can smile with this parable about judgmental, hence sinful, monks
metaphorically ready to cast stones—but given the usual societal, and monastic,
views about women, Ammonas's response is astonishing. In Arsenius 28, Arsenius
says to an upper-class woman who wants to talk with him, "Don't you know
you're a woman? Don't you know you should never go *anywhere*?" Later in the
story, Archbishop Theophilus, "pastorally" visiting her, reproves her: "Do you
not know that you are a woman? And that because of women the Enemy* [Satan]
wages war against the saints?" One may assume that neither Arsenius nor the
archbishop would have quietly covered the matter up here.

480. See Matt 7:14, where Jesus says, *The gate is narrow and the road is hard
that leads to life, and there are few who find it.*

481. your: SysAP X.116, our.

482. This sentence has biblical resonance: "forcefully constrain," *biázō*
(*biázomai*) means "inflict violence, on, dominate, constrain," "gain an object by
force, use force" (Bauer 175b–76a); see Matt 11:12 // Luke 16:16. "Cut off,"
kóptō, can indicate the cutting of branches (Matt 21:8), and when Jesus says *If
your hand or foot causes you to stumble [or: causes you to sin], cut it off and
throw it away* (Matt 18:5). In monastic terms: If your thoughts cause you to
stumble [or: cause you to sin], cut them off and throw them away.

483. Matt 19:27.

Concerning Abba Achilla (Achilles)[484]

1. [124] [X.18] One time three elders visited Abba Achilla. One of them had a bad reputation.[485] One of the elders said to Abba Achilla, "Abba, make me a large fishing net."[486]

Abba Achilla said, "I won't do it."

The second one now said, "Please perform an act of love* so we can have something to remember you by at the monastery."[487]

He said, "I don't have time."

The third one, the one who had a bad reputation, said, "Make me a net so I can have something you've made with your hands, abba."

Abba Achilla quickly responded, telling him, "I *will* make *you* one."[488]

The two elders spoke with Abba Achilla when they were alone with him, "Why when we asked* you did you refuse to make one for us but you said to *this* guy, 'Sure, I'll make *you* one'?"

The elder said to them, "I told you 'I won't make one,' and yet my refusing, because I don't have time, didn't make you sad. But this fellow—if I don't make one for him, he'll say 'It's because of my sin; the elder's heard about it, so he refused to make me a net.'

---

484. Achilla: Gk. *Achilâ*. A variant reading has *Achillâ* (PG 65:123–24, n. 72), and SysAP uses *Achillâ* or *Achillâs*. I have used *Achilla* here. See "Achilla / Achilles" in Dramatis Personae.

485. bad, *kakós*: or "evil." See n. 473.

486. A *sagēnē* was "a large net hanging vertically, with floats on the top and sinkers on the bottom" (Bauer 910a); in Matt 13:47-50 Jesus compares one to the kingdom of heaven "at the end of the age," so this story may also be an eschatological parable.

487. SysAP X.18 continues, Make us a fishing net.

488. I have made this emphatic because (1) the brother's request in Greek begins with an emphatic "for me make a net," (2) the other two responses do not have "you," and (3) the Greek begins the sentence emphatically with *egṓ*, "I," which is not in the first two responses; the pronoun, as in Spanish, and unlike in English, is not required.

If we do this, we're quickly cutting the rope.[489] So I raised up his soul[490] so someone like this won't be swallowed up by sorrow."

2. Abba Betimios[491] said, "When I was going down to Scetis* one time, some people gave me some small apples to give to the elders. So I knocked on Abba Achilla's cell in order to give him some, but he said, 'The rule is, brother, that I don't want you knocking on the door for me at this time of day, even if it were manna[492] you were bringing—and don't leave and go to somebody else's cell.'[493]

"So I withdrew* to my cell and later brought them to church."[494]

3. [IV.10] Abba Achilla one time entered the cell of Abba Isaiah* in Scetis* and found him eating; he was putting salt and water in a small dish. When the elder saw Abba Isaiah hide the dish behind the rope he was plaiting, he said to him, "Tell me, what were you eating?"

---

489. *Quickly* here picks up *quickly* in Abba Achilla's response earlier to the third monk. Perhaps *quickly* here means "all too quickly." We're quickly cutting: SysAP X.18, we have quickly cut. Achilla is metaphorically speaking about cutting the rope that connects the sinful monk with them, that is, the community. Since a *schoiníon* is a rope used in sailing, holding a ship's boat in place, we can see it as a lifeline: if the monks cut it, they will set the sinful monk adrift, probably to drown. See Acts 27:32; perhaps not incidentally, and important for monastic understanding, Paul there talks of being "saved." Three major themes of early monasticism come together here: (1) all are sinners, (2) thou shalt not judge, and (3) pastoral care within community.

490. raised up: in the NT *diegeírō* usually means "to rouse" from sleep.

491. Betimios: Gk. *Bētímios*, which is a variant reading (PG 65:123–24, n. 73); the text has *Bētímēs*. An Abba Bétimos is in SysAP XX.3.1.

492. See Exod 16.

493. It is likely that Betimios has come during a time set aside for prayer and silence.

494. brought: *anaphérō* (English *anaphora*) can have the sense of an offering, as in a sacrifice, the eucharistic sacrifice (Lampe 127ab). The etymology of the word is "bring or carry up," as in bringing a sacrifice up the steps of a temple or a hill or mountain.

Abba Isaiah said, "Forgive me, abba. Earlier I was cutting palm branches and, when I came home in the scorching heat, I put a small piece of bread* in my mouth with some salt. My throat had gotten dry on account of the heat, and the bread* wouldn't go down. So I had to add a little water to the salt so I'd be able to eat it. But forgive me."

The elder said, "Come on, everyone! See Isaiah using sauce in Scetis!*495 If you [sing.] want sauce, go back to Egypt."*

4. [IV.9] A certain one of the elders visited Abba Achilla and observed him spitting blood from his mouth, so he asked him, "What's going on, father?"

The elder said to him, "It's what a brother is saying;*496 it's saddened me."497 "I struggled* not to report this to him. I begged God498 to take this away from me, and what the brother had said became like blood in my mouth,499 so I spat it out and found myself at peace,* and I forgot about my sorrow."

5. Abba Ammoës used to say, Abba Betimios and I went to visit Abba Achilla, and we heard him meditating* on this verse,* *Do not be afraid, Joseph, to go down to Egypt,*500 and he continued to meditate on this verse for a long time. When we knocked, he opened the door to us and asked, "Where are you from?"

495. sauce: *zōmón* phonetically and thematically picks up the earlier "small piece of bread," *psōmón* (M. Gk. *psōmí*), thus emphasizing the fault of turning a humble piece of bread into a wealthy person's sauce.

496. saying, *lógos*: "had said" below. A junior monk would often ask an elder, literally, "Give me a word," that is, say something spiritually profitable, offer instruction, so the brother here is offering an "anti-word" that has saddened Achilla. See Spiritual Guidance in the Glossary.

497. saddened, *lupéō*: or "injured," "angered" (Lampe 814a). See n. 520.

498. begged, *déomai* (*déō*): or "ask," "pray" (NRSV). The word occurs frequently in the NT of petitions to God; see Bauer 218a.

499. like blood in my mouth: SysAP IV.9, blood in my mouth.

500. Gen 46:3. This saying shows that monks would meditate on Scripture by saying the words aloud.

We were afraid to say "From Kellia,"* so we said "From the monastic community* of Nitria."*⁵⁰¹

He said, "What can I do for you, seeing that you live so far away?" and he led us inside. We discovered that he'd been working* the whole night, plaiting rope, and we asked him to say something edifying* to us.

He said, "From late in the evening until now I plaited twenty fathoms of rope and, naturally, I don't need that much.⁵⁰² But maybe God is annoyed or angry with me and is accusing me, saying, 'Why, when you're able to work,* don't you work?'*⁵⁰³ Therefore I toil and make rope with all my might."

Having benefited* from what he said, we left.*

6. Another time a great elder came to visit Abba Achilla from the Thebaid* and said to him, "Abba, I'm having to wage war* on your account."⁵⁰⁴

Abba Achilla said to him, "Go on! You, too, elder? You're now at war* because of *me*?"

The elder, out of humility,* said, "Yes, abba."

Now there was sitting there by the door an elder who was blind and unable to walk, and the elder said to Abba Achilla, "I wanted to stay a few days, but because of this elder I can't."⁵⁰⁵

When Abba Achilla heard this, he marveled* at the elder's humility* and said, "This isn't sexual temptation.* No, it's the jealousy of evil demons."*⁵⁰⁶

---

501. I am not sure what his statement means.

502. fathom: an *orguía* was a fathom, or about six feet, so about 120 feet of rope here.

503. annoyed or angry: *aganaktéō* can mean either, or both. It and "accuse," *enkaléō*, occur often in the NT.

504. The "war" may be about sexual temptation or sin; see below.

505. The Greek is ambiguous here. Who is speaking to Achilla? From context, presumably it is the "great elder" who has just come for a visit.

506. This saying, to say the least, is elliptical. Wortley, *Give Me*, 66 n. 20, rightly wonders if the text is corrupt.

Concerning Abba Ammoë / Ammoës[507]

1. [125] [XI.11][508] They used to say about Abba Ammoës that when he was headed for church he wouldn't allow his disciple to walk near him, but only at a distance, and if the disciple started to ask about thoughts,* as soon as he began to speak Abba Ammoës would quickly drive him away, saying, "I don't allow you near me,[509] because while we're talking about something beneficial* I don't want us to accidentally fall into extraneous conversation."[510]

2. [XI.12] In the beginning Abba Ammoës would say to Abba Aseo, "How do you see me right now?"[511]

He would say to him, "You're like an angel, father."

Sometime later Abba Ammoës would say to him, "Now how do you see me?"

He would say, "You're like Satan. Even if you say* something good and beneficial,*[512] I'll regard you as a long and wide Thracian sword."[513]

3. [IV.11][514] They used to say about Abba Ammoës that he lay ill for many years. While he was sick in bed he never allowed his

---

507. Gk. *Ammōé(s)*.

508. A version of this story occurs in the Life of John the Little 8 (pp. 77–78).

509. I don't allow you near me: SysAP XI.11, I don't allow you to spend time around me.

510. fall into: I have followed the variant reading, PG 65:125–26 n. 74, of *parempíptō*, which SysAP XI.11 also has, instead of the text's *enkúptō*, "to stoop, bend over, lean over (to look at something)" (Bauer 588c). Extraneous conversation: see Amoun 2.

511. Aseo, Gk. *Aséō*: the text has *Isaiah*; a variant reading, PG 65:125–26 n. 75, has *Aséō*, as does SysAP XI.12 (uniquely here in the SysAP). It is likely that *Aséō* got assimilated into the more common *Isaiah*.

512. say something good: AP Sys XI.12 lacks "good and," *agathós*.

513. The Thracian sword, *romphaía*, had a blade 60–80 cm (2–2.5 feet) long. In Rev 2:16 Christ says to John concerning the church in Pergamum, "Repent, then. If not, I will come to you soon and make war against them with the sword [*romphaía*] of my mouth." See Gen 3:24 LXX; Bauer notes that Philo of Alexandria (ca. 20 BCE–ca. 50 CE) uses *romphaía* "always of the angel's flaming sword after Gen 3:24" (907a).

514. See the Life of John the Little 28 (pp. 89–90).

[128] thoughts* to turn to the interior of his cell to see what was there.[515] (People would bring him a lot of things on account of his illness.) When his disciple John came in and out, Abba Ammoës closed his eyes so he wouldn't see what John was doing; he knew that John was a faithful* monk.

4. Abba Poemen said, "A brother came to visit Abba Ammoës, asking for spiritual guidance* from him. He stayed with the abba seven days, but the elder didn't respond. Walking him to the door, Abba Ammoës said to him, "Go, watch out* for yourself. At this point, my sins have become a darkened wall between me and God."[516]

5. They used to say about Abba Ammoës that he made fifty *artabas** of bread* for use at some time in the future and set it out in the sun.[517] Before it dried completely, he saw something done there[518] that was of no benefit* to him, so he said to his young servants,[519] "Let's go; we're leaving here."

515. to turn to, *proséchō*: or "be concerned about."

516. darkened: *skoteinós*, "dark," is the opposite of *phōteinós*, "shining, bright, radiant, full of light," like angels' clothing or a "bright cloud indicating the presence of God" (Bauer 931b); see Matt 6:23; Luke 11:34, 36. *Skoteinós* can metaphorically indicate blindness, even "dark, evil," of paganism, hell-fire, heresies, and the Devil (Lampe 1241b).

517. bread: *sítos* can also mean "grain," of wheat or barley. Ammoës is here putting grain out in the sun to dry, or fresh-baked bread that would dry into hard loaves that lasted for months, up to a year, that the monks would eat with salt by moistening it. In Lausiac History 22.6 (Wortley, p. 60) Antony brings out such loaves, "each about six ounces, and dampened one of them for himself (for they were dry), but three for Paul." See Bread, dried in the Glossary.

518. something done there, *prágma*: or "something there."

519. servants, *paidárion*: from *país*, "child" or "slave." I am very uncertain of this translation. *Paidárion* could indicate a young boy or slave, or a little boy, metaphorically a "babe" in the sense of one who is humble (Lampe 995b). Wortley, *Give Me*, 67, translates "his boys," but male monks were opposed to having young boys around (see Isaac, the Priest of Kellia 5); Ward, *Sayings*, 31, translates "his servants," which is more likely. In Attic Greek (Aristophanes, Xenophon) *paidárion* can mean "young slave"; see Bauer 1518 ("slave" and "servant" both translate Gk. *doúlos*). The word occurs only once in the SysAP; in XVIII.8.5 (Guy 3.48) a *paidárion* gives Abba Zeno, who may be having a vision, some bread and a jug of water.

This greatly saddened them. When he saw them so sad, he said to them, "Are you sad because of the bread?"*520 "Look, I've seen people fleeing* their homes or cells,521 leaving open cabinet doors with dusty shelves filled with books* made of parchment; they didn't even close the doors to the place but took off, leaving them wide open."

Concerning Abba Ammoun of Nitria*522

1. [128] [XVII.3] Abba Ammoun of Nitria went to visit Abba Antony and said to him, "I labor harder than you.523 Why is your name more renowned among people than mine?"

Abba Antony said to him, "Because I love God more than you."

2. [XI.56] They used to say about Abba Ammoun that he made a measure524 of barley meal and lived on it for two months.525 He went to visit Abba Poemen and said to him, "If I leave my cell

520. "Sad" and "saddened" here, *lupéō*, could be "angry" and "angered," but "be sad, grieve" is the primary meaning. See n. 497.

521. I have added "their homes or cells." The Wadi Natrun* suffered numerous barbarian* invasions.

522. Ammoun: Gk. *Ammoûn*. See "Ammoun" in Dramatis Personae.

523. A variant reading, PG 65:127–28 n. 79 and SysAP XVII.3, I see that I labor harder than you. Labor: literally "I have labor." *Kópos* is multivalent: "labor, work"; "distress, trouble, difficulty" (Bauer 558b–59a).

524. The text has two words for "measure," *métē* and *mátē*. I have followed the Latin translation *mensura*, "measure." *Mátē*, "folly, foolishness, madness," is not possible. *Métē* does not occur in the SysAP. It is possible that *métē* is a loan word from Latin *metior*, "to measure," *mensa*, etymologically related to Greek *mêtis* (Liddell and Scott 1130a; Michiel de Vaan, ed., *Etymological Dictionary of Latin and the Other Italic Languages* (Leiden: Brill, 2008), 377). I wish to thank Mark Lamas for this suggestion.

525. This sentence is not in SysAP XI.56. Barley, as opposed to wheat, was part of the poor person's diet, but Lucien Regnault, *The Day-to-Day Life of the Desert Fathers in Fourth-Century Egypt* (Petersham, MA: St. Bede's, 1999), 68–69, notes that "barley bread was not restricted to monks; in some areas there was no other kind. Even today [1990] barley bread isn't hard to find in Egypt."

and go to my neighbor's or he visits me with some need, we're cautious about speaking with one another, afraid that extraneous conversation might raise its head."[526]

The elder said to him, "You're [sing.] doing the right thing. Youths need protection."*

Abba Ammoun said to him, "So what did the elders formerly do?"

Abba Poemen said to him, "The elders who were advanced in the spiritual life never had anything unusual within or anything strange on their lips that they would say."[527]

"So, then, if there's a good reason," Abba Ammoun said, "to speak with my neighbor,* do you want me to talk about the Scriptures,* or the sayings of the elders?"

The elder said, "If you're not able to maintain silence, it's better to speak about the sayings of the elders and not Scripture.* No small danger lies with the latter."

3. [AnonAP 422] A brother came from Scetis* to see Abba Ammoun[528] and said to him, "My father's sending me to perform a ministry,[529] and I'm afraid of committing sexual sin."*

The elder said to him, "Any time temptation* comes upon you, say 'God of power* and might,[530] through the prayers* of my father deliver me.' "[531]

---

526. Extraneous conversation: see Ammoës 1.

527. strange, *xénos*, also "foreigner," translated "extraneous" earlier ("extraneous" < Lat. *extrāneus* "external, foreign"; Sp. *extraño*, "strange"); see nn. 245, 325.

528. Ammoun: AnonAP 422, *Anóphōr*, which probably represents Coptic *Onofer*, Latinized On(n)ophrius. He does not have any sayings in the AlphAP.

529. ministry, *diakonía*: it is possible that this ministry could be "ministering poor-relief" (Lampe 351a.II [bii]).

530. God of power and might, through the prayers of my father deliver me: AnonAP 422, God of my father, help me and deliver me. God of power and might, *dýnamis*: *dýnamis*, "power,* might, authority," is an important word in the NT; "God of power and might" occurs often: see Matt 22:29; Rom 1:16, 20.

531. deliver: AnonAP 422, help. Deliver, *exairéō*: Bauer amplifies the sense with NT meanings: "to deliver someone from peril or confining circumstances,

One day, then, a young woman[532] closed the door behind him,[533] and he cried out with a loud voice,[534] "God of my father! Deliver me!" And immediately he found himself on the road to Scetis.*

Concerning Abba Anoub[535]

1. [XV.12] [129] Abba John told this story: Abba Anoub and Abba Poemen and the rest of their brothers from the same womb[536] became monks in Scetis.* When the Mazices* came the first time and laid it waste,[537] the brothers withdrew* from there and[538] went to a place called Terenouthis* while they decided where they should stay. They remained there a few days in an old temple. Abba Anoub said to Abba Poemen, "As an act of love,* you and your brothers, each living by himself, will remain in contemplative quiet.* We won't meet with one another this week."

---

set free, deliver, rescue" (344a). In Acts 7, in his speech to the council Stephen uses this verb of God's speaking to Moses: "I have surely seen the mistreatment of my people who are in Egypt and have heard their groaning, and I have come down to rescue them" (Acts 7:34). Exod 3:8; 18:4, 8–10 have God "delivering" Israel.

532. young woman, *párthenos*: or "virgin," that is, an unmarried woman, or, possibly, a female monastic. See Woman in the Glossary.

533. That is, either after he had visited her, or after he entered her dwelling.

534. "Cried out" occurs numerous times in the NT and LXX and "cried out with a loud voice" often; Mark 15:34: *At three o'clock Jesus cried out with a loud voice, "Eloi, Eloi, lema sabachthani?" which means, "My God, my God, why have you forsaken me?"*

535. Gk. *Anoúb*. Hist Mon 11.5 (p. 88) has a saying by Abba Anouph, who may be the same person. The SysAP has only *Anoub*.

536. from the same womb: SysAP XV.12 lacks. It is likely that the editor here added the phrase to make it clear that the brothers were from the same family. Anoub was the eldest (CE 1983a–84b).

537. laid waste: *erēmóō* is ironic here. It is cognate with *érēmos*, "wilderness, desert,"* the locale sought by monks. The destruction took place in 407 (CE 1983a–84b). See Barbarians in the Glossary.

538. became . . . and: SysAP XV.12 lacks.

Abba Poemen said, "We'll do as you ask," and they did.

There was there in that very temple a stone statue dedicated to a god. When the elder Abba Anoub[539] would get up early in the morning he'd throw rocks at the statue's face, and every evening he would say to the statue, "Forgive me." And he did this every day of the week.

On the Sabbath,[540] they met together, and Abba Poemen said to Abba Anoub, "I saw you this week, abba, throwing stones at the face of the statue and later asking it for forgiveness.[541] Does a person of faith* do such things?"

The elder replied, "I did what I was doing for your [pl.] sake. When you [pl.] saw me throwing stones at the statue's face did it speak or get mad?"*[542]

Abba Poemen said, "No."

"And again, when I prostrated* myself to it, did it get upset* and say 'I don't forgive you'?"

Abba Poemen said, "No."

So the elder said, "So, as for us, aren't we seven brothers? If you [pl.] want us to live with one another, we need to be like this statue: whether it's mocked or praised, it doesn't get upset.[543] If you [pl.] don't want to live like that, look—there are four doors in this temple: each person can go where he wants."

They threw themselves to the ground and said to Abba Anoub, "We'll do what you want, father. We hear what you're telling us."

Abba Poemen said, "We lived with one another our whole time together, working* in accordance with what the elder had told*

---

539. the elder: following a variant reading, PG 65:129–30 n. 30; SysAP XV.12 lacks.

540. That is, Saturday; in M. Gk. *Sábbaton* is still the word for "Saturday." It was, and is, common for monks to gather on Saturday for a synaxis* and meal together in preparation for Sunday.

541. asking . . . for forgiveness: literally "making repentance* [*metánoia*]."

542. The negative *mế* at the beginning of the sentence expects "No" for an answer.

543. or praised: SysAP XV.12 lacks. See Antony 8.

us. He appointed one of us steward;* whatever the steward set before us, we ate. It wasn't possible for one of us to say 'Bring us something different this time,'[544] or say 'We don't want to eat this.'[545] And we did this the whole time we were together and we lived with inward stillness."*

2. [XI.7] Abba Anoub said, "Since that time when the name of Christ[546] was invoked over me,[547] nothing false has come out of my mouth."

Concerning Abba Abraham[548]

1. [129] [X.19] They used to say about a certain elder that he spent fifty years neither eating bread* nor drinking water.[549] They also used to say that he killed sexual temptation* and avarice and the need for self-importance.* Abba Abraham came to see him, having heard that he'd said this,[550] and [132] said to him, "Did you say* you did this?"[551]

He said, "Yes."

544. SysAP XV.12 lacks "us."

545. We: a variant reading, PG 65:129–30 n. 64 and SysAP XV.12, I.

546. Christ: SysAP XI.7, the Lord.

547. invoked, *kaléō, call*: compare English *called* to a ministry or vocation, a *calling*. Bauer notes that in the NT the passive form, as here, has an ontological sense: "*be named* thus approaches closely the meaning *to be*" (503a [d]). Patristic use confirms this understanding of a divine calling: God "called us from non-being and wanted us from non-being to be" (2 Clement 1.8); "the things that were not, through his own will, God called into being" (Athanasius, *Orationes tres adversos Arianos* (*Three Discourses against the Arians*) 2.22 (Lampe 696b).

548. Gk. *Abraám.*

549. Bread with salt, and water, made up the customary monastic diet.

550. he'd said this: SysAP X:19, he was saying this, which has a sharper edge.

551. The sentence begins with "You," not necessary in Gk., so we might translate the question "Did you *really* say?"

Abba Abraham said to him, "Suppose you go into your cell and find on your sleeping mat a woman.* Can you conclude* that the woman's* not there?"[552]

He said, "No, but I fight* against the thought* so I don't touch her."

Abba Abraham said, "So, in fact, you haven't killed the passion;* it's alive and well,[553] but it's being held in check. Let's say again that you're out walking;[554] you see some rocks and potsherds and, in their midst, gold. Is your thinking disposed to conclude* that they're one and the same?"[555]

He said, "No, but I fight* against the thought* that says 'Take it.' "

The elder said, "The passion,* in fact, is alive and well, but it's being held in check."[556]

Once again Abba Abraham spoke: "Let's say you hear about two brothers. One loves* you, and the other one hates you and slanders you. If the two come to see you, do you think of them the same way?"

He said, "No, but I fight* against the thought* so I can do good for the one who hates me as well as the one who loves* me."

552. A variant reading, PG 65:131–32 n. 87, has the negative *mḗ* at the beginning of the sentence that anticipates a negative answer; thus: "Can you really conclude?"

553. you haven't killed the passion: SysAP X.19, the passion hasn't died.

554. you're out walking: a variant reading, PG 65:131–32 n. 88 and SysAP X.19, you're walking along the road. *Road*, then, becomes symbolic because Gk. *hodós* translates as both "road" and "way." In John 14:6 Jesus says *I am the way* (*hodós*); thus an ancient could read Abraham's response as a parable: "you're walking Christ's way, but the passions are a constant temptation along the way."

555. thinking: *diánoia* here, rather than *logismós*. In Life of Antony 12.1–2 (p. 87) and 40.4 (p. 145) the Devil presents Antony with illusory gold in order to tempt him.

556. The passion, in fact, is alive and well: I have followed the variant reading, PG 65:131–32 n. 89 and SysAP X.19, rather than the text's "It's alive and well."

Abba Abraham said to him, "So, then, the passions* are alive and well, only they're held in check by the holy ones."*

2. A brother asked Abba Abraham, "If it happens that I eat often, what does this mean?"[557]

The elder replied, "What are you saying, brother? Why do you eat like this? Do you think you've walked onto a threshing floor?"[558]

3. Abba Abraham used to talk about a certain brother at Scetis:* He was a scribe, and he didn't eat bread.* A brother came and asked* him to copy a book* for him. So the elder, in doing so, and keeping his mind focused on contemplative quiet,* copied the text in rows without breaks between words.[559]

After the brother picked up the book,* wanting to separate the words he found some verses* missing. So he said to the elder, "There aren't any spaces between the words, abba."[560]

The elder said to him, "Go away. First, work on understanding what the words* of Scripture* are saying; then come back, and I'll copy the rest for you."

Concerning Abba Are[561]

1. [132] [XIV.3] Abba Abraham paid a visit to Abba Are, and while they were sitting together a brother came to see the elder. He said to Abba Are, "Tell me what I should do to be saved."*

The elder said to him, "Go, spend the year doing this: each evening, eat bread* and salt. Then come back, and I'll talk to you."

---

557. I eat often: a variant reading, PG 65:131–32 n. 92, I eat often, and a lot.

558. Apparently Abraham is likening the brother to, say, a cow or a donkey eating what's on a threshing-room floor.

559. *Scriptio continua*, continual text without spacing between words or punctuation, was the norm in Late Antiquity.

560. One would expect here instead, There are some verses missing, abba.

561. Greek *Arḗ*; SysAP *Arí*, the two pronounced the same in Late Antiquity.

So the brother left and did so. When a year was up, he went back to see Abba Are once again. It so happened that at that time Abba Abraham was there, and the elder spoke once again to the brother: "Go, and fast* every other day this year."

After the brother had gone, Abba Abraham said to Abba Are, "Why do you give all the brothers here a light yoke, and put such a heavy load on this brother?"562

The elder said to him, "The brothers here come seeking counsel,* but they leave exactly the way they come. [133] This brother, however, because of God, comes to hear something beneficial.* He works* hard at it. If I say something specific to him, he eagerly does it. Therefore, I tell him the word* of God."563

Concerning Abba Alonius564

1. [133] [XI.13] Abba Alonius said, "If a person doesn't say in his heart, 'I alone and God are in the world,' he won't have inward stillness."*

2. He also said, "If I hadn't torn everything down, I would not have been able to build myself up."

---

562. See Matt 11:28-30, where Jesus says *Come to me, all you who are weary and are carrying heavy burdens, and I will give you rest. Take my yoke upon you, and learn from me; for I am gentle and humble [*tapeinós*] in heart, and you will find rest [anápausis] for your souls. For my yoke is easy, and my burden is light [*elaphrós*].* The Greek words, or cognates, are the same as the ones in this saying. Further, Jesus uses what became two key monastic terms: *humble** and *rest* (see Inward stillness in the Glossary). In other words, Abraham is worried that Are here is contradicting Jesus.

563. word: *something beneficial* translates *lógos*, as does *word** in "the word of God." Greek, therefore, yokes *something beneficial* and *word*. Are is saying, "I speak the word of God to him and he finds it beneficial," that is, Are's word, unlike that of the brothers there, makes a difference in this brother's spiritual life.

564. Gk. *Alốnios*.

3. [XI.14] He also said, "If a person wants to, from dawn to dusk that person can reach God's level."[565]

4. One time Abba Agathon asked Abba Alonius, "How can I get hold of my tongue so I don't lie?"[566]

Abba Alonius said to him, "Even if you don't lie, you're going to commit a lot of sins."

He said, "How?"

The elder said to him, "Look, two people have committed murder, and you're an eyewitness. One has fled to your cell. And now here comes the magistrate, looking for him, and he asks you, " 'Were you an eyewitness to a murder?' If you don't lie, you're handing the person over to death.[567] Better to leave him standing before God without shackles. God knows everything."[568]

Concerning Abba Apphu[569]

1. [133] [XV.14] The story was told about a bishop*[570] of Oxyrhynchus*[571] by the name of Abba Apphu that when he was a monk he would practice numerous austerities.[572] When he be-

---

565. SysAP XI.14 lacks "from dawn," which must be a mistake. Reaching God's level—and not worrying about the level, or measure, of others—is an important monastic theme.

566. See Jas 1:26 and 3:1-8. Lie: *laléō pseudós*: or "speak falsely," and throughout.

567. handing . . . over: *paradídomai* means "hand over, turn over, give up a person into the custody of" (Montanari 761b–63b). In Luke 22:6 // Matt 26:16, Judas "hands over" Jesus (NIV) or "betrays" him (NRSV).

568. See Ps 44:21; Acts 15:8; 2 Esdr 15:26.

569. Gk. *Apphú*.

570. a bishop: Sys AP XV.14, a certain bishop.

571. As the cases of Apphu and Ammonas show, monks became bishops. See Bishop in the Glossary.

572. austerities, *sklēragōgía*: or "take on numerous hardships"; *sklērós*: "hard, austere, severe" (Liddell and Scott 1612ab). In Classical Gk., *sklēragōgía* means

came bishop,* he wanted to submit himself to the same practice of austerity, even while living in the world, but he wasn't able to do so.[573] So he threw himself before God, saying, "Because of the episcopacy, has grace* left me?"[574]

It was revealed to him: "No. No, back then there was the desert* without a person in sight, and God would come to your assistance; but now, there is the world,* and people are coming to your assistance."[575]

Concerning Abba Apollo[576]

1. [133] There was a certain elder at Kellia by the name of Apollo, and if someone even began to ask him to do some kind of work* or another, he would go off joyfully, saying, "Today I have Christ working* with me on behalf of my soul![577] He is the soul's reward."*[578]

"hardy training" (Lampe 1612a), tough training, a term applied to the Laconians in the southeastern Peloponnese, a region dominated at times by the Spartans.

573. wasn't able, *ischúō*: in the AlphAP, Greek usually uses *dúnamai* for "can, be able," but here it is *ischúō*, so the meaning could possibly be "wasn't strong enough." Lampe notes, though, that the verb can have both meanings (697b).

574. The sentence begins with two negatives at the beginning (*mὲ ára*), thus expecting an emphatically negative answer, something like Paul's "Heaven forbid!" or "By no means!" (*mế génoito*). Grace: a variant reading, PG 65:133–34 n. 96; and SysAP XV.14, your grace.

575. are coming to your assistance, *antilambánomai*: in Luke 1:54 God "has helped Israel," and in Acts 20:35 Paul tells the Ephesian elders that through work "we must support the weak, remembering the words of the Lord Jesus." In other words, people, like God, are helping the monk-bishop.

576. Gk. *Apollố*. See Apollo in Dramatis Personae.

577. have Christ working: in Gk., "With Christ" emphatically begins the sentence.

578. reward: *misthós* also means "pay," so Apollo receives both payment and reward for his soul. See AlphAP *Aïố*.

2. They used to say about Abba Apollo in Scetis* that he was once a rough shepherd from the countryside. When he saw a pregnant woman in the field one time, possessed[579] by the Devil he said, "I want to see how the baby's lying in her womb," so he tore her open and saw the baby. Immediately his heart gave him an order,* so, moved to repentance, he went to Scetis* and reported to the fathers what had happened.[580]

He heard them singing the Psalms:* *The days of our lives are seventy years / or perhaps eighty if we are strong; / even then* [135] *they are filled with toil and work.*[581] So he said to them, "I'm forty years old and I've never prayed,* not even once. Now, if I live another forty years, I'll never stop praying* to God to forgive me my sins." As a result, he never worked with his hands but was always praying,*[582] "As a human being, I have sinned; you, as God, forgive me,"[583] and this became his prayer,* his practice night and day.[584]

---

579. possessed: *energéō* can mean possession by demons;* see Justin, *1 Apology* 62.1 and Eusebius, *Ecclesiastical History* 5.168. The verb is almost always positive in the NT, as in miraculous powers or God being at work* (*erg-*); see Matt 14:2 and Mark 6:14. The horrible irony here is that, with the pre-monastic Apollo, "work"* (*érgon*), the backbone of the monastic life, becomes demonic. The saying reinforces, however, that even the demonic can receive forgiveness. See nn. 56, 178, 204, 292, 304.

580. reported: the irony here is that *anangéllō* in the NT can mean "proclaim, teach" (*euangéllō*: proclaim the good news, the Gospel) by the power of the Holy Spirit (1 Pet 1:12) and proclaim "that God is light and in him there is no darkness at all" (John 1:5). "Reported" is in the imperfect tense, telling us that it was not a one-and-done report, but that Apollo was confessing his sin to various abbas.

581. Ps 90:10 LXX 89:1. Toil and work: or "work and affliction."*

582. Monks prayed as they did handiwork in their cells; perhaps this statement means that Apollo did not work outside of his cell.

583. "Forgive" is 2nd-person singular imperative, command, and not 2nd-person singular present tense. Apollo is asking God to forgive him.

584. practice, *melétē*: see Meditation in the Glossary.

There was a brother staying with Abba Apollo, and he heard him saying "I've begged you, Lord, forgive me so I can find a little inward stillness,"* and he felt assured that God had forgiven him all his sins,[585] even the sin concerning the woman. With regard to the child, assurance was not given him. One of the elders said to him, "God has forgiven you even the sin concerning the child, but he's allowing you toil and affliction[586] because it's profitable for your soul."[587]

3. The same elder said this concerning hospitality* for fellow brothers: "We must respectfully welcome[588] brothers who come to visit us, because we're not welcoming them but rather God. If you've seen your brother," he said, "you've seen the Lord your God.[589] And this," he said, "we've received from Abraham.[590] And when you welcome brothers, you're sustaining them with inward stillness.* This we've learned from Lot, who prevailed on the angels to enter his home."[591]

---

585. "He" is ambiguous but, given what follows, must refer to Apollo.

586. toil and affliction: *pónos*, "pain, distress affliction" (Rev 21:4c: "mourning and crying and pain [*pónos*] will be no more"). It can also mean "work that involves much exertion or trouble, (hard) labor, toil" (Bauer 852ab). Since both meanings are apposite here, I have used two words for the translation.

587. Both "forgiven" and "allowing" translate *aphíēmi*, saying that, in our parlance, forgiving does not require forgetting.

588. welcome: *proskunéō* means more than just "welcome" (*déchomai* is the usual word for "welcome"*). For *proskunéō* Bauer has "to express in attitude or gesture one's complete dependence on or submission to a high authority figure, (fall down and) worship, do obeisance to, prostrate oneself before, do reverence to, welcome respectfully" (Bauer 882b–83a). The wise men "pay homage" to newborn Jesus (Matt 2:2); one "worships" God (John 4:21-22).

589. See 1 John 4:20-21.

590. The story of Abraham welcoming the three visitors (Gen 18:1-8) is the archetype of monastic hospitality.

591. See Gen 19:3. "Sustain" and "prevailed on" translate *parabiázomai*, "force, prevail on, urge, strengthen, bolster" (Lampe 1008a).

Concerning Abba Andrew[592]

[136] [XI.120][593] Abba Andrew used to say, "These three things are appropriate for the monk: solitude and isolation* from the world,* voluntary poverty,* and patient* silence."[594]

Concerning Abba Aïö[595]

[136] They used to say about a certain elder in the Thebaid,* Abba Antonius, that he performed many ascetic practices* in his youth. In his old age he got weak and became blind, and the brothers, because of his weakness, would provide him with numerous physical comforts* and would even put food in his mouth.

Abba Aïö asked about this: "What becomes of all this care and comfort?"* So he told them, "I'm telling you, if a person's heart wants such comfort,* and he gladly agrees to it, if he eats a single date, God removes it from his labor,[596] and[597] if he doesn't agree to it and doesn't want to eat it,[598] God watches over and protects

---

592. Gk. *Andréos.*

593. Andrew is not named in SysAP XI.120.

594. Instead of "patient silence," literally "silence with / in patience," SysAP XI.120 has "silence with sober-mindedness" (*népsis*). *Népsis* does not occur in the NT, but its cognate verb *néphō* does; 1 Thess 5:6 fits a monastic context: "But since we belong to the day, let us be sober [*népsis*], and put on the breastplate of faith and love, and for a helmet the hope of salvation." Both are common in the SysAP (Guy 3.384–85).

595. Gk. *Aï.*

596. labor: *kópos* can mean "work, labor, toil," and also "distress, trouble, difficulty" (Bauer 558b–59a). The meaning one chooses significantly affects the import of the sentence. I take it to mean that if Antonius eats even a single date, God lightens his labor or distress.

597. and: or "but" (*dé*).

598. doesn't want: or "refuses."

his labor, keeping it safe and sound,[599] because he refuses to be forced to accept it. So, they have their reward."*[600]

Concerning Abba Ammonatha[601]

1. [136] A certain magistrate came one time to Pelusium* wanting to demand a head tax from the monks, just as he did from those living in the world.* As a result, all the brothers gathered together with Abba Ammonatha about the situation, and they voted to send certain fathers to the emperor. So Abba Ammonatha said to them, "There's no need to go to such trouble. No, instead, stay in your cells and keep contemplative quiet,* fast for two weeks, and by the grace* of Christ I'll take care of the matter myself."

So the brothers left, each to his own cell. [137] The elder also kept contemplative quiet* in his own cell.

When the fourteen days were up, therefore, the brothers became unhappy with the elder because they hadn't seen any movement at all from him, so they said, "The elder hasn't done a thing about our situation."[602] On the fifteenth day the brothers gathered together as they'd agreed, and the elder came and joined them, holding the imperial rescript signed and sealed by the emperor.

599. safe and sound, *sôs*: as in English *safe* and *save*, the adjective *sôs* is cognate with *sózō*, "to save." Gk. has the additional meaning of "healthy"; compare the English cognates *whole, healthy, heal*—and *holy*, as in William Byrd's hymn "I Have Longed for Thy Saving Health."

600. have . . . reward, *misthós*: see Apollo 1 and 1 Cor 9:17; Matt 5:46; 6:1. Aïṓ's final words suggest that whether or not Antonius eats the date, the brothers, with their good intentions, have their reward.

601. Gk. *Ammōnathá*.

602. done: *katergéō*: the root *–erg* is that of work,* so Ammonatha is, they believe, working against (*kat-* from *katá*) the brothers.

When the brothers saw it, they were astonished*[603] and said, "When did you bring this, abba?!"

The elder said, "Believe me, brothers: this very night I went to the emperor and he wrote the imperial rescript. So I went to Alexandria,* where I had it undersigned by the magistrates. And so I came back to you."

When they heard this, they were afraid,* and prostrated* themselves. So the matter was resolved, and the magistrate didn't bother them again.

---

603. astonished: the gospel writers often use *exhístēmi* to express astonishment or amazement* at Jesus and the miracle he has just done; see Matt 12:23; Mark 5:42; 12:2; Luke 8:56. Thus the saying here is likening Ammonatha to Jesus and, perhaps, the brothers with their lack of faith to the doubters in the gospels.

Chapter 2

B / Bêta / B

Concerning Basil the Great[1]

1. [137][2] One of the elders used to say that Saint Basil was visiting a cenobium.* After offering appropriate instruction, he said to the superior of the monastery, "Do you have a brother here who is obedient?"*

The superior said to him, "All your servants here are eager* to be saved,* master."*

Once again he said to him, "Do you, in fact, have someone who is obedient?"*

---

1. Gk. *Basileíos*. See Basil in Dramatis Personae.

2. Bracketed Arabic numerals before the sayings indicate the alphabetical *Apophthegmata Patrum* (AlphAP) in Migne's edition (PG 65:75–440). Bracketed Roman numerals followed by Arabic numerals (e.g., XII.3) identify the chapter and saying number in the systematic *Apophthegmata Patrum* (SysAP) (Jean-Claude Guy, ed., *Les Apophtegmes des Pères: Collection Systématique* [Paris: Cerf, 2013]). Other references in the work to Guy's edition (for example, Guy 3.219) give the volume and page number of the citation. AnonAP references come from the anonymous *Apophthegmata Patrum,* from John Wortley, trans., *The Anonymous Sayings of the Desert Fathers: A Select Edition and Complete English Translation* (Cambridge: Cambridge University Press, 2013). For a complete list of abbreviated entries, see Abbreviations (pp. xix–xxiii).

The superior brought him a brother, and Saint Basil had him wait on tables at breakfast. After they'd eaten, the brother made preparations for Saint Basil to wash up, and Saint Basil said to him, "Come, and I will make preparations for you to wash up." The brother consented to have Saint Basil pour water over his hands.

The saint said to him, "When I enter the sanctuary,³ come with me, and I will make you a deacon."*

After this had taken place, Saint Basil made him a priest because of his obedience* and took him with him to the episcopal residence.⁴

Concerning Abba Bessarion⁵

1. [137] [XIX.1] Abba Doulas, the disciple of Abba Bessarion, used to say, We were walking one time along the seashore. I got thirsty and said to Abba Bessarion, "Abba, I'm really thirsty."

So the elder offered a prayer* and said to me, "Drink from the sea," and the water had become sweet, so I drank it. With the flask I had, I got some water from the sea so I wouldn't get thirsty after we'd left there. When the elder saw this, [140] he said to me, "Why did you get water?"

I said to him, "Forgive me. So I won't get thirsty after we leave."

The elder said, "God is here, and God is everywhere."⁶

---

3. sanctuary: the *hierateîon* is the domain of the priest and other clergy; hence the word is cognate with *hieratía*, "priesthood"; *hierateúō*, "be a priest, function as one"; and *hieratikós* (English *hieratic*), "belong to the hierarchy, priestly, sacerdotal" (Lampe 609ab). Thus Basil's going into the sanctuary foreshadows what is soon to come.

4. For the biblical background and foreground to this story, see Matt 26:6-13 // Mark 14:3-9 // Luke 7:36-50 (a woman washes Jesus' feet); John 12:1-8 (Mary anoints Jesus' feet); and John 13:1-17 (Jesus washes the disciples' feet).

5. Gk. *Bisaríōnos*; variant readings: *Bēsaríonos* and *Bēssaríonos*.

6. Why did you get water? . . . The elder said: SysAP XIX.1 lacks.

2. [XIX.2][7] Another time, when he needed something, he offered a prayer* and crossed the Chrysoroa River on foot and crossed to the other side.[8] I was astonished.* I prostrated* myself before him, saying, "What did your feet feel like to you when you walked in the water?"

The elder said, "I could feel the water up to my ankles but otherwise it felt as though I were walking on solid ground."

3. [XIX.3] Another time, once again when we were going to see a certain elder,[9] the sun began to set. Praying,* the elder said, "I beg you, Lord, stop the sun until I reach your servant.'[10] And so it happened."

4. [XII.3, XX.1][11] Another time I again went inside his cell and found him standing in prayer* with his hands stretched out to heaven.[12] He remained there, praying* like that for fourteen days.[13] Afterwards, he called out to me and said to me, "Follow* me."

So, leaving the cell, we went out into the desert. When I got thirsty I said, "Abba, I'm thirsty." The elder took my sheepskin cloak* and went about a stone's throw away; after he offered a prayer,* he brought it back to me, filled with water.[14]

[XX.1][15] Walking on, we came down to a certain cave; going inside, we found a certain brother sitting and working,* plaiting rope. He just shook his head and refused to greet us; he refused

7. Sayings 2–5 continue with Abba Doulas telling stories about Bessarion.

8. See Matt 14:22-33 // Mark 6:45-52 // John 6:15-21.

9. A variant reading, PG 65:139–40 n. 5 and SysAP XIX.3: another (elder).

10. See Josh 10:1-15, esp. 12b–14.

11. Saying 4 melds together SysAP XII.3 and XX.1. Jean-Claude Guy divides Bessarion 4 into 4a and 4b (Guy 3.219). I have chosen to keep it as one saying and have noted the interfaces between XII.3 and XX.1. See n. 15.

12. This is the usual way monks prayed.

13. Fourteen days (the Sabbath number doubled) is often significant in the Bible: Exod 12:6, 8; Lev 23:5; Num 9:11; Ezek 45:21; Acts 27:33.

14. SysAP XII.3 continues here with a / the story about their going to Lykos to see Abba John (see below).

15. SysAP XX.1 begins here with "Abba Doulas told this story" and tells the story about the monk in the cave.

even to say a word us. So the elder said to me, "Let's go. Maybe the elder isn't confident enough to speak with us."

So[16] we continued on the road to Lykṓ[17] until we came to Abba John.[18] After we greeted him, we prayed* together. Then they sat down in order to discuss the vision* he'd had: Abba Bessarion said, "A decree has come forth to pull down the temples,"[19] and that's what happened. They were torn down."[20]

[21]As we headed back, we came once again to the cave where we'd seen the brother, so the elder said to me, "Let's go inside to visit him; maybe God's given him the confidence* to speak with us." So we went inside and found him dead, so [141] the elder said to me, "Come on, brother, let's wrap his body. This is why God sent us here."

As we were wrapping the body in order to bury it, we found that the brother was in fact a woman!* The elder was amazed* and said, "See how even women*[22] wrestle and pin Satan while we in the cities disgrace ourselves with our reprehensible behavior!" So, after giving glory to God, who protects those who love him, we left* there.[23]

5. [XIX.4] One time a person possessed* by a demon* came to Scetis.* The monks prayed* for him in church, but the demon* wouldn't come out. It was a particularly merciless one.[24] The

---

16. So: a variant reading, PG 65:139–40 n. 5 and SysAP XX.1: We left there.

17. *Lykṓ*: that is, Lycopolis.* To, *eis*: or "into."

18. John of Lycopolis.* Until we came to Abba John: SysAP XX.1, in order to visit Abba John.

19. On the Serapeum see Theophilus 3 and Epiphanius 1.

20. Then they sat down. . . . They were torn down: SysAP XX.1 lacks; the sentence is in XII.3.

21. SysAP XX.1 resumes now.

22. even women: or "women also."

23. protects, *hyperaspistḗs*: *Psalms of Solomon* 7:7 LXX uses the word of God, and *1 Clement* 45.7 uses *hyperaspistḗs* of God, "protector, champion" (Lampe 1438a).

24. merciless: *sklērós* can mean "hard, difficult," as in "hard to drive out" (Bauer 930ab). Both meanings apply here. *Shepherd of Hermas* (2nd cent.) 12.5.1: *sklērós* in referring to the Devil.

clergy were saying, "What are we going to do about this demon?*
No one's able to cast him out except Abba Bessarion, and if we
appeal* to him,[25] he's not going to enter the church. So, let's do
this! Abba Bessarion comes to the church early, before everyone
else. Let's have this fellow who's suffering sleep[26] in the abba's
place and, when he comes in, we'll stand for prayer* and say to
him, 'Wake the brother up, abba.' "

They did exactly that. When the elder came at dawn, they stood
for prayer* and said to him, "Wake the brother up,"[27] and the elder
said to him, "Get up! Leave him and get out!"[28] Immediately the
demon* left him, and the brother was healed from that time on.

6. [VII.4] Abba Bessarion said, "For forty days and nights I
stood in the middle of thorns, without sleeping."[29]

7. [IX.2] A certain brother who had sinned was removed from
the church by the priest. Abba Bessarion stood up and left with
him,[30] saying, "I'm a sinner, too."[31]

8. The same Abba Bessarion said, "For forty years I didn't lay
myself down to sleep but slept sitting or standing."[32]

---

25. appeal to him: a variant reading, PG 65:141–42 n. 8 and SysAP XIX.4,
continues with "concerning this" or "concerning him."

26. sleep, *koimáomai* (English *cemetery*): a variant reading, PG 65:141–42 n.
9, has the similar-sounding *kathízomai*, which means "sit," but also "dwell, live,"
as in a cell or monastery. Thus the variant reading is "Let's have this fellow who's
suffering dwell in the abba's place," that is, "stay in the abba's cell."

27. Wake the brother up: SysAP XIX.4, Wake up the brother, abba.

28. Leave him and get out: the NT often uses *exérchomai* "of spirits that come
or go out of a person"; see Mark 1:25; 5:8, and others. See Bauer 348a.

29. Forty: see Gen 7–8 (Noah and the ark); Exod 16:35 (the exodus from
Egypt); Exod 34:28; Amos 2:10; Mark 1:13; Acts 1:3; and many others. See
Bessarion 8.

30. left with, *synérchomai*, literally "go / come together." This is ironic. The
verb usually means "come together, assemble, meet" (Lampe 1324b), as in church,
so Bessarion and the brother are together forming an "anti- or extra-church," and
the monks are, so to speak, coming apart ("apart," the opposite of *syn-*, as in
sympathy ["suffer with"], Lat. *cum* [Sp. *con*], as in *community*).

31. I'm a sinner, too (*kaí*): or "Even [*kaí*] I am a sinner."

32. forty: see Bessarion 6 and n. 29.

9. The same elder said, "When you find yourself at peace* and not at war,* that's especially the time to be humble* so that some extraneous joy[33] doesn't come along with it so that we brag[34] about it and get handed over to warfare.* Oftentimes, on account of our weaknesses,* God won't allow us to be handed over to warfare;[35] otherwise, we'd be lost."

10. A brother living together with the brothers asked Abba Bessarion, "What should I do?"[36]

The elder said to him, "Maintain silence* and don't think too highly of yourself."[37]

11. [XI.15] When Abba Bessarion was dying, he would say, "The monk should be like the cherubim and seraphim, all eyes."[38]

12. [XV.116] [AnonAP 565][39] Abba Bessarion's disciples related that his life[40] took place in this manner: he always lived like the birds of the air or the fish in the sea or the animals that walk

---

33. extraneous, *allótrios*: "alien, foreign," of apostates and heretics, and / or "alien," as in *alienated from* (Lampe 77ab).

34. brag, *kaucháomai*: or "boast." The verb occurs often in Paul, both positively (1 Cor 1:31b; 2 Cor 10:17b), and negatively (Gal 6:13; 2 Cor 5:12) (Bauer 536b).

35. handed over to warfare: text "handed over," *paradídōmi*; I have followed the variant reading, PG 65:141–42 n. 11. See Hand on in the Glossary.

36. Often the question is "What should I do to be saved?" (see Abba Biare), which may be implicit here.

37. don't think too highly, *metréō*: literally "measure," joined with a reflexive pronoun as here, "yourself," means "size oneself up," "esteem oneself highly," which can lead to *kenodoxía*, self-importance* (Lampe 866b). The irony here is that an important monastic desire is literally "to reach the measure [*métron*] of God," be free of sins and the passions,* like God; see Alonius 3.

38. See Rev 4:6, 8.

39. The vocabulary and syntax of this saying are clearly more complex than most sayings, like those of the sayings and stories attributed to Syncletica; hers are drawn from a Life of Syncletica, so perhaps the saying comes from a Life or other work, as the saying's narrative structure suggests. This long story has fairy-tale qualities and gathers power as it progresses until Bessarion becomes an ancient version of the Ancient Mariner of Coleridge's poem "The Rime of the Ancient Mariner" (1834).

40. life: *bíos*, physical life, rather than *politeía*, the monastic term for "way of life."

the earth, untroubled and free from worry, all the days of his life.[41] He had no cares or concerns concerning a home, [144] nor did it seem that his soul's desire was to be lord and master over various properties or have an overabundance of luxuries[42] or acquire[43] houses or have the distractions of books.*

Yes, it seemed that he was completely free of all the bodily passions,* nourished by the hope* of things to come,[44] safe inside the stronghold of faith;* he would remain as steadfast as a prisoner here or there,[45] enduring cold and nakedness, being roasted by the scorching flame of the sun,[46] always in the open air. Pushing himself into the crags of the desert like a person who's lost, he took great delight in having himself carried along through uninhabited sandy expanses, like a person being tossed about in the sea.

If he happened to come to milder regions, where the monks had a similar way of life and lived a life in common,[47] he would sit weeping outside the gates, wailing like some castaway stranded by shipwreck.[48] Then, when one of the brothers came out and found him like this, Abba Bessarion would sit like a beggar, one of the world's* poor;* drawing near, the monk, feeling compassion,*[49]

---

41. These opening lines are similar to the first lines about Abba Serapion in SysAP XV.16; SysAP XV.16 is not in the AlphAP.

42. luxuries, *truphḗ*: a variant reading, PG 65:143–44 n. 12 has the similar-sounding *trophḗ*, "food(s)."

43. acquire: using the variant reading, PG 65:143–44 n. 13, *ktḗsis* (cognate with *ktáomai*, "own, possess"), "possession,"* rather than the homophone *ktísis*, "creation, creature."

44. See Heb 11:1.

45. It looks as though the author is comparing Bessarion to Moses in Heb 11:23-28, with some of the same language; see also Paul as a prisoner (Acts 23:18; Eph 3:1; Phil 1:1, 9).

46. See 2 Cor 11:27; Heb 11:38.

47. life in common, *koinós ho bíos*: *koinós* + *bíos* came to form *koinóbion*, *cenobium*,* where the monks lived in a more-regulated community.

48. This foreshadows what Bessarion tells a monk later.

49. feeling compassion, *eleinṓs*: or "pity." A number of important words in the NT are cognate, as here, with *éleos*, "kindness or concern for someone in need, mercy, compassion, pity, clemency"; *eleéō*, "have compassion, pity, mercy";

would say to him, "Why are you weeping, friend?[50] If you're in need of certain necessities, you'll have them, as we're able—only, come on in and share in our common table, obtaining some comfort and consolation."[51]

But he would reply, "I can't remain under a roof until I find my house and possessions,"* saying, "Many of my goods and a lot of my money were lost in various ways: I fell among pirates and suffered shipwreck.[52] I lost my noble birth and have gone from being esteemed and honored to being disgraced and dishonored."[53]

The brother, feeling miserable at what the fellow had said,*[54] went back inside the monastery, brought out some bread,* and offered it to him, saying, "Take this, father. God will remain steadfast, providing you again with the things you spoke about: homeland and family and wealth."[55]

But Bessarion still continued to grieve, all the more so, and, loudly gnashing his teeth,[56] cried out, "I don't know if I'll be able to find what I've lost and am looking for.[57] Nevertheless, all the

---

eleēmosúnē, "alms, charitable giving"; and *eleḗmos*, "merciful, sympathetic, compassionate" (Bauer 315b–16b). The Kyrie begins "Kyrie eleison," "Lord, have mercy [or: compassion]."

50. friend: literally "human being, person," *ánthrōpos*.

51. share in: *koinonéō* is cognate with *koinós*, "common, communal," earlier in the saying.

52. fell, *peripíptō*: in Luke 10:30 Jesus tells the parable ("The Good Samaritan") about the person who "fell [*peripíptō*] into the hands of brigands" (my trans.).

53. disgraced and dishonored: see shame.* Is this saying a parable about humanity's fallen state, the existential anguish of the human condition? I find it deeply moving.

54. feeling miserable: the Gk. has one word, *schetliázō*; the verb means "to complain, protest, be indignant"; I have taken "lamented" from the cognates *schetliásis* and *schétlios*, "unfortunate, unlucky, wretched, miserable" (Bauer 2069b).

55. The monk's response echoes what happens with Job (Job 42). Are these parabolic goods?

56. See Matt 8:12; 13:42, 50.

57. find . . . lost: see the story of the prodigal son in Luke 15:11-32; the same Gk. words for "lost" and "find / found" occur in v. 32.

more, I'll still give thanks,* always being in danger, each and every day, until death,[58] without relief from my immeasurable misfortunes. I have to continually wander here and there, until I finish my course."[59]

Concerning Abba Benjamin[60]

1. [144] Abba Benjamin used to say: "When we came down from the harvest to Scetis,* an offering[61] was brought to us from Alexandria*—for each person a jar with a pint of oil, sealed with plaster. When the time for the harvest came around again, if there was some oil left over the brothers would bring it to church. I did, too. I hadn't opened my jar but, piercing the jar with a needle, would pour out a little. My heart was bursting with pride at this great thing I'd done.[62] But when the brothers brought their own jars, still unopened, and with mine having been pierced, I found myself[63] filled with shame,* like someone who had sinned sexually."*

2. [IV.12] Abba Benjamin, the priest of Kellia,* said, "We went to visit a certain elder in Scetis* and wanted to bring him a little oil.[64] He said to us, 'Look where the small jar of oil you brought me three years ago is sitting. Once you put it there, there it remained.'

---

58. for always being in danger . . . until death: this is a common monastic topos.

59. *Wander* earlier translates the simplex *planáō* (English *planet*); here Gk. uses the compound verb *apoplanáō*, literally "wander away from" (*apó*), so I have added "here and there" so the compound verb intensifies the simplex.

60. Gk. *Beniamín.*

61. offering, *karpophoría*: "fruit-bearing," a "gathering of fruit," then an offering or sacrifice brought forward (*phérō*). So the word chimes nicely with "harvest." In *karpophoría*, *phor*- is cognate with *phérō*, "bear, bring."

62. That is, his moderation, even frugality.

63. I found myself, *heuréthēn* < *heurískō* (English *heuristics* and *eureka*): or "I was found."

64. SysAP IV.12 lacks "a little."

"When we heard this, we marveled* at the elder's way of life."*

3. The same elder said, "We went to visit another [145] elder; he prevailed on us to eat with him and served us some radish oil. So we said to him, 'Father, serve us instead a little oil we can use.'⁶⁵

"When he heard us, he crossed himself, saying, 'If there's some other oil besides this, I don't know what it is.' "

4. Abba Benjamin spoke to his sons⁶⁶ when he was dying: "Do these, and you can be saved:* rejoice always, pray* without ceasing, in every situation give thanks."⁶⁷

5. [VII.5] The same elder said, "Take the King's Highway, count the milestones, and you won't get discouraged."⁶⁸

Concerning Abba Biare⁶⁹

Someone asked Abba Biare, "What do I need to do to be saved?"*

He said to him, "Go, make your belly small and your handiwork great, and do not be troubled* as you sit in your cell. Do this, and you'll be saved."

---

65. That is, oil they would dip their bread* in. The Syriac here has *sweet oil* instead of *oil*, showing that the radish oil is inferior (Budge, *Paradise*, 23).

66. That is, monks, disciples.

67. See 1 Thess 5:16-18.

68. count the milestones, and you won't get discouraged: SysAP VII.5, and count the milestones. King's Highway, *basilikè hodós*: in Num 20:14-17 Moses asks Edom, after the people have come from captivity in Egypt, for permission to pass through the land, "we will go along the King's Highway" (17), but is refused (a variant tradition, Deut 2:1-8, has them marching through Edom); see also Num 21:22. In *De ecclesiastica theologica* 1.8, Eusebius* says "Therefore, the Church of God correctly expounds the King's Highway, while it rejects as unsuitable deviant paths." Lampe notes that the phrase can mean "the way of the Lord," and that "King" is used for "Christ" (292a–93a).

69. Gk. *Biarḗ*.

Chapter 3

G / Gámma / Γ

Concerning Gregory the Theologian[1]

1. [145][2] [I.3] [AnonAP 3][3] Abba Gregory[4] said, "These three things God demands from every person who has been baptized:[5] correct faith* from the soul,* truth from the tongue,[6] and good judgment and self-control* from the body.[7]

2. He also said, "The whole life of the person who labors with spiritual longing and desire is a single day."

---

1. Gk. *Grēgórios.*

2. Bracketed Arabic numerals before the sayings refer to the column numbers in the alphabetical *Apophthegmata Patrum* (AlphAP) in the Migne edition, PG 65:75–440.

3. Bracketed Roman numerals followed by Arabic numerals (e.g., XII.3) identify the chapter and saying number in the systematic *Apophthegmata Patrum* (SysAP) (Jean-Claude Guy, ed., *Les Apophtegmes des Pères: Collection Systématique* [Paris: Cerf, 2013]). Other references in the work to Guy's edition (for example, Guy 3.219) give the volume and page number of the citation. AnonAP references come from the anonymous *Apophthegmata Patrum*, from John Wortley, trans., *The Anonymous Sayings of the Desert Fathers: A Select Edition and Complete English Translation* (Cambridge: Cambridge University Press, 2013). For a complete list of abbreviated entries, see Abbreviations (pp. xix–xxiii).

4. Abba Gregory: SysAP I.3, Blessed Gregory.

5. has been baptized: literally "holds baptism."

6. See Jas 3.

7. good judgment and self-control, *sōphrosúnē*: see 1 Tim 2:9, 15.

Concerning Abba Gelasius[8]

1.[9] [145] [XVI.2] They used to say about Abba Gelasius that he had a book* made of parchment worth eighteen gold *aurei*;* it contained the complete Old and New Testaments. It lay in the church where any brother who wanted to could read it. A certain brother, a stranger* to the community, came to visit the elder. When he saw the book,* he coveted it,[10] so he stole it and took off. The elder, however, although he knew about the theft, didn't go after him in order to seize him.[11] So that fellow[12] went off to the city,[13]

---

8. Gk. *Gelásios*. See Gelasius in Dramatis Personae. The stories here have a more complex syntax and greater vocabulary than most sayings. See the first sentence in Gelasius 4, whose syntax I have rendered as the Greek has it.

9. This long tale seems to be Christian(ized) folk wisdom. The use of a recurring word linguistically intensifies the story. See the notes below.

10. coveted: *epithuméō*, "strongly desire," can also mean sexually lust after, so one could translate here "lusted after it"; see Walter Bauer, *A Greek-English Lexicon of the New Testament and Other Early Christian Literature*, ed. Frederick William Danker, W. F. Arndt, and F. W. Gingrich, 2nd ed. [Chicago: University of Chicago Press, 1979], 372b) (= Bauer). The use of *epithuméō* here has deep biblical resonance. In the Ten Commandments, Exod 20:17ab and Deut 5:21ab, "You shall not covet your neighbor's house; you shall not covet your neighbor's wife, or male or female slave, or ox, or donkey, or anything that belongs to your neighbor," the LXX uses *epithuméō*. In Matt 5:27-28 Jesus says, "You have heard that it was said, 'You shall not commit adultery.' But I say to you that everyone who looks at a woman with lust [*epithuméō*] has already committed adultery with her in his heart." In Acts 20:33 Paul tells the Ephesians, "I coveted [*epithuméō*] no one's silver or clothing."

11. in order to seize him: SysAP XVI.2 lacks. Seize: *katalambánō* can mean "arrest," so another translation could be "in order to have him arrested."

12. fellow: *ekeínos* means "that person," "that guy," so here and below the brother, now a thief, is no longer a "brother," *adelphós*, as he was when he first came to the monastery. *Ekeínos* can "refer to well-known or notorious personalities" (Bauer 302a).

13. Many sayings have monks going off to the city to sell their wares, but the city was also the epicenter of the world,* where monks faced temptation. So this monk, by his actions, is an anti-monk, even a parody of a monk, going to the city not to sell his simple wares but to proffer what he has purloined.

where he was looking to sell it.[14] When he found someone who wanted to buy it, he demanded[15] sixteen *aurei** as its price. The person who wanted to buy it said to him, "First give it to me; I'll appraise it so I can make you an offer regarding its price." So he gave it to him.

The potential buyer took it and brought it to Abba Gelasius for appraisal, telling him the amount the person who wanted to sell it had asked. The elder said, "Buy it. It's a good book,* and worth the price he was asking."[16] The person went[17] and told the seller a different story than what the elder had told him: "Look, I showed it to Abba Gelasius and he told me that what you're asking is too much. The book's* not worth the price you're asking."

When that fellow heard this, he said to him, "The elder didn't say anything else to you?"

He said, "No."

Then the brother said, "I don't want to sell it anymore."[18]

So, his conscience pricked,* he went[19] to the elder and repented, begging him to take the book* back, but the elder refused.

14. *Came, took off,* and *went off* translate three different iterations of the aorist past tense of *érchomai,* "to go, come." Thus the monk *came* to the monastery, stole from the monastery, *took off,* and *went* to the city to sell his thievery. His actions trample on the monastery's hospitality,* a grievous monastic sin. See nn. 17 and 19.

15. demanded, *aitéō:* or "asked," but the verb is the same as in Gregory 1 where he lists what God demands.

16. he is: I have used the variant reading of AlphAP XVI.2 and the reading of SysAP XVI.2 instead of the text's "you are" (sing.).

17. went: *elthṓn,* "having gone," is the aorist active participle of *érchomai* (see nn. 14, 19), which linguistically connects the potential buyer's mendaciousness and greed with the brother's equally bad behavior.

18. Now "that fellow," "his conscience pricked" (see the next sentence), is again a "brother."

19. went: *élthe* is the aorist past tense of *érchomai* (see nn. 14 and 17), thus his going is now redemptive.

Then the brother said, "If [148] you won't take it back, I won't have any peace or rest."[20]

The elder said to him, "If you won't be at peace—look, I'm taking it back."

So that brother[21] remained with Abba Gelasius until his death. He benefited* from the elder's monastic practice.[22]

2. A cell and the land around it was left one time to this Abba Gelasius by an old man who was also a monk and had a dwelling near Nicopolis.* A certain vine dresser in the employ of Bakatos[23] (at that time the chief magistrate of Nicopolis* in Palestine), a relative of the old monk who had died, approached this same Bakatos and demanded to have this property because, in very truth,[24] by law it ought to come to him. He,[25] being greedy,[26] tried to seize the land by force from Abba Gelasius.[27] Refusing to hand over a monastic cell to someone living in the world,* this same Abba Gelasius wouldn't concede the property.

20. peace or rest, *anápausis*, which I usually render "inward stillness."*

21. that brother: the text has *ekeínos*, "that person," but a variant reading has *ekeî*, "there"; SysAP XVI.2, "brother." *Ekeínos* and *ekeî* show textual confusion. Because of this and because the story has twice recently used *brother* to signal the monk's transformation from sinner to repentant and *that person* back to *brother*, I have followed the reading of SysAP XV.2. See n. 12.

22. practice: *ergasía* is cognate with *érgon*, "work."*

23. Bakatos: Gk. *Bakátos*. I have not been able to find information on him, so he may be a non-historical character.

24. in very truth: *déthen* is decidedly ambiguous. It has the meaning translated, but it can also mean "on the pretext that." Montanari 473ab says the word is "frequently ironic."

25. "He" is ambiguous, but below it becomes clear that Bakatos is the villain.

26. greedy, *drástēs*: Lampe 387b, citing this passage, gives "violent," but the cognate verb *drássomai* means "grasp, take hold of, take a handful" (Montanari 554a).

27. by force: literally "with his own hand," as opposed, it seems, to using legal means. Or, possibly, it means "by himself," because later he seems to have reinforcements.

Having closely observed[28] Abba Gelasius's work animals transporting olives from the land he'd been given, Bakatos forcibly[29] made off with the produce, taking the olives home with him.[30] (Shamefully,* he almost didn't release the animals along with their drivers.) The blessed elder, however, didn't respond[31] at all about the olives but also didn't relinquish ownership of the land, for the reason already given.

Bakatos, inflamed with anger and drawn to other matters needing his attention (because he was litigious), hurried off to Constantinople,* making the journey by foot.[32] He came to Antioch.* At that time Saint Symeon* shone brilliantly like a bright star. When Bakatos heard about him (Symeon was more than human), as a Christian he set his heart on setting eyes on the holy* man. When Saint Symeon from his pillar saw him hurriedly enter the monastery, he asked him, "Where are you from? And where are you going?"

Bakatos said, "I am here from Palestine and I am going to Constantinople."

Saint Symeon said to him, "Why?"

---

28. Having closely observed: the linguistic nuance, even double entendre, continues. *Paratēréō* has the translated meaning but can also mean, "watch for an opportunity," "watch maliciously, lie in wait for" (Bauer 771b). See Mark 3:2 and Luke 14:1 (the Pharisees looking for an opportunity to accuse Jesus of breaking the Sabbath). On *tēréō* see n. 77 below and chap. 1, nn. 180, 243, and 246.

29. forcibly, *biaíōs*: or "violently."

30. Not stated, but probably earlier and certainly now, Bakatos, after observing the harvest, had returned with (armed) support and wagons to haul.

31. respond, *antipoiéō*: or "retaliate."

32. There may be a play on words here: "hurried off," *hormáō*, will appear later. The cognate noun *hormḗ*, "desire, ardor," "act of getting in motion," can also mean a "violent movement towards, an assault, attack," thus referring to Bakatos's violent behavior—and, possibly, character. See Montanari 1485c–86a. See n. 36.

Bakatos said to him, "I need to do a number of things, and, through the prayers* of Your Holiness, I have hope* that I will return and venerate your holy footsteps.[33]

Saint Symeon said to him, "You have the least hope* of all people.[34] You refuse to acknowledge that you're approaching a person of God. No, your journey will not go well for you, nor will you ever see your home again.[35] If you take my advice, you will end your visit here and hurry to him,[36] repent, and ask his forgiveness—that is, if you even reach the place still among the living."[37]

Bakatos was suddenly seized by fear* and, put on a litter by those accompanying him, and, in accordance with what Saint Symeon had said,* was hurried off to reach the place,[38] repent,

33. footsteps, *íknē*: the cognate verb *iknéomai* means both "venerate" and "supplicate" (Montanari 973c–74a). The image may be that of one person grasping hold of another's sandals in petition. But the word can also mean the base of a statue, though the plural here makes translating it as "base" problematic (Montanari 996c).

34. the least hope: *anélpistos* has the root *elpís*, "hope"* + the negating prefix *–a / -an*, thus "hopeless." Symeon has given Bakatos a harsh rebuke. *Anelpistía* means "to despair" of salvation, "failure to expect, lack of hope" (Lampe 132b–33a). With Symeon echoing (mocking?) Bakatos, the magistrate, like Claudius in *Hamlet*, is "hoist with his own petard" (*Hamlet* III.iv). See n. 41.

35. The ironic allusions continue with the contrast of "people" and "person" (*ánthrōpoi* and *ánthrōpos* respectively); "home" picks up on Bakatos's earlier theft when he took his ill-gotten gains home with him; "approaching" translates *anérchomai*, "to go up," used of the ascension in Patristic Greek and in the Nicene Creed of Christ's ascension into heaven (Lampe 137a).

36. him: Gelasius. The non-specificity of the pronoun has a twofold result: (1) Gelasius's name has not come up and (2), without that context, "him" demonstrates Symeon's preternatural, and prophetic, discernment. "Hurry," *hormáō*, picks up the earlier use, reversing Balaktos's literal and figurative journey. See n. 32.

37. reach: *katalambánō* echoes "made off with" and "take" (*lambánō*) at the beginning of the story. The linguistic and thematic ironies continue to pile up with "the living," *zṓsin*: earlier, the cognate noun *zōa*, "animals," makes an appearance in this three-act play.

38. "hurried" reiterates "hurry" in the previous sentence and, ironically, Bakatos's earlier hurrying off on his greedy and litigious business trip. See nn. 32, 36.

and ask Abba Gelasius for forgiveness.[39] But when they reached Beirut, he died without laying eyes on his home,[40] in accordance with the holy man's prophecy. His son, also named Bakatos, after his father's death related these events to many trustworthy men.[41]

3. This story, too, many of his disciples told: One time a fish was brought to them. The cook fried it and brought it to the cellarer. Because of some urgent need, the cellarer left the storeroom, leaving the fish in a serving tray on the floor and telling the young disciple of blessed Gelasius [149] to guard* it for a while until he returned. The young man, however, gluttonous, set about eagerly eating the fish.[42]

When the cellarer came back to the storeroom and found the disciple eating the fish, he got angry at the young man sitting on the floor; without thinking of the consequences, he kicked him with his foot. Because of the working[43] of some demon,*[44] the young man, struck in a vital organ, lost consciousness and died.

---

39. "Seized," and "reach" in the next sentence, translate *katalambánō*. See n. 37.

40. "Laying eyes on" echoes "setting eyes on" earlier.

41. trustworthy, *axiópistos*: "worthy of belief, trust." *Pistós* is the adjectival form of *pístis*, "faith"* (see n. 34). The irony intensifies: these men "are worthy of trust" while Bakatos was, literally, *anélpistos*, "without hope," and vainly hoped (*elpízō*) that his journey would be successful.

42. The theme of gluttony connects with the theme of avarice in the preceding saying. In addition, "guard" may seem unimportant here, but guarding and keeping watch are integral and vital (that is, life-sustaining) actions. See Protect in the Glossary.

43. working, *energeía*: usually "work,"* *érgon*, is a positive monastic term, but "working" here clearly is not. Perhaps it suggests an "anti-work," that is, a working that works against the monks' good work. Wortley has "machination," which is good; see John Wortley, trans., *Give Me a Word: The Alphabetical Sayings of the Desert Fathers*, Popular Patristics Series (Yonkers, NY: St Vladimir's, 2014), 85.

44. I have followed the lead of Wortley here (*Give Me*, 85); the text has "someone," which, given what happens next, does not work.

The cellarer, gripped by fear,* laid this young man in his own bed and covered him. Leaving the cellar, he went and threw himself at Abba Gelasius's feet, telling him what had happened. Abba Gelasius told him not to say anything to anyone.[45] He ordered him, after everyone in the evening was keeping silence,* to bring the young man's body into the sacristy,* lay it in front of the altar, and withdraw.*

When the elder came into the sacristy,* he stood in prayer.* At the time appointed for the night office,* when the brothers had gathered together, the elder came out, followed* by the young man himself. No one knew what had happened except Gelasius and the cellarer, until the elder's death.

4.[46] They used to say about Abba Gelasius—not only his disciples but also the many people who continually came to see him—they told the story that, at the time of the ecumenical council in Chalcedon,* Theodosius,*[47] who instigated the schism in Palestine against Dioscorus,[48] going ahead of the bishops* when they were going to return[49] to their own churches (he himself was also in Constantinople,* having been driven out of his own country because he was always rejoicing in fomenting disturbances),[50]

45. "Telling," thematically and linguistically, connects the scenes in the story: the cellarer tells (*parangéllō*) the young man to guard the fish; the cellarer tells (*apangéllō*) Abba Gelasius what he has done; the abba in turn tells (*parangéllō*) him not to tell anyone, and now, with a stronger verb, *keleúō*, he will give him orders.

46. As I noted at the beginning of Gelasius 1, I have kept the Greek periodic syntax of this first sentence in order to show the more sophisticated style of the Gelasian pieces.

47. The Theodosius in this story is not the emperor but rather Theodosius of Jerusalem (see the Glossary).

48. Dioscorus (d. 454), was patriarch of Alexandria.

49. *Return* here foreshadows events later in the story when Theodosius commits unlawful acts before the bishops* can return.

50. There is a play on words here, the latter word reinforcing the former: *instigate* translates *prokatárxas*, from *prokatárchō*, and *disturbances* renders *tarachaîs*, from *tarássō*. The words are not related, but they sound similar.

rushed to Abba Gelasius at his monastery, and spoke against the Council as though it had ratified the opinion* of Nestorius.* By doing this he thought he could underhandedly mislead the holy* man into working with him to support his fraud and schism.

From the man's conduct, and because of his own understanding, characteristic of him, given to him by God, and fully grasping Theodosius's* corrupt and ruinous mind,[51] he was not led astray by his apostasy (as almost everyone was at that time) but, instead, appropriately ridiculed him and sent him on his way, doing this: he had brought into their midst the young man whom he had raised from the dead;[52] now he was speaking to Theodosius in a holy and respectful manner: "If you want to discuss matters of faith, you have this young man: he can listen to what you have to say and discuss things with you. As for me, I don't have time to listen to you."

Confused by what had taken place, Theodosius hurried to the Holy City,[53] where he deceived all the monks under the pretense of godly zeal.[54] He also deceived the Augusta,[55] who was there at that time. Gaining support this way, he took control of the see of Jerusalem, snatching[56] it away, accomplishing this with murders and other lawless and uncanonical acts that, even now, many people remember. Now in control, and accomplishing what he had set out to do, he ordained numerous bishops* and seized beforehand the sees of those bishops* who had not yet returned.

Now he summoned Abba Gelasius and urged him to enter the sanctuary, luring him and at the same time intending to cause him

---

51. mind, *gnṓmē* (*gi(g)nṓskō*, "to know"): and / or "opinion, view, doctrine" (English *gnomic*). See Lampe 317b.

52. See Gelasius 3.

53. That is, Jerusalem.

54. deceived, *sunharpázō*: the cognate noun *harpagḗ* means "robbery, plunder," and is used of the Devil suborning the soul (Lampe 1307a); see Matt 12:29 and Luke 8:29. Lampe notes that in Patristic Greek the word is "rarely used in a good sense." See n. 56.

55. Empress Aelia Pulcheria (d. 453).

56. snatching, *proharpázō*; see n. 54.

to be afraid.*[57] Once Abba Gelasius had entered the sanctuary, Theodosius said to him, "Anathematize Juvenal!"*

Not at all terrified, Abba Gelasius responded, "I know no other bishop* as the bishop of Jerusalem," he said, "than [152] Juvenal."*

Theodosius,* being careful and circumspect, so that others might imitate his pious zeal, cleverly ordered Abba Gelasius thrown out of the church. Those in on his scheme[58] piled wood around Abba Gelasius, threatening to burn him. But when they saw him not showing the least bit of concern, nor cowering in fear,* and, worried about stirring up the people because the man was famous (all this through divine providence), they let the martyr* go, unharmed, a voluntary whole-burnt offering* for Christ.

5. They used to say about him that while still a young man he embraced a life of poverty,* taking on the life of an anchorite.* There were along with him at that time numerous others in the surrounding areas sharing the same life with him. Among them was a certain elder who had reached the summit of simplicity and voluntary poverty,* living in a cell as a solitary until he died, even though he had disciples in his old age. This elder practiced* a life of asceticism:* he neither possessed* two tunics* nor worried about tomorrow his whole life.[59] (The two who were with him did the same.)

When, therefore, Abba Gelasius, with divine co-operation,* came to establish the cenobium,* a great deal of land was offered to him. He also acquired* the necessities needed for a cenobium:*

---

57. luring: *dealázō* has the sense "catch by bait, deceive"; it can also mean "to bait a hook" (Lampe 337a). Thus in Gk. *-azo* words of contumacy pile up in Theodosius's wake: "deceived," "snatching," and "luring."

58. I have made my own play on words here: *scheme* derives from Gk. *schḗma* (which, ironically, can mean the monastic dress, the habit). It can mean "appearance, as opposed to reality, semblance" (Lampe 1359b) and is thus like a scheme, a plot, to subvert what's actual. A variant reading, PG 65:151–52 n. 24: *schism*.

59. two tunics: Mark 6:9 // Matt 10:10; worry about tomorrow: Matt 6:34.

beasts of burden[60] and cattle. The one who called[61] to the divine Pachomius* in the beginning to establish a cenobium* was also working with* Abba Gelasius with regard to setting up everything the monastery needed.[62] When the elder spoken of above, therefore, saw Abba Gelasius amid all this activity, wanting to preserve[63] the genuine love* he had for him, he said to Abba Gelasius, "I fear,* Abba Gelasius, that your thoughts* are chained to the property and the rest of the cenobium's* possessions."*

Abba Gelasius said to him, "No, it's *your* thoughts* that are chained to the awl you use in your work,* not the thoughts* of Abba Gelasius with regard to possessions."*[64]

6. [VII.13][65] They used to say about Abba Gelasius that, troubled by thoughts* telling him to leave for the desert,* one day he said to his disciple, "As an act of love,* brother, whatever I do, bear with me, and don't speak to me this week."

So, taking a palm staff,* he began to walk around in the courtyard of his dwelling. Worn out, he sat down for a little while, then again stood up and was walking around. When evening came, he

---

60. beasts of burden, *kténos*: literally "possessions,"* which also means the flocks and herds in antiquity that constituted wealth.

61. called, *chrēmatízō*: this is an interesting word. It is cognate with *chrêma*, "goods, property, money, gear, chattels"; the verb originally meant "negotiate, transact business." It came to mean "consult," and then the response of an oracle (Liddell and Scott 2005ab). In the LXX (esp. in Jeremiah: see 33:2-3) and early Christian use, it can mean "utter a message," of God to prophets, then "call, name, call by name" (Lampe 1527b–28a).

62. In the Bohairic *Life of Pachomius* (SBo) 8 "the spirit of God" seizes Pachomius, and he is baptized; in 12 he has a "vision," and in 17 "a voice" comes to him "from heaven," saying "Pachomius, Pachomius, struggle, dwell in this place and build a monastery; for many will come to you to become monks with you, and they will profit their souls" (39).

63. preserve: *sōzō*, "save."*

64. Gelasius's rather dismissive response does not tell the whole monastic story: the monks, rightly, *did* have concerns about possessions and power.

65. SysAP VII.13 assigns this saying to Longinus; it is not in AlphAP Longinus.

said to the thought,* "The person who walks around in the desert*
doesn't eat bread* but rather plants.⁶⁶ So, Gelasius, eat some
chopped vegetables."

When he'd done this, he once again said to the thought,* "The
person out in the desert* doesn't sleep under a roof, but rather in
the open air. You too, then, do the same." So, lying down, he slept
in the courtyard.⁶⁷

So, after he'd spent [153] three days walking around in the
monastery, each evening eating some endive and sleeping at night
in the open air, he was worn out. Having rebuked the thought*
that was troubling him,⁶⁸ therefore, he refuted it,⁶⁹ saying, "If
you can't do the work* required in the desert,* sit in your cell
with patient endurance,* weeping for your sins, and don't go
wandering around.⁷⁰ The eye of God⁷¹ sees the works* that hu-
mans⁷² do *everywhere*, and nothing escapes God's notice: God
understands⁷³ who those are who are working* for the good."

Concerning Abba Gerontius⁷⁴

[153] [V.2] [AnonAP 178] Abba Gerontius of Petra* said:
"Many people, tempted by bodily pleasures, although they haven't

---

66. Plants are scarce in the Egyptian desert unless there is a water source like
a wadi or an oasis.

67. Courtyards were often where the livestock bedded at night.

68. rebuked: *epitimáō* can mean "subject to penitential discipline" (Lampe
537b); see Jude 9; Mark 8:33.

69. refuted, *elénchō*: or "exposed"; see Eph 5:13.

70. wandering around: *planáō* often has spiritual significance, and a monk
would probably hear that here. See chap. 1, n. 462.

71. the eye of God: see Ps 33:18; Prov 15:3; 1 Pet 3:12 (all "the eye/s of the
Lord").

72. humans: SysAP VII.13, we.

73. understands who those are who are working: SysAP VII.13, works* with
those who are working.*

74. Gk. *Geróntios*.

used their bodies for sexual relations, have committed sexual sin with their thought and intention.[75] While safeguarding* the virginity of their bodies, they commit sexual sin* with their soul.[76] It's good therefore, beloved, to do what's written, and for each person, always on guard,* to keep a watch on his own heart.[77]

---

75. See Matt 5:27-28.
76. On thoughts* and sexual intent, see Matt 5:28.
   77. to keep a watch on: in the LXX and NT *tēréō* often means "to persist in obedience, keep, observe," "fulfill; pay attention to, esp. of the law and teaching" (Bauer 1002ab [3]). See Prov 4:23.

Chapter 4
D / Délta / Δ

Concerning Abba Daniel[1]

1. [153][2] [X.21][3] They used to say about Abba Daniel that when the barbarians* came to Scetis,* the fathers fled.* The elder said, "If God doesn't care about me, why should I go on living like them?"

He passed through the midst of the barbarians,* and they didn't see him. Then he said to himself, "Look, God has shown concern for me, and I didn't die. So, Daniel, you too, do what people do and flee,* like the fathers."[4]

1. Gk. *Daniḗl.*

2. Arabic numerals in brackets before the sayings refer to the column numbers in the alphabetical *Apophthegmata Patrum* (AlphAP) in the Migne edition, PG 65:75–440.

3. Bracketed Roman numerals followed by Arabic numerals (e.g., XII.3) identify the chapter and saying number in the systematic *Apophthegmata Patrum* (SysAP) (Jean-Claude Guy, ed., *Les Apophtegmes des Pères: Collection Systématique* [Paris: Cerf, 2013]). Other references in the work to Guy's edition (for example, Guy 3.219) give the volume and page number of the citation. AnonAP references come from the anonymous *Apophthegmata Patrum,* from John Wortley, trans., *The Anonymous Sayings of the Desert Fathers: A Select Edition and Complete English Translation* (Cambridge: Cambridge University Press, 2013). For a complete list of abbreviated entries, see Abbreviations (pp. xix–xxiii).

4. So, Daniel, you too, do what people do and flee, like the fathers: a variant reading, PG 65:153–54 n. 27, continue, So he got up and fled. SysAP X.21, So I too should do what humans do and flee, like the fathers.

2. A brother asked Abba Daniel, "Give me one commandment,* and I'll keep* it."

So Abba Daniel said to him, "Never dip your hand in a dish where a woman* is doing so and eat with her.⁵ By refraining from doing this, you'll be able to flee the demon* of sexual sin*—at least for a little while."

3. [XV.15] Abba Daniel said, There was in Babylon* a daughter of a chief magistrate who had a demon.* Her father held in high esteem a certain monk whom he loved,* who said to him, "No one can heal your daughter except some anchorites* I know.⁶ If you call on* them for help, they, out of humility,* will refuse to heal her. But—let's do this: when they come to the marketplace, act as though you want to buy something from them; [156] when they come to collect the payment, we'll ask them to offer a prayer,* and I believe* she'll be healed."⁷

So the magistrate and the monk left for the marketplace and found a disciple of the elders [that is, the anchorites] sitting and selling the goods the elders had made. They took him, along with the baskets, so he could collect the payment owed them. When the monk entered the house, the daughter possessed* by a demon* came and slapped him on the cheek. But he just turned the other cheek, following the Lord's commandment.*⁸

The demon, tormented, cried out, "The violence you're doing to me! Jesus' commandment* is throwing me out!"⁹ And imme-

---

5. Those eating would take bread* and dip it into a common bowl. See Matt 26:23 where Jesus refers to Judas, so Daniel may unfortunately be making a connection between women and Judas: they both betray? On woman as temptress, see Evagrius S3 and Theodore 17.

6. There is word play here with *échō,* "to have, hold": "had" in the previous sentence translates *échousa* and "held" in this sentence is *eîche;* in the next sentence, "refuse" translates *anéchontai.*

7. Here too there may be wordplay: *do, act,* and *offer* render forms of *poiéō,* emphasizing that the monks' actions will lead to action by the anchorite.

8. See Matt 5:38-42.

9. throwing . . . out, *ekbállō:* "force to leave, drive out, expel," "cast out," often said in the NT of driving demons out of people; see Matt 8:31; 9:33-34. See Walter Bauer, *A Greek-English Lexicon of the New Testament and Other*

diately the woman* was made clean.[10] When the elders came, those in the house told them what had happened. So the elders gave glory* to God and said, "This happens all the time—the Devil's arrogance falls before the humility* commanded* by Christ!"[11]

4. [X.22] Abba Daniel would also say, "As much as the body flourishes, the soul just as much grows thin, and as much as the body grows thin, the soul flourishes."

5. [XI.16] One time Abba Daniel and Abba Ammoës were on the road and Abba Ammoës said, "When are we going to settle down in a cell like other monks, father?"

Abba Daniel said to him, "Who's snatching God away from us right now? God's in the cell and, likewise, God's outside the cell."

6. [X.23] Abba Daniel related this story: When Abba Arsenius was in Scetis,* there was a certain monk there who was stealing the elders' things.[12] So Abba Arsenius took the thief into his cell, wanting to win him over[13] and get the elders some peace and quiet.[14] He said to the monk, "If you want something, I'll get it for you—only, don't steal." So he gave him money, both gold and bronze, and clothing, and everything he needed, but the monk left and started stealing again.

When the elders, therefore, saw that he hadn't stopped stealing,[15] they drove him away, saying, "If a brother is found

---

Early Christian Literature, ed. Frederick William Danker, W. F. Arndt, and F. W. Gingrich, 2nd ed. (Chicago: University of Chicago Press, 1979), 299ab.

10. woman, *gynḗ*: a variant reading, SysAP XV.15, "young woman" (*kórē*).

11. the humility commanded by Christ: literally "the humility of Christ's commandment."

12. things: *tà skeúē* (sing. *skeúos*) can non-specifically indicate "things," but, as in Daniel 3, it can mean "goods, wares."

13. win him over, *kerdaínō*: or "gain."* In the NT the verb can mean gain someone for the kingdom of God (Matt 18:15; 1 Cor 9:19-22); a person can also "gain Christ" (Phlm 3:8). So Arsenius, wanting to win the monk over, has salvific intentions.

14. peace and quiet, *anápausis*: see Inward stillness in the Glossary. See n. 15.

15. stopped, *epaúsato* (< *paúō*): there is a play on words here: "peace and quiet" earlier translates *anápausis*, "inward stillness,"* greatly desired by the

morally flawed because of some weakness,* we need to bear with him. But if he steals and, even though admonished, doesn't stop,[16] drive him away, because he's both damaging his own soul and upsetting* everyone here."

    7.[17] [XVIII.4] [AnonAP 761B] Abba Daniel the Pharanite*[18] told this story: Our father Abba Arsenius said that a certain brother

---

monks. The thief's not stopping (*epaúsato*) is thwarting the monks' peace and quiet (*anápausis*) and, concomitantly, "damaging his own soul." See n. 14.

    16. and, even though admonished, doesn't stop (*paúetai* < *paúō*, as above): I have adopted the variant reading, PG 65:155–56 n. 32, which continues with this phrase. See nn. 14 and 15.

    17. The story here requires a preface. Pliny the Elder (23/24–79) comments that the Christians "take food of an ordinary, harmless kind" (Epistle 10.96; Pliny, *Letters*, trans. Betty Radice [Cambridge, MA: Harvard University Press, 1969], 288–89), but Paul F. Bradshaw and Maxwell E. Johnson note that Pliny's account is "secondhand" and comment, "The emphasis put by the Christians on the food's being an ordinary and harmless kind was no doubt intended to counter common accusations from their pagan contemporaries" (Bradshaw and Johnson, *The Eucharistic Liturgies: Their Evolution and Interpretation* [Collegeville, MN: Liturgical Press, 2012], 25 n. 1). On this subject see Andrew B. McGowan, "Eating People: Accusations of Cannibalism against Christians in the Second Century," JECS 2 (1994): 413–42. See also McGowan, "Feast as Fast: Asceticism and Early Eucharistic Practice," in *The Eucharist—Its Origins and Contexts*, vol. 2, *Patristic Traditions, Iconography*, ed. David Hellholm and Dieter Sänger (Tübingen: Mohr Siebeck, 2017), 829–43. Minicius Felix (2nd–3rd cent.) reports on and defends against accusations against the Christians; see *Octavius*, 8.4, 5; 9.2, 4–7; 10.2, 5; 12.5. See Bradshaw and Johnson, *Eucharistic Liturgies*, "Eucharistic Presence," 44–50, and "Eucharistic Sacrifice," 50–58. They note, "The sayings of Jesus recorded in the New Testament writings that refer to bread and wine as being his body (or flesh) and blood were recalled by a number of second-century writers" (44). Justin,* *First Apology* 66.2, states that "the food . . . is both the flesh and blood of that incarnate Jesus" (cited by Bradshaw and Johnson, *Eucharistic Liturgies*, 45). Tertullian (ca. 160–ca. 225), *Against Marcion* 4.40.3–4, says that Jesus says "this is my body," that is, in Tertullian's words, "the figure of my body" (Bradshaw and Johnson, *Eucharistic Liturgies*, 48). Later, Cyril of Jerusalem (ca. 315–86) speaks of "the spiritual sacrifice, the bloodless worship," and says that the Holy Spirit makes "the bread Christ's body and the wine Christ's blood" (*Mystagogical Catechesis* 5.6–9, cited by Bradshaw and Johnson, *Eucharistic Liturgies*, 79). In Egypt, Serapion* of Thmuis (Sarapion of Tmuis) (ca. 350)

in Scetis* was a great monk because he did good works[19] but was
naïve with regard to matters of [157] faith:* he was prone to error
on account of his overly simple understanding. For example, he
would say, "The bread we receive isn't really[20] the body of Christ
but is, rather, a symbol."[21]

Two elders heard that he was saying* this. Knowing that he
was a great monk in the way that he practiced the monastic life,*
they reckoned that he was simply saying this out of guilelessness
and simplicity, so they went to him and said to him, "Abba, we've
gotten word that you've been saying something that a non-believer
would say: that the bread we partake of[22] is not really the body of
Christ but is, rather, a symbol."

---

says that the eucharistic bread and wine are the "likeness" (*homoíoma*) of Christ's
body and blood (Bradshaw and Johnson, *Eucharistic Liturgies,* 81). They note,
133, that in addition to "likeness," in the 4th–5th cent. other terms appear: *figure,
sign, symbol, type,* and *antitype.* It is clear that Christians in the first five centuries
were shaping, adapting, and bending language to define what many consider the
ineffable. The "naïve" brother here declares, "The bread we receive isn't really
[*phýsei*; by nature] the body of Christ but is, rather, a symbol." On *phýsei,* see
nn. 20 and 25. "Symbol," *antítypos,* is one of the apparently orthodox terms for
the body and blood; see the list above. On this term, see Lampe 158b–59b; he
notes that "in later writers, [it is] applicable only to unconsecrated elements"
(159a [4b]). I wish to thank Ruth Meyers for bibliographical help here.

18. SysAP XVIIII.4 notes that *the Pharanite* is lacking in some manuscripts.

19. did good works: *praktikós* indicates an active rather than a contemplative
life; *praktikḗ* means "an active life of good works" (Lampe 1127ab). This is not
the sense that the word has in Evagrius's *Praktikos.*

20. really: *phýsei* is an adverbial dative of *phýsis,* "nature" (English *physical,
physics*); it became a key word in the Christological discussion—and controversy—over the nature/s of Christ. See nn. 17 and 25.

21. symbol, *antítypos:* or "representation"; see Montanari 210a. As Lampe
shows, *antítypos* is a complex word. It can be positive: "symbol of things to come"
(as figures and events in the HB are symbols of realities in the NT), "earthly form
corresponding to a heavenly reality." Or it can negatively mean "a mere symbol,"
that is, "not the reality itself" (Lampe 159ab). Context shows that it may be the
latter here.

22. partake of, *metalambánō:* that is, in the Eucharist (Lampe 852b [B2]).
Earlier, "receive" translates the simplex *lambánō.*

The elder said, "Yes, I'm the one who's saying that."

They pleaded* with him, saying,* "Don't hold these views, abba! No, hold to what the Church catholic has handed on* as tradition.[23] We believe* that the bread is itself the body of Christ and the cup is itself the blood of Christ,[24] in very truth,[25] and is *not* a mere symbol. No, just as in the beginning God, taking dust, fashioned the human being according to his image,[26] and no one can say that that is *not* the image of God—even if it's incomprehensible—in the same way, we believe* that the bread that he said 'is my body' is, in truth, because he said so, the body of Christ."[27]

The elder said, "Unless I'm persuaded by seeing some event, I won't be convinced."[28]

They said to him, "We'll ask God this week about this mystery,* and we believe* that God will reveal the answer to us."[29]

The elder joyfully welcomed what they had said,* so he asked God, "Lord, you know that it's not from some evil intention[30] that I don't believe,*[31] but because I don't want to be led astray by ignorance. Reveal the answer to me, Lord Jesus Christ!"

The two elders went into their own cells,[32] each one calling on* God, saying, "Lord Jesus Christ, reveal this mystery* to the elder so he'll come to believe* and not waste all his effort."

---

23. See 1 Cor 11:27-29.

24. See Luke 22:19-20; 1 Cor 10:16.

25. in very truth, *phýsei*; see nn. 17 and 20.

26. Gen 1:27; 2:7.

27. is my body: Matt 26:26 // Luke 22:19.

28. See John 2:18 and 4:48 on the demands for a sign from Jesus.

29. the answer: the Gk. here lacks a direct object, so I have provided "the answer"; another possibility is "the truth," which would go nicely with "really" and "in very truth" earlier in the story.

30. evil, *kakía*: "guilelessness" above translates *akakía*, literally "no / lack of evil."

31. don't believe: *apistéō* combines an alpha-negative + *pístis*, "faith,"* so "be faithless, deny the faith." See nn. 36 and 40.

32. "Went into their own cells" foreshadows the end of the story.

God listened to them both. When the week was up, they went to the church on the Lord's Day and the three stood together . . . with the elder in the middle.[33] Their eyes were opened[34] and when the bread was placed on the holy table it appeared to the three alone as a child.

When the priest stretched forth his hands to break the bread— suddenly an angel of the Lord came down from heaven with a knife, slew the child as a sacrifice, and poured its blood into the chalice! When the priest broke the bread into small pieces, the angel also was cutting the child into small pieces. When the three came forward to receive the holy sacraments,[35] to the elder alone was given a bleeding piece of flesh. Seeing this, he was afraid,* and cried out "I believe,* Lord, that the bread *is* your body and the chalice *is* your blood!"[36] Immediately the flesh in his hand

33. The stage directions here seem to have them facing the altar. For the ellipses the text has *hèn embrímin*; *embrímin* is probably a form of *embrímion*, "pillow, cushion" (Montanari 669a), but the entry cites only AlphAP Joseph of Panephysis 1 (PG 65:228B), where *embrímin* clearly means "cushion"; E. A. Sophocles, *Greek Lexicon of the Roman and Byzantine Periods* (Cambridge, MA: Harvard University Press, 1914), 453b, cites three uses of the two words in the AlphAP. But the text says that the three here are standing; it would make more sense if they were kneeling on a long cushion. SysAP XVIII.4 has "stood." Wortley, *Give Me*, 91, translates "the three were standing together in a separate group"; in Joseph 1, he translates the plural as "cushions." In the other examples in the SysAP (Guy 3.314b) the words mean "cushion" or "pillow." In an email, Apostolos N. Athanassakis suggests that the word derives from Latin *umbra*, "shade," and that in "Greek military slang it means a temporary wooden structure where one may sleep relatively secure." Since the monks are in the church, *shade* does not seem right, but perhaps they are standing under a wooden structure.

34. their eyes were opened: a variant reading, AlphAP XVIII.4, the eyes of their intelligence were opened.

35. the holy sacraments: literally "the holies" (*hagíōn*). Gk. *hágios*, "holy, sacred," can refer to the bread and wine (Lampe 18b [B2b]).

36. The healing of the child with the unclean spirit in Mark 9:14-29 // Matt 17:14-20 // Luke 9:37-43a lies linguistically and thematically in the background: earlier in the story the elder says "I don't believe" (*apistéō*: *a*-, "not," + *pístis*);

became bread in accordance with the mystery,* and he partook of it, [160] blessing God.[37]

The elders said to him, "God understands human nature,[38] that it's not possible to eat raw meat; because of this, then, he transforms the body[39] into bread and his blood into wine for those who receive it in faith."*[40] And they gave thanks[41] to God concerning what had taken place because God didn't allow the elder's hard work to come to nothing.[42]

8. [XVIII.5][43] The same Abba Daniel related this story about another great elder who lived in Lower Egypt.* Because of his naïve and simple understanding, he would say, "Melchizedek* is Son of God."

Blessed Cyril,* the archbishop of Alexandria, was told about it,[44] so he sent for him. Knowing that the elder was a miracle-worker,*[2] and that if he asked something of God, God would reveal it to him, and that the elder had said what he'd said* out of a simple and naïve understanding, the archbishop, employing great wisdom, said, "Abba, I entreat* you—since I have a thought* that tells me that Melchizedek* is Son of God, while another thought*

---

in Mark 9:19 Jesus exclaims "You faithless (*ápistos*) generation!" In 9:23 Jesus says to the boy's disbelieving father, "All things can be done for the person who believes." Then the boy's father immediately cries out "I believe [*pisteúō*]! Help my unbelief [*apistía*]." Here, the elder also *cries out,* and the meat becomes bread *immediately.* See nn. 31 and 40.

37. blessing, *charistóō* is cognate with *cháris,* "grace."*

38. nature, *phýsis*: see nn. 15, 18, and 23.

39. the body: a variant reading, SysAP XVIII.4, his body.

40. faith, *pístis*: earlier "belief" and "believe." See nn. 31 and 36.

41. gave thanks: *eucharistéō* is cognate with *eucharistía,* "thanksgiving, Eucharist."

42. come to nothing, *apóllumi*: translated earlier as "*waste* all his effort."

43. Daniel 7 and 8 offer intriguing looks into two disputes in Late Antique Christianity.

44. it: or "him."

says 'No. No, he's a human being, God's high priest'—since I am not certain about this, then, I sent for you so you could ask God. This way, God will reveal the answer to you."[45]

The elder, confident because of his ascetic way of life,* said with confidence,* "Give me three days; I'll ask God about this and tell you who Melchizedek* is." So he left and talked to God about this matter. After three days, he came back and said to blessed Cyril, "Melchizedek* is a human being."[46]

The archbishop said to him, "How do you know, abba?"

He said, "God revealed to me all of the patriarchs; each of them, one by one, passed by in front of me, from Adam to Melchizedek,* and the angel said to me, 'This is Melchizedek,*[47] and rest assured that this is so.' "[48]

So the elder left and proclaimed[49] that Melchizedek* is a human being. So blessed Cyril greatly rejoiced.

Concerning Abba Dioscorus[50]

1. [160] [IV.13] It was related about Abba Dioscorus of Nachiastis[51] that his bread* was made from barley and lentils.[52] Each

---

45. A variant reading, SysAP XVIII.5, continues, *and we will know the truth.* (What is true is very important in Daniel's sayings.)

46. human being: *ánthrōpos* is the first word in the Gk. sentence, thus emphatic.

47. and the angel said to me, 'This is Melchizedek': using the variant reading in SysAP XVIII.5.

48. rest assured: *tharséō* picks up the elder's earlier "confident" (*tharrôn*; same vb. with different spellings), thus gently correcting the elder's earlier (over-)confidence.*

49. proclaimed: *kērússō* can also mean "preach," "proclaim the Gospel" (Mark 16:15).

50. Gk. *Dióskoros.*

51. I have not been able to locate this place.

52. That is, not from fine wheat flour.

year he would take on a new ascetic practice,[53] saying, "I'm not going to meet anyone this year,"[54] or "I'm not eating boiled vegetables," or "I'm not eating fruit or vegetables at all." And he would do this with every activity.* When he finished one, he would take on another. He did this each and every year.

2. [III.23] A brother once asked Abba Poemen, "My thoughts* trouble* me, and they won't allow me to be concerned[55] about my own sins; they make me focus on [161] the shortcomings of my brother instead. What should I do?"[56]

The elder told him about Abba Dioscorus: He was in his cell, weeping for himself. His disciple was sitting in the other cell. When he went to see the elder, therefore, he found him weeping and said to him, "Father, why are you weeping?"

The elder replied, "I'm weeping for my sins."

So his disciple said to him, "You don't have any sins, father."

The elder answered, "To be truthful, child, if I'm allowed to see my sins, three or four people won't be enough to weep for them."

3. Abba Dioscorus said, "If we wear our heavenly apparel,[57] we will not be found naked, but if we're not found wearing that apparel, what will we do, brothers? We, too, have to hear that

---

53. ascetic practice: *politeía* usually means a monastic way of life,* but here it is more like a practice,* although, as we will see, each new practice changes Dioscorus's way of life.

54. meet: *apantáō* can mean "meet, encounter," or "entertain" (a guest) (Lampe 173b).

55. be concerned about: *phrontízō* can also mean "get control of" (Lampe 1491a). I have followed the variant reading of SysAP III.23.

56. Implied here is "What should I do?" so I have added it.

57. heavenly apparel: this phrase does not occur in the NT. Bauer 333a points out that the *Shepherd of Hermas* (2nd cent.) transfers the meaning to refer to "one's inner life."

voice that says 'Throw this person into "the outer darkness, where there will be weeping and gnashing of teeth."'[58]

"But now, brothers, great shame* is ours, after wearing the monastic habit all this time, to be found at this time of distress not having our wedding apparel.[59] What need for repentance will be coming to us! What darkness will be falling[60] on us as we stand before our fathers and brothers as they watch us being punished[61] by the Punishing Angels!"[62]

Concerning Abba Doulas[63]

1. [161] [II.13] Abba Doulas said, "If the Enemy* is committing violence against us, preventing us from practicing contemplative quiet,* let's just not listen to him.[64] There's nothing like contemplative quiet.* And fasting*—when the two join forces,

---

58. Matt 22:13. This is the penultimate sentence in Jesus' parable of the wedding banquet, Matt 22:1-14. It is likely that a monastic audience would know what comes next: "For many are called, but few are chosen."

59. See Matt 22:1-14; 22:11. Distress: *anánkē* rather than *tarachḗ* (*tarássō*), "disturbance, trouble."* In 1 Cor 7:26 Paul speaks of the "present distress" (*anánkē*).

60. falling, *epipíptō*: or "attacking, assailing," or "will befall us" (Bauer 377ab).

61. punished: *timōréō* and its cognate noun *timōría* can also carry the sense of retribution and vengeance.

62. Punishing Angels: or "Angels of Retribution." Heb 10:26-31 may well be in the background; it concludes "It is a fearful thing to fall into the hands of the living God." Words common to both: *fall, sin, what will be coming,* and *vengeance.* Gustav Davidson, *A Dictionary of Angels, including the Fallen Angels* (New York: Free Press / Macmillan, 1971), has catalogued angels from a variety of sources, including Jewish, and found seven Angels of Punishment / Punishing Angels. See 2 Enoch 10:1-3 (online).

63. Gk. *Doulâs.*

64. listen to him: SysAP II.13, listen to him at all.

they fight* as allies against him and provide[65] us with keen interior vision."

2. [II.14] He also said, "Cut off relationships with the multitude[66] so that the warfare* within your mind doesn't beleaguer you[67] and disturb* your practice of contemplative quiet.*

---

65. provide, *parérchomai*: or, possibly, "promise."

66. multitude: *hoi polloí* can have the same meaning as *hoi polloi* in English, which may be the intention here. Another translation could be "Cut yourself off from your numerous relationships."

67. doesn't beleaguer you: SysAP II.14, never beleaguers you / doesn't beleaguer you at all.

Chapter 5
E / Épsilon / E

Concerning Saint Epiphanius, Bishop of Cyprus[1]

[2]1. [161][3] Saint Epiphanius the bishop*[4] told this story: In the time of blessed Athanasius the Great,* crows were flying around the temple of Serapis,* crying out without ceasing, [163] "Cras, Cras." Standing before the blessed Athanasius,* as adversaries defending the temple, was a crowd of pagans, and they cried

---

1. Gr. *Epiphánios*. See "Epiphanius" in Dramatis Personae.

2. A version of this story, without naming the Serapeum, occurs in Sozomen,* *Ecclesiastical History* 4.10 (https://www.newadvent.org/fathers/26024.htm).

3. Arabic numerals in brackets before the sayings refer to the column numbers of the alphabetical *Apophthegmata Patrum* (AlphAP) in the Migne edition, PG 65:75–440. Bracketed Roman numerals followed by Arabic numerals (e.g., XII.3) identify the chapter and saying number in the systematic *Apophthegmata Patrum* (SysAP) (Jean-Claude Guy, ed., *Les Apophtegmes des Pères: Collection Systématique* [Paris: Cerf, 2013]). Other references in the work to Guy's edition (for example, Guy 3.219) give the volume and page number of the citation. AnonAP references come from the anonymous *Apophthegmata Patrum,* from John Wortley, trans., *The Anonymous Sayings of the Desert Fathers: A Select Edition and Complete English Translation* (Cambridge: Cambridge University Press, 2013). For a complete list of abbreviated entries, see Abbreviations (pp. xix–xxiii).

4. A variant reading, AlphAP the bishop of Cyprus.

out,[5] "You wicked old man![6] Tell us why the crows are crying out!"

In reply he said, "The crows are crying out 'Cras, cras.' In Latin, *cras* means 'tomorrow.'" And he added, "Tomorrow you will see the glory of God!"

Then, the next day the death of Emperor Julian* was announced. When this happened, the pagans came running and, forming a crowd, were crying out against Serapis,*[7] "If you didn't want him, why did you welcome everything he gave you?"

2. The same person told this story: There was a certain charioteer among the Alexandrians,* whose mother was [named] Mary. This charioteer, as the race was coming to a conclusion, fell to the track.[8] Then he got up and passed the charioteer who had knocked him to the ground, and won the race. As a result, the crowd shouted out "The Son of Mary has fallen[9] and gotten up and won!"[10]

While the crowd was still saying this, a rumor spread[11] through the crowd about the temple of Serapis* that Theophilus* the Great had gone up to the idol of Serapis*and torn it down and the temple was now in his possession.[12]

5. cried out, *krázō*: the same verb occurs for the crowd and the crows. The crowd's crying out is ignorant; by ironic contrast, the crows, given the bishop's upcoming linguistic work, turn out to be not ignorant but prophetic. See n. 7.

6. wicked old man: in a monastic context, *kakógeros* could mean "wicked elder" (*gérōn*), but here it means "wicked old man," as it does in John Moschus, *The Spiritual Meadow of John Moschus (Pratum Spirituale)*, trans. John Wortley, CS 139 (Kalamazoo, MI: Cistercian Publications, 1992), 45 (p. 36), where a demon spits this at Abba Theodore. In other words, the pagans are like demons.*

7. crying out against, *katakrázō*; see n. 5 above

8. fell to the track, *katapíptō*: literally "fell down." See nn. 10 and 12.

9. fallen: *píptō*; see nn. 9 and 12.

10. gotten up: in the passive voice *egeírō* in the NT means "be raised," as from the dead; see Matt 28:7, among many.

11. spread: *empíptō*; see nn. 9 and 10.

12. possession: *enkrátēs*: by the time of the monks, this word also meant "moderate, continent"; English "self-possessed" shows something of the connec-

3. [XII.6] It was made known to blessed Epiphanius, the
bishop* of Cyprus,[13] by the abbot of the monastery he had in
Palestine,* "With your prayers,* we have not neglected our rule
of faith, but with eagerness we complete the monastic Office*[14]
at the first,[15] the third, the sixth, and the ninth hour."[16]

When blessed Epiphanius discovered this, he made the following clear[17] to them: "You clearly are being negligent by not doing
your prayers* at the other hours of the day. The real monk must
at all times have prayer* and psalmody* in his heart."[18]

4. [IV.15] Saint Epiphanius[19] one time sent for Abba Hilarion,[20]
summoning* him: "Come, let us see one another before we depart
from the body."

So after Abba Hilarion arrived, they rejoiced with one another.
While they were eating, a cooked bird was served.[21] Taking it, the
bishop* gave it to Abba Hilarion.

---

tion. Its cognates *enkrateía* (n.), "temperance, continence, abstinence," and *en-
krateáomai* (vb.), "practice self-restraint* / abstinence," became important
monastic terms (Lampe 402b–3b).

13. bishop: a variant reading, PG 65:163–64 n. 46, archbishop.

14. monastic Office: *kanṓn* instead of *sýnaxis*.

15. the first: the text lacks, but the next word is *kaí*, "and," which suggests that
"the first" has dropped out. The editor, PG 65:163 n. 47, suggests adding "the
first."

16. and the ninth hour: a variant reading, PG 65:163–64 n. 46 and SysAP XII.6,
continues, and at lamp-lighting. *Luchnikós*, Lat. *lucernarium*, Vespers, "or more
exactly the first part of the office, taking place after sunset when lamps are lit to
give light and for symbolic reasons" (Lampe 817a). So the monks pray at about
6 and 9 a.m., noon, 3 p.m., and dusk. For David's schedule of prayer as the pro-
totype of the monastic Office, see Epiphanius 7.

17. made . . . clear, *dēlóō*: translated earlier in the saying as "made known";
thus the verb reinforces Epiphanius's rejoinder, which becomes a rebuke.

18. at all times, *adialeíptōs*: in 1 Thess 5:17 Paul tells the Christians of Thes-
salonica to "pray without ceasing" with the same adverb.

19. Saint Epiphanius: SysAP IV.15, Epiphanius was the bishop of Cyprus.

20. Hilarion has one saying under his name in the AlphAP.

21. was served: SysAP IV.5, was served them.

The elder said to him, "Forgive me. Since I took the monastic habit, I haven't eaten slaughtered food."

The bishop* said to him, "Since I too took the habit, I have not allowed anyone to go to sleep who has something against me, nor have I gone to sleep having something against anyone."[22]

The elder said to him, "Forgive me; your way of life* is better than mine."[23]

5. The same bishop* used to say, "The image of Christ,[24] Melchizedek,* the root of the Jews, blessed Abraham.[25] How much more does Christ, who is Truth itself, bless and sanctify all those who have faith* in him?"[26]

6. [165] The same bishop* used to say, "The Canaanite woman cries out and is heard, and the woman with a hemorrhage remains silent and is blessed.[27] The Pharisee cries out and is pronounced guilty; the tax collector does not open his mouth and is heard."[28]

7. He used to say, "The prophet David[29] used to pray* at a very late hour, getting up at midnight. He would call on* God before

---

22. See Eph 4:26.

23. With "Forgive me" the first time, Hilarion places himself above Epiphanius; the second time, in humility* he places himself below the bishop.

24. image: *eikṓn* (English *icon*) occurs often in the NT. In Gen 1:26 LXX "image and likeness" are *eikṓn* and *homoíōsis*.

25. See Gen 14:17-24. On Melchizedek, see Dan 8.

26. See John 14:6; truth, *alḗtheia*, occurs 22 times in the gospel of John.

27. See Matt 9:20-22 and 15:21-28.

28. See Luke 18:9-14.

29. On David as prophet in the NT see Acts 1:16 ("the Scripture had to be fulfilled, which the Holy Spirit through David foretold concerning Judas"); 2:29-30 ("our ancestor David . . . was a prophet"). See also Acts 4:25; Mark 12:36-37; and *Barnabas* 12:10 (late 1st cent.). Justin,* *First Apology* 40.1, speaks of David as "prophet and king" speaking "by the Spirit of prophecy," and quotes Ps 19:2-4. Other patristic writers who see David as prophet are Clement, Origen, and Gregory of Nyssa (Lampe 1196a). In the Qurʾān, David is a prophet, a fact that makes one wonder about Christian influence. For early Jewish and Christian views see James L. Kugel, "David the Prophet," in Kugel, ed., *Poetry and Prophecy: The Beginnings of a Literary Tradition* (Ithaca, NY: Cornell University Press, 1990), 45–55.

dawn; standing at dawn, he would be making his plea at the first hour.[30] In the evening and at midday he would beseech* God.[31] On account of all this, he would say 'Seven times a day I praised you.' "[32]

8. He also said, "The possession of Christian books* is a necessity for those who can afford it. The very sight of the books,* in and of themselves, works* to make us hesitant to sin; instead, it urges us to rouse ourselves towards righteousness."*[33]

9. He also said, "A great place of safety and security that prevents sinning is the reading of the Scriptures."*

10. He also said, "A great precipice and deep pit is ignorance of the Scriptures."*[34]

11. He also said, "It is a great and treacherous betrayal of salvation* to not know even one of God's commandments."*[35]

12. The same person used to say, "The transgressions of the righteous* have to do with the lips,[36] while those of the impious involve the whole body. Thus David sings in the Psalms,* 'Lord, place a guard* with my mouth, keep watch over the door of my lips,'[37] and 'I said "I will guard* my ways so I do not sin with my tongue." ' "[38]

---

30. That is, dawn.

31. On these "hours," see in the LXX Pss 118:62 ("midnight"), 107:3 and 118:148 ("dawn"), 129:6 ("early in the morning"), 54:18 ("evening" and "midday"). See Epiphanius 3.

32. Ps 118:164 LXX. Ps 118:164 LXX has "seven," but the number in our text seems to be about five.

33. urges, *protrépō*: or "persuade," "invites, summons," "warns, admonishes."

34. precipice, *bárathron*: or "gulf, pit." Liddell and Scott 306a notes that the word indicated "at Athens a cleft behind the Acropolis into which criminals were thrown."

35. God's commandments: or "the divine / holy [*theíos*] commandments."

36. transgressions, *hamártēma*: in the NT it is often difficult to distinguish this word from its cognate *hamartía*, "sin." The Wisdom literature in particular says a great deal about the lips; see Prov 6:2; Sir 12:16; 20:20. With regard to similar teachings about the tongue, see Sir 5:15; 20:18; Wis 1:6, 11; and, in the NT, Jas 3:1-10.

37. The Gk. of the LXX here is not clear to me, so I have used the NRSV version.

38. See, respectively, Pss 141:3 (LXX 140:3) and 39:1 (LXX 38:2).

13. The same abba was asked, "Why are there ten Commandments* regarding the Law, but nine Beatitudes?"[39]

He said, "The Decalogue numbers the same as the plagues against the Egyptians,[40] while the number of Beatitudes is a representation of the Trinity times three."[41]

14. He was also asked whether one just* person could win over God,[42] and he said, "Yes. God himself said, 'Seek out one person practicing justice* and righteousness,* and I will be graciously disposed to all the people.'"[43]

15. The same elder said, "God forgives the debts of sinners who repent, like the prostitute[44] and the tax collector.[45] With regard to the righteous,* however, he [167] also demands interest.[46] This

---

39. Ten Commandments: Exod 34:1-7; Deut 5:1-21; 10:4. Beatitudes: Matt 5:1-12.

40. plagues: a *mástix* was originally a horsewhip, and then metaphorically a "scourge" or "plague" (Liddell and Scott 1083ab). On the plagues against the Egyptians, see Exod 7:14–11:10; the LXX, however, does not use the word *plague*. In the NT *mástix* can mean a "whip, lash" and "torment, suffering," but apparently *1 Clement* (late 1st cent.) first uses it for the Egyptian plagues.

41. representation: an *eikón* was originally a "likeness, image, picture," as on coins (Matt 12:20; Rev 13:14-15). It is not clear that Epiphanius means a painted icon here.

42. See Jer 5:1; Rom 3:10 (Ps 14:1-3; 53:1-3; Eccl 7:20).

43. See Jer 5:1; 23:5; Ezek 33:14.

44. prostitute, *pórnē* (English *pornography*): see John 8:1-11 (although v. 3 says that she was "caught in adultery [*moicheía*]"; in v. 4 the Gk. uses *autóphoros* to emphasize that she was "caught in the act" (*phōr* = "thief," one who carries [*phérō*] off).

45. the tax collector: a variant reading, PG 65:165, and the brigand;* see Luke 23:39-43. See Luke 18:1-14; 19:1-10 (Zacchaeus). As Bauer 999a notes, "The prevailing system of tax collection afforded a collector many opportunities to exercise greed and unfairness. Hence tax collectors were particularly hated and despised as a class." See Naphtali Lewis, *Life in Egypt under Roman Rule* (Oxford: Clarendon, 1983), 160–63, 178–79.

46. Given that in a system of tax farming (see the previous n.), as in Roman Palestine and Egypt, tax collectors (or, rather, their underlings) charged usurious rates, the image of God demanding interest seems odd (see Exod 22:25 and Lev

is why he would say to the apostles, 'Unless your righteousness*
exceeds that of the Scribes and the Pharisees, you will never enter
the kingdom of heaven.' "[47]

16. He also used to say this: "God sells a great deal of righteousness* for very little to those who are eager to buy it. You,
however, will spend what little you have[48] for a small crust of
bread or some inferior clothing, or even a cup of cold water."[49]

17. In addition, he used to say this: "A person who because of
his poverty, or because he wants to become prosperous, borrows
money from a person expresses gratitude when receiving the
money, but when he pays it back, he does so secretly, because he
is ashamed.* God, our Lord and Master,* does just the opposite:
he borrows it in secret and returns it in front of angels and archangels and those who are just and righteous.[50]

Concerning Saint Ephraim[51]

1. [168] [XVIII.6] When Abba Ephraim[52] was a child, he had
a dream or a vision:* a grapevine sprouted up from his tongue; it
grew and, with very abundant fruit, filled the whole earth under

---

25:36, among many). But see the Parable of the Talents (Matt 25:14-30 // Luke
19:11-27). Perhaps the moral here is, "Yes, you righteous / just, God does forgive
the sins of those who repent, but of you God demands even more (so put away
the laurels you were resting on)." See Epiphanius 16–17.

47. Matt 5:20.

48. what little you have: literally, "one *obolos*," one-sixth of an Athenian
drachma (see Montanari 1423a).

49. inferior: *entelés* can be positive: "thrifty, frugal, simple." But it can also
mean "vile"; its cognate noun can mean "of low estate, inferiority, state of deg-
radation" (Bauer 577ab). This second sentence is a paraphrase; it seems that some
words are missing.

50. I have used both *just* and *righteous* here for *díkaios*; see Epiphanius 14–16.

51. Gk. *Ephraím*. See "Ephraim" in Dramatis Personae.

52. Abba Ephraim: SysAP XVII.6, blessed Ephraim.

heaven.[53] All the birds of heaven were coming and were eating the fruit of the vine, and, while they were eating, the vine kept producing more and more fruit.

2. [XVIII.7] Another time a certain one of the saints* had a vision: a rank of angels was descending from heaven in accordance with a command of God,[54] and the angels were holding a scroll in their hands, that is, a book* with writing on both sides of the page.[55] They were saying to one another, "Who ought to be entrusted with this?"[56]

Some were saying "this person," while others were saying "that person." The angels answered one another and said, "In all truth, these are all holy and righteous*—but no one can be entrusted with it except Ephraim."[57]

The elder[58] saw that they'd given the scroll to Ephraim. When he got up early the next morning, he heard Ephraim composing a book:* it was[59] as though a spring of water were flowing from his mouth.[60] The elder[61] knew then that what was issuing forth from the lips of Ephraim was the Holy Spirit.

3. [X.26] Another time, when Ephraim was once again passing by, at someone's instigation a prostitute approached him, wanting

---

53. Here and in Ephraim 2, in Greek one "sees" a dream or vision (*vision* derives from Lat. *videre*, "to see"; Ger. *wissen*, "to know," is cognate).

54. "Rank," *tágma*, and "command," *próstaxis*, are cognate.

55. On a scroll held by an angel see Rev 10:1-11. Scrolls figure prominently in Isaiah and Jeremiah.

56. entrusted, *encheirízō*, "enhanded," has "hand" (*cheír*) within it: thus the angels want to hand over the scroll into the hands of someone trustworthy.

57. but . . . Ephraim: a variant reading, PG 65:167–68 n. 64 and SysAP IV.15, but they were unable to entrust it [to anyone]. Having said many other saints' names, they finally said, "No one can be entrusted with it except Ephraim."

58. the elder: SysAP IV.15, the elder who had had the vision.

59. he heard Ephraim composing a book: it was: SysAP IV.15, he heard Ephraim teaching and he / it was.

60. spring of water: see possibly Rev 21:6.

61. the elder: SysAP IV.15, the elder who had had the vision.

to flatter him into having obscene intercourse[62] with her or, if not, to provoke him to anger,* because no one had ever seen him get angry.*[63] So he said to her, "Follow* me." As he approached a very crowded area, he said to her, "Right here, come on, we'll do exactly what you wanted."

But that woman,* when she saw the crowd, said to him, "How can we do it here, with so many people standing around, and not be ashamed?"*[64]

He said to her, "If we're ashamed* in front of people,[65] how much more ought we be ashamed* before God,[66] who brings to light 'what's hidden in darkness.' "[67]

So she went away, shamed,[68] without accomplishing a thing.[69]

Eucharistus, Who Lived in the World*[70]

1. [168] [XX.2] Two of the fathers appealed* to God to [169] make clear to them what stature they had reached, and a voice

---

62. obscene: *aischrós* can also mean "shameful";* see below.

63. get angry: a variant reading, PG 65:167–68 n. 65 and SysAP X.26, get angry or fight with anyone.

64. and not be ashamed: SysAP X.26 lacks.

65. we're ashamed: SysAP X.26, you're ashamed.

66. how much more ought we be ashamed: SysAP X.26, how ought we not be ashamed.

67. brings to light: see 1 Cor 4:5. *Elénchō* means "expose, set forth," metaphorically "bring to light," then "to bring a person to the point of recognizing wrongdoing, convict, convince" and "reprove, correct," "punish, discipline" (Bauer 315ab). All are apposite here; I have chosen the metaphor "bring to light" because that is what Paul says in 1 Cor, though with a different verb (*phōtízō*).

68. shamed: the synonym *entrépō* rather than *aischúnomai*; see Shame in the Glossary. In the NT, 1 Cor 4:14; 2 Thess 3:14; Titus 2:8.

69. So she went away, shamed, without accomplishing a thing: SysAP X.26, She went away, ashamed. There could well be a strong linguistic irony here: "without accomplishing a thing" translates *ápraktos*, whereas *práktikos* means to practice* an active life of works.

70. Gk. *Eucharístos*.

came to them, saying, "In such-and-such village in Egypt* is a certain person who lives in the world,* Eucharistus by name,[71] and his wife is called Maria. You two haven't yet reached their stature."[72]

So the two elders got up and went to the village and, having inquired, found his cell and his wife. So they said to her, "Where's your husband?"

She said, "He's a shepherd, he's tending his flock." And she brought them into his cell.[73] When evening came, Eucharistus came with his flock and, seeing the elders, prepared a table for them and brought water to wash their feet.[74]

The elders said to him, "No, we won't eat anything until you tell us what sort of work* you do."

Eucharistus with humility* said, "I'm a shepherd, and this is my wife."

The elders continued to appeal* to him, but he didn't want to tell them.[75] So they said to him, "God sent us to you."

When he heard what they had said,* he became afraid* and said to them, "See, we got these sheep from our parents. And if with the Lord's guidance we prosper and make money from them, we divide it into three parts: one part for the poor, one part for hospitality,* and the third part for our own needs. From the time I took my wife, neither I nor she has been defiled; each of us is a

---

71. Eucharistus's name nicely fits the moral of the story; it can mean "thankful, grateful," esp. towards God (Lampe 580b); *eucharistía* means "thanksgiving," then *Eucharist*.

72. The theme of (more-)righteous non-monastic folks occurs several times in the AlphAP and other early monastic literature; see Antony 24.

73. A variant reading, PG 65:169–70 n. 67, her cell; Sys AP XX.2, her home.

74. See John 13:4-5, and the shepherd with his flock can symbolically be Jesus (John 10:1-21).

75. didn't want to: *thélō* with a negative can also mean "refuse." That is, this continues to emphasize that the shepherd here is modeling monastic humility.

virgin.[76] Each of us sleeps separately from the other. We wear sackcloth at night and our regular clothing during the day. Until now, nobody knew any of this."

When the elders heard this, they were amazed,* and withdrew,* glorifying God.

Eulogius[77]

1. [169] [VIII.4] A certain Eulogius became a disciple of blessed Bishop John.[78] Eulogius was a priest and great ascetic;*[79] fasting* two days at a time, often even prolonging it for a week, eating only bread* and salt and drinking water, he was constantly being praised by people.

He went to visit Abba Joseph of Panephysis, expecting to find in him an even more austere ascetic* discipline. After joyfully welcoming Eulogius, the elder made a little something from what he had to provide him some comfort,* so Eulogius's disciples said, "The priest doesn't eat anything except bread* and salt."[80] Abba Joseph, keeping quiet, set about eating.

Eulogius and his disciples, staying three days, never heard the monks singing the Psalms* or praying,* because the monks kept

---

76. defiled, *miaínō*: a passage like this is difficult today: Eucharistus "took" his wife; sexual intercourse as defilement. And the thinking here must be independent of Augustine's teaching on original sin. In John 18:28 Jesus' accusers do not enter Pilate's headquarters "so as to avoid ritual defilement and to be able to eat the Passover." *Miaínō* occurs frequently in the HB, esp. in Leviticus (a priestly document) and Ezekiel (who was from a priestly family).

77. Gk. *Eulógios*.

78. Bishop John: a variant reading, PG 65:169–70 n. 68, Archbishop John; SysAP VIII.4, Saint John, the archbishop.

79. great ascetic: SysAP VIII.4, ascetic.

80. bread and salt: SysAP VIII.4, bread and water and salt.

hidden their way of life.⁸¹ So they left, without receiving any benefit* from their visit.

But, in accordance with divine governance,* a darkness⁸² came upon them, they got lost,⁸³ and they came back to the elder's monastery. But before they could knock, they heard the monks singing the Psalms.* They remained outside a long time and then knocked again. The monks became silent, stopped the psalmody,* and then welcomed* the visitors, rejoicing.⁸⁴

Because of the scorching heat, Eulogius's disciples⁸⁵ put water into a flask⁸⁶ and gave it to him,⁸⁷ but because the water was a mixture of salt and fresh water, he couldn't drink it. Coming to his senses, he fell down before the elder, wanting to learn⁸⁸ [172] his way of life,⁸⁹ and said, "Abba, what's going on? First you [pl.] weren't singing the Psalms,* but now, after we left, you are. And the flask I just now received—when I tasted the water, I discovered it was salty!"⁹⁰

81. way of life: here *ergasía* instead of *politeía*, "a monastic way of life."* *Ergasía*, cognate with *érgon*, "work,"* generally means "activity." *Ergasía* returns at the end of the story. See n. 98.

82. darkness: in patristic writers such as Gregory of Nyssa,* *gnóphos* can, in a mystical understanding, indicate "divine darkness where God dwells," and "the contemplation of mysteries," of Moses and the Exodus (in Gregory's *Life of Moses*) (Lampe 317a).

83. lost: *planáō*, "wander," of planets, can also mean "go astray," "be at a loss" (Lampe 1088b–89a). Other meanings of *planáō* in the passive voice are apposite here: "be mistaken, deceive oneself," "be deceived, misled" (Bauer 822a). See n. 94.

84. The monks became silent, stopped the psalmody, and then welcomed the visitors, rejoicing: SysAP VIII.4, the elder welcomed them, rejoicing.

85. Eulogius's disciples: SysAP VIII.4, those with Eulogius.

86. flask: a *baukálion* / *baukálē* was the Alexandrian* name for a flat, narrow-necked, earthenware vessel (Lampe 294b).

87. and gave it to him: SysAP VIII.4, and gave it to him because he was thirsty.

88. wanting to learn: SysAP VIII.4, and begged to learn.

89. way of life: *diagōgḗ* this time.

90. And the flask I just received—when I tasted the water, I discovered it was salty!: Wortley, *Give Me*, 100–101 n. 39, notes that one tradition has, "Likewise,

The elder[91] said to him, "The brother who gave you the flask is
an idiot[92] and, in error,[93] he mixed fresh water with sea-water."
Eulogius begged* the elder, wanting to learn the truth, so the
elder said to him, "That small cup of wine was for the love* feast,[94]
while this water—this is what the brothers always drink." In this
way the elder taught Eulogius the discernment* of thoughts,* and
he cut away from Eulogius all merely human thinking.

So Eulogius became more accommodating[95] and from then on
would eat everything set before him. He also learned to keep his[96]
way of life.[97] So he said to the elder, "Truly, your [pl.] way of life
is the true one."

---

then, you were drinking wine in our presence, but now I tasted your water and
found it scarcely drinkable." The irony is sweet: "salty" here translates *halmurós*,
"salty, briny," "brackish, bitter, distasteful" (Liddell and Scott 72a), whereas
earlier Eulogius's disciples told the elder that their abba would eat only bread
and salt (*hálas*).

91. The elder: SysAP VIII.4, Abba Joseph.

92. idiot, *salós*: there could be a word-play between *hálas*, "salt," and *salós*,
"fool, idiot" ("salt" is *sal* in Latin), suggesting that it is not the brother but rather
Eulogius who is the idiot. This interpretation gets support from the sentence now
following.

93. error: *planḗ*, cognate with *planáō*; see n. 84. The noun reinforces the idea
that Eulogius has seen the error / wandering of his way(s).

94. cup: *potḗrion* can also refer to a eucharistic cup, chalice (Lampe 1124b
[6]).

95. accommodating, *oikonomikós*: a variant reading, PG 65:171–72 n. 69 and
SysAP VIII.4, have *synkatabatikós*, "respectful, diplomatic," but its cognate noun
synkatábasis provides an interesting twist that seems to undercut the moral of
the story: "going down to the level of, accommodation, concession, condescen-
sion" (Montanari 1982c). The variant reading also undercuts a play on words:
oikonomikós, cognate with *oikonomía* (see "governance" early in the Saying and
in the Glossary). This word play signals that Eulogius is more in tune now with
God's wishes (concerning humility and accepting hospitality). Gk. lacks "more,"
which I have added for smoother English.

96. his: apparently the elder's.

97. keep his way of life (here and in the next sentence): *ergázomai*, cognate
with *ergasía*; see n. 82 and Work in the Glossary.

Concerning Abba Euprepius[98]

1. [172] Abba Euprepius said, "Since you have within yourself God, who is faithful* and powerful,[99] have faith* in him, and you'll share in what is God's.[100] If you get discouraged, you lack faith.*[101] We all believe* that God is powerful,* and 'we believe* that with God all things are possible.'[102] But with regard to your own actions and circumstances, have faith* in God there, too. God works wonders* in you, too."

2. When this same elder was being robbed, he helped the thieves carry away his things. After they had hauled off what had remained in the cell, leaving behind his staff,* Abba Euprepius saw it. He was weighed down with grief, so, taking the staff,* he went running after them, wishing to give it to them. He caught up with them,[103] but they refused to accept it, afraid* that something might happen to them. Meeting some people who were headed the same way as the thieves, he thought it would be good if they handed over the staff* to the thieves, so he asked them to do so.[104]

---

98. Gk. *Euprépios.*

99. faithful* (*pistós*) and powerful* (*dynatós*): in the NT, Paul especially speaks of God "who is faithful": 1 Cor 1:9; 10:13; 2 Cor 1:18; 1 Thess 5:24. "Powerful": in the Magnificat, Luke 1:49, Mary speaks of God as the "Mighty One" (*ho dynatós*). See Power in the Glossary.

100. share in what is God's: the same phrase occurs in Heb 2:14, sharing in Jesus' flesh and blood (not eucharistically).

101. lack faith: or "you're lacking in faith."

102. possible, *dynatós*: see n. 100 and Power in the Glossary. We believe . . . possible: Jesus says this in Matt 19:26.

103. I have added this sentence for continuity.

104. Wortley, *Give Me*, 102 n. 41, notes that "very similar stories" occur in AlphAP Zosimas 12 (SysAP XVI.21; AnonAP 337); Moschus, *Spiritual Meadow*, 212 (pp. 190–91); and AlphAP Macarius the Great 18 and 40.

3. Abba Euprepius said, "Bodily things are material. The person who loves* the world* loves stumbling-blocks.[105] So, then, if someone happens to lose something, that person should accept the matter with joy and give thanks, like those set free from cares and concerns."

4. [I.28] A brother asked Abba Euprepius about life.[106] The elder said, "Eat what cows eat, dress in what cows eat; sleep on it, too. That is, despise everything and acquire a heart made of iron."

5. [I.29] A brother asked this same elder, "How does the fear* of God come into the soul?"

The elder said, "If a person has humility* and voluntary poverty,* and doesn't judge,* the fear* of God comes to that person.

6. [I.30] The same elder said,[107] "Let fear,* humility,* the diet of those in need, and sorrow* stand by you.

7. [X.24] When he was young,[108] Abba Euprepius went to visit a certain elder and said* to him,[109] "Abba, give me some counsel:* How can I be saved?"*

The elder said to him, "If you want to be saved,* when you visit someone, don't speak before he gets a good look at you."[110]

Pricked* by what the elder had said, he prostrated* himself, saying,* "It's a fact that I've read a lot of books,* but I never knew teaching like this."

Greatly benefiting* from the visit, he left.[111]

---

105. stumbling block, *próskomma*: in Rom 4:13 Paul uses this word and the more common *skándalon* ("stumbling block or hindrance").

106. Abba Euprepius: SysAP I.28, an elder.

107. The same elder said: SysAP I.30, an elder said.

108. young: *archḗ*, "beginning," as in Gen 1:1 LXX and John 1:1, can also be "when he was a novice."

109. When he was young, Abba Euprepius went to visit a certain elder and said to him: SysAP X.24, A brother went to visit a certain elder.

110. gets a good look at you: perhaps "before he sizes you up."

111. "Greatly" and "a lot" in the previous sentence both translate *pollá* (*polús*), "many." Thus the words reinforce the theme that the elder's teaching supersedes the reading of many books. SysAP X.24 lacks "greatly."

Concerning Abba Helladius[112]

1. [173] [IV.16] They used to say about Abba Helladius that he spent twenty years at Kellia,*[113] and not once did he lift his eyes upwards to see the roof of the church.[114]

2. They used to say about this same Abba Helladius that he would eat only bread* and salt. When Easter[115] arrived, therefore, he would say "The brothers are eating bread* and salt, but I ought to make a little extra effort because it's Easter. Since I eat sitting down the rest of the year, now that it's Easter I'll make an effort to eat standing up."[116]

3.*[117] On a Saturday of joy,[118] the brothers came together* to eat in the church at Kellia. When the dish with porridge was

112. Gk. *Helládios*.

113. at Kellia: SysAP IV.16 lacks.

114. not once did he lift: SysAP IV.16, not once lifted.

115. It seems that *Easter* should be *Lent* three times in this saying. Maged S. A. Mikhail agrees, but tells me that *Easter* may be a reference to the roughly 40 hours from the cross to the empty tomb, which were observed with greater austerity, bread and salt or complete abstinence. Whatever the case, the saying shows that Helladius was a diligent faster.* Mikhail adds, "from roughly the 330s to the 650s the fast* was 40 days, and Lent included Passion Week; it was a six-week observance ending with Easter, introduced by Athanasius based on the Roman model."

116. There may be a play on words here: "ought" translates *ópheilon*, from *opheílō*, "owe, ought," (*owe* and *ought* are different tenses of the same verb in English), while "benefiting" in Euprepius 7 translates *ōphelētheís*, from *ōpheléō*, "benefit, profit." What the monk ought to do benefits himself or herself.

117. Jean-Claude Guy, *Recherches sur la tradition grecque des Apophthegmata Patrum* (Brussels: Bollandistes, 1962), 44.

118. Saturday of joy: this could possibly be when all the monks gather together, even the anchorites, for a common meal (as does Abouna Lazarus at St. Antony's by the Red Sea in Egypt today). Maged S. A. Mikhail suggests that it may indicate the Saturday between Good Friday and Easter: "I have not seen the term 'Saturday of Joy' except in Arabic, but one of the designations for that Saturday is: *sabt al-farah* / Saturday of joy (Coptic *rashe* often comes into Arabic as *farah* / 'joy')."

served, Abba Helladius the Alexandrian* began to weep. In response, Abba Jacob said to him, "Why are you weeping, abba?" He said, "Because the joy of my soul has passed away, that is, fasting,* and the comfort* of the body has arrived."

Concerning Abba Evagrius[119]

1. [173] [III.2, III.5][120] Abba Evagrius said: As you sit in your cell, gather your thoughts.*[121] Think about the day of your death. Then observe the decaying of your body.[122] Imagine the calamity, accept the pain. Come to realize[123] the world's foolishness[124] so you can always be disposed towards and maintain your intention

119. Gk. *Euágrios*. See Evagrius in Dramatis Personae. The SysAP gives several of Evagrius's apophthegms here (1, 3, 4, 6) to other abbas, showing the disappearing of Evagrius from the tradition. Many after his death considered him, along with Origen, a heretic. See nn. 120, 133, 145, 147, 151, and 153.

120. SysAP III.2 gives this saying to Antony. See nn. 119, 133, 145, 147, 151, and 153. As Guy notes, SysAP 1.149 n. 1, "This piece is not by Anthony but Evagrius (*Rerum mon. rationes* 9, PG 40:1261 = AlphAP Evagrius 1 . . .). Pelagius translates [into Latin] a not yet 'corrected' model, which does not divide the text into two parts and preserves its attribution to Evagrius." On the subject matter here, see Theophilus 4.

121. thoughts: SysAP III.2, mind.

122. decaying, *nékrōsis*: in English, therefore, the image becomes even more striking when we think of necrotic flesh.

123. Come to realize: the morphology and possibilities of *kataginōskō* are important here. The root is *gnō-*, as in *gnōsis*, "knowledge,"* vitally important to Paul, Clement* and Origen,* the Gnostics,* and Evagrius. Its first meaning is "to remark, discover, esp. something to one's prejudice"; it can also mean "to give a judgement, pass sentence against a person, pass sentence (of death)" (Liddell and Scott 355a); "contemplative and mystical knowledge" (Montanari 437bc). Thus Evagrius could be saying to first realize the world's* foolishness, then pass judgment* on it.

124. foolishness: *mataiótēs* occurs often in the Psalms* and Eccl (1:2: "All is foolishness"). The world's foolishness so you can: SysAP III.2, the world's foolishness. Take care to be gentle and forbearing and diligent so you can.

to remain in contemplative quiet*[125] and not become sick and incapacitated.[126]

Keep in mind also the state of things in Hades* now.[127] Give thought to how the souls there are doing: the most terrible kind of silence,[128] the most bitter kind of moaning and groaning,[129] the magnitude of the fear* and struggle,* the awful expectation,[130] the unceasing pain and distress,[131] and the boundless tears of the soul.[132]

[133] [SysAP III.5] But remember also the day of resurrection and your appearance before God.[134] Picture in your mind[135] that terrify-

---

125. be disposed towards and maintain: *próthesis* has a number of meanings apposite here, so I have used two definitions in the translation: "free choice, inclination," "disposition," "purpose, intention, plan" (Montanari 1764ab).

126. Presumably he means spiritually.

127. now: SysAP III.2, lacks.

128. Silence: *siōpḗ* is usually much desired by the monks; perhaps here it means some kind of existential void.

129. the most terrible kind of silence, the most bitter kind of moaning and groaning: SysAP III.2, the most bitter kind of silence, the most terrible kind of moaning and groaning.

130. expectation, *prosdokía*: its verb *prosdokáō* can be neutral, but both can also refer to coming judgment* (Lampe 1166b).

131. unceasing: a monastic audience could well hear the irony here; *ápauston* is the negative of *anápausis*, the inward stillness* the monks so desire.

132. the unceasing pain and distress; SysAP III.2, their expectation of unceasing pain and distress. See Theophilus 4 and the (Ethiopic) *Apocalypse of Peter* (http://www.earlychristianwritings.com/text/apocalypsepeter-mrjames.html).

133. SysAP III.5 begins here, attributed to Abba Theodore. The editor of the SysAP or its tradition is "disappearing Evagrius." See nn. 119, 120, 145, 147, 151, and 153.

134. There could well be a play on words here: *resurrection* is *anastáseōs* < *anástasis*, and *appearance* translates *parastáseōs*, from *parástasis*, thus emphasizing the idea that resurrection brings with it a "court appearance" and Judgment.*

135. Picture in your mind, *phantázomai*: or "contemplate" (Lampe 1470b–71a). See Vision (*phantasía*) in the Glossary.

ing and fearful* Judgment.*[136] Observe what is in store there for sinners: shame* before God and the angels and archangels and the whole human race—that is, punishment,[137] unending fire, the worm that never sleeps,[138] Tartarus,* darkness, the gnashing of teeth,[139] the fears* and the punishments.

But now observe also the good things in store for the just and righteous:*[140] the ability to speak freely and fearlessly* before God the Father,[141] the angels and archangels, and the entire company of the saints, the kingdom of heaven and its gifts: its joy and pleasure.[142]

Take to heart[143] and be mindful of both of these: on the one hand, weep over the Judgment* of sinners, be sorrowful,* be afraid* that you too will be found among them. On the other hand, rejoice and delight in what awaits the just and righteous.*[144] Do your fullest to share in their joy and pleasure and separate yourself from those others. See to it that you never forget all this, whether you are within your cell or even outside it somewhere, keeping these things in mind so that, because of them, you may flee from foul and harmful thoughts.*

136. terrifying, *phrikṓdēs*: "that which strikes terror; horror, terrible, dreadful, fearful" (Montanari 2306c); "something that causes shuddering or trembling" (Lampe 1490a). See Jas 2:19.

137. punishment: SysAP III.5, all the punishment.

138. the worm that never sleeps: SysAP III.5, the everlasting worm. See Jdt 16:17; Sir 7:17; Mark 9:48 (referring to Isa 66:24).

139. the gnashing of teeth: SysAP III.5, for all these (sinners) the gnashing of teeth; see Matt 8:12 and others.

140. the just and righteous: SysAP III. 5, the good and the just and righteous.

141. before God the Father, the angels and archangels: SysAP III.5, before God and his Christ and the angels and archangels.

142. SysAP III.2 ends here.

143. Take to heart: literally, with *ágō* as twice before ("observe"), "observe in yourself." This saying is structured around the threefold use of *ágō*.

144. awaits, *anakeímai*: translated earlier as "lies in store for."

2. He also said, "Cut off your relationships with the multitude so that your mind does not become dependent on them and disturb* your practice of contemplative quiet."*

3. [XI.17][145] He also said, "It is a great thing to pray* without distraction, and[146] it is even better to sing psalms* without distraction."

4. [XI.18][147] He also said, "Always be mindful of your departure,[148] and do not forget that there will be eternal Judgment.*[149] If you do these, there will be no error or sin in your soul."

5. [176] He also said, "Take away temptations,* and no one gets saved."*[150]

6. [I.4, XVII.35][151] He also said, "One of the fathers used to say, 'A frugal and regular diet,[152] yoked with love,* brings the monk quickly into the safe harbor of being without the passions.' "*[153]

---

145. SysAP XI.17 assigns this saying to Daniel; it occurs in Evagrius, *Praktikos* 69 (p. 35). See nn. 119, 120, 133, 147, 151, and 153.

146. and, *dé*: or "but."

147. SysAP XI.18 assigns this saying to Daniel. See nn. 119, 120, 133, 145, 151, and 153.

148. departure: that is, death; see Evagrius 1.

149. See Evagrius 1. Heb 6:2 speaks in passing of "eternal judgment."

150. no one gets saved: literally "no one is being saved."

151. SysAP I.4 and XVII.35 expunge Evagrius as the speaker; it is part of Evagrius, *Praktikos* 91 (p. 39). See nn. 119, 120, 133, 145, 147, and 153.

152. This phrase is not certain. The word for "frugal," *xērotéra*, is not in any of the lexicons I consult; its root is *xērós*, "dry" (English *xeriscaping*), and *xērótēs* can mean "harshness, hardness." The other adjective for "diet" is *anốmalos*, "irregular" (English *anomalous*). I have followed Guy, "Un régime alimentaire sec et constant" (SysAP I.4; Guy 1.103) and "Une nourriture frugale et régulière" (SysAP XVII.35; Guy 3.37).

153. As Guy notes, I.103 n. 1, "The anonymous author of this saying and of the following is Evagrius Ponticus. The scribe has suppressed his name, suspected of heterodoxy, while maintaining the two pieces in their normal alphabetical

7. [XVI.3][154] A council took place in Kellia one time concerning some matter, and Abba Evagrius spoke. The priest said to him, "We're fully aware, abba, that if you were in your homeland, you would,[155] perhaps, be a bishop* and would be in charge of a lot of people. But now you sit here a stranger."*[156] Abba Evagrius, though stung,* didn't get upset; instead, he nodded his head and said to him, "That is the truth, father. 'I have spoken once; I will not add anything to it.'"[157]

7.* [Guy, *Recherches*, 21] He also said, "The starting point of salvation* is condemnation of yourself."[158]

8.* [Guy, *Recherches*, 50] He also said that a certain elder had said, "Because of this, I do away with pleasures in order to cut off pretexts for anger.*[159] I know for a fact that anger* is always waging war* with regard to pleasures, making my mind agitated, and driving away knowledge.*[160]

---

order." Guy adds that the two pieces (SysAP I.4 and I.5) are extracts from Evagrius, *Praktikos* 91 (p. 39). See nn. 119, 120, 133, 145, 147, and 151.

154. SysAP XVI.3 is in Latin.

155. would, *échō*: or "could."

156. sit, *kathézomai*: or "dwell, live."

157. Job 40:5. Job's response follows God's answer to him "out of the whirlwind" in Job 38:1–40:2.

158. condemnation, *katágnōsis*: a harsh word (see Bauer 516a; Lampe 706b, "condemnation, censure, rejection"). See n. 162. The noun does not occur in the NT, but the cognate verb *katagignṓskō* occurs at 1 John 3:20 ("condemn").

159. pretexts: *próphasis* can mean "having an opportunity for," but its more common meaning is "pretext, excuse"; the cognate noun *prophasízomai* means "adduce pretexts or excuses" (Montanari 1840c–41a). Therefore I have used the sharper meaning.

160. The saying has an important play on words: "knowledge"* translates *gnôsis*, while "condemnation" earlier is *katágnōsis* (see n. 159). Evagrius, *Chapters on Prayer* 86 (p. 69, inclusivized) is apropos here: "Knowledge! A human being's great possession. It is a fellow-worker with prayer, acting to awaken the power of thought to contemplate the divine knowledge."

9.* [Guy, *Recherches*, 50] "One of the brothers," he also said, "inquired of one of the elders, asking whether he could eat with his mothers and sisters when he went home to visit.

" 'Never eat,' he said, 'with a woman.' "*161

Concerning Abba Eudaemon

[176] Abba Eudaemon said this concerning Abba Paphnutius, the father of Scetis: "I went down there as a young man, and he wouldn't let me stay there, saying with regard to me, 'Because of the war with the Enemy, I will not allow a woman's face to stay in Scetis.' "

161. eat: *bibrōskō* is not the usual word for "to eat," so the translation here may be timid: "devour, eat greedily" (Montanari 387b). In John 6:13, however, the only use of the word in the NT, in the story of the feeding of the 5,000, the word does not have negative implications, and it clearly means simply "eat" in the LXX. On woman as temptress, see Arsenius 28, Ammonas 3, Ephraim 13, and esp. Daniel 2 and Theodore 17.

Chapter 6
Z / Zêta / Z

Concerning Abba Zenon[1]

1. [176] [2] [VIII.5][3] Abba Zenon, the disciple of blessed Silvanus,[4] said, "Don't live in a famous place; don't dwell with a person of great renown; don't ever lay a foundation to build a cell for yourself."

2. They used to say about Abba Zenon that from the beginning he refused to accept from anyone anything whatsoever. Because of this, those bringing something for him went away saddened because he wouldn't accept what they had brought. Others came

---

1. Gk. *Zénōn.*

2. Arabic numerals in brackets before the sayings give the column numbers in the alphabetical *Apophthegmata Patrum* (AlphAP) in the Migne edition, PG 65:75–440.

3. Bracketed Roman numerals followed by Arabic numerals (e.g., XII.3) identify the chapter and saying number in the systematic *Apophthegmata Patrum* (SysAP) (Jean-Claude Guy, ed., *Les Apophtegmes des Pères: Collection Systématique* [Paris: Cerf, 2013]). Other references in the work to Guy's edition (for example, Guy 3.219) give the volume and page number of the citation. AnonAP references come from the anonymous *Apophthegmata Patrum,* from John Wortley, trans., *The Anonymous Sayings of the Desert Fathers: A Select Edition and Complete English Translation* (Cambridge: Cambridge University Press, 2013). For a complete list of abbreviated entries, see Abbreviations (pp. xix–xxiii).

4. Silvanus has 12 sayings in the AlphAP.

to see him, wanting to receive something as from a great elder, but he didn't have anything to do with them,[5] and they went away saddened.

The elder said, "What should I do? Both those who bring something and those who want to get something go away saddened. This will be more beneficial:* if someone brings something, I'll take it, and if someone looks for something, I'll provide it for him."[6]

So, by doing this, he found inward stillness,* and everyone was completely satisfied.

3. A brother, an Egyptian, went to visit Abba Zenon in Syria* and made accusations against his own thoughts* to the elder. Abba Zenon was amazed* and said, "The Egyptians hide the virtues* they have, and[7] they don't hide the faults they have—they're always accusing themselves of these. The Syrians and Greeks, on the other hand, talk about the virtues* they don't have and hide the faults they do have!

4. [X.27] Brothers came to him and asked him, "What does what's written in Job mean—*Heaven is not pure before God?*"[8]

In reply the elder said to them, "The brothers have set aside their sins and go looking for the things of heaven. This, then, is the interpretation of the verse: God alone is pure; therefore he said *Heaven is not pure.*"[9]

5. [177] [XVIII.8] They would say about Abba Zenon that, while living in Scetis,* he left his cell one night as though going to the marshy meadow. He spent three days walking around lost. Getting exhausted, he stopped and fell to the ground to die. Sud-

---

5. he didn't have anything to do with them: or "he couldn't give them anything."

6. provide: *paréchō* may be nullifying a previous *échō* ("have"), "he didn't have anything to do with them."

7. "And" (*dé*) here and in the last sentence of the saying can mean "but."

8. This is what one of Job's friends, Eliphaz, tells Job in Job 15:15 (see 15:1-35).

9. pure, *katharós* (English *cathartic*): in Job and the HB *katharós* indicates "pure" and also "clean," as in the desire for covenant holiness by keeping oneself "clean." "He" could be referring to God, but probably refers to Eliphaz.

denly a young boy stood before him, holding bread* and a flask of water, and said to him, "Get up and eat."

Abba Zenon stood and prayed,* thinking that it was an illusion.[10] The boy said to him, "You've done well." So Abba Zenon again prayed,* a second and a third time, and the boy said to him, "You've done well."

The elder stood up, therefore, took the bread,* and ate.[11] Afterwards, the boy said to him, "The more you walked around, the farther you got from your cell, but get up and follow* me."[12]

Immediately Abba Zenon found himself at his cell, so he said, "Come inside, offer a prayer* for us."

When the elder went inside, that boy had vanished.

6. [IV.17] Another time, the same Abba Zenon was out walking in Palestine. Getting tired, he sat down next to a bed of cucumbers in order to eat, and a thought* said to him, "Take a cucumber for yourself and eat it. What's the big deal?"

In reply, Abba Zenon said to the thought,*[13] "Thieves go down[14] to punishment,"[15] so find out if, in the future, you can endure punishment. So he got up and stood in the scorching heat[16] and,

---

10. illusion: *phantasía* can also mean a "vision."* A variant reading, PG 65:177–78 n. 75, *phántasma*, "apparition, phantom." See Lampe 1571b.

11. "Took" and "ate" here are the same words as in Matt 26:26 when Jesus says, "Take, eat. This is my body."

12. This also echoes Matt 4:19 when Jesus says *Come, follow me.*

13. This question and answer is reminiscent of Jesus' temptation by the Devil in Matt 4:1-11 // Luke 4:1-13.

14. go down: *hypágō*; in classical Gk., *hypágō* can mean "to bring a person before the Judgment seat" (the *hypó* refers to the person being set under or below the judge); see Liddell and Scott 1850ab, 1850b [II]). In the NT, the verb can be a euphemism for "to die" (Matt 26:24 // Mark 14:21); see Bauer 1028b (3). Matt 25:46 uses *kólasis*, "punishment," in "eternal punishment."

15. There may be an echo here of 1 Cor 6:10, where thieves, among others, will not inherit the kingdom of God.

16. scorching heat: *kaûma* (English *caustic*) occurs only twice in the NT: (1) in Rev 7:16, "those who have come out of the great ordeal will hunger and thirst no more and will not experience scorching heat." (2) In Rev 16:8 when the seven

having fried himself as if in a frying pan,[17] said, "I can't bear the punishment!"[18]

So he said to the thought, "If you can't take the heat, don't steal something and eat it."[19]

7. Abba Zenon said, "When the person who wants God quickly to hear his prayer* stands and stretches out his hands to God, he will pray* for his enemies before everything else, even before praying* for his own soul. If he prays* properly this way, whenever he asks* something of God, God will listen to him."

8. It was said that there was a certain person who lived in a village who was fasting* a great deal, so much so that he was called "the Faster."* When Abba Zenon heard about him,[20] he sent for him. The fellow gladly came.[21] So after praying together, they sat down.

The elder then began to work* in silence. Not finding a way to speak with Abba Zenon, the Faster* began to be disturbed by *acedie.*[22] So he said to the elder, "Pray for me, abba. I want to leave."

The elder said to him, "Why?"

---

angels pour out the seven bowls "of the wrath of God," the fourth angel pours his bowl on the sun, and it "scorches" the sinners with "fierce heat."

17. I have added "as if in a frying pan" because *tēganon* is a frying pan (and later an instrument of torture), and the verb here, *tēganízō*, means "roast, fry" (Bauer 1392b).

18. I can't: using the variant reading, PG 65:177–78 n. 76, *dýnamai* instead of the text's *dýnasai* ("you can't").

19. If you can't take the heat: the Gk. text has "if you can't"; given the context, I have added "take the heat" with its double entendre. Another translation can be "if you can't bear the punishment."

20. him: or "it."

21. gladly, *metà charâs*: or "joyfully," "with joy."

22. disturbed, *ochléō*: the cognate noun *óchlos* means a "crowd"; as Bauer says, "a relatively large number of people crowded together" (745a). In a monastic context, it was thoughts* that were crowding in on the Faster. At Acts 6:16, the NRSV and NIV translate the passive participle of *ochléō* as "tormented": "those tormented by unclean spirits."

In reply he said, "Because my heart is burning up,²³ and I don't know what's going on. When I was living in the village, I fasted* until late in the day, and nothing like this ever happened to me." The elder said, "In the village, you were fed by the sounds and activities of the village. But go, and from now on eat at three in the afternoon—and, whatever you do, do in secret."

When he began to fast* this way, he had a hard time waiting until three, and those who knew him were saying, "The Faster's* possessed by a demon."* He went and told the elder everything. The elder said to him, "This path accords with what God wants."

Concerning Abba Zachariah²⁴

1. [177] [I.6] Abba Macarius²⁵ said to Abba Zachariah, "Explain to me what the work* of the monk is."

He said to him, "You're asking *me*, father?"

Abba Macarius said, "I have confidence in you, Zachariah my child. There's someone who's urging me to ask you."

Zachariah said to him, "In my opinion, father, it's to keep a handle on himself in everything. This is the monk."²⁶

2. [XII.7] Abba Moses went to draw water one time and found Abba Zachariah praying beside the cistern, and the Spirit of God was seated above him.²⁷

3. [XV.19]²⁸ Abba Moses said to Brother Zachariah one time, "Tell me what I should do."

---

23. burning up, *kaíō*: the cognate noun *kaûma* figures in Zenon 5.

24. Gk. *Zachária*.

25. This is probably Macarius the Great (Macarius of Egypt), who has 41 sayings in the AlphAP, or it may be Macarius of Alexandria, who has three.

26. See Zachariah 3.

27. The Spirit (or "spirit") of God occurs over 50 times in the Bible; see Gen 1:2 (in creation), Matt 3:16 (descending on Jesus at baptism), and Rom 8:14 ("all who are led by the Spirit of God are children of God").

28. A version of this saying is found in the Life of John the Little 11 (p. 79).

When he heard this, Zachariah threw himself to the ground at Abba Moses' feet and said, "You're asking me, father?"

The elder said to him, "Believe me, Zachariah my child, I saw the Holy Spirit come down on you;[29] because of this, I have to ask you."

Zachariah then took his cowl, put it under his feet, and stomped on it. He said, "If a person doesn't crush himself like this, he can't be a monk."

4. [XV.18] When Abba Zachariah was living in Scetis* one time, a vision* came to him, so he got up and told his abba, Charion. The elder, who was a practical person, involved in day-to-day activities, wasn't sure such things were real. So he got up and beat Zachariah, saying that it came from the demons.*

But the thought persisted, so Abba Zachariah got up and went to Abba Poemen at night and told him about it, and how it was burning within him. When the elder saw that the vision* was from God, he said to him, "Go to such-and-such elder and whatever he tells you—do it."

So he went to the elder. Before the elder asked him any questions, he knew beforehand what was going on and told Abba Zachariah everything, acknowledging that the vision* was from God. "But go," he said, "obey* your father."

5. [XV.20] Abba Poemen said that Abba Moses asked Abba Zachariah,[30] who was about to die, "What do you see?"

Abba Zachariah said to him, "Isn't it better to keep silent, father?"

Abba Moses said, "Yes, child, be silent."

At the moment Abba Zachariah died, Abba Isidore was sitting there. Looking up to heaven, he said, "Be glad and rejoice, my child Zachariah: the gates of the kingdom of heaven have opened for you."

---

29. See Matt 3:16 // Mark 1:10 // Luke 3:22 (Jesus' baptism); Acts 2:1-4 (Pentecost).

30. A variant reading, AlphAP, Brother Zachariah.

Chapter 7

H / Êta / Ē

Concerning Abba Isaiah[1]

1. [180][2] Abba Isaiah said, "Nothing profits [181] a novice so much as a rebuke: just as a tree is watered each day, so too a novice is rebuked and submits to it."[3]

2. He also used to say to novices who were doing well and were submitting* to holy fathers, "The best dye, such as purple, doesn't fade." And, "Just as young branches are easily directed elsewhere and bent, so too are novices when they submit to the fathers."[4]

3. He also used to say, "A novice moving from monastery to monastery is like an animal in a halter being driven here and there."

4. [XII.8][5] He also said, "The priest of Pelusium,* when there was an agape meal* and the brothers were in the church eating and

1. Gk. *Ēsaías*. The long "e" in Greek, along with other vowels and diphthongs, became a long "i" sound, ī; thus in English "Isaiah."

2. Arabic numerals in brackets before the sayings give the column numbers in the alphabetical *Apophthegmata Patrum* (AlphAP) in the Migne edition, PG 65:75–440.

3. are submitting: submit, *hypoménō*. Bauer suggests that in Rom 12:12 and 8:24 (a variant reading), the verb could mean "put up with"; see Bauer 1039a (2).

4. This sentence could have originally been a separate saying, joined here because of the theme of submission.

5. Bracketed Roman numerals followed by Arabic numerals (e.g., XII.3) identify the chapter and saying number in the systematic *Apophthegmata Patrum*

talking with one another, rebuked them and said, "Be quiet, brothers. I saw[6] a brother eating with you and drinking as many cups as you,[7] and his prayer* was going up into God's presence like fire."

5. They used to say about Abba Isaiah that he took a basket once and went to the threshing floor and said to the landowner, "Give me some grain."

He said to Abba Isaiah, "And did you work at the harvest, abba?"

He said, "No."

The landowner said to him, "So how can you want to get some grain when you didn't work the harvest?"

The elder said to him, "So then, if someone doesn't harvest, that person doesn't receive a reward?"*

The landowner said, "Nope."

So the elder went away.* When the brothers saw what he'd done, they prostrated* themselves before him, asking* him to teach them why he'd done this. The elder said to them, "I did it as an example: if someone doesn't work,* that person will not receive a reward* from God."

6. The same Abba Isaiah summoned one of the brothers, washed his feet,[8] and threw a handful of lentils into a pot; when it came to a boil, he served the lentils. The brother said to him, "The water hasn't boiled long enough, abba."

(SysAP) (Jean-Claude Guy, ed., *Les Apophtegmes des Pères: Collection Systématique* [Paris: Cerf, 2013]). Other references in the work to Guy's edition (for example, Guy 3.219) give the volume and page number of the citation. AnonAP references come from the anonymous *Apophthegmata Patrum,* from John Wortley, trans., *The Anonymous Sayings of the Desert Fathers: A Select Edition and Complete English Translation* (Cambridge: Cambridge University Press, 2013). For a complete list of abbreviated entries, see Abbreviations (pp. xix–xxiii).

6. saw, *eîdon*: SysAP XII.8 has the similar-sounding *oîda,* "I know."

7. and drinking as many cups as you: SysAP XII.8 lacks, perhaps because of a concern about cups of wine.*

8. See John 13:1-17.

He said to him, "Isn't it enough for you that you fully saw the brightness? This in and of itself is a great comfort.*

7. He also used to say, "If God wants to have compassion* for a soul but it resists and won't accept the help but instead follows its own will, God allows it to suffer* what it doesn't want to suffer.* In this way the soul will seek after God."

8. He also used to say, "Whenever someone wishes to repay evil for evil,⁹ that person can, with merely a wave of the hand,¹⁰ harm the brother's conscience."

9. [XXI.1] The same Abba Isaiah was asked,¹¹ "What is love of money?"¹²

He answered, "Not to have faith* in [184] God, that God cares for you and watches over you, not to have faith* in God's promises,¹³ and to be arrogant."¹⁴

10. [XXI.2] He was also asked, "What is backbiting?"¹⁵

He answered, "To be ignorant of the glory of God,¹⁶ and to envy your neighbor."

11. [XXI.3] He was also asked,¹⁷ "What is anger?"*

He answered, "Strife, lying, and ignorance."¹⁸

---

9. See 1 Pet 3:9.

10. wave of the hand, *neûma*: "sign of actions that are empty signs without significance" (Lampe 905b); thus I have added "merely."

11. The same Abba Isaiah was asked: SysAP XXI.1, an elder was asked.

12. See Luke 16:14; 1 Tim 6:10; 2 Tim 3:2.

13. God's promises, *epangelía*: the phrase occurs numerous times in the NT, esp. in Paul's letters; see Rom 4:13, 16; Acts 2:39.

14. to be arrogant: a variant reading, PG 65:183–84 n. 81 and SysAP XXI.1, to love harmful pleasures.

15. backbiting, *katalalía*: or "slander"; see 2 Cor 12:20 and 1 Pet 2:1.

16. To be ignorant of the glory of God: variant readings, PG 65:183–84 nn. 83, 84, not to know God or his glory; SysAP XXI.2, not to know God or the glory of God. See Ps 97:1; 106:20; John 11:40; Rom 1:23.

17. He was also asked: SysAP XXI.3, An elder was asked.

18. Strife: a variant reading, AlphAP 184, n. 84, Heresy; SysAP XXI.3 has "strife." The Greek words sound similar.

Concerning Abba Elijah[19]

1. [184] [III.6] Abba Elijah said, "I'm afraid* of three things: when my soul's going to leave the body, when I'm going to meet God, and when Judgment* is going to be issued against me."

2. [XIX.5] The elders used to speak to Abba Elijah in Egypt about Abba Agathon,* saying that he had been a good abba.[20] The elder said to them, "In his generation he was good."

They said to him, "Why only among monks of old?"

In reply he said, "I said to you, 'He was good *in his generation.* Among the monks of old I saw a person in Scetis* who could stop the sun in the heavens, just as Joshua the son of Nun did.'"[21]

When they heard this, they were astounded* and gave glory to God.

3. Abba Elijah, a member of the diaconate,* asked, "What strength does sin have where there is repentance? What benefit* does love give when there's arrogance?"

4. Abba Elijah said: "I saw some person who was carrying a gourd filled with wine under his arm. In order to put the demons* to shame* (this was a vision*), I said to the brother, 'As an act of love,* take that off—it's mine.' When he took off his pallium,* it was clear that he wasn't carrying anything.

"I said this because even if you [pl.] see something with your eyes or hear something, don't believe it. Even more—watch out for arguments[22] and the thoughts* and intentions of the heart,[23] knowing that the demons* throw out these things in order to stain* the soul, causing it to think things that aren't useful or beneficial*

---

19. Gk. *Ēlías.*

20. abba: a variant reading, PG 65:183–84 n. 85 and SysAP XIX.5, brother.

21. See Josh 10:12-15.

22. See 1 Tim 2:8: people should pray "lifting up holy hands without anger or argument."

23. "Thoughts and intentions" is a direct quotation from Heb 4:12; the verse follows with "of the heart," so I have added the phrase. In Heb 4:12 "the word of God" judges these thoughts and intentions.

and in order to distract the mind* from considering its sins and thinking of God."

5. He also said, "People have their minds* focused either on their sins or on Jesus or on other people."

6. He also said, "If the mind* doesn't sing in tune with the body, its labor is in vain.[24] If someone loves affliction,* it later leads that person into joyfulness and inward stillness."*

7. He also said, "A certain elder was staying in a temple, and the demons* came and said to him, 'Get out of here! This place* is ours!'"[25]

"The elder said, 'You don't have a place.' "*

So they began to scatter his palm branches all over the place. The elder, however, stayed there, collecting them.

Later, the demon* [*sic*] grabbed him by the hand and started to drag him outside. When the elder got near the door, with his other [185] hand he grabbed hold of the door and cried out, "Jesus, help me!" Immediately the demon* fled. The elder began to weep, and the Lord said to him, "Why are you weeping?"

The elder said, "Because they dared to grab hold of a human being and treat him this way!"

The Lord said to him, "It's you who were neglectful.[26] When you sought me, you saw how I was with you."

The elder said, "I'm telling you this because the need for hard work[27] is great: without it, a person can't have God with him.[28] He was crucified for our sake."[29]

---

24. sing: *psállō*, from which "psalm" derives, can also mean "sing the psalms."

25. place: since *tópos* can also indicate a monastic community, the demons are claiming that this particular space is for *their* community.

26. neglectful, *ameléō*: two NT passages are apposite here: Heb 2:3 ("if we disregard so great a salvation") and 1 Tim 4:14 ("do not neglect the [spiritual] gift that is in you").

27. hard work, *kópos*: translated as *labor* earlier in the saying.

28. have God with him: I have used the variant reading, AlphAP XIX.5, rather than the text's "have his God."

29. See Rom 4:25.

8.[30] A brother visited Abba Elijah, who kept contemplative quiet* in the cenobium of the Cave of Abba Sabas,* and said to him, "Abba, offer me counsel."*

The elder said to the brother, "In the days of our fathers, they loved these three virtues:* lack of possessions,* gentleness and being considerate, and self-control.* But now greed seizes hold of the monks, along with gluttony and indolence and arrogance. Seize hold of whichever you want."[31]

Concerning Abba Heraclius[32]

1. [185] [XIV.30] A brother, embattled,*[33] told Abba Heraclius about it.[34]

He said this to that brother in order to strengthen him: A certain elder had a disciple who had been very obedient* for many years. One day, then, the disciple, embattled,* prostrated* himself before the elder, saying, "Make me a monk."

The elder said to him, "Find a place,* and we'll make a cell for you."[35]

30. A shorter version of this saying is in John Moschus, *The Spiritual Meadow of John Moschus (Pratum Spirituale)*, trans. John Wortley, CS 139 (Kalamazoo, MI: Cistercian Publications, 1992), 52.

31. Seize hold of: *kratéō* linguistically and pastorally (and nostalgically) picks up the earlier use of the verb when Elijah lists all the vices monks "seize" now. Thus the verb reinforces the theme of emulating the fathers of old. The monk has to choose which he will seize, virtues or vices.

32. Gk. *Ērákleios,* or possibly *Ērákleion.* In the SysAP he is Heracleides.

33. embattled: a variant reading, PG 65:183–84 n. 90 and SysAP XIV.30, embattled (with the thought of) living by himself.

34. Heraclius: a variant reading, PG 65:183–84 n. 91 and Sys AP XIV.30, Heracleides.

35. A variant reading, PG 65:183–84 n. 92 and SysAP XIV.30 continue, "and you'll be / become a monk."

So he went off a mile distant and found a place, and they left and made him a cell.[36] The elder said to the brother, "Whatever I tell you to do—do it. When you're hungry, eat; drink; sleep. Only, don't leave your cell until Saturday. Then come and stay near me."[37]

The brother spent two days following the elder's orders.*[38] On the third day, suffering from *acedia*,* he said, "Why did the elder do this to me?"[39] Standing up, he sang a large number of psalms. When the sun set, he ate. Getting up, he went to go sleep on his mat. He saw an Ethiopian* lying on it, gnashing his teeth at him.[40] He ran full speed, filled with fear,* and came to the elder. Knocking on the door, he said, "Abba, have mercy on me! Open the door!"[41]

The elder, knowing that the brother didn't follow[42] what he had ordered* him, didn't open the door for him until dawn. When he opened it at dawn, he found the brother outside, begging* for help. Then, feeling compassionate,* he brought him inside.

Then the brother said,[43] "I beg* you, father: I saw a dark-skinned Ethiopian* on my mat when I went to go to sleep!"

The elder said, "You suffered* this[44] because you didn't follow the counsel* I gave you." Then, to the best of the brother's ability,*

---

36. they left and made him a cell: SysAP XIV.30, he made a cell.

37. come and stay near me: literally "come near me." A variant reading, Alph. AP: come quickly. SysAP XIV.30 continues, The elder returned to his own cell.

38. the elder's orders: SysAP XIV.30, what the elder had said.

39. Why did the elder do this to me?: SysAP XIV.30, Why did the elder do this to me, [telling me] not to pray?

40. In Mark 9:18 an evil spirit "grinds his teeth" at a boy whom Jesus then heals (9:14-29). Matthew six times (Luke once) uses a different verb for the gnashing of teeth in the outer darkness (see Matt 8:12 and 13:42).

41. A variant reading, PG 65:183–84 n. 95 and SysAP XIV.30 continue, Open the door for me—hurry!

42. follow: *phylássō*, and below. See Protect in the Glossary.

43. said: SysAP XIV.30, said to the elder.

44. You suffered this: SysAP XIV.30, this happened to you.

the elder provided him monastic formation[45] so he could follow a solitary life, and little by little he became a good monk.[46]

45. provided him monastic formation: *typóō* is cognate with the noun *týpos* (English *typology*), a "stamp or mold." So Heraclius is molding the brother in how to follow the monastic life, what we today call "monastic formation."

46. and little by little he became a good monk: a variant reading, PG 65:183–84 n. 97, and released him, and little by little he became a good monk. SysAP XIV.30, and released him, and little by little he became a tried and true monk. "Tried and true," *dokimázō*, can also mean "respected, esteemed" (Bauer 256a).

Glossary

Vocabulary, Places, People

Because some Greek words in context require different words in English, a number of words have cross-references. Sometimes different words in Greek translate as the same word in English, so occasionally the same word in English will have an asterisk, leading one to the Glossary, and sometimes not, because it is a different Greek word from the one in the Glossary. For example, words in the Glossary related to work have Greek *–erg* as their root (English *ergonomics*); *hard work* (not in the Glossary), is either *kópos* or *pónos*.

Examples from the Septuagint and New Testament are rarely exhaustive; for more examples, see the page numbers supplied from Bauer (full citations of abbreviated works are found in the Abbreviations, pp. xix–xxiii).

The names of the ammas and abbas of the Greek Alphabetical Apophthegmata are not given here. For a selection, see Dramatis Personae.

Cross-references below in **boldface** refer to entries in the Glossary.

Abba. The Aramaic word for *father* used by Jesus and Paul in the New Testament (Mark 14:36; Rom 8:15; Gal 4:6), transferred as a title of respect to respected or venerated monks. On the pedagogy of the abbas and ammas, see Graham Gould, *The Desert Fathers on Monastic Community* (Oxford: Clarendon, 1993), chap. 2, "The Abba and His Disciple," 26–87; André Louf, "Spiritual Fatherhood in the Literature of the Desert," in J. R. Sommerfeldt, ed., *Abba: Guides* *to Wholeness and Holiness East and West*, CS 28 (Kalamazoo, MI: Cistercian Publications, 1982); and Gabriel Bunge, *Spiritual Fatherhood: Evagrius Ponticus on the Role of Spiritual Father* (Yonkers, NY: St Vladimir's, 2018).

Ability. Gk. *dýnamis*. See **Power**.

Acedia. Gk. *akēdía*, Lat. *acedia*, "the noonday demon," "indifference, apathy"; "weariness, torpor" (Montanari 67bc); *kêdos*, "care, thought"; "anxiety, worry, pain, agonizing suffering, grief" + *a-*, alpha-privative negative (Montanari 1122a). See Ps 91:1-6 and 90:1-6: Those "who live in the shelter of the Most High / . . . will not fear / . . . the pestilence that stalks in darkness, / or the destruction that wastes at midday." The "noonday demon," *de daemonio meridiano*, comes from Jerome's Vulgate (Latin) translation; the modified Vulgate has *pernicie quae vastat meridie*, "the destruction that wastes at midday" (*Biblia Sacra iuxta Vulgatem Clementiam: Nova Editio* [Madrid: Biblioteca de Autores Cristianos, 1977], 531). Cassian devotes the Tenth Book of the *Institutes* to "The Spirit of Acedia"; he defines it as "a wearied or anxious heart" and continues that it "is akin to sadness and is the peculiar lot of solitaries and a particularly and frequent foe of those dwelling in the desert. It disturbs the monk especially around the sixth hour [noon]" (219).

Donald Grayston, *Thomas Merton and the Noonday Demon: The Camaldoli Correspondence* (Eugene, OR: Cascade Books, 2015), chap. 1, 12–32, gives a good survey; on p. 13 he gives good reasons to transliterate rather than translate *acedia*. Kathleen Norris states it well: "Acedia is not a relic of the fourth century or a hang-up of some weird Christian monks, but a force we ignore at our own peril."[1] *Acedia* is a key monastic term. Lampe 61b–62b is instructive: "fatigue, exhaustion; weariness, inertia"; "listlessness; torpor, boredom." Its causes can be natural (B3a) or preternatural (B3b), attributed to a particular demon. With its effects (B4) it "causes monks to leave monasteries"; its remedies are (B5): "prayer and work."[2] Dom Bernardo Olivera offers this etymological insight: in

---

1. Kathleen Norris, *Acedia & Me: A Marriage, Monks, and a Writer's Life* (New York: Riverhead Books, 2008), 130.

2. See further Siegfried Wenzel, "Ἀκηδία: Additions to Lampe's Patristic Greek Lexicon," *Vigiliae Christianae* 17 (1963): 173–76, available online.

Latin "there is a family of words related to acedia, such as *acer* (sharp, bitter), *acetum* (vinegar), and *acerbum* (harsh), which, taken figuratively, [make] us think that persons suffering from acedia have received a high dose of acidity," and thus, Norris adds, "are incapable of appreciating the sweetness of life."[3]

Evagrius says that "the demon of acedia—also called the noonday demon—is the one that causes the most serious trouble of all."[4] Mary Schaffer argues for "the pervasive and undeniable influence of Evagrius" on the *Life of Syncletica* and sees a "close harmony" with Cassian, *Conference* 14. She states that acedia is "one of the [*Life*'s] major themes."[5] See Cassian, *Institutes* 10.[6] See Gabriel Bunge, *Despondency: The Spiritual Teaching of Evagrius Ponticus on Acedia* (Yonkers, NY: St Vladimir's, 2011). For modern reflections and many insights on acedia, see Grayston, *Thomas Merton*; Norris, *Acedia & Me*; and Andrew Solomon, *The Noonday Demon: An Atlas of Depression* (2001; New York: Scribner, 2015). Norris speaks highly of Aldous Huxley's essay "Accidie"; I could not find it, but "Mind Your Maker, Aldous Huxley on Accidie" appears to have portions of it (mindyourmaker.com/2008/10/03/aldous-huxley -on-accidie-aka-melancholy-boredom-ennui-despair/).

Acquire. See **Possess / Possessions**.

Activity. Gk. *ergasía* is cognate with *érgon*; see **Work**.

Act of love. Gk. *agápē*. See **Love**.

Action. Gk. *érgon*. See **Work**.

Active. Gk. *energéō*. See **Work**.

Adversary, the. Satan

---

3. Olivera, "The Sadness Corroding Our Desire for God," 2007 circular letter, http://www.aimintl.org/en/2015-05-29-13-29-49/bulletin-96/acedie; Norris, *Acedia*, 203.

4. Evagrius Ponticus*, Praktikos & Chapters on Prayers*, trans. John Eudes Bamberger, CS 3 (Kalamazoo, MI: Cistercian Publications, 1981).

5. Mary Schaffer, *The Life and Regimen of the Blessed and Holy Syncletica by Pseudo-Athanasius, Part Two, A Study of the Life* (Eugene, OR: Wipf and Stock, 2005; Peregrina Publishing, 2001), 11.

6. John Cassian, *John Cassian: The Institutes*, trans. Boniface Ramsey, ACW 58 (New York: Paulist Press, 2000), 217–34.

Afflict. Gk. *thlíbō* can also mean "crush," of crushing corn. The etymology of English *oppress*, from Latin *opprimere*, "press down, crush," is apposite here. *Thlíbō* and its cognate noun *thlípsis* occur frequently in the NT, especially in Paul's letters; see 2 Cor 1:6; 2 Cor 7:5. See 2 Cor 4:8: "We are afflicted in every way, but not crushed" (*stenochōroúmenoi < stenochōréō*; *stenós*, "narrow, a strait," as in English "straitened circumstances"). Lampe 653a notes that some found affliction's origin in sin, and others declared that God was not its source.

Afraid, be. Gk. *phobéomai*. See **Fear**. The aorist aspect often has the sense "become frightened" (Bauer 1060b–61a).

Agape meal. Gk. *agápē*, "love" (see **Love**). Early Christians used the word for a communal meal, often combined with or following Communion. See Jude 12; Bauer 7a notes that "the details are not discussed in the NT, although Paul implicitly refers to it in 1 Cor 11:17-33." As a technical term, Lampe 8a, explains it as "denoting a common meal of fellowship to which the poor were invited or from which distribution was made to those supported by the Church." In early monasticism the term also refers to such a meal, often on Saturday, when the **anchoritic** and **semi-anchoritic** monks would leave their cells and gather in a central location. In Arsenius 11 and 20 *agápē* indicates "an act of love or charity," especially of helping those in need.

Age. Gk. *aíōn*. Aíōn is a laden term in the NT; see Bauer 32a–33a. For Paul it designates the present age, nearing its end (1 Cor 3:18), the world, as opposed to God (Rom 12:2; 1 Cor 1:20): "The god of this world [*aíōn*] has blinded the minds of the unbelievers" (2 Cor 4:4). It and *kairós* (see **Opportune time**) can be eschatological.

Alexandria. Alexandria was "the pre-eminent emporium for trade and commerce" in the eastern Mediterranean. "Yet Alexandria underwent considerable change across Late Antiquity, and it was appreciably different from the city that had once been the dynastic capital of the Ptolemies" (*The Oxford Dictionary of Late Antiquity*, ed. Oliver Nicholson, 2 vols. [Oxford: Oxford UP, 2018], 1.47b–49b). It was the home of such great early Christian thinkers as Clement and Origen. See Christopher Haas, *Alexandria in Late Antiquity: Topography and Social Conflict, Ancient Society and History* (Baltimore: Johns Hopkins University Press, 1996). Ewa Wipszycka,

The Second Gift of the Nile: Monks and Monasteries in Late Antique Egypt, trans. Damian Jasiński, The Journal of Juristic Papyrology Supplements (Warsaw: The University of Warsaw, 2018), 9, argues that in "writing about the history of Christianity in Egypt, it is possible—and indeed necessary—to abandon the distinction between Alexandria and Egypt." See **Egypt**. I believe her dichotomy is incorrect.

Amazed, be. See **Astonished, be.**

Amma. "Mother"; used of venerable female monks. See **Abba.**

Anchorite. Gk. *anachōrētḗs*, cognate with *anachōréō*, "to **withdraw**." Anchorites were monks who lived by themselves or with only a disciple or two. Athanasius's Life of Antony 3.1–3; 11.1 (pp. 61–63, 85) claims that Antony's great innovation was to withdraw from village **asceticism** into the **desert**.

Anger. Gk. *orgḗ* (n.), *orgízomai* (vb.). Anger is a chief concern of the ammas and abbas. See Matt 5:22; Rom 2:5; 2 Cor 12:20; Jas 1:19-20. See Cassian, *Institutes* 8 (pp. 191–208). See Gould, *Desert Fathers*, 107–37, esp. 112–20. Gould correctly observes, "With the exception of the conduct of the teaching relationship, there is no area of personal relationships with which the Desert Fathers show themselves more concerned than the problems arising from anger, judgement, dispute, and slander" (112).

Antioch. Antioch on the Orontes (modern Antakya, Turkey) was "Metropolis of Syria Prima (Syria Coele, seat of the Comes Orientis, the principal civil administrator of the Dioecesis of Oriens), frequently in the 3rd and 4th centuries an imperial residence, a leading literary centre, and the home of a distinctive school of Christian theology" (ODLA 1:84a–85b, here 1.84a).

Apatheia. It's unfortunate that English has turned Gk. *apátheia* into *apathy*, because *apathy* is the opposite of a sustained spiritual life striving for *apátheia*. Norris correctly points out that *apátheia* "has nothing to do with apathy, but is a blessed state of equilibrium, free from distraction or regret."[7] *Apátheia* comes from the Greek word

---

7. Norris, *Acedia*, 280; see 280–82. The OED online basically equates *apatheia* with *apathy*, but a sidebar notes that the entry hasn't been updated from the 1885 edition.

páthos, "incident, accident, change," then "calamity," "disease," then "emotion, passion," + -*a*, a negative. See **Passions**. Lampe 170a uses "impassibility"; another traditional translation is "passionlessness." But these are formidable words. Easier equivalents are "freedom from emotion," "absence of sin or sinful emotions," hence "mastery over the passions, detachment, tranquility." The NT uses neither *apátheia* nor its cognate *apathês*, "free of suffering," "without suffering, uninjured" (Bauer 95b). One should carefully note the emphasis among the monastics on removing *sinful* emotions; the monks are not advocating catatonia. *Apatheia* literally means to be "without passion," a much-desired state. The monks considered passions to be disordered desires that distract a person from (literally "draw away from") following God. In his discussion of self-care and philosophy in Antiquity and Late Antiquity, Zachary Smith makes this connection: "The final state in philosophies of self-care finds the tranquil, passionless body and soul in perfect harmony and under perfect **self-control**, expressed in the AlphAP as *apatheia*."[8] See Evagrius, *Praktikos* 63–89 (pp. 33–39). See John Behr, *Asceticism and Anthropology in Irenaeus and Clement* (Oxford: Oxford University Press, 2000), esp. chap. 6, 185–207.

Apostle, the. The Apostle Paul, a common reference in early Christianity.

Appeal. Gk. *parakaléō*. See **Ask**, and **Comfort**.

Arabia of Egypt. This phrase probably indicates the "Arabian desert," that is, the desert places east of the Nile; the western desert was called the "Libyan desert."

Arcadius and Honorius. Sons of **Theodosius** and, later, emperors. Arcadius Flavius (ca. 377–408) was the elder son of Theodosius and Eastern Roman emperor 395–408 (ODLA 1:119–20); Honorius, the younger son (384–423), was the Western Roman emperor from 395–423 (ODLA 1:739–40). Both have entries in *The Prosopography of the Later Roman Empire*, ed. A. H. M. Jones, et al. (Cambridge: Cambridge University Press, 1971), 1:99 and 1:442, respectively.

---

8. Zachary Smith, *Philosopher-Monks, Episcopal Authority, and the Care of the Self: The* Apophthegmata Patrum *in Fifth-Century Palestine*, Instrumenta Patristica et Mediaevalia 80 (Turnhout: Brepols, 2017).

Archbishop. See **Bishop.** "In the 4th and 5th c. the title was applied to the patriarchs and holders of other outstanding sees [the episcopal seat, that is, where the archbishop presided]. Later its use was extended to metropolitans (or primates) having jurisdiction over an ecclesiastical province" (ODCC 81a).

Artábē. Gk. *artábē* is, like *paradise*, a Persian loan-word, quantity uncertain, that became an Egyptian measurement, later equally an amphora, 39 liters, which is too large a quantity for the amount in Ammoës 5; there he makes 50 artabas of bread, 2000 liters = 528 gallons. R. P. Duncan-Jones, "The Choenix, the Artaba and the Modius," *Zeitschrift für Papyrologie und Epigraphik*, 21 (1976): 43–52, 50, speaks of "the confusion in available sources about the absolute size of the attested artaba measures." He calculates that the artaba consisted of 3 modii of 8.62 liters each, equaling about 26 liters or 7 US gallons.

Ascetic activity. Gk. *politeía*. See **Way of life, monastic.**

Ascetic practice. Gk. *politeía*. See **Way of life, monastic.**

Ascetic practice. Gk. *en askḗsei, askḗsei.* The origins of *ascesis* are athletic—"exercise, practice, training"—and by the time of Lucian in the 2nd cent. CE it could mean "mode of life, profession" (Liddell and Scott 257b). On ascesis as self-care, see Smith, *Philosopher-Monks,* chap. 4.5, 203–50. C. Wilfred Griggs, *Early Egyptian Christianity* (Leiden: Brill, 1990), 64, makes an important observation: "One should observe that while **Clement** considered asceticism one of the main indicators of Christian gnostic heresy, Eusebius (certainly looking back through the perspective of a developing ascetic tradition within the monastic movement—and looking favorably at that) mentions in positive terms **Origen**'s own tendency towards asceticism." See Teresa M. Shaw, *The Burden of the Flesh: Fasting and Sexuality in Early Christianity* (Minneapolis: Fortress, 1998), esp. the Introduction, 5–10; Behr, *Asceticism and Anthropology,* esp. 129–207.

Ashamed, be. See **Shame.**

Ask. Gk. *parakaléō*: "call to one's side," "call upon for help," "appeal to, request, implore, entreat" (Bauer 765b–66a). See also **Comfort.**

Astonished, Astounded, Amazed, be. Gk. *thaumázō* (vb.), *thaumastós* (n.); *exhístēmi*, and *ekthambéomai*. Also, "marvel." "To be extraordinarily impressed or disturbed by something" (Bauer 444b–45a). The word occurs often in the NT for those amazed or impressed by

things Jesus does (Matt 15:31; Luke 8:25; John 3:7). The American
poet Galway Kinnell concludes his poem "Astonishment" with
"Before us, our first task is to astonish / And then, harder by far, to
be astonished" (*The New Yorker*, 23 July 2012; www.newyorker
.com/contributors/galway-kinnell).

Athanasius. Lived about 296 to 373. Archbishop of Alexandria and
author of the *Life of Antony*. See CE 298a–302b; ODCC 101b–12a;
ODLA 1:170b–72b. For an introduction, see Alvyn Pettersen, *Athanasius* (Harrisburg, PA: Morehouse, 1995).

Attendants. Gk. *diakonētēs* (*diákonos*: deacon), those who attended to
a senior monk in a monastery (Lampe 351a).

Attention, pay. See **Concerned, be**.

Attitude. Gk. *logismós*. See **Thought/s**.

Aureus / Aurei. The *aureus* (pl. *aurei*) was the standard gold coin of
Rome. At 18 aurei, the book in Gelasius 1 was fabulously expensive;
the numbers probably reflect storytelling hyperbole. "In Constantine's reform of AD 312, the aureus was replaced by the solidus as
the basic monetary unit" (www.britannica.com/topic/aureus); see
ODLA 1:182a.

Awe-inspiring. Gk. *thaumastós*. See **Astonished**.

Babylon. Upper Babylon is "the oldest part of the city of Cairo . . .
situated on the east bank of the Nile, to some extent on the border
between Upper and Lower Egypt. . . . In late antiquity 'Babylon'
designated the settled country between Heliopolis and the Roman
fortress situated to the south" (CE 317a–23b).

Bandit. Gk. *lēstēs*. Bauer 594a correctly points out that *lēstēs*, etymologically connected with the word for "booty, spoils," does not mean
a simple thief, whereas *lēstēs* means "robber, highwayman, bandit,"
"revolutionary, insurrectionist, guerrilla." The old translation of *thief*
for *lēstēs* is inaccurate; some of them were, as we say, freedom-
fighters. See Luke 23:39-43. As Jesus is being crucified, one of the
two criminals says to him: "Jesus, remember me when you come
into your kingdom," and Jesus replies, "Truly I tell you, today you
will be with me in Paradise." The Roman state executed Jesus as a
lēstēs. So Jesus was crucified not with two thieves but with two
bandits / insurrectionists (Matt 27:38); John 18:40 identifies Barab-
bas as a bandit.

Barbarians. Nomadic tribes from the west (the Libyan desert), including the **Mazices**, invaded **Scetis*** a number of times in the 5ᵗʰ and 6ᵗʰ centuries. The first invasion took place in 407–8. See Derwas Chitty, *The Desert a City* (Crestwood, NY: St Vladimir's, 1966), 60–61; CE 2102b–6a: "Scetis was raided by barbarians, with destruction of buildings and temporary dispersal of the monks, in 407, 434, and 444." For a good discussion, see Hugh G. Evelyn-White, ed., Walter Hauser, *The Monasteries of the Wâdi 'N Natrun*, vol. II, *The History of the Monasteries of Nitria and Scetis* (New York: Metropolitan Museum, 1932; repr. Arno Press, 1973), 2.150–67.

Basket. Gk. *thallís*; see Montanari 923a. Wortley, *Give Me a Word* (Yonkers, NY: St Vladimir's, 2014), 43 n. 12, footnotes *thallís* as "A dry measure of uncertain dimension; a basket made of palm-fronds." *Thállos* indicates a young shoot, a young branch, but it also seems to indicate a basket or bag made from palm branches, as in Arsenius 17. W. E. Crum and H. I. Bell, eds., *Wadi Sarga: Coptic and Greek Texts from the Excavations Undertaken by the Byzantine Research Account* (Hauniae: Gyldenaske Boghandel-Nordisk Vorlag, 1922), 226 (archive.org/stream/wadisargacopticg00crumuoft?ref=ol#page/n8/mode/2up), cite 15 occurrences of Coptic *thall(ion)* in the texts; the word occurs often in receipts. They translate the word as either "sack" or "bag."

Bear. Gk. *bastázō* is the word in John 19:17 for bearing the cross. In the parable of the laborers and the vineyard (Matt 20:1-16), some of the workers complain that they have "borne [*bastázō*] the burden of the day and the scorching heat." See **Support**.

Be at peace. Gk. *anápausis*. See **Inward stillness**.

Beg. See **Ask**.

Believe. Gk. *pisteúō*, cognate with *pístis*, "faith, trust (in)," "have faith." See **Faith**.

Beneficial / Benefit. Gk. *ōpheléō*. Having and doing beneficial things and being benefited by something or someone is very important in early monasticism.

Beseech. See **Ask**.

Bishop. In the NT, an *epískopos* (English *episcopate*) is "one who has the responsibility of safeguarding or seeing to it that something is done in the correct way, guardian" (Bauer 379b–80a); *episkopéō* (vb.) means "to give attention to, look at, take care, see to it," "to accept responsibility for the care of someone, oversee, care for" (Bauer 379a). See Acts 20:28; Phil 1:1; 1 Tim 3:2; Titus 1:7. As Bauer notes, "The ecclesiastical loanword 'bishop' is too technical and loaded with late historical baggage for precise signification of usage of *epískopos* and cognates in our literature, esp. the NT" (379b). See Lampe 532b–34a. "The first witness to monepiscopacy (only one bishop at the head of each local church) is found in the letters of Ignatius of Antioch [early 2nd c.]. . . . By the middle of the second century, the Ignatian type of church order, with a single bishop at the head of each Christian community, was generally observed" (EEC 150b–54a, here 151b). On the Alexandrian episcopacy, see chaps. 2, 5, 9–12 in Ewa Wipszycka, *The Alexandrian Church: People and Institutions*, JJP Supplements (Warsaw: Journal of Juristic Papyrology, 2015). See David Brakke, *Athanasius and the Politics of Asceticism* (Oxford: Oxford University Press, 1995), esp. 80–141. Monks became bishops quite early, for example, Serapion of Thmuis (bishop mid-4th cent.), but it is uncertain when bishops started to come exclusively from the monasteries, as they do in the Coptic Church today. See Zachary Smith, *Philosopher-Monks*, 65–122; he partially concludes, "Travelogues, histories, and monastic sources suggest debates in late antiquity about the relationship between monks and bishops in Egypt. Taken together, the texts present a muddled view of the relationship between monks and ecclesiastical authorities in Egypt." See Griggs, *Early Egyptian Christianity*, 79–115. For a detailed focus on Egypt, see Stephen J. Davis, *The Early Coptic Papacy: The Egyptian Church and Its Leadership in Late Antiquity* (Cairo / New York: AUC Press, 2004), esp. 43–84. See also "Monasticism, monks" in his Index, 249a.

Bishoy, Abba. *Pshoi* in Coptic and *Paḯsios* in Greek. A fourth- to fifth-century Egyptian monk who gathered a community around him in Scetis.* See Tim Vivian and Maged S. A. Mikhail, eds., *The Life of Bishoi* (Cairo: AUC Press, 2021). He does not have any sayings in the AlphAP or SysAP. See CE 2029a–30a (under "Pshoi of Scetis").

Black man. See **Ethiopian(s)**.

Blessed. Greek *makários*, often used to pun on **Macarius**'s name. Each verse of the Beatitudes, Matt 5:3-11, begins with *Makárioi* ("Blessed").

Book(s). The monks had varying views about books, and their efficacy—or lack thereof; for example, see Bessarion 12, Ephraim 8, Epiphanius 8, and Euprepius 7. See Lucien Regnault, *The Day-to-Day Life of the Desert Fathers in Fourth-Century Egypt*, trans. Étienne Poirier, Jr. (Petersham, MA: St. Bede's, 1999), 92–93. In the Arabic AlphAP 26, Antony, whom the tradition often sees as illiterate (Life of Antony 1.1 [p. 57], 72.1 [p. 209], and 73.3 [p. 211]), advises "If you sit in your cell, don't neglect these things: reading books, beseeching God, and working with your hands." (A volume on the Greek, Coptic, and Arabic AlphAP is forthcoming, with Lisa Agaiby, from Cistercian Publications).

Bread. Bread, with salt, was the main part of the monastic diet. See Regnault, *Day-to-Day Life,* 65–69.

Bread, dried. Gk. *paximátion* or *paximádion*. In Historia Lausiaca 22.6, "Paul the Simple" (p. 60), the loaves of dry bread weigh six ounces each; Antony, "who had adopted a way of life more severe than he had ever practiced in his younger days," moistens one to eat and gives three to his hungry guest, who has not eaten in three days. Life of Antony 12.4 (p. 89) states that Antony lays away "enough bread for six months (those from the **Thebaid** do this, and often the bread is stored for even an entire year without harm)."

Call / call on. See **Ask,** and **Comfort**.

Canopus. A "city located on the northern coast of the western Delta, 15 miles (24 km) northeast of Alexandria. . . . Rufinus (*Historia ecclesiastica* 2.26–27) relates that in his day (second half of the fourth century) the Egyptian god Serapis still held sway in Canopus. . . . Jerome relates that monks from the monasteries of Pachomius settled in Canopus and followed the Pachomian rule. . . . In order to avoid the pagan associations evoked by the name Canopus, the monks changed the name of their dwelling to Monastery of the Metanoia" (CE 31b–32a). This monastery was probably outside of, not in, Canopus. Arsenius 42 says that he spent three years in Canopus but does not specify this monastery.

Careful watch. Gk. *phylakḗ*. See **Protect / Protection**.

Carry. Gk. *bastázō*. See **Bear**.

Cassian, Abba. Cassian (about 360 to 435) came to Egypt in the late fourth century; he later wrote two great monastic books, *Institutes* and *Conferences*, drawing on his experience in Egypt.

Catechumen. Gk. *katēchéō* and related words. In the early church the catechumenate became a rigorous and lengthy time of instruction (*katēchéō*). The catechumenate could last up to three years, and catechumens left the church before the Eucharist began. See Luke 1:4; Acts 21:24; 1 Cor 14:19; Gal 6:6. See EEC 185–86. The verb occurs only once in the SysAP (Guy, 3.55; Wortley, *Book*, 37): X.176.2 (AlphAP Mios 3).

Cause to sin. Gk. *skandalízō*. See **Scandalize**.

Cells, the. See **Kellia**.

Cenobium. Gk. *koinóbion*, "common life." A monastic community where the monks lived together (as opposed to **anchorites** and **semi-anchorites**) under an **abbot** and a **Rule**. See **Pachomius**.

Chalcedon. The Council of Chalcedon took place in 451. Its history, with the Christological fisticuffs and even bloodshed, is complex; see Frances M. Young, *From Nicaea to Chalcedon: A Guide to its Literature and Background*, 2nd ed. (Ada, MI: Baker, 2010). The Council issued a Definition, affirming the authority of the three previous councils, and affirmed "that in Christ there are two perfect natures, divine and human . . . . The definition resulted in a schism in the East between those who maintained that the council had betrayed **Cyril** in affirming a duality of natures, and those who believed that it had upheld his teaching" (ODLA 1:314ab). (See "Miaphysite," ODLA 2:1016b–17a.) While the majority in Egypt were Miaphysite, the majority in Palestine embraced the Chalcedonian Definition. Thus Gelasius 4 clearly shows a Palestinian setting.

Cilicia. Cilicia Prima and Secunda were "Provinces of southeast Anatolia" (the peninsula of Asia Minor) in the Diocese of Oriens. The area was evangelized early (Paul was from there; see Acts 21:39; 22:3), and "Numerous bishops from the region attended the Council of Nicaea in 325" (ODLA 1:345ab). See Gal 1:21; Acts 6:9.

Clement. Clement of Alexandria (ca. 150–ca. 215), a theologian, "agreed with the Gnostics in holding 'gnosis,' religious **knowledge** or illumination, to be the chief element in Christian perfection. But for him the only true 'gnosis' was that which presupposed the faith of the Church" (ODCC 303ab). See Johannes Quasten, *Patrology*, 3 vols. (Westminster, MD: Christian Classics, 1984), 2.5–36, and Behr, *Asceticism and Anthropology*.

Cloak. See **Clothing, monastic.**

Clothing, monastic. The sources, written and pictorial, are often not clear or consistent about monastic dress. See R.-G. Coquin, "A propos des vêtements des moines egyptiens," *Bulletin de Société D'Archéologie Copte* 31 (1992): 3–23; and Karel C. Innemée, *Ecclesiastical Dress in the Medieval Near East*, vol. 1 (Leiden: Brill, 1992), esp. 91–129.

Coat. Gk. *melótē*. See Innemée, *Ecclesiastical Dress*: "The melote is used as a traveling-coat which one takes off at arrival" (106–7).

Combatant. See **War.**

Comes. Gk. *deílēs*: "Although often translated as 'count,' the root meaning of *comes* is 'companion,' an allusion to proximity to the emperor. As such it was a term which had long been used informally to refer to those who accompanied the emperor when travelling. In Late Antiquity, however, it became a formal title for a range of offices associated with the imperial court, most prominently" financial offices. "A specifically military usage also emerged (*Comes Rei Militaris*), referring to officers commanding detachments of the field army" (ODLA 1:375a).

Comfort. In John 14:16 Jesus tells the disciples that he will send "another Paraclete [*paráklētos*]," usually translated "advocate, intercessor, spokesman"; "comforter, consoler" (Lampe 1018b); Bauer 766ab: "mediator, intercessor, helper." In Matt 2:18 and 5:4, in the context of mourning, the verb means "comforted." Lampe 1017a also suggests "summon, exhort." A *paráklētos* originally meant a person "called to one's aid" (literally "called [*kaléō*] to one's side (*pará*)" (Liddell and Scott 1313a); see John 14:16. Also "appeal to" and "call on," "summon," "entreat."

Command / Commandment. Gk. *entolḗ* (n.) and *entéllō / entéllomai* (vb.) occur 56 and 6 times, respectively, in the SysAP. See Exod 15:26; Isa 48:18; Matt 22:38-40.

Compassion. Gk. *eleéō* (vb), *éleos/eleēmōn* (n.), translated in the literature (usually) as "mercy," "have mercy on." But the words also mean "compassion," "have compassion for" (Bauer 315b and 316ab); I usually use the latter. I am not clear on the distinctions in

Greek between *eleéō, éleos / eleémōn* ("mercy") and *splanchnízomai* (vb.), *splánchnon* / pl. *splánchna* (n.) ("compassion"). Bauer 938b points out that *splánchnon* / *splánchna* initially means "the inward parts of a body, including esp. the viscera, inward parts, entrails," and continues, "as often in the ancient world, inner body parts served as referents for psychological aspects . . . ; of the seat of the emotions, in our usage a transference is made to the rendering 'heart.'" For *splánchnon* / *splánchna* Bauer gives "love, affection," and not "compassion," but perhaps our *empathy* better captures the sense. See Matt 9:27; 15:22; 18:27; 20:29-34; Rom 12:8. See AnonAP 281–89 (pp. 187–95).

Concerned, Be. Gk. *proséchō* has a wide variety of meanings in the NT apposite here: "be concerned about, care for, take care," with the reflexive pronoun, as here, "be careful, be on one's guard," "pay close attention to, give heed to" (Bauer 879b–80a). It occurs numerous times in the LXX; see Deut 4:9: "But take care and watch yourselves closely." See Acts 20:28 and Luke 17:3.

Conclude. Gk. *logízomai*; see **Thoughts**.

Confidence. Gk. *parrēsía* is a linguistic mixed bag: "freedom of speech, free speaking, frankness"; "power, faculty, liberty" (see Montanari 1590b). It and its cognate verb *parrēsiázomai* are positive in the NT: in addition to the meanings above, it can also mean "courage, confidence, boldness, fearlessness" (Bauer 781b). But the word can also mean "license, [over-]confidence, impudence" (Montanari 1590b). *Parrēsía* is an important virtue in the NT, in John and Paul especially, and passed into monasticism: "a use of speech that conceals nothing and passes over nothing, outspokenness, frankness, plainness," "a state of boldness and confidence, courage, confidence, boldness, fearlessness" (Bauer 781ab). Paul uses the term often: 2 Cor 3:12; 7:4; Phil 1:20; Phlm 8, and in the Pauline or deutero-Pauline Eph 3:12; 6:19. Douglas Burton-Christie, *The Word in the Desert: Scripture and the Quest for Holiness in Early Christian Monasticism* (New York: Oxford University Press, 1993), 110, says that "freedom of speech [*parrēsía*] . . . characterized the elders of the desert and the authority their words enjoyed." See Thomas Merton, "Free Speech (*Parrhesia*)," in Merton, *The New Man* (New York: Noonday / Farrar, Straus & Giroux, 1961), 71–98.

Conscience-stricken. See **Contrition**.

Consider. See **Thoughts**.

Constantine. "The Great" (d. 337) became emperor in 312. He legalized Christianity in the Roman Empire. See ODLA 1:383b–87a.

Constantinople. Modern Istanbul, Turkey, founded "by **Constantine I** in 324 on the site of the small city of Byzantium. . . . During the 4th century the rulers of the eastern half of the Empire often resided in Constantinople and lived there permanently from" 395–641 (ODLA 1:389a, here 1:389a–404b).

Constantius. Constantius II (317–361), Roman Emperor from 324 to 361. See ODLA 1:405a–6b.

Contemplation. Gk. *theōría*, literally "seeing," "beholding"; in the NT "to come to the understanding of something, notice, perceive, observe, find" (Bauer 454b [2]); see Acts 17:22; John 4:19. Later, the higher level of **ascetic practice**, gained through *hēsychía*, "**contemplative quiet**," "quiet contemplation"; meditation whose goal is union with God.

Contemplative quiet. Gk. *hēsychía*, contemplative quiet, outer and inner silence and peace; live a life of contemplative quiet, *hēsycházō* (English *hesychast* and *hesychasm*). *Hēsychía* is a key monastic term and concept, and a word difficult to capture in English: "silence, of God prior to the revelation of his mysteries"; "tranquility, quiet, as a state of the soul necessary for contemplation"; "tranquility as a state of separation from the world, = solitude" (Lampe 609ab). In the NT see (vb.) 1 Thess 4:11, and (n.) 2 Thess 3:12, although the words in the NT do not reflect later developments. On *hēsychía* see SysAP II.1–35, lines 124–47 (John Wortley, *The Book of the Elders: Sayings of the Desert Fathers: The Systematic Collection*, CS 240 [Collegeville, MN: Cistercian Publications, 2012], 15–24); AnonAP 133–43 (Wortley, *The Anonymous Sayings of the Desert Fathers: A Select Edition and Complete English Translation* [Cambridge: Cambridge University Press, 2013], 93–99). See Gould, *The Desert Fathers*, 167–77, esp. 171–77, for a good discussion of *hēsychía* vis-à-vis personal and communal relationships.

Contend. Gk. *agōnízomai*. See **Fight**.

Contrition. Gk. *katánuxis*, often translated "compunction" (Lat. *compungere*, "severely sting, prick," English *puncture*), "stung to the heart." See **Pricked**. The base meaning of *katanússomai* (vb.) is "to sting, prick, goad," and the cognate adjective *katanuktikós* can indicate a "piercing bird song," then "causing compunction, heart-searching," so I have used the metaphor "stung to the heart" to capture the sense. In patristic Greek, *katanússomai* can specifically indicate "of moving to repentance." Its noun, *katánuxis*, means "compunction," so "stab of conscience" and "conscience-stricken" are good (all Lampe 713a). See SysAP III.1–56, lines 148–83 (Wortley, *Book*, 25–37) and AnonAP 519ff. (Wortley, *The Anonymous Sayings*, 353–75).

Control / Get control of. Gk. *enkratḗs*: "self-control" or "moderation" (often translated "abstinence"). *Enkratḗs* and *enkráteia* are key monastic terms; see **Self-control**. On *enkráteia* see SysAP IV.1–104, lines 184–239 (Wortley, *Book*, 38–58).

Co-operation. Gk. *synergía* (English *synergy*), literally "working together." See **Work**.

Counsel. Literally, "Tell me a word [*lógos*]." See **Spiritual Guidance**.

Cross. Make the Sign of the Cross, Gk. *sphragízō* (vb.), *sphragís* (n.) "sign, seal." The earliest examples that Lampe (1354b [B]) adduces for making the sign of the cross are *The Acts of John* and *The Acts of Matthew* (ca. 260–ca. 339), but in *The Acts of Paul and Thecla* 22, possibly as early as 100 CE, Thecla, about to be martyred (God rescues her), "having made the sign of the cross . . . went up on the pile [of wood, to be burned]";[9] Eusebius (d. 339) writes, in *Demonstratio evangelica* 7:14: "it is the custom for us to be sealed with the sign of Christ"; Life of Antony 13.5 by Athanasius (d. 373): "You will seal yourselves" or "Seal yourselves," or "cross / will cross yourselves" (89); Tertullian (ca. 160–ca. 225), *De corona* 3: "At every forward step and movement, at every going in and out, . . . in all the ordinary actions of daily life, we trace upon the forehead the sign"; see Life of Antony 80 (pp. 225, 227).

Cyril of Alexandria. Patriarch of Alexandria (412–444), "one of the most powerful churchmen of his age, and a sublime theologian known especially for his exposition of Christology" (ODLA 1:444b, here 444b–45b). See also CE 671b–75b.

Deacon. Gk. *diákonos.* See **Diaconate**.

---

9. New Advent, Fathers of the Church, online.

Deed. Gk. *érgon.* See **Work.**

Deceitful One. Satan

Demon/s. Gk. *daimōnízomai < daímōn, demon.* The verb occurs in 14 passages in the NT; see Mark 5:18; Luke 8:36. The subject of demons and early monasticism is vast. The words occur 154 times in the SysAP (Guy, 3.294). In Life of Antony 21–44 (pp. 107–51), Antony gives a long discourse on the Devil and demons. As Gould notes, *Desert Fathers,* 173, "Isaac [the Theban 2] shares with Agathon [see Agathon 9] that it is the aim of the demons to distract a monk from prayer—that prayer is, in effect, an extension of combat" (see **War**). Michael A. Williams points out that in *Life* 21.3 (p. 109), Antony quotes Eph 6:12, as does the Gnostic Nag Hammadi text *The Hypostasis of the Archons* at the beginning, saying that the evil powers' "chief is blind."[10] See the role of demons in Evagrius, *Praktikos* 15–39, 40–62 (pp. 20–33).

John Eudes Bamberger in Evagrius, *Praktikos,* 4, notes that of "the hundred chapters that make up the *Praktikos,* demons are mentioned in sixty-seven." See his discussion, 4–10. For an introduction, see Regnault, *Day-to-Day Life,* 174–93; and Jeffrey Burton Russell, *Satan: The Early Christian Tradition* (Ithaca and London: Cornell University Press, 1981), esp. 149–85, chap. 6, "Dualism in the Desert." See David Brakke, *Athanasius and the Politics of Asceticism* (Oxford: Oxford University Press, 1995), and Evagrius of Pontus, *Talking Back: A Monastic Handbook for Combating Demons,* trans. David Brakke, CS 229 (Collegeville, MN: Cistercian Publications, 2009). Norris provides two good insights for moderns about demons: she wonders "why, if we have effectively banished the word *demon,* we are still so demon-haunted," and comments, "A friend who is a monk, a scholar, and, like some contemporary Benedictines, the client of a psychiatrist and a user of psychotropics, once remarked that what we call 'issues' the early monks called 'demons.' It's probably not that simple, but I'm tempted to brandish my poetic license and say

10. Michael A. Williams, *"The Life of Antony and the Domestication of Charismatic Wisdom,"* JAAR Thematic Studies 48, nos. 3, 4 (1982): 23–45, 31. *The Hypostasis of the Archons,* trans. Bentley Layton, The Gnostic Society Library (gnosis.org/naghamm/hypostas.html).

that he's right."[11] Demons figure very prominently in Life of Antony; see especially 4, 8, 9, 21–35 and the Genreal Index, pp. 283–84.

Desert / Deserted places. Gk. *érēmos.* "Wilderness" or "desert" is where humans do not normally live and where demons* often are. This is where John the Baptist emerges from, "The voice of one crying out in the wilderness [*érēmos*]" (Matt 3:3; Isa 40:3), and where Jesus goes out to a "deserted place" (Matt 14:13, 15). See Susanna Elm, *"Virgins of God": The Making of Asceticism in Late Antiquity* (Oxford: Clarendon, 1996), 260; she quotes **Origen**: the desert is where "the air is more pure, the sky more open, and God more familiar" (*Homilies on Luke* 1, in Latin).

Desire(s). Gk. *epithymía* can indicate "forbidden or inordinate" desire, "craving, lust" (Bauer 372ab). See Gal 5:17-21. As the great Anglican phrase has it, "the devices and desires of our own hearts." See Mark Sheridan, "The Desert Was Made a City: The Role of the Desert in Early Egyptian Monasticism and Christian Hagiography" (www.academia.edu/19952744/).

Diaconate. Gk. *diakonía.* Deacons were ministers who attended to the needs of the monks and the monasteries, handling such things as money, charitable relief, and caring for the sick, dying, and dead. In Phil 1:1 Paul greets "all the saints," with the **bishops** (*epískopos*) and deacons (*diákonos*); 1 Tim 3:8-13 lists the qualifications to be a deacon. The terms *deacon* and *diaconate* are not prolific in the SysAP, with only 14 instances for the former and 8 for the latter (Guy 3.298).

Diocletian. Roman Emperor from 284 to 305. He instituted the last great persecution of the church, especially in Egypt. See ODLA 1:485b–87; CE 904a–8a.

Dioscorus. Dioscorus (d. 454), was Patriarch of Alexandria. See ODLA 1:491a; CE 912b–15b.

Discernment. Gk. *diákrisis.* In Arabic Antony, Letters XI Antony teaches, "Therefore beseech the Lord with tears by day and by night to have the spirit of discernment, so that you may abound in every good thing and attain perfection." Discernment is a vital part of monastic practice; the *locus classicus* is *Praktikos* 6–14 (pp. 16–20), where Evagrius discusses the eight kinds of evil thoughts, and 15–39

---

11. Norris, *Acedia*, 131 (emphasis hers), and 33, respectively.

(pp. 20–26) where he offers antidotes for them. The discussion of the medicine there is almost twice as long as that for the disease(s). See esp. Antony Rich, *Discernment in the Desert Fathers:* Diákrisis *in the Life and Thought of Early Egyptian Monasticism* (Waynesboro, GA: Paternoster, 2007); and John Wortley, "Discretion: Greater Than All the Virtues," *Greek, Roman, and Byzantine Studies* 51 (2011): 634–52. On *diákrisis* see SysAP X.1–194 (2.14–135) and Wortley, *Book*, 143–88; AnonAP 216–56 (Wortley, *Anonymous Sayings*, 155–75); Cassian, *Conferences* 2 (pp. 77–112); and Gould, *Desert Fathers*, 48–52. See **Judge**.

Dispirited. Gk. *akēdía*. See **Acedia**.

Disturb. Gk. *tarássō* has a wide range of meanings; in Matt 14:26 the word indicates what the disciples experience when they see Jesus calm the waters and walk on the water. Bauer 990b–91a offers these synonyms for various biblical passages: "to cause inner turmoil, stir up, disturb, unsettle, throw into confusion." One can stir up a crowd (Acts 17:8), and, in the passive voice, the verb means "be troubled, frightened, terrified" (Matt 2:3; 14:26).

Domitius. See **Maximus**.

Duke. In the fourth century a Roman military commander in frontier areas.

Dwell. See **Sit**.

Eager. Gk. *spoudázō* has a number of nuances apropos to early monasticism: "hurry, hasten"; "be zealous / eager"; "take pains, make every effort, be conscientious" (Bauer 939ab). See Gal 2:10 and Eph 4:3, among many.

Eating early. The usual meal time for **anchorites** and **semi-anchorites** was the ninth hour, about 3 p.m.

Ecstasy. Gk. *ékstasis* can be positive or negative: "alienation or separation of mind, trance," or mystical ecstasy, combined with visions. Patristic writers use the term with reference to Adam, Christ, David, the apostles, and martyrs (Lampe 438b–39a). See Life of Antony 37; Gould, *Desert Fathers*, 177–82, chap. 6.2, "Ecstasy."

Edifying. Gk. *lógos*. See **Spiritual Guidance**.

Effort, make every. Gk. *agōnízomai*. See Matt 7:13 // Luke 13:24 (NIV). See **Fight**.

Egypt. Wipszycka argues, *Second Gift,* 9, that in "writing about the history of Christianity in Egypt, it is possible—and indeed necessary—to abandon the distinction between Alexandria and Egypt," but in monastic parlance, "Egypt" usually represents the "civilized" places away from **Scetis,** the **world,** that is, **Alexandria** or **Babylon** (Old Cairo) or other settled areas.

Eighth hour. The ancients reckoned the beginning of each day at sunup, roughly 6 a.m., depending on the time of the year. The eighth hour, then, was approximately 2 p.m.

Eleutheropolis. "A titular see in Palaestina Prima. . . . Its first known bishop is Macrinus (325); five others are mentioned in the fourth and two in the sixth century. . . . At Eleutheropolis was born St. Epiphanius, the celebrated bishop of Salamis in Cyprus; . . . he established a monastery which is often mentioned in the polemics of St. Jerome with Rufinus and John, Bishop of Jerusalem. The city was, moreover, an important monastic centre at least till the coming of the Arabs" (*Catholic Encyclopedia* [New Advent, www.newadvent .org/cathen/05380a.htm]).

Embattled. See **War / Wage War**.

Enaton. The Enaton, or Ennaton, nine miles west of Alexandria, figures in the *Sayings* and was one of the most famous monastic settlements of the 6th and 7th centuries; it was a collection of monasteries, hermitages, and churches, rather than a single monastery. See CE 954b–58b.

Endurance. See **Patience / Patient Endurance**.

Enemy, the. Gk. *ho echthrós,* that is, Satan, the Devil. *Echthrós* carries "hateful, hatred, hostile" with it (Lampe 187b.2.5). *Echthrós* as an appellation of the Devil does not occur in the NT; Acts 13:10 comes close when Paul there says to a magician, "You son of the devil, you enemy [*echthré*] of all righteousness." *Echthrós* occurs 82 times in the SysAP. "Enemies" can mean the demons, but can also be generic. A modern reader should be aware that a monastic listener or reader would easily make the connection between "enemy" and the "Enemy." See Burton Russell, *Satan,* esp. 149–85.

Equanimity. See **Inward stillness**.

Ethiopian(s). The belief that the Devil and demons took the form of Ethiopians was common in early monastic literature; as Regnault points out, "The form [that the Devil] appears to like best is that of an Ethiopian man or woman whose dark skin evokes the black tint of malice (*Day-to-Day Life*, 187); see Arsenius 32–33, Heraclius, and Moses 3. See Brian Noell, "Race in Late-Antique Egypt: Moses the Black and Authentic Historical Voice," *Eras Journal* (www. monash.edu/arts/philosophical-historical-international-studies/eras/ past-editions/edition-six-2004-november/race-in-late-antique-egypt-moses-the-black-and-authentic-historical-voice), and the notes at the end for further resources.

Eusebius. Eusebius of Caesarea (ca. 260–ca. 339): "Biblical exegete, Christian apologist in the era of the Great Persecution, author of various historical and geographical works, and (from ca. 313) Bishop of Caesarea of Palestine" (ODLA 1:565b–657b, here 565b). He is best known for his *Ecclesiastical* (or *Church*) *History, Life of Constantine*, and *Demonstration of the Gospel*.

Evil one. Gk. *ho ponērós*: *ponērós* can mean "evil" or "the evil one." See the end of the Lord's Prayer at Matt 6:13: "And do not bring us to the time of trial, but rescue us from the evil one." See **Enemy**.

Fast / Fasting. For an introduction to monastic fasting, see Regnault, *Day-to-Day Life*, 61–65; on fasting and hospitality, see Gould, *Desert Fathers*, 142–49. See especially Shaw, *Burden of the Flesh*.

Faith. Gk. *pístis*. NT: "faithfulness, reliability, fidelity, commitment," "trust, confidence, faith" (Bauer 818b–20b); Matt 23:23; 1 Thess 1:8. For a discussion of faith and Paul, see N. T. Wright, *Paul and the Faithfulness of God* (Minneapolis: Fortress Press, 2013), 75–195. See **Faithful**.

Faithful. Gk. *pistós* has biblical resonance. It can mean "trustworthy, dependable, inspiring trust / faith," and, with emphasis on its cognate *pístis*, "trust, faith," it can refer to a person of faith or to God "as the one in whom we can have full confidence" (Bauer 820b–21b). See **Faith**.

Father. A spiritual father. The term also hearkens back to the father-son advice in the Wisdom literature of the Hebrew Bible. See Gould, *The Desert Fathers*, 26–87.

Fear / Be frightened. Gk. *phóbos* (noun), *phobéomai* (verb), English *phobia*. The fear of God or the Lord is a common theme in both the HB and NT. Numerous biblical passages refer to the fear of God or fear of the Lord: Exod 18:21; Deut 6:24; 31:12-13; Ps 112:1; Matt

10:28; Luke 1:50; 2 Cor 7:1; and 1 Pet 2:17. See Gould, *Desert Fathers*, 62–63, 90–91. As Gould notes, 91, "The fear of God, for the Desert Fathers, was generally a positive quality, a means to the attainment of virtue."

Fearlessly, Speak freely and. Gk. *parrēsía.* See **Confidence.**

Fight. Gk. *agōnízomai.* As in Paul, early Christianity uses athletic metaphors. Originally, an *agón* was "a place of contest, the arena," then "a contest for a prize at the games" (see Phil 3:14), then generally "any struggle, trial, or danger" (Liddell and Scott 18b–19a). Early monastics used these athletic metaphors to connote spiritual struggle, engagement, in the spiritual life.

Fighter. Gk. *agōnistḗs.* See **Fight.**

Flee. Gk. *pheúgō* has important biblical meanings. Bauer 1052ab gives three apposite definitions: (1) "to seek safety in flight, flee" (Matt 26:56, where the disciples desert Jesus and flee); (2) "to become safe from danger by eluding it or avoiding it, escape" (Mark 14:52); (3) "to keep from doing something by avoiding it because of its potential damage, flee from, avoid, shun" (1 Cor 6:18: "shun fornication!").

Flesh. Gk. *sárx* (n.), *sarkikós* (adj.). Lampe 115a–16a says that the term can be neutral but can also mean "carnal," that is, "worldly" and "sensual" (as opposed to the spiritual); moderns often misconstrue the word as having to do with sex. *Sarkikós* and *sárx* figure prominently in Paul's writing. The NRSV translates the former as either "material," belonging to the physical realm (Rom 15:27; 1 Cor 9:11), or "(merely) human" (1 Cor 3:4; 2 Cor 10:4). Rom 7:7-25; 7:17: "For I know that nothing good dwells within me, that is, in my flesh. I can will what is right, but I cannot do it."

Follow. Gk. *akolouthéō.* In the New Testament *akolouthéō* can mean "to follow someone as a disciple, be a disciple" (Bauer 36b–37a); see Matt 9:9, Mark 1:18; Luke 5:40, 43. Compare English *acolyte.*

Foreigner. See **Stranger.**

Fourth hour. The ancients reckoned the beginning of each day at sunup, roughly 6 a.m., depending on the time of the year. The fourth hour, then, was approximately 10 a.m.

Free (from the passions). Gk. *apátheia,* "without the passions." See **Apatheia** and **Passion/s.**

Fulfill. Gk. *plēróō*, "to make full, fill"; "fill (up), complete"; "complete, finish"; "fulfill" (Bauer 827b–29b). See Matt 1:22; 3:13-15; Rom 13:8.

Fulfill, wanting to. Gk. *tēréō*. Often used in "keeping the word" (*tēréō* + *lógos*), or commandment. See Matt 19:17, where Jesus says "If you want to enter life, keep [*tēréō*] the commandments." In the NT, *tēréō* has a number of meanings: "keep watch over, guard"; "keep, hold, reserve, preserve"; "keep, observe, fulfill, pay attention to" (Bauer 1002ab). See especially John 15:9: "If you keep [*tēréō*] my commandments." See **Protect**.

Gain. Gk. *kerdaínō*. In the NT a person gains his or her neighbor for the kingdom of God (Matt 18:15; 1 Cor 9:19-22; 1 Pet 3:1) or gains Christ or makes Christ one's own (Phil 3:8) (Bauer 541a [1b]). It can also mean "keeping, fulfilling commandments" (Lampe 545b). See **Fulfill, wanting to**, and **Protect**. See Gould, *The Desert Fathers*, 93–95.

Gift. Gk. *eulogía*. The basic meaning is "blessing, blessing as a mark of favor bestowed by God," then "benefit, gift"; see Rom 15:29; Gal 3:14. In the Eucharist, it means "consecration" and thence "gift of blessed bread" (Lampe 569a–70b). Eulogia is still passed out regularly at the end of the Coptic eucharistic liturgy, and the term *eulogia* is used, especially by the younger clergy, but *luqmat baraka*, "blessed bread," the Arabic equivalent, also occurs frequently and is normative with the older generation. There is a great deal of evidence that monks received a ration / measure of **wine** as part of their weekly supplies well into the 8th cent., but it is not clear that it was part of the eulogia in the 4th–5th cent.; it is not part of the eulogia today or for some time, perhaps because of Muslim criticism. **Wine** also appears as a normative aspect of the monastic table in Egypt at least until the 11th cent. I wish to thank Maged S. A. Mikhail for the Coptic information.

Glory / Glorify. Gk. *dóxa* (n.), *doxázō* (vb.). In the NT *dóxa* can mean "fame, recognition, renown, honor, prestige" (Bauer 256b–58a), but it and its cognate verb *doxázō* often mean "to praise, honor, extol" God the Father and "glorify" the Son and the Father; *doxázō* "is a favorite term in John . . . in which the whole life of Jesus is depicted as a glorifying of the Son by the Father" (Bauer 258ab; 258b [2]).

Gnostics. Gnosticism is a "Generic term in modern scholarship for a diverse set of religious teachings and sects within and on the margins of Christianity in the 2nd to 5th centuries AD. It includes those opposed by heresiologists from Irenaeus onwards as being 'Gnostics' (from Gk. *gnôsis*, a higher knowledge, theoretical or mystical" (ODLA 1:669ab). See **Knowledge**. The scholarship is vast: see David Brakke, *The Gnostics: Myth, Ritual, and Diversity in Early Christianity* (Cambridge, MA: Harvard University Press, 2012); and Elaine Pagels, *The Gnostic Gospels* (New York: Vintage, 1989). For an up-to-date bibliography, see ODLA 1:669ab.

Go away. See **Withdraw**.

Governance. Gk. *oikonomía* (from *oíkos*, "house"; English *economy*) has a wide range of meanings: "ministration, management, charge"; "good management," "disposition, organization, constitution," "dispensation, ordering" (Lampe 940b–43a). Patristic theologians came to talk about God's "economy" in ordering the things of heaven and earth. An *oikónomos* was a steward in a monastery, helping to keep things running smoothly in the community.

Governor. Gk. *árchōn*. The NT itself shows the "civilizing," even forgetful, embracing of "governor," that is, the state (the NT almost always uses *hēgemón* for "governor" instead of *árchōn*). Except for the neutral use of "governor" in Luke 2:2, the term is always negative in the Synoptic gospels (John does not use it): "governors persecute and kill, and Pilate is their archetype" (Matt 27:2). In John 12:31 Jesus says, "Now is the judgment of this world; now the ruler [*árchōn*] of this world will be driven out." In 1 Cor 2:6, 8, Paul speaks negatively of "the rulers [*archóntōn* < *árchōn*] of this age." The writer of 1 Peter, though (late 1st–early 2nd cent.), no longer sees things this way: "For the Lord's sake accept the authority of every human institution, whether of the emperor as supreme, or of governors [*hēgemón*]" (1:13-14). In the 4th–5th cents., with Christ as governor, we see the apotheosis of the term. In Rev 1:5 Christ is "the ruler / governor [*árchōn*] of the kings of the earth."

Grace. Gk. *cháris*. Grace of Christ: see Rom 5:15; 16:20; 2 Cor 13:3; Gal 6:18; Eph 4:7.

Guard. Gk. *phylássō*. See **Protect**.

Guidance. See **Spiritual Guidance**

Hades. Gk. *hádēs*. In Classical Greek, Hades is the god of the under-world (*Odyssey* 4.834: "the house of Hades") and occurs in Sopho-cles and Aristophanes (Montanari 29bc). The word occurs often in the LXX, esp. in Job, Proverbs, and Isaiah ("Sheol"); in Isa 14:11 the prophet warns, "Your pomp is brought down to Sheol, / and the sound of your harps; / maggots are the bed beneath you, / and worms are your covering." The word occurs 8 times in the NT: "the nether world," the place of the dead (Bauer 19b). In the story of Lazarus and the rich man, Luke 16:19-30, the rich man is being "tormented" there; in Rev 20:14, "Death and Hades were thrown into the lake of fire. This is the second death, the lake of fire." The other 6 refer-ences offer no details.

Hand on (as Tradition). Gk. *paradídōmi*: in 1 Cor 11:23 Paul says, "I received from the Lord what I also handed on [*paradídōmi*] to you," then discusses the Lord's Supper / Eucharist. In Patristic Greek the cognate noun *parádosis* came to mean "teaching, tradition" (Bauer 762b [3]–63a). Ironically, the verb and the noun can also mean "to betray" and "betrayal," respectively, "hand over" (to the police or courts). See the note about "betrayal" at Bauer 762 (2b).

Hermopolis Magna. Modern el-Ashmunein, on the west bank of the Nile in the **Thebaid**, between al-Minya and Asyut (**Lycopolis**).

Hesychast. From Greek *hēsychía*, "silence, quiet, stillness, tranquility," an important monastic term for interior stillness, contemplative peace. A hesychast was one who practiced *hēsychía*. See **Contem-plative quiet**.

Highwayman. See **Bandit**.

Himation. Gk. *himátion*. An outer garment worn by the ancient Greeks over the left shoulder and under the right.

Holy, Holy ones. Gk. *hágios* in the plural, *hágioi*, can mean "the saints," "those of outstanding virtue," living or dead (Lampe 18b); "worship-pers of the true God" (18b); "the saints," meaning "fellow Chris-tians" in the NT; or the angels (Bauer 10b–11b). See Peter Brown, *The Cult of the Saints: Its Rise and Function in Latin Christianity* (Chicago: University of Chicago Press, 2014).

Hood. Gk. *koukoúlion*. See Innemée, *Ecclesiastical Dress*, 106.

Hope. Gk. *elpís*; have hope: *elpízō*. Noun and verb occur numerous times in the NT: "to look forward to something, with the implication of confidence about something coming to pass" (Bauer 319ab). Thus the word is stronger than the usual meaning of "hope" now. See 1 Cor 13:13: "And now faith, hope, and love abide, these three."

Hour, this. The normal time for eating was the ninth hour, about 3 p.m., but it could be later on Friday or put off until the **synaxis** on Saturday.

Humble. Gk. *tapeinóō.* See **Humility.**

Humility. Gk. *tapeinóō* (vb.), *tapeínosis* (n.), *tapeinosophrúnē* (n.): A key monastic aspiration, practice, and virtue. In the gospels the words specifically refer to Jesus (Matt 11:29; 21:5). Three passages illustrate the centrality of humility in the New Testament: (1) In Luke 1:48 God "has looked with favor on Mary's lowliness [or "humility," *tapeínosis*]." (2) Paul, perhaps quoting from an early Christian hymn, declares that Christ "humbled [*tapeinóō*] himself and became obedient to the point of death—even death on a cross" (Phil 2:8). (3) In Luke, Jesus, with his use of contraries, sounds like an early monastic: "all who exalt themselves will be humbled, and those who humble themselves will be exalted" (Luke 14:11). *Tapeinophrosúnē* does not occur in the gospels, but its cognate verb, *tapeinóō,* occurs numerous times (Bauer 990ab), esp. in the Pauline (Phil 2:3), deutero-Pauline, and Pastoral Epistles (Bauer 989b). It can also mean "constrain, mortify" (Bauer 990a). On humility, see Burton-Christie, *Word in the Desert,* 236–60: "Humility was the starting point for the desert monks" (236). AnonAP 298–334 (Wortley, *Anonymous Sayings,* 201–18) are on humility. Chap. 5 of Gregory Boyle, *Barking to the Choir* (New York: Simon & Schuster, reprint edition, 2018), 91–105, is on humility.

Hypostasis (pl. **hypostases**). A concrete manifestation of an abstract reality: being, substance, reality. For its many nuances, with patristic citations, see Lampe 1454–61.

Implore. Gk. *parakaléō.* See **Appeal.**

Inner cell. Many monastic dwellings consisted of two rooms: a front room for work and receiving guests and a back room for prayer and sleep.

Intention. Gk. *lógos.* See **Thoughts.**

Interior way of life. "Interior," *tò éndon,* "within," can refer to the interior spiritual and moral life (Lampe 468b).

Inward stillness. Gk. *anapaúō* and *anapaúomai* (vb.), *anápausis* (n.): a condition or state much desired by the monks. *Anápausis* comes to mean "cessation from wearisome activity for the sake of rest; rest, relief"; "repose, rest, refreshment"; "a result of training in practice of virtue" (Bauer 69a). It can mean "rest in eternity" and "tranquility, peace" (Lampe 115a–16a). Matt 11:29 gives us the biblical resonance: "Take my yoke upon you, and learn from me; for I am gentle and humble in heart, and you will find rest [*anápausis*] for your souls." For the synonym *katápausis*, see Heb 3:11, 18; 4:1-10.[12]

Isaiah of Scetis. Died 491. Also known as Isaiah the Hermit, and "possibly to be identified with Isaiah of Gaza" (ODLA 1:788a), he was a "fifth-century anchorite whose spiritual advice to other monks greatly influenced the Eastern churches. . . . Of all the Isaiahs mentioned in Egyptian monastic sources of the fourth and fifth centuries, the most renowned is the author of the ascetic treatises that had a wide vogue in the Christian Orient. Unfortunately, we do not find in these treatises much in the way of autobiographical information. We learn merely that Isaiah had begun his life as a monk in Egypt, probably at **Scetis**, where he was in contact with several personalities mentioned in the Apophthegmata Patrum" (CE 1305a–6b). He later moved to Gaza. On Isaiah see John Chryssavgis and Pachomios (Robert) Penkett, *Abba Isaiah of Scetis: Ascetic Discourses*, CS 150 (Kalamazoo, MI: Cistercian, 2002).

John of Lycopolis. John was a well-known monk who, oddly, does not have any sayings in the AlphAP. He appears numerous times in the SysAP (see Guy, 3.243). See Historia Lausiaca 35 (pp. 81–85) and Hist Mon 1 (pp. 52–62).

Judge / Judgment. Gk. *krínō* (vb.), *krísis* (n.): "select, prefer"; "to pass judgment upon (and thereby seek to influence) the lives and actions of other people, judge, pass judgment upon, express an opinion about"; "criticize, find fault with, condemn"; "reach a decision, decide, propose, intend" (Bauer 567b–69a). In Greek, "judge," "justice," and "righteousness" (root: *dik-*) are etymological siblings. See Matt 7:1; Rom 2:1. See SysAP IX.1–26, lines 426–49 (Wortley,

---

12. I wish to thank Graham Gould, *Desert Fathers*, 131, for "inward stillness."

Book, 133–42), and AnonAP 475–518 (pp. 304–51). See Gould, *Desert Fathers,* 107–37, esp. 123–37.

Julian. Julian, dubbed "the Apostate" by Christians, died on June 26, 363. See Robert Browning, *The Emperor Julian* (Berkeley: University of California Press, 1976), 159–86, chap. 9, "Julian and the Christians"; ODLA 2:839a–40a.

Just. See **Righteous / Just.**

Justin. Justin, ca. 100–ca. 165, known as Justin Martyr, was an early Christian apologist and author of the *First* and *Second Apology*, and *Dialogue with Trypho*.

Justinian I. Roman emperor from 527 to 565.

Keep (a commandment). Gk. *phylássō*. See **Watch.**

Kellia. Kellia (Cells), a monastic settlement about 18 km. south of **Nitria,** "is one of the most important and most celebrated monastic groupings in Lower Egypt." Palladius reports that "nearly 600 monks were living in Kellia at the end of the fourth century" (CE 1396b–1410a, here 1396b). See Evelyn-White, *Monasteries,* 2.24–27; and Wipszycka, *Second Gift,* 306–8, 313–15, 487–89.

Keration. A small coin.

Knowledge. Gk. *gnôsis* occurs 27 times in the SysAP (Guy 3.292). Wipszycka, *Second Gift,* 89, in what may be an overstatement, says "In Egypt it was widely believed at the time that true piety was founded on knowledge (*gnosis*) and that this knowledge could be attained solely by people who renounced the world." Pagels prefers "insight" or "understanding," since she believes that *gnôsis* "refers to 'knowledge of the heart.' "[13] Evagrius gives a monastic understanding of knowledge in *Praktikos* 32 (p. 24), "contemplative knowledge," and 68 (p. 66), "immaterial knowledge." In *Chapters on Prayer* 86 (p. 69, modified) Evagrius exclaims: "Knowledge! A human being's great possession. It is a fellow-worker with prayer, acting to awaken the power of thought to contemplate the divine knowledge." See Everett Ferguson, "The Christian Gnostic," in *Gnosticism in the Early Church,* ed. Everett Ferguson, et al. (Lon-

---

13. Elaine Pagels, *Why Religion? A Personal Story* (San Francisco: Ecco / HarperCollins, 2018), 28.

don: Routledge, 1993), 78–79; and, for *gnôsis* and **Origen**, "Gnostics," in John Anthony McGuckin, *The Westminster Handbook to Origen* (Louisville and London: Westminster John Knox, 2004). See also Behr, *Asceticism and Anthropology,* esp. 185–207. In the Life of Antony 77 (pp. 219–23), Athanasius downplays the *gnôsis* of the philosophers and shows that true *gnôsis* is faith in God.

Leave. Gk. *anachōréō*. See **Withdraw**.

Lebiton. Gk. *lebitón*. According to E. A. Sophocles, *Greek Lexicon of the Roman and Byzantine Periods* (Cambridge: Harvard University Press, 1914), *lebitón* is the same as *kolóbion*, and is Semitic in origin.

Linen. Gk. *linárion*, a diminutive of *línon*, is "anything made from flax" (Lampe 1051b). So possibly "thread," with another possibility being linen sails (Lampe). In the New Testament *línon* can mean "lampwick," "linen garment," or "fish-net" (Bauer 596b). Because of the ambiguity, I have rendered it more generally as "linen," which means some linen product. Cassian, *Institutes* 1.4 (p. 24) says that "the wearing of linen clothing is to teach them that they have utterly died to a **worldly** way of life." See CE 2210b–30b. Naphtali Lewis, *Life in Egypt under Roman Rule* (Oxford: Clarendon, 1983), 134, notes that "Egypt was famous for two of its manufactures, linen and papyrus." An early fourth-century papyrus, P. Berl. inv. 13897 (Naldini, no. 36), has "Didyme and the sisters," possible monastics, writing about linen and a linen-weaver (Mario Naldini, *Il Cristianesimo in Egitto: Lettere private nei papyri dei secoli II–IV* [Florence: Nardini, 1968]).

Listlessness. See **Dispirited**.

Live. See **Sit**.

Love (n.). Gk. *agápē*, cognate with the verb *agapáō* (see below), "esteem, affection, regard, love" (Bauer 6a–7a). The word occurs perhaps 50 times in the NT and is the word for love in Paul's memorable profession in 1 Cor 13. *Agápē* and *agapáō* occur 40 and 122 times, respectively, in the SysAP (Guy 3.253) for a total of 162, while *philía*, "friendship, love," and *philéō* occur respectively only 10 and 4 times (Guy 3.452) for a total of 14, thus demonstrating the key importance of *agápē* in monastic thought and spirituality. Norris, *Acedia*, 110, calls freedom to love "the ultimate freedom." See Behr,

Asceticism and Anthropology, esp. 185–207, chap. 6. See **Love** (vb.) and **Love, act of.**

Love (vb.). Gk. *agapáō,* cognate with *agápē.* See Matt 22:37-38; John 3:16. See **Love** (n.) and **Love, act of.**

Love, act of. Gk. *agápē.* When making a request, monks often literally say "Do an act of love." This can equal "Please," but the NT understanding of *agápē* (see **Love** [n.]) intensifies the sense. *Agápē* especially indicates "fraternal love." Lampe 7a notes, "denoting especially God's or Christ's love for [humans], [humans'] love for God, and fraternal charity of Christians." *Agápē* evolved from an abstract noun (although Paul's list of what love is and is not is not abstract) to a noun of praxis, an *agápē.* See AnonAP 334–58 (Wortley, *Anonymous Sayings,* 225–35), and Gould, *Desert Fathers,* 96–102. The first instances that Lampe gives (8a [B]) for the "act of love or charity" are the *Sibylline Oracles* 8.497 (2nd–3rd cent.) and John Chrysostom (d. 407).

Loved / Beloved. Gk. *agapētós* < *agápē,* "love" (n.); see John 21:20, of "the disciple whom Jesus loved [*agapētós*]."

Lycopolis. Coptic Siout, now Asyut, was a metropolis "in Middle Egypt strategically located on the west bank of the Nile at a bend in the river and at a terminus of a Western Desert route. . . . The hermit, prophet, and healer John of Lycopolis lived on the Western Mountain" (ODLA 2:929ab). Lycopolis, "home of a Christian community since at least as early as the great persecution of Diocletian at the beginning of the fourth century, became one of the most important centers of Christianity in Egypt during the Roman and Byzantine periods" (CE 296a–97b).

Macarius. See **Blessed.** "Macarius" usually refers to either Macarius of Egypt / Macarius the Egyptian / Macarius the Great (CE 1491a–92a) or Macarius of Alexandria (CE 1489b–90b). Both have sayings in the AlphAP.

Mad. See **Anger.**

Magister officiorum. An "official [office] created by Constantine. . . . He controlled the imperial couriers (*agentes in rebus*) and the inspectors of the post (*curiosi*) . . . and issued postal warrants (*evectiones*)" (OCD 638b).

Maintain. Gk. *phylássō.* See **Protect.**

Manichean. Manichaeism (a heresiological term coined by its opponents) was a late-antique religion founded by Mani (216–ca. 276); it was heavily influenced by Zoroastrianism. "Mani taught a theogonic myth detailing a universal conflict between the powers of Light and Darkness." See ODLA 1:950b–53a, here 952a.

Martyr. Gk. *mártyr* originally meant "witness." Martyrs were those who witnessed to their faith. During the periodic and sporadic persecutions against Christians until the early 4th cent., those who died for their faith were "martyrs," while those, like Gelasius in Gelasius 4, who bore witness but were not killed, were "confessors."[14] The AlphAP deals with the period beginning about a hundred years after the persecutions ended, but see Life of Antony 46 (pp. 157–59), and the word's meaning has broadened. On the monk as martyr, see Edward E. Malone, *The Monk and the Martyr: The Monk as the Successor of the Martyr* (New York: Literary Licensing, 2011 [repr.]).

Marvel. Gk. *thaumázō*. See **Astonished**.

Master. Gk. *despótēs* (English *despot*): "one who has legal control and authority over persons, such as subjects or slaves, lord, master"; "ruler of a city." Luke 13:25 (in Papyrus 75), 2 Pet 2:1, and Jude 4 use it of Christ; The Song of Simeon 2:29 uses it of God.

Matins. The late-night **Office**.

Mazices. According to Evelyn-White, *Monasteries*, 2.151–53, the fifth-century Mazices were probably the Mastikos or Marikos, Berbers who dwelled in the western desert of Egypt. Sometimes the sources differentiate them from the **barbarians** and sometimes seem to conflate them.

Meditate / Meditation. Gk. *meletáō* (vb.) / *meleté* (n.) The basic meaning is "practice, exercise," giving "care or attention" to, "usage, habit"; in monastic Gk. meditation (*meletáō*), to meditate on Scripture is quietly to utter on one's lips the words of **Scripture**, most commonly the Psalms. Burton-Christie, *Word*, 123, notes, "Meditation was not, as the word has come to imply today, an interior

---

14. Though a bit dated now, on the persecutions see W. H. C. Frend, *Martyrdom and Persecution in the Early Church: A Study of a Conflict from the Maccabees to Donatus* (New York: New York University Press, 1967).

reflection on the meaning of certain words. It was first and foremost the utterance, or exclamation of words, which were originally digested and interiorized." *Meletáō* can also mean "take thought, take pains," "practice"; "train oneself" (Bauer 627a). See **Psalm(s)**. With regard to the importance of the Psalms, Norris paraphrases Jeremy Driscoll: "The psalter is not merely a collection of prayers; it is meant to be a song that resonates in the monk's soul, accompanying him on life's journey and illuminating his path." She quotes Luke Dysinger: the psalms are "a vision of the whole of creation" and "the training-ground of the Christian contemplative."[15]

Melchizedek. Melchizedek was the king of Salem who blessed Abram (Gen 14:17-18); in Ps 110:4 God says (of Simon Maccabeus?), "You are a priest forever according to the order of Melchizedek." "Thus Melchizedek," Michael C. Astour points out, "is here not only the human archetype of the ideal-priest king of Jerusalem, but the eternal priest of Yahweh, a supernatural being engendered by Yahweh and comparable to the mythological figure of Day Star, son of Dawn" (Isa 14:12). The Essenes "gave Melchizedek a very high place in their heavenly hierarchy and eschatology." He is less exalted in Philo and Josephus. See Michael C. Astour, "Melchizedek (Person)," Anchor 4.684b–86b; see 685b–86a, "D. The Letter to the Hebrews," for a discussion of Melchizedek in that book. Heb 5:6, 10; 6:20; 7:1, 10-11, 15, and 17 connect Jesus and Melchizedek. The Nag Hammadi Library contains a very fragmentary Coptic tractate, "Melchizedek"; see Birger A. Pearson, trans., "Melchizedek," in *The Nag Hammadi Library*, ed. Marvin Meyer (San Francisco: HarperOne, 2007), 595–605. See CE 1583b–84a.

Memphis. "The Greek name of the city known in Egyptian as Mennufer and in Coptic as *membe* or *menf* (variant spellings of the name abound in Coptic documents). The city was one of the most populous places in ancient Egypt and played an important part in the administrative and religious life of the Egyptian people. The remains of Memphis, which include a number of temples, a palace, an embalming house, tombs, and necropolises, are located near the modern

---

15. Norris, *Acedia*, 277 and 276, respectively (sources not given).

village of Mit Rahinah on the west side of the Nile about 12 miles (19 km) south of Cairo" (CE 1586b–87b).

Mind. Gk. *noûs* represents the habitation of the interior, spiritual life. As Bauer shows, *noûs* in Greek is multivalent: "the faculty of intellectual perception, mind, intellect," "way of thinking, mind, attitude," "result of thinking, mind, thought" (680ab).

Miracle-worker[1]. The more common Gk. word for "wonder-worker" is *thaumatoúrgos*; *thaumatoúrgos* occurs in only one saying in the SysAP (Guy 3.425), parallel with AlphAP Daniel 8, and, strikingly, *sēmeióphoros* (see **Miracle-worker[2]**) occurs not at all (Guy 3.339). Neither term occurs in the NT. *Thaumatoúrgos* occurs in the title of SysAP XIX.1–26, lines 426–49 (Wortley, *Book*, 351–57), "Concerning Wonder-Working Elders"—but, oddly, not in the book itself.

Miracle-worker[2]. Gk. *sēmeióphoros*, literally a "sign / miracle-worker": *sēmeía*, "signs, wonders," are very important in John's gospel; see **Wonders**. *Sēmeióphoros* can also mean a "standard-bearer," a "confessor for the Faith, of the Fathers of Nicaea" (Lampe 1231a). Given **Cyril's** role in Christological controversies, it could certainly mean that in Daniel 8.

Monastic community / Monastery. As Wipszycka notes, *Second Gift*, 4, "In Greek sources the whole desert zone is referred to as *óros*, which normally means 'a mountain' or 'a hill,' but in Egypt took on the meaning of 'a desert'. . . . the very same word *óros* (and its Coptic equivalent *toou*) was also used to denote monastic communities, both hermitages and monasteries, which resulted from the fact that they came into existence primarily in the desert."

Monastic settlement. Gk. *tópos*, literally "place" (English "topography").

Mother. See **Amma**.

Mountain. In monastic parlance, "mountain" (Coptic *toou* and Greek *óros*) signifies a place away from the fertile and inhabited Nile flood plain. See **Monastic community / Monastery**.

Moved, deeply. Gk. *katanússō, katanússomai*. See **Pricked**.

Movement(s). In his first letter, Antony speaks of the soul's movements; see Antony, Letters, 197–202.

Mysteries, holy. Communion, the Eucharist.

Mystery. Gk. *mystĕrion, mystĕria* (pl.): "the unmanifested or private counsel of God, (God's) secret" (Matt 13:11: "To you it has been given to know the secrets [*mystĕria*] of the kingdom of heaven"). "That which transcends normal understanding, transcendent / ultimate reality, secret, with focus on Israelite / Christian experience" (Bauer 661b–63b).

Neglect. Gk. *améleia* (n.), *ameléō* (vb.). Neglect is an important monastic concern (compare *forgetfulness* in the Qur'ān): neglect of salvation (Heb 2:3); neglect of a (spiritual) gift (1 Tim 4:14).

Neighbor. Gk. *plēsíon* has deep biblical resonance, beginning with Lev 19:18. Several times in the NT Jesus says "Love your neighbor as yourself" (Mark 12:31, 33; Matt 19:19; 22:39; Luke 10:27), and Paul reiterates, "the whole law is summed up in a single commandment: 'You shall love your neighbor'" (Rom 13:9; Gal 5:14). See Gould, *Desert Fathers*, 88–106. See Kengo Akiyama, *The Love of Neighbour in Ancient Judaism: The Reception of Leviticus 19:18 in the Hebrew Bible, the Septuagint, the Book of Jubilees, the Dead Sea Scrolls, and the New Testament* (Leiden: Brill, 2018).

Nestorius and Nestorianism. Nestorius (d. 451) was "Patriarch of Constantinople from 428–31. He subscribed to a dual-nature Christology rejected at the First Council of Ephesus in 431 and not affirmed at the Council of Chalcedon in 451" (ODLA 2:1068b–69b). See CE 1786a–87b.

Nicopolis. Biblical Emmaus, west of Jerusalem; a city with the name of Nicopolis dates from 221. There was a Late Antique basilica there and a martyrium (ODLA 2:1074b).

Night Office. Gk. *nukterínĕs* (< *núx, nuktós*, "night") is not in Lampe, Montanari, or Sophocles. But it must equal *nuktereîa*, "night service" (Montanari 1407c). The Latin renders the word *hora nocturnae psalmodiae*, "the hour of / time for the nighttime psalmody, the saying of the night psalms." See **Office**.

Ninth hour. The ancients reckoned the beginning of each day at sun-up, roughly 6 a.m., depending on the time of the year. The ninth hour, then, was approximately 3 p.m. The usual time for the daily meal.

Nitria. The famous monastic settlement northwest of **Scetis**, "with Scetis and Kellia, one of the principal monastic habitations, founded about 325–330 by Amun" (CE 1794b–96a). "It is located in the western part of the Delta, about 10 miles (15 km) south of Daman-hur, where the village of al-Barnuji stands today" (CE 1794b–96b, here 1794b). As Chitty, *Desert*, notes, "The term 'Scetis' is some-times used in our sources to cover **Nitria** as well. But the term 'Nitria' is *never* used to cover Scetis" (12; emphasis his). See Chitty, *Desert,* 11–13, 29–34, 46–53, 57–60, 66–67; Evelyn-White, *Mon-asteries,* 2.17–24, 43–59.

Nubians. Those of (black) African descent who lived in upper (south-ern) Egypt and Nubia. See **Ethiopian**.

Obedience / Obedient. Gk. *hypakoḗ / hypotagḗ*. In a society like ours with the bumper sticker "Question Authority," obedience may have for many a bitter taste. But as Gould, *Desert Fathers*, 57, states, monastic texts "see obedience and self-disclosure as heroic activities directed to the end of personal development in the virtues of the monastic life, not as something supine, passive, or signifying im-maturity or lack of individuality." Obedience is very important in early monastic literature. Synonyms such as *dutiful* and *devoted* may help. A main theme in early monasticism is the effort to overcome the ego; following Scripture or the wisdom of the elders can help mightily in this. *Hypakoḗ* occurs 47 times in the SysAP (Guy 446ab). It is important to add that in the NT *hypakoḗ* is "predominantly of obedience to God and God's commands" (Bauer 1028b); see Rom 6:16b. On *hypakoḗ* and *hypotagḗ* see Phil 2:8; SysAP XIV.1–32 (Guy 1.252–83; 233–45); AlphAP Hyperechius 8 (Wortley, *Give Me*, 312); AnonAP 291–97; and Gould, *Desert Fathers*, 27–36. See **Obey**.

Obey. Gk. *hypotássō*. The verb occurs often in the NT: submitting to or being subject to God; see 1 Cor 15:28b; Heb 12:9; Jas 4:7. See **Obedience**.

Offend / Take offense. Gk. *skandalízō*. See **Scandalize**.

Offering, whole burnt. The verb *holokautóō*, "to offer a whole burnt offering," does not occur in the NT, but its cognate noun *holokaútōma* ("holocaust") occurs twice: in Mark 12:33, Jesus, following the prophets (see Amos 5:22), says that loving God is "more important than all whole burnt offerings and sacrifices"; in Heb 10:6, 8, where the author says that when Christ came into the world, quoting Ps 40:6, he said of God, "in burnt offerings and sin offerings / you have taken no pleasure." The noun occurs well over a hundred times in the HB.

Office. An "Office" indicates a set time during the day when monks prayed (often set prayers or services) individually or together, as today. The first Office was at dawn; thus, depending on the season, the monastic Offices took place around 6 and 9 a.m., noon, and 3 and 6 p.m. See Cassian, *Institutes* 2–3 (pp. 35–55, 57–74); see Robert Taft, "Praise in the Desert: The Coptic Monastic Office Yesterday and Today," *Worship* 56 (1982): 513–36.

Opinion. Gk. *dógma* has a wide range of meanings: "opinion," "fixed belief, tenet," "precept, ordinance"—and "of beliefs of pagan religions."

Opportune time. Gk. *kairós* is an important term in the NT: "a moment or period as especially appropriate; the right, favorable time," "a period characterized by some aspect of special crisis; time" (Bauer 497b–98a). See Col 4:5: "Conduct yourselves wisely towards outsiders, making the most of the opportune time" (NRSV: "time.")

Oppress. Gk. *thlílbō*. See **Afflict**.

Order(s). See **Command / Commandment**

Origen. "Origen (185–255) was one of the greatest Christians who ever lived, and certainly among the greatest of Egyptian Christians. Only Athanasius can rival him in stature among the sons of Christian Egypt. . . . Though Origen started writing late in his life, his output was enormous. Much of it survives in the original Greek, and even more in Latin translations made during the two centuries after his death, some by Rufinus and Jerome" (CE 1846b–55a). Origen was a great influence on the early monastics, especially Evagrius. The scholarship on Origen is immense; for starters, see Joseph Trigg, *Origen* (New York: Routledge, 1998). See also John Behr, *Origen: On First Principles* (Oxford: Oxford University Press, 2018). On the controversies surrounding Origen, see the brief entry by E. M. Harding, "The Origenist Crises," in *The Westminster Handbook to Origen*, ed. John Anthony McGuckin (Louisville: Westminster John Knox, 2004), 162b–67a; and Elizabeth A. Clark, *The Origenist Controversy: The Cultural Construction of an Early Christian Debate* (Princeton: Princeton University Press, 1992).

Over-confidence. See **Confidence**.

Pachomius. Pachomius, the founder of cenobitic (see **Cenobium**) monasticism, lived 292–346. He does not have any sayings in the AlphAP and appears 4 times in the SysAP (Guy 3.257b). For an introduction, see William Harmless, *Desert Christians: An Introduction to the Literature of Early Monasticism* (Oxford: Oxford University Press, 2004), 115–63; see also James A. Goehring, *Ascetics, Society, and the Desert: Studies in Early Egyptian Monasticism* (Harrisburg, PA: Trinity, 1999), 89–109. Cistercian Publications has published *Pachomian Koinonia I–III*, ed. Armand Veilleux, CS 45–47 (Kalamazoo, MI: Cistercian Publications, 1980, 1981, 1989).

Palestine. In Late Antiquity, Palaestina Prima, Secunda, and Tertia covered a larger area than Palestine today. Prima included Samaria and the bulk of Judaea; Secunda, "the Jezreel Valley and Lower Galilee west of the Jordan"; and Tertia "the Sinai Peninsula, the Negev, and southern Transjordan" (ODLA 2:1125b–26a). Monasticism in Palestine was essentially contemporaneous with that in Egypt; see Yizhar Hirschfeld, *The Judean Monasteries in the Byzantine Period* (New Haven and London: Yale University Press, 1992); and John Binns, *Ascetics and Ambassadors of Christ: The Monasteries of Palestine, 314–631* (Oxford: Clarendon, 1994).

Paphnutius Kephalas. In AlphAP Macarius 28 and 37, a Paphnutius (Coptic *papnoute*, "the one belonging to God") is described as "the disciple of Abba Macarius"; in the *Life of Macarius of Scetis* 36, he is described as "the holy man Abba Paphnutius, who was the greatest of the saint's disciples. It was he who assumed the fatherhood in the holy places after Abba Macarius." There were a number of known monks named Paphnutius. A Paphnutius has five sayings in the AlphAP. For a discussion of the various Paphnutii, see Tim Vivian, *Paphnutius: Histories of the Monks of Upper Egypt and the Life of Onnophrius,* CS 140 (Kalamazoo, MI: Cistercian Publications, 2000), 42–50. See Guy 1.59–61.

Passion(s. Gk. *páthos* (sing.), *páthē* (pl.). English *pathos* and *pathetic*. The monks considered "passions" to be disordered desires that distract (literally "draw away") a person from following God. The word should not be equated with the modern English *passion*, as in "a passion for" or "a passionate kiss." Since "distract" comes from Lat. *traho* (passive participle *tractum*), "draw, pull, drag," a good image in English is a tractor drawing / pulling a person away from God and **Contemplative quiet.** Rowan Williams, "The Theological World of the *Philokalia,*" in *The* Philokalia*: A Classic Text of Or-*

thodox Spirituality, ed. Brock Bingaman and Bradley Nassif (Oxford: Oxford University Press, 2012), 105, offers a good definition: "it could be said that the essential character of sin or fallenness in the *Philokalia* is our inability to see the world, including our fellow-humans, without 'passion,' without the compulsion, that is, to see them in terms of our own supposed needs and fantasies." The NT generally differentiates *páthē* from *pathḗmata*, "sufferings" or "misfortunes." **Apatheia** is the state of having defeated, being without, the passions. Clement of Alexandria prefigured some of the monastic teaching on the passions: "But Clement goes beyond the cardinal freedom from passion. . . . Clement links the passions (principally desire, pleasure and anger) to the irrational parts of the soul and to the physical senses. He says many times that the Logos cures the passions (*Paedagogus* I.1.2; I.3.1; I.3.3; I.5.1; I.6.1–4). Control of the passions is not enough; the aim is to be freed from them altogether. To this end asceticism and self-discipline are the keys (*Stromateis* 2.20)" (John Ferguson, "The Achievement of Clement of Alexandria," *Religious Studies* 12, no. 1 [1976]: 59–80. See **Free (from the passions)**.

Patience / Patient Endurance. Gk. *hypomonḗ* (n.), *hypoménō* (vb.). Also "steadfastness, perseverance." A less-used word is *makrothymía*; it and related words occur 19 times in the SysAP (Guy 3.372b), while *hypomonḗ* and cognates occur 54 times (Guy 3.448b). As Bauer notes, 1039b–40a, in the NT it is used "especially during trouble, affliction, persecution." Matt 10:22 is especially resonant for the monks; Jesus tells them "you will be hated by all because of my name. But the one who endures to the end will be saved." See SysAP VII.1–31, lines 336–97 (Wortley, *Book*, 98–122) and AnonAP 192–215 (pp. 139–55).

Pay. See **Reward**.

Peace and quiet. Gk. *hēsychía*. See **Contemplative quiet**.

Pelusium. Modern Tell el-Farama, Pelusium was "the largest Late Antique city in the Nile Delta, apart from Alexandria" in the eastern Nile delta (ODLA 2:1156b); Elm, "*Virgins*," 266, believes that the Pelusium in Ammonathas 1 "is most likely" the one in the Fayoum / Fayyum / Faiyum (Arsinoite), south of modern Cairo, "near Theadelphia, close to an eastern arm of the Nile, not the metropolis of Augustamnica."

Perfection. Gk. *teleiótēs*. See SysAP I.1–37, lines 103–23 (Wortley, *Book*, 7–14).

Petras. Possibly Petra, Jabal Khashm al-Qu'ud, a "mountainous site about 20 miles to the west of the Wadi al-Natrun, that is to say, from the salty lake farthest to the west" (CE 1315b–16a).

Pharan / Pharanite. Pharan (Faran) is an "oasis in the south of the Sinai Peninsula, a little to the north of the town of al-Tur (Raïthou) and to the west of the Greek monastery of Saint Catherine" (CE 1925b–53a); "a wilderness . . . with anchorites at the beginning of the 5th century, and an oasis city with a bishop by the late 4th / early 5th century, visited by Egeria" (ODLA 2:1182; for Egeria, 1:524).

Pherme. "There is a mountain[16] called Pherme in Egypt, on the way to the great desert of Scetis. About five hundred men live on that mountain, practicing spiritual discipline" (Historia Lausiaca 20.1, p. 51). It was probably in the Delta (though "**Egypt**" can designate areas outside of **Scetis**, **Kellia**, and **Nitria**), and "lay on one of the routes connecting the Delta to **Scetis**. Unfortunately, there is nothing in this to suggest the direction in which Pherme lay" (Evelyn-White, *Monasteries*, 2.36).

Philosophy. Gk. *philosophía*. The use of "philosophy" to designate the monastic life is common in early monastic literature. In monastic parlance, *philósophos* can indicate a monk or ascetic, although Lampe 1483b (B) does not cite a use before the fourth century; Basil the Great (ca. 330–379), Gregory of Nyssa (ca. 330–95), and Eusebius (ca. 260–ca. 340) use *philosophía* of the spiritual life or asceticism (1483a [B5]). In his *First Apology* (New Advent: www.newadvent.org/fathers/0126.htm), Justin Martyr (mid-2nd cent.) declares right away that "Reason [*lógos*] directs those who are truly pious and philosophical to honour and love what is true" (II), emphasizes reason and philosophy (III), and argues that Christians with their beliefs fit in with the "diverse" views of philosophers (IV).

Clement of Alexandria saw philosophy as Christian, a prolegomenon to Christianity; in *Stromateis* 1.5.28 he states, "Before the coming of the Lord philosophy was necessary to lead the Greeks to righteousness, and it is still useful in drawing them nearer to the worship of God. . . . God is the origin of all good things . . . including philosophy' " (Ferguson, "Achievement of Clement," 89).

---

16. mountain: or "monastic settlement." See **Monastic community** and **Mountain**.

See J. T. Muckle, "Clement of Alexandria on Philosophy as a Divine Testament for the Greeks," *Phoenix* 5, no. 3–4 (Winter 1951): 79–86. For the first-century background, see N. T. Wright, *Paul and the Faithfulness of God* (Minneapolis: Fortress Press, 2013), 197–245. For the *Apophthegmata*, see Zachary Smith, who connects philosophy with self-care: "If the goal of *philosophia* is wisdom itself, the path to wisdom is self-care" (Smith, *Philosopher-Monks*, 170–250, here 170).

Place. Gk. *tópos* can also mean a "monastic place," that is, a settlement or community of monks.

Poor. The usual word for the noun *poor* in the NT and the AlphAP, as in "the poor," is *ptōchós*, "economically disadvantaged," "dependent on others" (Bauer 896ab). See Matt 5:3 // Luke 6:20, and Luke 4:18; 7:22. When speaking of the monastic ideal of voluntary poverty, the monks tend to use *aktēmosunē*. See **Poverty.**

Pope. Gk. *pápa* / *pápas* / *papâs* / *pappâs*. This honorific title apparently first occurred in Egypt; the earliest known example comes from Dionysius, bishop of **Alexandria** (247–264), quoted by Eusebius, *Ecclesiastical History* 7.7.4: "I inherited this rule and example from our blessed pope Heraclas [231–247]." "Pope," however, may be anachronistic in Eusebius's *History*. See Lampe 1006a (2b). See Stephen J. Davis, *The Early Coptic Papacy: The Egyptian Church and its Leadership in Late Antiquity* (Cairo: The American University in Cairo Press, 2004), 27. He makes an important point on 28: "the use of the title 'Pope,' from its inception, evoked the process by which Alexandrian episcopal authority was consolidated and expanded during the first half of the third century."

Possess / Possessions. Gk. *ktáomai* (vb.) and *ktêsis*, *ktêma* (n.). Possessions, and avoiding them, are important in early monasticism, as is being poor, without possessions, *aktḗmōn*, and (spiritual) **poverty**, *aktēmosúnē*, "lack of possessions." In the NT, *ktáomai* and *ktêma* do not have the later, monastic, sense. In 2 Cor 8:2 and 8:9, Paul uses *ptōchía* for the Macedonians' and Christ's poverty.

Possessed (by a demon). Gk. *daimōnízomai* < *daímōn*, "demon": see, among many, Mark 5:18 and Luke 8:36. Bauer 209b translates as "be possessed by a hostile spirit." See **Demon.**

Poverty, voluntary. In Greek, "poverty" (*aktēmosunē*) is related etymologically to *possess*, *ktáomai*; *poverty* is literally "lack of possessions."

In monastic parlance, it almost always means voluntary poverty. The cognate adjective is *aktḗmōn* (*aktḗmōn bíos*, a "life of poverty"), and the verb "to live a life of poverty" is *aktēmonéō*. Lampe 67b notes that the word also designates one who is "spiritually poor, detached," and cites Evagrius: "Blessed is the mind that at the time of prayer becomes numinous [or: spiritual] and detached." Coptic monasticism has had two famous monks named "Matthew the Poor," one ancient and one modern, Abouna Matta'l Meskeen; for the former see CE 1571b–72a; for the latter, Bishop Epiphanius, "The Human & Spiritual Legacy of Father Matthew the Poor," presented at St Athanasius College, 5th International Symposium of Coptic Studies, Melbourne, Australia (13–16 July 2018), forthcoming in book form. I wish to thank Lisa Agaiby for this source. See SysAP VI.1–35, lines 314–35 (Wortley, *Book*, 89–97).

Power / Powerful. Gk. *dýnamis* (n.) and *dynatós* (adj.) (English *dynamite*, *dynamic*) occur dozens of time in the NT. Although the word often means "ability, capability" (Bauer 263a), it often refers to divine power or the receiving of it; in Acts 1:8, after the resurrection Jesus tells the disciples, "you will receive power when the Holy Spirit has come upon you." See Mark 5:30; Matt 22:29; Rom 15:13.

Practical. In Evagrian thought, *praktikós* "starts from acute observation of the psychology of the solitary, the vices which threaten him, [and] the ascesis that purifies his heart and thoughts" (EEC I.306a). See Evagrius, *Praktikos*.

Practice. Gk. *phýlax*, cognate with *phylássō*. See **Protect / Protection**.

Praise. See **Glory / Glorify**.

Prayer. Gk. *eúchomai*, *proseúchomai* (vbs.), *proseuchḗ* (n.). "Pray" and "prayer" occur over 150 times in the NT; see Matt 5:44; 6:5, 9; 14:23; 26:36-44. See Cassian, *Conferences* 9–10 (pp. 323–63 and 365–93), and Evagrius, "Chapters on Prayer, in *Praktikos* (43–80). See Gould, *Desert Fathers*, 167–77.

Prefect. Various kinds of Roman officials. A prefect's office, department, or area of control was called a prefecture.

Prescribe. Gk. *entéllomai*. See **Command**.

Present age. Gk. *kairós*. See **Age**.

Pricked. Gk. *katanússomai*. See Acts 2:37, "cut to the heart." In Acts, the pricking, or cutting, leads Peter's audience to repent and be baptized. See **Contrition**.

Prison. Gk. *phylakḗ*. See **Protect**.

Procurator. Procurators were agents of the emperor in the civil administration and were posted to minor provinces such as Judaea.

Proscribe. Gk. *entéllomai*. See **Command**.

Prostrate / Prostration. Gk. *bállō metánoia*, literally "throw / put / place repentance" (*metánoia*), or *metanoéō*. Prostration is the outward and visible sign of an inward repentance. See Lampe 858b.

Protect / Protection. Gk. *phylássō* (vb.), *phylakḗ* (n.). Lampe 1493a: "maintain, uphold, observe, keep; pay heed to." The basic meaning of *phylássō* is "guard," "protect," "defend"; the original meaning of *phýlax* is "guard, watchman," and can mean "the night watch." In the NT, *phylássō* also means "observe, follow" a commandment (Bauer 1068ab).

Psalms(s). With regard to the importance of the Psalms, Norris paraphrases Driscoll: "The psalter is not merely a collection of prayers; it is meant to be a song that resonates in the monk's soul, accompanying him on life's journey and illuminating his path." She quotes Luke Dysinger: the psalms are "a vision of the whole of creation" and "the training-ground of the Christian contemplative."[17] See **Meditate**.

Raïthou. A "Monastic area at a harbor oasis on the southwest coast of the Sinai Peninsula, active from at least the 5th to the 11th century. Late Antique sources blame **barbarian** raids for the martyrdom of 40 monks" there (ODLA 2:1267b).

Reflect on. Gk. *logízomai* is a multivalent word. Cognate with *lógos*, "reason," and *logikós*, "rational," it can mean "calculate, count, reckon," "take into account, calculate, consider," "conclude by reasoning, infer" (Liddell and Scott 1055b). See **Thought(s)**.

Remain. Gk. *phylássō*. See **Guard**.

Renounce. Gk. *apotássō*, or "withdraw." The cognate nouns *apotaktikoí / apotaktikaí* represent male and female renunciants who had withdrawn from the world. The word became a technical term, at first apparently for village renunciants who lived an ascetic life. See James A. Goehring, *Ascetics, Society, and the Desert: Studies in Early Egyptian Monasticism* (Harrisburg, PA: Trinity, 1999), 53–72.

Renowned. See **Glory / Glorify**.

---

17. Norris, *Acedia*, 277 and 276, respectively (source not given).

Repentance. Gk. *metánoia*. **Prostration**: "making or doing a *metánoia*," literally a "repentance." This Egyptian practice appears to have traveled to Syria: John of Ephesus, in "Lives of Thomas and Stephen," *Lives of the Eastern Saints* 13, Patrologia Orientalis 18.204, describes one act of penance this way: "During every [interval], he would make thirty Egyptian *metunâyê* [= *metanoiai*] which are called prayers, until he accomplished five hundred during the night with the service of matins, and these I myself on many nights secretly counted."

Rest. Gk. *anápausis* (n.), *anapaúō* (vb.). See **Inward stillness**.

Reward. Gk. *misthós* also means "pay." See Matt 5:12; 6:1-6; Luke 6:23, 35; 1 Cor 3:8, 14; 9:18; Heb 11:26. In Matt 6:1 Jesus speaks about a person having a reward from God.

Righteous / Just. Gk. *díkaios*, *dikaiosúnē*, "righteousness." *Díkaios* means both "righteous" *and* "just" (Bauer 246a–47a; Lampe 368a–69). There are 21 words in Lampe with *dikaio-* at the beginning, a fact that shows its importance; *ádikoi* is the negative. In translating I often use both English words to capture the full meaning of *díkaios*.

Rule. The monastic Rule, or governing ordinances of a monastic community or monastery. See **Cenobium** and **Pachomius**.

Sabas. Or "Saba." "Monk (439–532) and founder of monasteries in Palestine" (ODLA 2:1315ab). See the Index in Hirschfeld, *Judean Monasteries*, 304.

Sacristy. The *diakonikón* (*diákonos*, "deacon") was a sacristy or vestry where sacred vessels were kept; it could be a building separate from the church (Lampe 351b).

Safeguard. See **Protect**.

Safeguarding. Gk. *phylakē̇*. See **Protect / Protection**.

Salvation. Gk. *sōtēría*. See **Save**.

Save. Gk. *sōzō*. Asking how to be saved is a common question among the early monks, from one monk to an elder and from an elder to God. We hear *saved* primarily in terms of (eternal) salvation, but the word in Greek is really holistic: body and soul; its meaning is to be saved "from sickness or afflictions" (Lampe 1361b). See English "whole," "holistic," "heal," and "healthy"—and "holy," all cognate. See Isa 53:7: "Surely it is God who saves me." Smith,

Philosopher-Monks, 249, makes an important point: "Because of [the connection between the deformation of the soul and the Fall], the proper goal of the self shifts from access to wisdom and knowledge to the salvation of the soul through a close connection with the divine." See John Wortley, "What the Desert Fathers Meant by 'being saved,' " *Zeitschrift für Antikes Christentum* 12 (2008): 322–43.

Say / Saying. Gk. *lógos* or *rêma.* See **Spiritual Guidance.**

Scandalize. Greek *skandalízō. Skandalízō* has degrees of fault: "cause to fall, lead into sin; cause offense to; shock, hurt one's feelings" (Lampe 1235b). The verb and the noun *skándalon* occur often in the NT; *skándalon* means "trap; an action or circumstance that leads one to act contrary to a proper course of action or set of beliefs, temptation to sin, enticement to apostasy" (Bauer 926a); cause one to sin, "scandalize." Given Jesus' commandment (Matt 5:29; 17:27), in Antony 9, Antony may be intimating that even the slightest offense to one's (monastic) neighbor is an affront to Christ. See Matt 18:6, 8; 2 Cor 11:29.

Scetis. The Wadi al-Natrun has been the site of continuous monastic life for over 1600 years. Its ancient name, Scetis, comes from the Coptic *shi hēt,* "to weigh the heart," a most appropriate name for a place long dedicated to silence, prayer, and contemplation. Its southeast end is about 40 miles northwest of Cairo. See CE 2102b–6a: "historically designated the area of monastic settlement extending about 19 miles (30 km) through the shallow valley known in the medieval period as Wad Habb, now called Wadi al-Natrun, which runs southeast to northwest through the Western or Libyan Desert, about 40 miles (65 km) southwest of the Nile Delta. In a very broad sense, 'Scetis' or the 'Desert of Scetis' also designated the ensemble of monastic colonies in the wilderness or on the edge of the desert southwest of the Delta, thus including Nitria or the 'Mountain of Nitria'. . . ; Kellia, in the desert south of Nitria; and Scetis in the narrower and more proper sense, still farther into the desert, south of Kellia." See Chitty, *Desert,* 12–13, 33–36, 38–39, 52–53, 56–61, 66–74, 78–80, 144–49; Evelyn-White, *Monasteries,* 2.27–36, 60–66.

Scripture. Gould, *Desert Fathers,* 79: "[Hermann] Dörries comments that the Desert Fathers did not inherit Origen's interest in the speculative interpretation of Scripture. [But in the anti-Origenist persecution and later *damnatio memoriae*, we probably lost a great deal of monastic Origenist writings.] In a sense this is obviously true. What these sayings do suggest is that for the Desert Fathers the interpretation of Scripture was not something to be lightly entered upon, not something to be regarded as an automatic subject of discussion. An easy approach to Scripture may hide your own real needs and your own real state of mind. Where the proper attitude is not present, it is implied, silence, the absence of teaching or dialogue between abba and disciple, may be the best course of action." See Antony 17. Ethiopic AP 13: "A brother asked an elder and said to him: 'Do you wish me to meditate on what people read in the Scriptures when I go to church?' The Elder said to him: 'You are going to the source of life.' " See John Wortley, ed., *More Sayings of the Desert Fathers* (Cambridge: Cambridge University Press, 2019), 4. See Elizabeth A. Clark, *Reading Renunciation: Asceticism and Scripture in Early Christianity* (Princeton: Princeton University Press, 1999), and esp. Burton-Christie, *Word*.

See that. Gk. *phylássō*. See **Protect / Protection**.

Self-control. Gk. *enkráteia* is traditionally translated "abstinence, continence" (Lampe 402), but for the cognate verb *enkrateúomai* Lampe 403b offers "practice self-restraint." See SysAP IV.1–104, lines 184–239 (Wortley, *Book*, 38–58), and AnonAP 144–63 (pp. 99–109). **Clement** offers a very measured statement; in *Stromata / Stromateis* III.4 he praises both "continence / self-control" (*enkráteia*) and marriage: "Continence is an ignoring of the body in accordance with the confession of faith in God. For continence is not merely a matter of sexual abstinence, but applies also to the other things for which the soul has an evil desire because it is not satisfied with the necessities of life. There is also a continence of the tongue, of money, of use, and of desire. It does not only teach us to exercise self-control; it is rather that self-control is granted to us, since it is a divine power and grace. Accordingly I must declare what is the opinion of our people about this subject. Our view is that we welcome as blessed the state of abstinence from marriage in those to whom this has been granted by God. We admire monogamy and the high standing of single marriage, holding that we ought to share suffering with another and 'bear one another's burdens,' lest anyone who thinks he stands securely should himself fall. It is of second marriage that the apostle says, 'If you burn, marry' " (https://www.newadvent.org/fathers/02103.htm). See Carolyn M. Schneider, *The Text of a Coptic Monastic Discourse*, On Love and Soul Control: *Its Story from the Fourth Century to the Twenty-First*, CS 272 (Collegeville, MN: Cistercian Publications, 2017).

Self-importance. Gk. *kenodoxía*. *Kenodoxía* is an intriguing word. It is formed of *kenós*, "empty, vain," and *dóxa*, "opinion, judgment." It does not occur in the LXX, but *kenós* does. In the NT see Phil 2:13 ("empty conceit"). The earliest patristic uses meaning "senseless opinion" that Lampe cites are **Clement** of Alexandria (d. before 215) and the *Shepherd of Hermas* (2nd cent.). The earliest use meaning "vainglory" (the traditional translation) is Life of Antony 55.3 (p. 175: "false pride"). On vainglory and pride, see Cassian, *Institutes* 11 and 12, pp. 239–51 and 253–79.

Self-moderation. See **Self-control.**

Send / Send back. Gk. *apostéllō,* cognate with *apóstolos*, "apostle"; one sent forth (by Christ).

Serapeum. The sanctuary dedicated to Serapis, the Serapeum consisted of "a temple surrounded by a colonnade with a famous library. It dominated the acropolis [in Alexandria], and was embellished with a monumental column dedicated to Diocletian in 298. . . . It was destroyed during a conflict between pagans and Christians (led by the Patriarch Theophilus) in 391/392" (ODLA 2:1539a). For later Christian and non-Christian relationships and violence, see Edward J. Watts, *Riot in Alexandria: Tradition and Group Dynamics in Late Antique Pagan and Christian Communities* (Berkeley: University of California Press, 2017).

Serapion. Serapion of Thmuis (Sarapion of Tmuis) was a "fourth-century bishop of Tmuis who supported" **Athanasius** "in the Arian controversy. . . . Sarapion wrote numerous works, most of which have not survived" (CE 2095b–96b). See Oliver Herbel, *Sarapion of Thmuis:* Against the Manicheans *and* Pastoral Letters (Strathfield, NSW, Australia: St. Paul's Publications, 2011).

Serapis. See Lesley Adkins and Roy A. Adkins, *Dictionary of Roman Religion* (Oxford: Oxford University Press, 1996), 202: "Serapis was a conflation of the god Osiris and the sacred bull Apis. The cult[18] of Serapis seems to have arisen at Memphis in Egypt, in the temple where the sacred bull Apis was kept." See **Serapeum**.

Settlement, monastic. Gk. *tópos*. See **Place**.

Sexual Temptation / Sin. Gk. *porneía* (English *porn, pornography*). The usual translation is "fornication," but that seems outdated now. See Matt 15:19; 1 Cor 5:1; Gal 5:19. On *porneía* see SysAP V.1–54, lines 240–313 (Wortley, *Book*, 59–88), one of the longest chapters, and AnonAP 454–74 (pp. 293–302). It is usually not clear whether *porneía* indicates thought, word, and / or deed; see Matt 5:28; Rom 1:24. See Cassian, *Institutes* 6.151–66. In his translation of the *Diadache* (around 100 CE), Bart Ehrman translates *porneía* as "sexual immorality," which is good. See *The Apostolic Fathers*, vol. 1, ed. and trans. Bart D. Ehrman, Loeb Classical Library 24 (Cambridge, MA: Harvard University Press, 2003).

Shaken. Gk. *tarássō*. See **Disturb**.

Shame / Feel shame / Be ashamed. Gk. *aischúnē* (n.), *aischúnomai* (vb.) shame, disgrace, ignominy (Bauer 29b–30s). See 1 Cor 11:14; 15:43; 2 Cor 6:8. On honor and shame, see Bruce J. Malina, *The New Testament World: Insights from Cultural Anthropology*, 3rd ed., rev. and exp. (Louisville: Westminster / John Knox, 2020), 27–57; and Malina and Richard L. Rohrbaugh, *Social-Science Commentary on the Synoptic Gospels*, 2nd ed. (Minneapolis: Fortress, 2003), 369–72.

Shamefulness. See **Shame**.

Silence, keep. Gk. *hēsycházō*. See **Contemplative quiet**.

Sit. Gk. *kathízomai/kathézomai*, which can mean "sit" and "dwell, live."

Solidus / pl. Solidi. "A Roman gold coin introduced by **Constantine** in 309–310, replacing the *aureus* as the main gold coin of the Roman Empire. The name *solidus* had previously been used by Diocletian* (284–305) for the gold coin that he introduced, which is different from the solidus introduced by Constantine. The coin was struck at a theoretical value of 1/72 of a Roman pound (about 4.5 grams). Solidi were wider and thinner than the aureus. Interestingly, the word

---

18. In the study of religion, "cult," from Latin *cultus*, does not have its modern English sense. It means the practice (worship, organization, etc.) devoted to a god or to God.

soldier is ultimately derived from *solidus*, referring to the solidi with which soldiers were paid" (ODLA 2:1402b–3a).

Solitude. Gk. *xeniteía*: "sojourn or travel in a foreign land, exile," "solitude, isolation from world" (Lampe 931b–32a). Since the word means both "solitude" and "separation from the world," I have used both meanings in the present translation. The word is cognate with *xénos*, "foreigner, **stranger**"; thus monks are "outsiders." This could, and probably often did, have a price: Wipszycka explains that because of a "model of social life" that was very limited (by modern Western standards), people "were on their own only rarely—they would work and rest in groups. Ascetics, driven by religious motives, could find solitude only at a price: they had to leave the settlements behind them" (*Second Gift*, 7).

Son. A spiritual son. The term also hearkens back to the father-son advice in the Wisdom literature of the HB.

Sorrow. Gk. *pénthos*: "sorrow as experience or expression, grief, sadness, mourning" (Bauer 795b). The word occurs only five times in the NT (the cognate verb *penthéō* occurs more often). The key passage for monastic spirituality is Jas 4:6-9.

Sozomen. Sozomen, ca. 400–after 445, was a Church historian who wrote the *Ecclesiastical History* (ca. 445). See ODLA 2:1406ab.

Speak freely. Gk. *parrēsía*. See **Confidence**.

Spirit of God. "The Spirit of God" and "Spirit of the Lord" occur often in the HB (Num 24:2; Isa 11:2), especially in Judges. In Matt 3:16, at his baptism Jesus sees "the Spirit of God descending on him," and in Luke 4:18 he says, "the Spirit of the Lord is upon me."

Spiritual contemplation. Gk. *theōría*. See **Contemplation**.

Spiritual guidance. Gk. *lógos* or *rêma*. Many sayings begin with a monk asking an elder, "Give me a word" [*lógos*; sometimes *rêma*]. In the HB words can signify the covenant with Israel. In Exod 34:27-28 LXX, God tells Moses, "in accordance with these words [*rêma*] I have made a covenant with you and with Israel. . . . And [Moses] wrote on the tablets the words [*rêma*] of the covenant, the ten commandments." In Deut 4:13 and 10:4 the ten commandments are the ten words [*rêma*].

With "Give me a word" the monks are asking for spiritual guidance, so I am translating the expression with "spiritual guidance" to make that clear. *Lógos* is multivalent in the *Sayings*; it often

means "say" or "speak," and, more important, it is the root of
Thoughts, *logismós* / *logismoí*, and **Thinking**, *logízomai*. To hear
something edifying: literally "to hear a word [*lógos*]." In the sayings
translated here I am using *edifying* and *beneficial*. Wortley, *Give
Me*, understandably titles his translation of the AlphAP *Give Me a
Word*. See Gould, *Desert Fathers*, 26–87.

Staff. In Cassian's symbolic interpretation of monastic wear in *Institutes*
1.8 (p. 25), he traces the monastic staff back to the story of Elisha
and Gehazi in 2 Kgs 4:29-31.

Stain. Gk. *miaínō*. As Bauer points out, "the primary sense 'to stain'
(as of dye . . .) prepares the way for the transferred sense of causing defilement through socially or cultically unacceptable behavior.
It is well to keep in mind in connection with the use of the term and
cognates that in the Greco-Roman world harmonious relations with
the transcendent realm were understood to be dependent on careful
observance of certain moral and ritual proprieties. Individuals were
subordinate to interests of the community and violations of standard
moral and ceremonial expectations could jeopardize the delicate
balance between an entire populace and its deities" (650a). See
Shame.

Steadfastness. Gk. *hypomonḗ*. See **Patience / Patient endurance**.

Steward. Gk. *oikónomos*. The monk in a monastery or monastic settlement who was in charge of business matters.

Sting. See **Prick**.

Stranger. Gk. *xénos* (n.), *xenikós* (adj.). See **Solitude**. One's thoughts
go immediately to the numerous biblical verses that command taking care of strangers and aliens, but the LXX in these places uses
not *xénos* but *prosḗlytos* (English *proselyte*). Heb 13:2, however,
does use the participial form of *xenízō*, "to be a stranger": "Do not
neglect to show hospitality to strangers, for by doing that some have
entertained angels without knowing it," a reference to Abraham and
Sarah, who welcome the two visitors (Gen 18). For hospitality and
the care for strangers in Paul's communities, see Rom 12:9-13; Phil
2:1-5; 1 Thess 4:9-12.

Struggle. Gk. *ágōn* (n.), *agōnízomai* (vb.) See **Fight**.

Stung to the heart. See **Contrition**.

Submit. See **Obey**.

Suffer. Gk. *páschō*, cognate with *páthos*. See **Passion/s**.

Summon. See **Comfort.**

Support. Gk. *bastázō* can also mean "bear, endure" (Lampe 293b) and can mean "support heaven" (Bauer 171ab).

Surprised. See **Astonished.**

Symeon. Symeon Stylites the Older (Symeon the Stylite) lived ca. 390–459. He was the "first of the stylite saints, perched on the top of columns." Because of his intercessory prayer, he "attracted a continuous stream of pilgrims and was widely imitated" (ODCC 1276a). See ODLA 2:1435a; and Robert Doran, *The Lives of Symeon Stylites*, CS 112 (Kalamazoo, MI: Cistercian Publications, 1992).

Synaxis. Gk. *sýnaxis*. Literally "gathering"; the same Greek root gives *synagogue*. The word had a wide range of meanings: "gathering, assembly for public worship and instruction, religious service," "form of worship or prayer obligatory upon monks and nuns, perhaps sometimes referring to the Eucharist but also to a [monastic] office" (Lampe 1302a–3a); "any assembly for public worship and prayer, inclusive of the Eucharist, or 'liturgical synaxis'" (ODCC 1331b–32a). See Robert Taft, "Praise in the Desert: The Coptic Monastic Office Yesterday and Today," *Worship* 56 (1982): 513–36.

Syria. In Late Antiquity, Syria was "roughly equivalent to modern Syria and Lebanon" (ODLA 2:1440a–42a; here 1440a).

Talking with everyone. Gk. *parrēsiázomai*, cognate with *parrēsía* (n.); see **Confidence.** In the NT, these words are positive: "a use of speech that conceals nothing and passes over nothing, outspokenness, frankness, plainness," "a state of boldness and confidence, courage, confidence, boldness, fearlessness" (Bauer 781ab). Paul uses the term often: 2 Cor 3:12; 7:4; Phil 1:20; Phlm 8; and in the Pauline or deutero-Pauline Eph 3:12; 6:19. But *parrēsiázomai* can also mean that a person is *too* confident: "be over-confident, presume" (Lampe 1046a). The noun and verb occur 38 times in SysAP (Guy, "Index des mots grecs," 3.403) and can be positive or negative (e.g. I.34 [Guy 1.120]).

Tartarus. In classical Greek mythology, Tartarus is either a deep, gloomy place, a pit or abyss used as a dungeon of torment and suffering that resides within Hades or the entire underworld, with

Hades being the hellish component. In Plato's *Gorgias*, souls are judged after death, and those who received punishment are sent to Tartarus. A lengthy description of Tartarus occurs in Hesiod, *Theogony* 721–819; see David M. Johnson, "Hesiod's Description of Tartarus *(Theogony* 721–819)," *Phoenix* 53, no. 12 (Spring/Summer 1999): 8–28 (available on JSTOR). Second Peter 2:4 uses the verb *tartaróō*: "God did not hold back from punishing the angels that sinned, but, by throwing them into Tartarus, delivered them into pits of dense darkness to be reserved for judgment." See Bauer 991a. See the (Ethiopic) *Apocalypse of Peter*, M. R. James, trans., Early Christian Writings, www.earlychristianwritings.com/text/apocalypse peter-mrjames.html.

Task. See **Work**.

Tell. Tell us a word (*lógos*). See **Thoughts** and **Spiritual Guidance**.

Temptation. Gk. *peirasmós*. The NT uses the verb *peirázō* for the temptation of Jesus (Matt 4:1 and par.) and the noun in the Lord's Prayer (Matt 6:13; Luke 11:4). *Peirasmós* can also mean "trial," as in "undergoing a trial." Lampe 1056b notes that temptation or trial was caused especially by **demons**.

Tempter, the. Satan

Test / Put to the test. Gk. *dokimázō* (vb.), *dokimós* (n.). See 1 Cor 11:28 ("Examine yourselves"); 2 Cor 8:22; Jas 1:12.

Thebaid. The Thebaid was "the administrative unit of southernmost Egypt," named after the Pharaonic city **Thebes** (Luxor); Thebes "remained a significant provincial city in Late Antiquity" (ODLA 2:1470). For an extensive treatment, see Roger S. Bagnall and Dominic W. Rathbone, *Egypt from Alexander to the Early Christians: An Archaeological and Historical Guide* (Los Angeles: The J. Paul Getty Museum, 2004), 183–208.

The division of Egypt into two parts, Lower and Upper Egypt, goes back to Pharaonic antiquity. The Sa'id, Upper Egypt, may be divided into (a) the lower Sa'id (or Lower Thebaid), from Cairo to al-Bahnasa (Oxyrhynchus), (b) the middle Sa'id (or Thebaid), from al-Bahnasa to Akhmim, and (c) the Upper Sa'id (or Upper Thebaid), from Akhmim to Aswan. See CE 2080ab; ODLA 2:1470ab.

Thebes. A great Egyptian city, it was located about 800 km south of the Mediterranean, on the east bank of the Nile. Thebes was the capital of Waset, the fourth upper-Egyptian nome. See CE 2080ab; ODLA 2:1470ab.

Theodosius. Theodosius I, "the great," was Augustus from 379–395 (ODLA 2:1483).

Theodosius of Jerusalem. Theodosius (d. 457), patriarch of Jerusalem (451/2–453), was an "Anti-Chalcedonian monastic leader in Palestine, installed as patriarch during the revolt of the monks against Juvenal" after the Council of Chalcedon (ODLA 2:1486; on Juvenal, see 2.850a).

Theophilus. Theophilus of Alexandria was the 23rd patriarch of Alexandria (385–412). "Throughout his career, Theophilus was on good terms with various groups of ascetics in Nitria and Scetis. . . . Jerome observes (Epistle 82) that the monks rushed to greet Theophilus on the occasion of his visits. In both the Coptic and Greek versions" of the AlphAP, "the patriarch and the monks consult each other" (CE 2247b–53b). Tito Orlandi comments that "Theophilus of Alexandria is one of the most poorly preserved authors in Greek Patrology, in spite of his importance." See "Theophilus of Alexandria in Coptic Literature," *Studia Patristica* 16 (1985): 100–104, here 100; on his writings, see Quasten, *Patrology*, 3:100–106. See Wipszycka, *Second Gift*, 122–23, 126; and Norman Russell, *Theophilus of Alexandria* (Oxford: Routledge, 2007). On the destruction of the **Serapeum**, and the "Christianization of space," see Russell, *Theophilus*, 7–11.

Think / Thinking. Gk. *logízomai*. See **Thoughts**.

Thought(s). Gk. *logismós* (sing.), *logismoí* (pl.) < *lógos* (the translation here often translates the singular as a plural). Thoughts, and their discernment, are key in early monasticism. Once again, Evagrius offers a systematic analysis: see Evagrius, *Praktikos*. In *Praktikos* 6–14 (pp. 16–20), he discusses the eight kinds of evil thoughts, and in 15–39 (pp. 20–26) he offers antidotes for them. One notes that the discussion of the medicine is almost twice as long as that for the disease(s). On discernment of thoughts, see the Index in Rich, *Discernment*, 325; and Tim Vivian, *Words to Live By: Journeys in Ancient and Modern Egyptian Monasticism*, CS 207 (Kalamazoo, MI: Cistercian Publications, 2005), 11–21. For a good modern reflection, see Mary Margaret Funk, *Why Thoughts Matter: Discovering the Spiritual Journey* (Collegeville, MN: Liturgical Press, 2013).

Time. See **Opportune time.**

Timothy. Timothy of Alexandria: an elderly monk elected as archbishop, serving from 380–385 (CE 2263).

Tranquility. See **Peace and Tranquility.**

Transgression. Gk. *anomía*, literally "not law, without law," therefore "lawlessness" (English *anomie*). Bauer 85ab prefers "a lawless deed"; in fact, one scholar has suggested that the Lawless One (*ho ánthrōpos tês anomías*) in 2 Thess 2:3 is a translation of Beliar, a name in Patristic Greek used for an "antichrist" (173b).

Tremissis. A small gold coin worth 1/3 of the **aureus.** The *keration* was another small coin. According to Moschus, *Spiritual Meadow,* 184, twenty-four *keratia* equaled one *tremissis*; see also 154.

Trial. See **Temptation.**

Tried and tested. See **Test.**

Tried and true. See **Test.**

Trouble. See **Disturb.**

Trust. Gk. *ēlpikénai* < *elpízō*; its cognate noun *elpís* is a key Christian term meaning "**hope.**"

Tunic. Gk. *lébition*. See Innemée, *Ecclesiastical Dress,* 101–4.

Turn to. See **Concerned, be.**

Upset. Gk. *tarássō*. See **Disturb.**

Urge. See **Comfort.**

Verse. Gk. *lógos* or *rêma*. See **Spiritual Guidance.**

Vigil, keep. Gk. *agrupnéō* (English *agrypnia*): a monastic (night) vigil or prayer (Lampe 24a), but other meanings, instead of or in addition, are apposite: "to be vigilant in awareness of threatening peril, be alert" (about, for example, the Devil) (Bauer 16a); see Mark 13:33 (Jesus: "Beware, keep alert; for you do not know when the time will come"); Luke 21:36 (Jesus: "Be alert at all times, praying that you may have the strength to escape all these things that will take place, and to stand before the Son of Man").

Virtue / Virtues. Gk. *aretḗ* (sing.), *aretaí* (pl.). The Virtues were an important spiritual concept to the early monks: they tried to cultivate them in themselves and in others. The Virtues were sometimes grouped together: *Pistis* (Faith), *Elpis* (Hope), *Agapē* (Love), and

Parthenia (Virginity), *Thbbio* (Humility), *Tbbo* (Chastity), *Mntrm-rash* (Gentleness),[19] *Gratia* (Grace), *Hypomonē* (Patience), and *Sophia* (Wisdom). See Tim Vivian, "Ama Sibylla of Saqqara: Prioress or Prophet? Monastic, or Mythological Being?" in Vivian, *Words*, 377–93.

Vision(s)[1]. Gk. *theōría* means both "spiritual contemplation" and "a vision, such as the patristic writer saw in the prophets and the apostles" (Lampe 648a–49b). He also notes, "of visions of prophets and apostles . . . which can be rightly interpreted only by minds detached from earthly things" (649a [D1]). It and its cognate verb, *theōréō,* do not have either meaning in the NT but rather have the words' root meaning of "see, look at, observe" (Bauer 454b–55a).

Vision(s)[2]. Gk. *phantasía. Phantasía* (English *fantasy*) also has negative implications: "unreal appearance, illusion, delusion" (Lampe 1471a). The verb *phantázō* means "delude" but in the middle and aorist passive voices means "form a conception of, picture to oneself" (1470b). *Phantasía* occurs eight times in the SysAP, and it is positive only in XVIII.8.7. In SysAP V.25 **demons** show a monk visions / illusions / delusions / fantasies of women; in V.54 (Historia Lausiaca 23; pp. 62–64) Pachon is troubled by "thoughts and nocturnal visions [or: delusions]," so much so that he thinks of forsaking the desert. Visions occur in five of the AlphAP sayings; only Antony 12 mentions demons with them. See Gould, *Desert Fathers*, 42–46.

Wadi. In Egypt a strip of land amid the arid desert with a good water supply and water table.

Wadi Natrun. See **Scetis**.

War / Wage War. Gk. *pólemos* (n.), *poleméō* (vb.) (English *polemic*). See Matt 24:6; Jas 4:1. Revelation uses the noun and verb 8 and 7 times each respectively. The theme of waging spiritual warfare is

---

19. *Thbbio, Tbbo,* and *Mntrmrash* are Coptic words; the others, except for Latin *Gratia,* are Greek.

very important in early monasticism; the SysAP uses the noun 59 times and the verb 65 (Guy 3.411).

Watch / Keeping watch. Gk. *phylakḗ.* See **Protect / Protection.**

Watch Out. See **Concerned, be.**

Watchfulness. Gk. *phylakḗ.* See **Protect / Protection.**

Way of life, monastic / ascetic. Gk. *politeía* (from *pólis*, "city"), English *political,* is an important monastic term; like *diagōgḗ* in the phrase "monastic way of life," it can simply mean "way of life," but as a monastic term it has additional resonance: "conduct oneself; live as a member of community, share a particular mode of life" (Lampe 1114a). It often appears in the titles of monastic hagiographical Lives.

Weakness. Gk. *asthéneia* (English *neurasthenia*). From Plato on, *asthéneia* can indicate "the frailty to which all" humans are heir. In the NT it can contrast with *dýnamis,* "**power,** strength." In 2 Cor 12:5-9 Paul speaks of his weaknesses, and in verse 9 the Lord says to him, "My grace is sufficient for you, for power is made perfect in weakness."

Welcome. Gk. *déchomai*: this word has deep resonance with the gospels' "receive as guest, welcome." See Matt 10:14, 40-42. In John 4:45, "the Galileans welcomed [Jesus], since they had seen all that he had done in Jerusalem." In Matt 18:4-5 Jesus says, "Whoever becomes humble [*tapeinóō*] like this child is the greatest in the kingdom of heaven. Whoever welcomes one such child in my name welcomes me." *Déchomai* can also "indicate approval or conviction by accepting, be receptive of, approve, accept" (Bauer 220ab).

Wilderness. Gk. *érēmos.* See **Desert.**

Wine. The monks had varying views on wine. Regnault, *Day-to-Day Life,* 76, has an amusing take on the drink: "We find some fifty mentions of wine in the apothegms and almost all attest to the fact that, even if it was not generalized, the use of wine in the desert was nonetheless not as rare as one would be led to believe." Citing the Life of Antony 7.6 (p. 75), Regnault continues, "Antony, like his ascetic companions, never drank wine. But we scarcely quote other names which the anti-alcohol brigade might claim as role models." The statement in the Life of Antony may be idealized, or not. See Antony 22 and Theodore of Pherme 6. See Chitty, *Desert,* 44 n. 29.

Withdraw (from the world). Gk. *anachoréō* (English *anchorite*). Lampe 128b: "withdraw from the world to live a religious life." It could mean "withdraw from the world" as early as Plato. In Matt 14:13 Jesus "withdrew from there in a boat to a **desert**ed place by himself." Monks withdrew from the world to live a life of **contemplative quiet** in the **desert** / remote places. Jesus often withdraws in Matthew (4:12; 15:21). "Deserted place" translates" *érēmos*, also "desert." Thus Jesus is the archetype and exemplum for the desert mothers and fathers.

Woman. The desert "was a world of men. Women had no place in such an environment. Not only that: the desert world, in its complete isolation, had been created in part for the exact purpose of escaping from women and all they represented" (Elm, *"Virgins,"* 257).[20] See further Elm, *"Virgins,"* 268–71 and 269 n. 51. Although the AlphAP has sayings by three female monastics, "woman" in the abstract often takes a beating. See Arsenius 28, Daniel 2, Evagrius S3, Ephraim 3, and Theodore of Pherme 17. Women, less abstract, are sometimes the locus of forgiveness and healing; see Ammonas 8, Daniel 3, Epiphanius 6, John the Little 40, John of Kellia. Several of these stories concern prostitutes and their redemption—or not; see Benedicta Ward, *Harlots of the Desert: A Study of Repentance in Early Monastic Sources*, CS 106 (Kalamazoo, MI: Cistercian Publications, 1987). The three women in the AlphAP are Sarah, Syncletica, and Theodora (in volume 2, forthcoming). See Tim Vivian, "Courageous Women: Three Desert Ammas—Theodora, Sarah, and Syncletica," ABR 70, no. 2 (June 2019): 75–101, and Vivian, " 'We Sail by Day': Metaphor and Exegesis in the Sayings of Amma Syncletica of Egypt," CSQ 54, no. 1 (2019): 3–24.

In Historia Lausiaca 41 (pp. 102–4), Palladius "commemorates" "some courageous women" whom he sees as equal to men. Modern scholarship on early female monastics (or proto-monastics) is volu-

---

20. This appears to me to have two overstatements: (1) The *Sayings* show that the monks did not live in "complete isolation." (2) I do not believe that flight from women was "the exact reason" that (male) monks went out into the desert; the flight was from "the world," and both men and women primarily sought to live Gospel lives, alone and together. (3) There *were* women out there, apparently in large numbers; see below.

minous. See David Brakke, *Athanasius and the Politics of Asceticism* (Oxford: Oxford University Press, 1995), esp. 17–79; Laura Swan, *The Forgotten Desert Mothers: Sayings, Lives, and Stories of Early Christian Women* (New York: Paulist, 2001). On female monastics, see Elm, *"Virgins,"* and, esp. for this volume, 253–82. See also Ward, *Harlots*; Tim Vivian, "The Origins of Monasticism," in *The T&T Clark Handbook to the Early Church* (London: T&T Clark / Bloomsbury, forthcoming 2021); Shaw, *The Burden of the Flesh*; Alanna Emmett, "Female Ascetics in the Greek Papyri," *Jahrbuch der österreichischen Byzantinistik* 32, no. 2 (1982): 507–15; and Ross S. Kraemer, ed., *Maenads, Martyrs, Matrons, Monastics: A Sourcebook on Women's Religions in the Graeco-Roman World* (Philadelphia: Fortress, 1988). For Syncletica, see The Life of Syncletica; and Schaffer, *The Life & Regimen*. It's right to finish this entry with comments by Elm, *"Virgins,"* 281: "As in Asia Minor, women in Egypt pursued their ascetic life within the confines of their own home and their own family . . . or else in community with others, whether men or women." Women, she says, broke their "confines." See now Rachel Wheeler, *Desert Daughters, Desert Sons: Rethinking the Christian Desert Tradition* (Collegeville, MN: Liturgical Press, 2020).

Wonders. Gk. *sēmeía* (pl.; sing. *sēmeío*). "Signs, miracles, wonders" are important in the gospels, especially in John, where the word occurs 16 times (see 2:11; 6:2; 20:30).

Word. Gk. *lógos* or *rêma*. See **Spiritual guidance**.

Work / Working. Gk. *érgon* (n.), *ergasía* (n.), *ergázomai* (vb.). The three are important words and concepts in early monasticism. Jas 2:14-26 uses *érgon* numerous times. See Lisa Agaiby, *Manual Labor in Early Egyptian Monasticism: From the Late Third to Mid-Fifth Century* (Cairo: Saint Cyril of Alexandria Society Press, 2015).

Work with. Gk. *synergía* (English *synergy*). See **Co-operation**.

World, the. Gk. *kósmos*. A, perhaps the, main theme of the sayings of AlphAP Arsenius is "the world." In the NT, *kósmos* often means "the world and everything that belongs to it, . . . that which is hostile to God, i.e. lost in sin, wholly at odds with anything divine, ruined and depraved" (Bauer 562b [7]). See esp. John (1:10; 8:23, among many) but also 1 Cor 2:12 and Jas 1:27. See **World, those living in the world**.

World, those living in the world. Gk. *kosmikós*. See **World, the**. *Kosmikós* occurs only twice in the NT: Heb 9:1 ("an earthly sanctuary") and Titus 2:11-12; in the latter it means "worldly": "For the grace of God has appeared, bringing salvation to all, training us to renounce [*arnéomai*] impiety and worldly [*kosmikós*] passions [*epithymía*]." The three bracketed words, and their concepts, are key to monastic spirituality. In patristic Greek *kosmikós* has positive, negative, and neutral meanings (Lampe 769b).

Worldly. Gk. *kosmikós*. See **World, the**.

Dramatis Personae

Brief Biographies of Selected Ammas and Abbas of the Greek Alphabetical Apophthegmata[1]

An asterisk (*) in the entries indicates a person in this list.

Achilla / Achilles. A "monk at Scetis in the golden age of monasticism (fourth-fifth centuries). Saint Achillas was outstanding among all the great ascetics. Theodore of Pherme said of him, 'He was like a lion at Scetis, considered formidable in his own day.' The *Apophthegmata Patrum* gives some examples not only of his austerity but also of his wisdom and the sensitivity of his charity" (CE 56a). See Derwas Chitty, *The Desert a City* (Crestwood, NY: St. Vladimir's, 1966), 78 n. 64; 80 n. 117; Guy 1.63–64.[2]

Agathon. Agathon was a "fourth-fifth century anchorite. The different collections of the *Apophthegmata Patrum* include about fifty items in which an Abba Agathon appears, but it is justifiable to doubt whether they all concern the same person, for in a collection preserved in Ethiopic he is designated 'Agathon the Great' . . . and 'the one from early times'" (CE 64b–65a).

---

1. Because the Greek and English alphabets do not always coincide, the alphabetical order here is different from that in the Sayings.

2. Full citations of works abbreviated here appear in the Abbreviations (pp. xix–xxiii).

Ammonas. "Anchorite and Bishop. The Apophthegmata Patrum in-cludes about fifteen items relating to a fourth-century Abba Ammo-nas who spent at least fourteen years at Scetis and was in touch with Saint Antony" (CE 113ab). See Chitty, *Desert*, 38.

Ammoun / Amoun / Amun. A fourth-century anchorite. Tradition holds that "around the year 320, Amoun became the first monk to settle in the desert of Nitria" (CE 119a). See Chitty, *Desert*, 11, 29; Hugh G. Evelyn-White, *The Monasteries of the Wâdi 'N Watrun*, vol. II, *The History of the Monasteries of Nitria and Scetis*, ed. Walter Hauser (New York: Metropolitan Museum, 1932; repr. Arno Press, 1973), 45–49; Hist Mon XXII, pp. 111–12; Historia Lausiaca, 8 (pp. 20–22); ODLA 1:65a; Susanna Elm, *"Virgins of God": The Making of Asceticism in Late Antiquity* (Oxford: Clarendon, 1996), 253.

Antony. The "father of monasticism" lived from about 251 to 356. Scholars used to consider the *Life of Antony* by Athanasius to be the main source for his life, but this is now very much open to question;[3] see David Brakke, *Athanasius and the Politics of Asceti-cism* (Oxford: Oxford University Press, 1995). For the letters, see Antony, Letters. On Antony's monastery, see Tim Vivian, "St. Ant-ony and the Monastery of St. Antony at the Red Sea, ca. 350–ca. 1322 / 1323," in Elizabeth S. Bolman, ed., *Monastic Visions: The Wall Paintings at the Monastery of St. Antony at the Red Sea* (New Haven, CT: Yale University Press, 2002), 3–20. See CE 149a–51a; Chitty, *Desert*, 1–7, 9–11, 13–17, 19–20, 27–29, 31–32, 34–36, 38–39, 68–69, 85–86, 96–97; Evelyn-White, *Monasteries*, 13–16, 67–68; ODLA 1:89b–90a.

Apollo. A monk at Scetis. "Our knowledge of Saint Apollo is limited to the Apophthegmata Patrum" (CE 175–76a). Guy 1.64 notes the various spellings of Apollo and persons by that name at various locales. See Guy 1.64–65; Hist Mon VIII, pp. 70–79.

Arsenius. "They used to say about Abba Arsenius that no one could understand his monastic way of life" (Arsenius 45*). Arsenius lived from approximately 354 to 449. He had been tutor to the princes Arcadius* and Honorius but in 394 came to Scetis* and lived in the

---

3. See Life of Antony, xxiv–xxx.

community of Abba John the Little.* See CE 40a–41b; Guy, 1.74–77; Evelyn-White, *Monasteries,* 122–24, 160–64.

Basil. Basil (the Great) lived roughly from 330 to 379, bishop of Caesarea in Asia Minor (now Turkey) and famous monastic founder. See ODLA 1:217b–20a.

Ephraim. Ephraim (Ephraem, Ephrem) Syrus (ca. 306–73) was "one of the most productive spiritual writers of the fourth century. Lives of Saint Ephraem . . . are late and provide us with no objective information about him. His portrait can best be traced through the considerable quantity of his works. . . . The work of Ephraem appeared at the same time in Syriac and in Greek, and it is not easy to establish the priority for his thought, which was certainly first given expression in Syriac" (CE 963a–64b). He is not connected with the Monastery of the Syrians (Dayr al-Suryan) in the Wadi Natrun. See Historia Lausiaca 40 (pp. 101–2); ODLA 1:542b–43b; Sebastian P. Brock, *Singer of the Word: Ephrem the Syrian and His Significance in late Antiquity* (Piscataway, NJ: Gorgias Press, 2020).

Epiphanius. Lived about 315 to 403. Bishop of Salamis on Cyprus, writer against heresy, and supporter of monasticism. See ODLA 1:548a–49a; Andrew S. Jacobs, *Epiphanius of Cyprus: A Cultural Biography of Late Antiquity*, Christianity in Late Antiquity (Berkeley: University of California, 2016). See also Frank Williams, ed. and trans., *The Panarion of Epiphanius of Salamis*, Books I–III, Nag Hammadi Studies (Leiden: Brill, rev. eds., 2008–2012); for an overview of Epiphanius's life, see xi–xvi.

Evagrius. Evagrius Ponticus (Evagrius of Pontus), 345–399, is a preeminent early-monastic theologian and writer on spirituality. He came to Egypt "around 383. After a sojourn of two years at Nitria, he established himself in the desert of the Kellia, where he remained until his death in 399. With Ammonius, one of the 'Tall Brothers,' he was the soul of the community of monks whom their adversaries called 'Origenists' because of their sympathy for the opinions of Origen, judged heterodox." He "wrote numerous books, the transmission of which suffered from his condemnation in 553. Only some have been preserved in Greek, the original language, sometimes under the name of Saint Nilus" (CE 1076a–77b). See Chitty, *Desert,* 49–53, 59–60; Evelyn-White, *Monasteries,* 85–88; Historia Lausiaca 38, pp. 94–98; ODLA 1:571b–72a; Ewa Wipszycka, *The*

Alexandrian Church: People and Institutions, JJP Supplements (Warsaw: Journal of Juristic Papyrology, 2015), 151–55; Johannes Quasten, *Patrology*, 3 vols. (Westminster, MD: Christian Classics, 1984), vol. 2, *The Ante-Nicene Literature after Irenaeus* (Westminster, MD: Christian Classics, 1984), 37–101.

Gelasius. A Gelasius was connected with the Great Laura in Palestine; Binns does not give much information about him, probably because there is very little to be had (John Binns, *Ascetics and Ambassadors of Christ: The Monasteries of Palestine, 314–631* [Oxford: Clarendon, 1994], 272a). The six sayings in the AlphAP do not allow us to firmly connect him to the Gelasius in Palestine, but because they were both Palestinians, the connection seems probable.

Hilarion. Hilarion was a "fourth-century monk of Palestine," born about 296. "Almost our only source of information about Saint Hilarion is the *Vita Hilarionis* written in Latin by Saint Jerome shortly after 390" (CE 1232a–32b). See Binns, *Ascetics,* 154–55; Chitty, *Desert,* 13–14, 37–38; ODLA 1:721a.

John the Little. "John Colobos, the Little or the Dwarf (fourth and fifth centuries), is one of the most striking figures among the desert fathers. He is known principally from the *Apophthegmata Patrum* and from a Life in the form of a panegyric composed by Zacharias, the bishop of Sakha, at the end of the seventh century in Coptic, in Lower Egypt. See Life of John the Little. This Life adds certain extra information to the data in the apothegms, the value of which it is difficult to assess with any precision. Some of the apothegms also should be handled with caution. In the fourth century there were many monks in Egypt bearing the name John, and it is not easy to be sure of the establishment of the role each played" (CE 1359b–62a). See *John Cassian: The Institutes,* trans. Boniface Ramsey, ACW 58 (New York: Paulist Press, 2000), 4.23–26 (pp. 90–92); Evelyn-White, *Monasteries,* 107–11; Guy 1.66–68.

Selected Bibliography

Dictionaries and Encyclopedias

The Anchor Bible Dictionary. Ed. David Noel Freedman. New York: Doubleday, 1992.

Bauer, Walter. *A Greek-English Lexicon of the New Testament and Other Early Christian Literature*. Ed. Frederick William Danker, W. F. Arndt, and F. W. Gingrich. 2nd ed. Chicago: University of Chicago Press, 1979. A 3rd ed. is now available.

The Coptic Encyclopedia. Ed. Aziz S. Atiya. New York: Macmillan, 1991. *The Claremont Coptic Encyclopedia*. https://ccdl.claremont.edu/digital/collection/cce/search.

De Vaan, Michiel, ed. *Etymological Dictionary of Latin and the Other Italic Languages*. Leiden: Brill, 2008.

Encyclopedia of Early Christianity. Ed. Everett Ferguson. New York and London: Garland, 1990.

Goh, Madeleine, and Chad Schroeder, ed. *The Brill Dictionary of Ancient Greek*. English edition. Leiden / Boston: Brill, 2015.

The HarperCollins Dictionary of Religion. Ed. Jonathan Z. Smith. San Francisco: HarperSanFrancisco, 1995.

Lampe, W. G. H. *A Patristic Greek Lexicon*. Oxford: Clarendon, 1961. archive.org/details/LampePatristicLexicon/mode/2University Press.

A Latin Dictionary. Ed. Charlton T. Lewis and Charles Short. 1879; Oxford: Clarendon, 1975. www.perseus.tufts.edu/hopper/text?doc=Perseus%3atext%3a1999.04.0059.

Liddell, Henry George, and Robert Scott. Rev. Henry Stuart Jones. *Greek English Lexicon*. Oxford: Clarendon, 1977. www.perseus.tufts.edu/hopper/text?doc=Perseus%3atext%3a1999.04.0057.

Montanari, Franco, Stefanos Matthaios, and Antonios Rengakos. *Vocabolario della lingua greca*. Turin: Loescher Editore, 2013.

The Oxford Classical Dictionary. Ed. N. G. L. Hammond and H. H. Scullard. 2nd ed. Oxford: Clarendon, 1978.

Oxford Dictionary of the Christian Church. Ed. F. E. Cross and E. A. Livingstone. 2nd ed. Oxford: Oxford University Press, 1988.

Oxford Dictionary of Late Antiquity. 1st ed. Oxford: Oxford University Press, 2018.

Oxford English Dictionary. www.oed.com/public/freeoed/loginpage.

Sophocles, E. A. *Greek Lexicon of the Roman and Byzantine Periods.* Cambridge, MA: Harvard University Press, 1914. archive.org/details/cu31924021609395/page/n10/mode/2up.

Editions and Translations

Agaiby, Elizabeth, and Tim Vivian, trans. *Door of the Wilderness: The Greek, Coptic, and Copto-Arabic Sayings of Antony of Egypt.* Collegville, MN: Cistercian Publications, forthcoming.

Alphabetical Apophthegmata Patrum. Ed. J.-P. Migne. *Patrologia Graeca* 65. Turnhout: Brepols, 1864. 65:75–440.

Athanasius. *Life of Antony: The Coptic Life and the Greek Life.* Trans. Tim Vivian and Apostolos N. Athanassakis. CS 202. Kalamazoo, MI: Cistercian Publications, 2003.

———. *Vie D'Antoine.* Ed. G. J. M. Bartelink. SCh 400. Paris: Cerf, 1994. 123–377.

Budge, E. A. Wallis, trans. *The Paradise of the Holy Fathers.* Vol. 2. *The Counsels of the Holy Men and the Questions and Answers of the Ascetic Brethren Generally Known as the Sayings of the Fathers of Egypt.* London: Chatto & Windus, 1907.

Cassian, John. *John Cassian: The Conferences.* Trans. Boniface Ramsey. ACW 57. New York: Paulist Press, 1997.

———. *John Cassian: The Institutes.* Trans. Boniface Ramsey. ACW 58. New York: Paulist Press, 2000.

Evagrius Ponticus. *Praktikos & Chapters on Prayers.* Trans. John Eudes Bamberger. CS 3. Kalamazoo, MI: Cistercian Publications, 1981.

———. *Talking Back: A Monastic Handbook for Combating Demons.* Trans. David Brakke. CS 229. Collegeville, MN: Cistercian Publications, 2009.

Guy, Jean-Claude. *Les Apophtegmes des Pères: Collection Systématique.* Ed. Jean-Claude Guy. 3 vols. SCh 387, 474, 498. Paris: Cerf, 2013.

————. *Recherches sur la tradition grecque des Apophthegmata Patrum.* Brussels: Bollandistes, 1962. suciualin.files.wordpress.com/2012 /01/guy-recherches-sur-la-tradition-grecque-des-apophtegmata -patrum.pdf.

"Histoires des Solitaires Égyptiens." Trans. Frédéric Nau. *Revue de l'Orient Chrétien.*

Histories of the Monks of Upper Egypt and the Life of Onnophrius. Ed. and trans. Tim Vivian. CS 140. Kalamazoo, MI: Cistercian Publications, 1993.

The Life and Regimen of The Blessed and Holy Syncletica: Part One, The Translation. Trans. Elizabeth Bryson Bongie. Eugene, OR: Wipf and Stock, 2005; Peregrina Publishing, 2003.

The Lives of the Desert Fathers: The Historia Monachorum in Aegypto. Trans. Norman Russell. CS 34. Kalamazoo, MI: Cistercian Publications, 1981.

Meyer, Marvin, ed. *The Nag Hammadi Scriptures: The International Edition.* New York: HarperCollins, 2007.

Mikhail, Maged S. A., and Tim Vivian, eds. *The Holy Workshop of Virtue: The Life of John the Little by Zacharias of Sakha.* CS 234. Kalamazoo, MI: Cistercian Publications, 2010.

Moschus, John. *The Spiritual Meadow of John Moschus (Pratum Spirituale).* Trans. John Wortley. CS 139. Kalamazoo, MI: Cistercian Publications, 1992.

Palladius of Aspuna: *The Lausiac History.* Trans. John Wortley. CS 252. Collegeville, MN: Cistercian Publications, 2015.

Regnault, Lucien, trans. *Les sentences des pères du desert: Collection alphabétique.* Solesmes: Bellefontaine, 1981.

Rubenson, Samuel, trans. *The Letters of St. Antony: Monasticism and the Making of a Saint.* Studies in Antiquity & Christianity. Minneapolis: Fortress Press, 1995.

The Sayings of the Desert Fathers: The Alphabetical Collection. Trans. Benedicta Ward. CS 59. Kalamazoo, MI: Cistercian Publications, 1975.

St Macarius the Spiritbearer: Coptic Texts Relating to Saint Macarius the Great. Trans. Tim Vivian. Popular Patristics Series. Crestwood, NY: St Vladimir's, 2004.

Vivian, Tim. *Words to Live By: Journeys in Ancient and Modern Egyptian Monasticism.* CS 207. Kalamazoo, MI: Cistercian Publications, 2005.

Wortley, John, trans. *The Anonymous Sayings of the Desert Fathers: A Select Edition and Complete English Translation.* Cambridge: Cambridge University Press, 2013.

————, trans. *Give Me a Word: The Alphabetical Sayings of the Desert Fathers.* Popular Patristics Series. Yonkers, NY: St Vladimir's, 2014.

————, ed. *The Book of the Elders: Sayings of the Desert Fathers: The Systematic Collection.* CS 240. Collegeville, MN: Cistercian Publications, 2012.

————, ed. *More Sayings of the Desert Fathers.* Cambridge: Cambridge University Press, 2019.

Studies

Bagnall, Roger S. *Egypt in Late Antiquity.* Princeton: Princeton University Press, 1993.

Behr, John. *Asceticism and Anthropology in Irenaeus and Clement.* Oxford Early Christian Studies. Oxford: Oxford University Press, 2000.

Binns, John. *Ascetics and Ambassadors of Christ: The Monasteries of Palestine, 314–631.* Oxford Early Christian Studies. Oxford: Clarendon, 1994.

Boyle, Gregory. *Barking to the Choir: The Power of Radical Kinship.* New York: Free Press, 2017.

————. *Tattoos on the Heart: The Power of Boundless Compassion.* New York: Free Press, 2010.

Brakke, David. *Athanasius and the Politics of Asceticism.* Oxford Early Christian Studies. Oxford: Oxford University Press, 1995.

————. *Demons and the Making of the Monk: Spiritual Combat in Early Christianity.* Cambridge, MA: Harvard University Press, 2006.

Brown, Peter. *The Cult of the Saints: Its Rise and Function in Latin Christianity.* Chicago: University of Chicago Press, 2014.

————. *The Making of Late Antiquity.* Cambridge, MA: Harvard University Press, 1978.

Burton-Christie, Douglas. *The Word in the Desert: Scripture and the Quest for Holiness in Early Christian Monasticism.* New York: Oxford University Press, 1993.

Charleston, Steven. *The Four Vision Quests of Jesus.* New York: Morehouse Publishing, 2015.

Chitty, Derwas. *The Desert a City.* Crestwood, NY: St Vladimir's, 1966.

Clark, Elizabeth. *Reading Renunciation: Asceticism and Scripture in Early Christianity.* Princeton: Princeton University Press, 1999.

Cooper, Alan. "Imagining Prophecy." In *Poetry and Prophecy: The Beginnings of a Literary Tradition,* edited by James L. Kugel. Ithaca, NY: Cornell University Press, 1990. 26–44.

Coquin, R.-G. "A Propos des vêtements des moines egyptiens." *Bulletin de la Société d'archéologie copte* 31 (1992): 3–23.

Elm, Susanna. *"Virgins of God": The Making of Asceticism in Late Antiquity.* Oxford Classical Monographs. Oxford: Clarendon, 1996.

Evelyn-White, Hugh G. *The Monasteries of the Wâdi 'N Natrun.* Vol. II. *The History of the Monasteries of Nitria and Scetis.* Ed. Walter Hauser. The Metropolitan Museum of Art Egyptian Exhibition. New York: Metropolitan Museum, 1932; repr. Arno Press, 1973.

Ferguson, Everett. "The Christian Gnostic." In *Gnosticism in the Early Church,* edited by Everett Ferguson, David Scholer, and Paul Corby. London: Routledge, 1993.

Ferguson, John. "The Achievement of Clement of Alexandria," *Religious Studies* 12, no. 1 (1976): 59–80.

Goehring, James A. *Ascetics, Society, and the Desert: Studies in Early Egyptian Monasticism.* Studies in Antiquity and Christianity. Harrisburg, PA: Trinity, 1999.

Gopnik, Adam. "Sacred Arts: Reading the Great Good Books, from the Torah to the Quran." *The New Yorker,* 28 January, 2019: 69–75.

Gould, Graham. *The Desert Fathers on Monastic Community.* Oxford Early Christian Studies. Oxford: Clarendon, 1993.

Graiver, Inbar. *Asceticism of the Mind: Forms of Attention and Self-Transformation in Late Antique Monasticism.* Studies and Texts 213. Toronto: Pontifical Institute of Mediaeval Studies, 2018.

Griggs, C. Wilfred. *Early Egyptian Christianity from its Origins to 451 C.E.* Leiden: Brill, 1990.

Harmless, William. *Desert Christians: An Introduction to the Literature of Early Monasticism*. Oxford: Oxford University Press, 2004.

Hausherr, Irénee. *Spiritual Direction in the Early Christian East*. CS 116. Kalamazoo, MI: Cistercian Publications, 1990.

Hirschfeld, Yizhar. *The Judean Monasteries in the Byzantine Period*. New Haven and London: Yale University Press, 1992.

Kaplan, Edward K. "Scholarship, Community, and Communion: A Jewish Perspective." In *We Are Already One: Thomas Merton's Message of Hope, Reflections to Honor His Centenary (1915–2015)*, edited by Gray Henry and Jonathan Montaldo. Louisville, KY: Fons Vitae, 2014. 51–54.

Kelty, Matthew. *My Song is of Mercy: Writings of Matthew Kelty, Monk of Gethsemani*. Ed. Michael Downey. New York and Oxford: Rowman & Littlefield, 1995.

Lekan, Todd. "The Marriage of Ideals and Strenuous Actions: Exploring William James' Account of Significant Life," *Transactions of the Charles S. Peirce Society: A Quarterly Journal in American Philosophy* 52, no. 4 (Winter 2016): 576–97.

Lewis, Naphtali. *Life in Egypt under Roman Rule*. Oxford: Clarendon, 1983.

Luijendijk, AnneMarie. *Greetings in the Lord: Early Christians and the Oxyrhynchus Papyri*. Harvard Theological Studies. Boston: Harvard University Press, 2008.

Nerburn, Kent. *The Girl who Sang to the Buffalo: A Child, an Elder, and the Light from an Ancient Sky*. Novato, CA: New World Library, 2013.

———. *Neither Wolf Nor Dog: On Forgotten Roads with an Indian Elder*. Novato, CA: New World Library, 1994, 2002.

———. *The Wolf at Twilight: An Indian Elder's Journey through a Land of Ghosts and Shadows*. Novato, CA: New World Library, 2009.

Norris, Kathleen. *Acedia & Me: A Marriage, Monks, and a Writer's Life*. New York: Riverhead Books, 2008.

Pagels, Elaine. *Adam, Eve, and the Serpent*. New York: Vintage, 1989.

———. *The Gnostic Gospels*. New York: Vintage, 1989.

Quasten, Johannes. *Patrology*. 3 vols. Westminster, MD: Christian Classics, 1984.

Rapp, Claudia. "Storytelling as Spiritual Communication in Early Greek Hagiography: The Use of *Diegesis*." *Journal of Early Christian Studies* 6, no. 3 (1998): 431–48.

Regnault, Lucien. *The Day-to-Day Life of the Desert Fathers in Fourth-Century Egypt*. Trans. Étienne Poirier, Jr. Petersham, MA: St. Bede's, 1999.

Rich, Antony D. *Discernment in the Desert Fathers:* Diákrisis *in the Life and Thought of Early Egyptian Monasticism*. Studies in Christian Theology and Thought. Waynesboro, GA: Paternoster, 2007.

Rubenson, Samuel. "To Tell the Truth: Fact and Fiction in Early Monastic Sources." CSQ 48, no. 3 (2013): 317–24.

Russell, Norman. *Theophilus of Alexandria*. The Early Church Fathers. Oxford: Routledge, 2007.

Schaffer, Mary. *The Life & Regimen of the Blessed and Holy Syncletica by Pseudo-Athanasius*, Part Two, *A Study of the Life*. Eugene, OR: Wipf and Stock, 2005; Peregrina Publishing, 2001.

Shaw, Teresa M. *The Burden of the Flesh: Fasting and Sexuality in Early Christianity*. Minneapolis, MN: Fortress Press, 1998.

Smith, Zachary. *Philosopher-Monks, Episcopal Authority, and the Care of the Self:* The Apophthegmata Patrum *in Fifth-Century Palestine*. Instrumenta Patristica et Mediaevalia 80. Turnhout: Brepols, 2017.

Swan, Laura. *The Forgotten Desert Mothers: Sayings, Lives, and Stories of Early Christian Women*. Mahwah, NJ: Paulist Press, 2001.

Vivian, Tim. "St. Antony and the Monastery of St. Antony at the Red Sea, ca. 350–ca. 1322 / 1323." In *Monastic Visions: The Wall Paintings at the Monastery of St. Antony at the Red Sea*, edited by Elizabeth S. Bolman. New Haven, CT: Yale University Press, 2002. 3–20.

———. "The Origins of Monasticism." In *T&T Clark Handbook to the Early Church*, edited by Piotr Ashwin-Siejkowski, Ilaria L. E. Ramelli, and John Anthony McGuckin. New York: T&T Clark / Bloomsbury, forthcoming 2021.

———. *Words to Live By: Journeys in Ancient and Modern Egyptian Monasticism*. CS 207. Kalamazoo, MI: Cistercian Publications, 2005.

Williams, Rowan. *A Silent Action: Engagements with Thomas Merton*. Louisville, KY: Fons Vitae, 2011.

———. "The Theological World of the *Philokalia*." In *The* Philokalia*: A Classic Text of Orthodox Spirituality*, edited by Brock Bingaman and Bradley Nassif. Oxford: Oxford University Press, 2012. 102–21.

Wimbush, Vincent L., and Richard Valentasis, eds. *Asceticism*. Oxford: Oxford University Press, 1995.

Wipszycka, Ewa. *The Alexandrian Church: People and Institutions*. The Journal of Juristic Papyrology Supplements. Warsaw: Journal of Juristic Papyrology, 2015.

———. *The Second Gift of the Nile: Monks and Monasteries in Late Antique Egypt*. Trans. Damian Jasiński. The Journal of Juristic Papyrology Supplements. Warsaw: Journal of Juristic Papyrology, 2018.

Wiseman, James A. "Thomas Merton and Theravada Buddhism." In *Merton and Buddhism: Wisdom, Emptiness, and Everyday Mind*, edited by Bonnie Bowman Thurston. Louisville, KY: Fons Vitae, 2007. 31–50.

Wortley, John. "Discretion: Greater Than All the Virtues." *Greek, Roman, and Byzantine Studies* 51 (2011): 634–52.

Scripture Index

Scriptural references are indexed by page and / or note number.

Old Testament / Hebrew Bible

New Testament

General Index

Entries are indexed by page numbers; asterisks indicate the presence of the term in a note on the numbered page. An asterisk after a range of page numbers indicates the presence of a note on at least one of those pages. **Boldfaced** page numbers indicate sayings collected under the name of the cited father. Greek, Coptic, and Latin words are italicized. In lists of Greek terms, nouns and adjectives appear first, followed by the first person present singular form of the verb.